Monetary Policy, Capital Flows and Exchange Rates

Max Fry was known internationally for his research on international and domestic financial issues. This book is a tribute to his work and draws together contributions from a range of academic and policy-making friends and colleagues who were fortunate enough to experience the depth of knowledge and insights which Max provided.

This volume covers a wide number of issues, from monetary policy and financial regulation, through exchange rate behaviour, to the forces determining, and the impacts of, international capital flows. As with Max's own work, the emphasis is on highly topical policy-making perspectives, both from a practitioner and academic viewpoint. The papers are divided into four themes:

- *Monetary policy* with contributions from William A. Allen, DeAnne Julius, Peter Sinclair and Charles Goodhart.
- *The financial sector* with contributions from Andrew Crockett, Jerry Caprio, Patrick Honohan and Andy Mullineux.
- *Exchange rates* with contributions from Ronald McKinnon, Jeffrey Frankel and Menzie Chinn.
- *Country studies* with contributions from Jim Ford and Katherine Hsu, Eric Girardin and Nick Horsewood, Chang Shu, David G. Dickinson.

David G. Dickinson is Senior Lecturer and Director of Money, Banking and Finance programmes in the Department of Economics at the University of Birmingham.

William A. Allen is a Deputy Director of the Bank of England. He is responsible for the central bank's dealing operations in financial markets and for its Centre for Central Banking Studies.

Routledge International Studies in Money and Banking

1 **Private Banking in Europe**
Lynn Bicker

2 **Bank Deregulation and Monetary Order**
George Selgin

3 **Money in Islam**
A study in Islamic political economy
Masudul Alam Choudhury

4 **The Future of European Financial Centres**
Kirsten Bindemann

5 **Payment Systems in Global Perspective**
Maxwell J. Fry, Isaak Kilato, Sandra Roger, Krzysztof Senderowicz, David Sheppard, Francisco Solis and John Trundle

6 **What is Money?**
John Smithin

7 **Finance**
A characteristics approach
Edited by David Blake

8 **Organisational Change and Retail Finance**
An ethnographic perspective
Richard Harper, Dave Randall and Mark Rouncefield

9 **The History of the Bundesbank**
Lessons for the European Central Bank
Jakob de Haan

10 **The Euro**
A challenge and opportunity for financial markets (Published on behalf of *Société Universitaire Européenne de Recherches Financières* (*SUERF*))
Edited by Michael Artis, Axel Weber and Elizabeth Hennessy

11 **Central Banking in Eastern Europe**
Nigel Healey

12 **Money, Credit and Prices Stability**
Paul Dalziel

13 **Monetary Policy, Capital Flows and Exchange Rates**
Essays in honour of Maxwell Fry
Edited by David G. Dickinson and William A. Allen

14 **Adapting to Financial Globalisation**
Edited by Morten Balling, Eduard H. Hochreiter and Elizabeth Hennessy

15 **Monetary Macroeconomics**
A new approach
Alvaro Cencini

Monetary Policy, Capital Flows and Exchange Rates

Essays in honour of Maxwell Fry

Edited by
David G. Dickinson
and William A. Allen

London and New York

First published 2002
by Routledge
11 New Fetter Lane, London EC4P 4EE

Simultaneously published in the USA and Canada
by Routledge
29 West 35th Street, New York, NY 10001

Routledge is an imprint of the Taylor & Francis Group

Typeset in 10/12 pt Times by Newgen Imaging Systems (P) Ltd., Chennai, India
Printed and bound in Great Britain by TJ International Ltd., Padstow, Cornwall

British Library Cataloguing in Publication Data
A catalogue record for this book is available
from the British Library

Library of Congress Cataloging in Publication Data
A catalog record for this book has been requested

ISBN 0-415-25135-4

Contents

Figures

Tables

Contributors

William A. Allen, Deputy Director, Financial Market Operations and Centre for Central Banking Studies, Bank of England.

Jerry Caprio, Director, Financial Strategy and Policy Group, and Manager, Financial Sector Research, World Bank.

Menzie Chinn, Professor of Economics, Department of Economics, University of California, Santa Cruz.

Andrew Crockett, General Manager, Bank for International Settlements.

David G. Dickinson, Senior Lecturer, Department of Economics, University of Birmingham.

James Ford, Emeritus Professor, Department of Economics, University of Birmingham.

Jeffrey Frankel, James W. Harpel Professor of Capital Formation and Economic Growth, John F. Kennedy School of Government, Harvard University.

Eric Girardin, Professor of Economic, CEDERS, University of Aix-Marseilles II.

Charles Goodhart, Norman Sosnow Professor of Banking and Finance, London School of Economics.

Patrick Honohan, Lead Economist, Development Research Group, World Bank.

Nicholas Horsewood, Lecturer, Department of Economics, University of Birmingham.

Katherine Hsu, Research Officer, Research Department, Joint Credit Information Centre, Taipei, Taiwan.

DeAnne Julius, Former Member of UK Monetary Policy Committee, Bank of England.

Ronald McKinnon, William D. Eberle Professor of Economics, Department of Economics, Stanford University.

Andrew Mullineux, Professor of Global Finance, Department of Accounting and Finance, Business School, University of Birmingham.

Chang Shu, Manager (Economist), Hong Kong Monetary Authority, Hong Kong.

Peter Sinclair, Director, Centre for Central Banking Studies, Bank of England and Professor of Economics, University of Birmingham.

Foreword

Very sadly, Maxwell Fry died of a brain tumour, on 22 February 2000, aged 56, while this book was in preparation. Max Fry was an Englishman whose career as a monetary and international economist took him all over the world. He held academic posts in the United Kingdom, the United States of America, Singapore, and Turkey and advised the governments or central banks of Afghanistan, Bangladesh, Mauritius, Nepal, Portugal, Turkey, and the United Kingdom. At the untimely end of his career, he combined the posts of Director of the Bank of England Centre for Central Banking Studies and Professor of International Finance at the University of Birmingham.

His temperament and career experiences gave him an optimistic and enterprising outlook, and an awareness of what things were like outside large industrial democracies. He had countless friends all over the world whom he would telephone, fax or e-mail at a moment's notice to tell them of some new project or other. He energised his colleagues and collaborators. The Bank of England benefited greatly from his presence as an Adviser in 1990 and Senior Houblon-Norman Fellow in 1997. His last and most important role at the Bank of England was at the Centre for Central Banking Studies, which he directed from 1997 until his enforced retirement in 1999. Under his direction and thanks to his vision, the CCBS took a large step in its development from an institution offering mainly basic training to central bankers from Eastern Europe and the former Soviet Union to a forum in which central bankers from all over the world can meet and exchange ideas on the latest developments in central banking. This is an achievement for which all central bankers can be profoundly grateful.

The present volume of papers on the subjects to which Max devoted his career, by a group of Max's friends, is a fitting tribute to his work.

E. A. J. George
Governor
Bank of England

Introduction

Max Fry was born on 12 February 1944 and died on 22 February 2000. In 1989 he joined the Business School at the University of Birmingham, from which time I was fortunate to have the opportunity to work with him. From 1997 he was Director of the Centre for Central Banking Studies (CCBS) at the Bank of England. It was in discussions with Bill Allen at the CCBS (and latterly Peter Sinclair who took over from Max as director) that it was decided to organize this volume in his honour.

Max's academic career began at the London School of Economics. From there he moved to the University of California (Los Angeles) to take an MSc, before returning to the LSE to complete a doctorate (in finance and development). The influence of Harry Johnson at the LSE stayed with Max throughout his career and made him always open to new ideas, allied to an ability to see their relevance to his investigation of the interaction between finance and development.

After the LSE he worked extensively in the developing countries which were to be the focus of his research over the years before returning to the US, firstly in Hawaii, latterly, back in California, at Irvine. It was during this time that he produced his most well-known book, *Money, Interest and Banking in Economic Development*, without doubt the leading text in the field and one unlikely to be surpassed in terms of its breadth of coverage or insightful analysis. It was, of course, a culmination of his voluminous original research, detailed in the long list of publications which can be found at the end of this introduction.

This book is a celebration of the great contribution which Max Fry made to the study of economics. The papers it contains cover the broad range of topics on which Max himself worked. Therefore, in keeping with these interests, contributors to this volume look at monetary policy and its operation, the behaviour of exchange rates and policy options in the foreign exchange market, and the implications of international financial market movements and the forces which influence them. A recurring topic which appears in a number of the papers is the way in which structural changes in the international financial system are providing challenges for policy. The importance of careful and rigorous analysis of the effects of global economic developments on economic policy was, of course, something for which Max was renowned.

The chapters are divided into four themes: monetary policy, bank regulation, exchange rates, and empirical single- or multi-country studies. In the first are contributions by Bill Allen, DeAnne Julius, Peter Sinclair, and Charles Goodhart. The second group contains papers from Andrew Crockett, Jerry Caprio and Patrick Honohan, and Andrew Mullineux. The exchange rate theme contains work by Jeffrey Frankel and Menzies Chinn, and Ronald McKinnon. Finally, there are four papers employing a range of econometric techniques to examine empirical issues relating to monetary policy, exchange rates and capital flows.

Bill Allen considers the issue of inflation targeting and, in particular, the experience of the UK. He reviews why inflation targets were adopted in the UK and analyses the circumstances in which inflation targets are superior to money supply or exchange rate targeting. As he points out, adopting inflation targets means that low inflation is made the primary objective of monetary policy, and hence the key to successful operation of monetary policy using an inflation target is the measurement of inflation itself. In this regard, he examines whether asset prices should be included and draws the conclusion that existing measures of inflation may be imperfect, but they still provide a suitable basis for policy operation. He also examines whether it is sensible to use a target band for inflation and the time horizon over which monetary policy should operate. Allen views the issue of openness and transparency of policy to be critical to success. He argues that the credibility of monetary policy in the UK is enhanced by the way in which policy is conducted. He concludes that, while adopting inflation targets does not make monetary policy any easier, they do focus interest on the technical issues which need to be resolved in order to make monetary policy operate more successfully in the future.

The paper by DeAnne Julius provides insights into the challenges facing members (like herself until recently) of the UK Monetary Policy Committee. The ideas presented formed the basis of the first Maxwell Fry Global Finance Lecture held at the University of Birmingham in 1999. She discusses the evidence for a decline in inflation world-wide and relates this to the structural economic and policy changes which have taken place over the last twenty years. However, she points out that the economic factors which characterize the current structural changes in the world economy (globalization, new technologies, price transparency) are very similar to those which persisted before and after the turn of the twentieth century, and hence the 1990s have seen the return to low inflation rather than the realization of a 'new' economy. As long as the structural changes result in improved productivity, she foresees a long period of price stability. The challenge for monetary policy makers is to identify whether the long-run improvements in productivity are actually taking place. Although she analyses the UK carefully, she is forced to conclude that the answer to that may take 10 years to appear. Hence monetary policy, always dogged by uncertainty about what is actually happening in the economy, is going to be especially difficult over the first decade of the new millennium. A prescription offered to overcome the risks involved, proposes not taking forecasts based on past performance too seriously, learning from what is actually happening in the economy, paying specific attention to what is happening to prices, and finally acting quickly but not aggressively.

Peter Sinclair provides a discussion of the potential for monetary policy to influence real growth. This is particularly interesting in the context of the emphasis given by both Allen and Julius on using monetary policy to combat inflation. Sinclair provides a comprehensive analysis of why inflation control is a sensible objective, by showing that higher inflation can increase or reduce real growth but the latter is a much more likely outcome. By developing an endogenous growth model with money explicitly incorporated, Sinclair is able to demonstrate that a number of competing forces are at work. Whether inflation raises or lowers growth depends upon the driving force behind economic growth, the ability of real capital to provide liquidity services as money does, the resource costs of training and the way in which money operates on agents' utility.

Sinclair provides a number of possibilities and argues that, since human capital development is likely to be an important component of growth, this involves time as well as physical resources and as money is used to save time in transactions, this leads to a negative long-run relationship between inflation and growth. The driving force for this result is that lower real money balance induces higher time costs of transactions, and hence, reduced time for human capital development.

In a piece from another (former) member of the UK Monetary Policy Committee (MPC), Charles Goodhart reviews particular features of the operation of UK monetary policy and contrasts those with the institutional framework in which the European Central Bank makes its decisions. The chapter is based on a lecture given in 1999 and so, like that from De Anne Julius, represents the thoughts of Charles Goodhart while he was actually working on the committee. He points out that the MPC meets much more regularly than other monetary policy making institutions in response to the fact that members of the committee take joint responsibility for published inflation forecasts. He sees this as providing a number of benefits: that members recognize how imprecise are forecasts; that by engaging members' attention on the forecasts they are improved as a result; that the public nature of the process ensures that pressures on the MPC, beyond the need to control inflation, are reduced; that the process ensures greater accountability; and that the process provides transparency. Having set out the benefits of the UK approach, Goodhart turns his attention to the European Central Bank (ECB). He regards the juxtaposition of a federal monetary policy institution alongside nation-states which have most other economic powers as being the unique feature of the European monetary system. He focuses on certain operational aspects of the ECB. He highlights the call for financial regulation to be conducted at a European level given the likely consolidation in the industry which will result from the creation of a single currency. In the context of lender of the last resort, he argues however, that the responsibility to provide finance to support the banking system in the event of a systemic crisis must be maintained at the level of the nation-state since the ECB does not have the necessary powers or access to resources to effectively carry out this function. Beyond this, he points out a number of potential inconsistencies between fiscal and monetary policy and in terms of the impact of asymmetric shocks across Europe which he regards as increasing, the risks associated with the single currency project.

Andrew Crockett provides an overview of the future for the structure of the international financial system. He argues that this incorporates not only the institutions, but also the framework of rules and regulations in which they operate. The main focus of his paper is on how this framework needs to change in the future in order to maintain and enhance the efficiency of an international financial system which is subject to periodic market failure. He considers, first, the problem of dealing with international financial crises. He assesses that most emerging market economies will have to adopt flexible exchange rate regimes but, in addition, must ensure that accurate information is available to market participants. Beyond this macroeconomic transparency, he also regards as crucial the provision of information about private sector decisions (particularly in the banking industry). If this information is available, the onus is on the market to resolve the pricing of risks and also the moral hazard associated with lending transactions. This emphasis on the market leads him to emphasize the importance of markets for tradeable financial assets. Once again, the provision of information is seen as the key to development. In order to ensure that international standards of disclosure are maintained across the global economy, he recommends an approach similar to the Basle Rules on bank supervision. Although the market can self-enforce these rules, it is also seen as important to develop an international institutional facility to ensure compliance. Beyond the World Bank and IMF, Crockett also envisages a role for something akin to the Financial Stability Forum. Crockett's view is that national agencies will, for the foreseeable future, have responsibility for ensuring that domestic financial markets and institutions operate efficiently. A set of international rules and regulations emphasizing transparency can greatly assist them in exercising that responsibility.

Jerry Caprio and Patrick Honahan also consider the issue of financial regulation but pose the question whether the existing Basle Committee framework needs to be strengthened in the light of recent financial crises in a number of emerging market economies. In their analysis they use the insight that deposit insurance is equivalent to the state giving a put option on insured bank deposits. This provides a useful way of examining both existing regulations and the decision by regulators to close a bank down. For example, capital adequacy rules can be seen as a way of reducing the cost of the option by increasing the non-insured liabilities relative to the banks' total assets. However, in the interests of keeping the rules transparent and easily verifiable, regulators have not attempted to devise a coherent strategy based on the put option principle. Caprio and Honahan then move onto discuss the interpretation of the existing Basle Rules for preserving financial sector stability in developing economies. They argue that, although Basle standards appear to be pretty well universally adopted, there is a substantial divergence between what is reported and actually practiced. For example, they suggest that the measurement of capital is open to flexible interpretation. Beyond this, they regard the measurement of risks faced as being problematic – these should be based on a forward-looking perspective whereas it is often the result of looking at past experience only. They also suggest that risk-weights used in assessing capital adequacy are often not well-connected with the true risk position based on past experience and future projections. They do not regard the use of credit-rating agencies as alleviating this problem. In particular, they highlight that capital adequacy should be measured against unexpected loan losses while much of the information provided by credit ratings will help to guide loan loss provisions against expected loan defaults. In the case of developing countries, they argue for a much more systematic (centralized) approach to calculating the risks faced and state that the current approach is too informal to provide this. However, they also recognize the need to create incentives for the private sector to achieve the necessary risk reduction and flag up a number of ways that this can be achieved. Deposit holders do monitor bank behaviour; similarly, and with even more reason, so do holders of subordinated debt. Hence, the market can provide a mechanism to control bank risk exposure. Beyond this, agreed rules between bank managers and regulators, which will involve penalties if the managers fail to meet the established criteria, is another mechanism for controlling the risk-taking activities of banks. Third, they discuss the incentives for supervisors to behave appropriately, by enhancing pay and reducing the ability to forbear. Forbearance may open supervisors to outside pressure, although reducing the ability to use it has negative consequences if it increases the risk of bank runs. Overall, they view the search for optimal regulation as a continually evolving process and feel that recent financial crises have emphasized that further evolution at a faster pace is going to be necessary to keep the rules ahead of market attempts to exploit them.

Andy Mullineux uses his contribution to speculate about the future of the banking system. He argues that what is regarded as money and what constitutes banks, or banking, is in the process of changing as a result of financial innovation, driven by the 'IT revolution' and increasing competition in the financial sector. Despite continuing speculation, however, he suggests that a world without money and banks is some way off. Elimination of these central institutions of the current financial system requires full information. At present, there is a rapidly expanding amount of information but with considerable doubts about the quality of much of it. Cash, and 'clicks and mortar' or 'bricks and clicks' banks, may appear to be outdated and ready for replacement, but he argues that their extinction is not imminent.

Ronald McKinnon examines why emerging markets find monetary policy and financial management so difficult. McKinnon argues that it is the way in which the world financial system operates and, in particular, the existence of a dollar standard which can explain these problems. He provides an explanation of why the dollar has such a pre-eminent role in the global financial system, based partly on historical legacy and partly on the efficiency of using a single currency for inter-bank transactions, issue of sovereign debt, pricing of commodities and invoicing of individual country trade. But this implies that the dollar can supplant the domestic currency within the domestic financial system, and for emerging economies this can be a source of problems. McKinnon points out that the dollar now exists as a medium of exchange as well as a store of value in many countries in Latin America, Asia and elsewhere. But the latter implies that it is necessary for domestic issuers of financial assets to pay a significant premium over the equivalent dollar instruments. Towards the longer end of the market, the risk premium may be so large as to make the issue of domestic currency assets prohibitively costly. The emphasis on short-term assets poses serious problems for bank regulators since banks have incentives to borrow short in foreign currency and lend long in domestic currency without covering for foreign exchange risk. These problems, together with ones associated with using the dollar as a unit of account, lead to the necessity to peg to the dollar as exchange rate policy. McKinnon goes on to consider the implications of alternative policy responses. Either countries can adopt an open capital account, in which case an exchange rate peg should be maintained to preserve financial stability, or they can impose capital controls and similarly peg the exchange rate in order to provide an anchor to the foreign exchange market. A third case where banks are regulated in order to keep foreign exchange exposure at zero also leads to high volatility of the exchange rate and hence a requirement to adopt a peg. McKinnon finishes with a discussion of an issue which Max Fry regarded as most important, namely moves to lengthen the term structure of finance. He suggests that macroeconomic stability is a key requirement; a currency board may be one mechanism through which this can be achieved. One outcome of a currency board is a long-term credible commitment to a pegged exchange rate. This is something which the Asian economies did not have and it is the failure here which McKinnon regards as having hindered the recovery of these economies from the speculative attacks which they faced. Furthermore, such a commitment to maintaining purchasing power stability, allied to appropriate legal and accounting frameworks, would encourage the development of loan term debt markets. A *virtuous* circle can evolve whereby a commitment to exchange rate stability encourages the development of long-term debt, creating an economy less vulnerable to currency and banking crises, with enhanced monetary control.

Menzies Chinn and Jeffrey Frankel examine survey data to ascertain how well exchange rate expectations predict the future. The particular innovation of their study is that their data goes far beyond the usual countries which previous studies have examined. The fact that their data set incorporates a number of developing economies makes it specially relevant for a volume in honour of Max Fry. They are concerned with four particular questions. The first is the predictability of exchange rates using the survey data. They find that there is some evidence that forecasts do have predictive power, that the forecasts are of the correct sign but they are biased – there is too much variability in expected depreciation, particularly at the three-month time horizon. Second, they find that the risk premium is time-varying, most noticeably at the twelve-month horizon; however, the risk premium does not appear to be as variable as expected depreciation. Third, at five-year horizons, there is little evidence for expectations converging towards purchasing power parity levels. Finally, using survey expectation in an equation of exchange rate determination meets with a complete lack of success. Overall, their paper is consistent with earlier results that the analysis of foreign exchange markets is awaiting further theoretical explanation.

Max was deservedly known for his ability to apply original ideas not just to a single case but to multiple examples, drawing out the key general conclusions in the process. It is therefore appropriate that the remaining papers in this volume turn their attention to empirical analysis of countries and regions for which Max, himself, provided original and perceptive analysis.

Jim Ford and Katherine Hsu (one of Max's former PhD students) look to East Asia for their work, a region which Max himself examined in many papers. They are particularly concerned with the case of Taiwan. They employ semi-structural VARs and VECs (with tests of Granger-causality) to examine the transmission process of monetary policy. They are able to characterize how the Central Bank of China can adjust its operating targets or instruments in response to different disturbances to the economy, and how monetary disturbances in their turn affect the macroeconomy. They use different measures of monetary aggregate as an intermediate target. The direct instrument of monetary policy is found to be most aptly described by the monetary base. The conclusion of their study is that control of the price level is an overriding policy objective although output, and by implication its rate of growth, is also given prominence. Policy has been very successful both in terms of achieving low inflation and high growth. The evidence they present indicates that the intermediate monetary target either should be the narrowest monetary aggregate or the broadest (where the latter is best defined in terms of a Divisia index). Indeed, the evidence is slightly in favour of the latter. There are indications that the authorities attach importance to the foreign exchange rate. The movements of the monetary base, and through it of the intermediate targets (monetary aggregates, especially M1A and Divisia), provide indirect evidence that this operates via a sterilization process. They also find evidence of the importance of asset markets to monetary policy operation. This echoes a topic of more general current concern and something which will become increasingly important with the realization of a fully global financial system.

Eric Girardin and Nick Horsewood look at a situation which, no doubt, intrigued Max, namely, the existence of a zero-interest rate in Japan over the last few years. They use VAR methodology to investigate what are the transmission mechanisms for monetary policy during the period of zero interest rates. They identify three possible channels: interest rate, asset price and credit. Given that they are using the VAR approach, they are able to uncover the effects of monetary shocks. Their key finding is the importance of asset prices in explaining the behaviour of the Japanese economy. Furthermore, and as a consequence of this observation, they do not regard a policy of yen depreciation as being effective since their estimated model shows a dominating fall in share prices and a consequent fall in demand and output. Hence, they regard a combined policy of yen depreciation and support for share prices as much more likely to get Japan out of its liquidity trap than one which focuses on a yen depreciation alone.

Chang Shu (another former PhD student of Max) considers the issue of the impact of capital flows on real exchange rates. She uses panel data to examine both short-run and long-run dynamics using an error correction framework. Perhaps not surprisingly, she finds that capital flows to Africa have had little effect on the real exchange rates while for Latin America and Asia they have played a much more important role. Capital flows have tended to generate real exchange rate appreciation, particularly for the case of Latin America; this may reflect the time period chosen and also rely on the fact a substantial part of capital flows have been foreign direct investment, in the case of Asia.

David Dickinson analyses the effects of uncertainty on foreign direct investment into a selection of European Countries. This work stems in part from a long-term interest in the transforming economies of Central and Eastern Europe which led him to work closely with Max during his time at Birmingham, on a number of projects funded under the ACE initiative within the PHARE programme of the European Commission. The particular focus of the paper here is the extent to which a number of the 'new' members of the European Union benefited from the stability which membership brought them. It is demonstrated that stability did seem to provide an impetus to inflows of direct investment, and lessons are drawn for the potential new members of the European Union from Central and Eastern Europe.

Even as he was losing the battle against his illness, Max continued to show interest in the project and appreciation to his friends and colleagues who showed such spontaneous willingness to contribute papers. The number who agreed is a testimony to his standing in the profession and the long-lasting contribution he has made.

The publications of Maxwell J. Fry

Books

Finance and Development Planning in Turkey (Leiden: Brill, 1972), pp. xv + 231.

The Afghan Economy: Money, Finance and the Critical Constraints to Economic Development (Leiden: Brill, 1974), pp. xii + 332.

Resource Mobilization and Financial Development in Nepal (Kathmandu: Centre for Economic Development and Administration, 1974), pp. ix + 94.

Portuguese Monetary Problems (Lisbon: Banco de Portugal, 1976), pp. xi + 172.

Portuguese Monetary Reforms (Lisbon: Banco de Portugal, 1977), pp. xxvi + 218.

Money and Banking in Turkey (Istanbul: Bogazigi University Press, 1979), pp. xiii + 385.

Financial Intermediation in Small Island Developing Economies (London: Commonwealth Secretariat, Commonwealth Economic Papers, No. 16, September 1981), pp. vi + 75.

American Money and Banking (New York: John Wiley, 1984) (with Raburn M. Williams), pp. xi + 483.

Improving Domestic Resource Mobilization through Financial Development (Manila: Asian Development Bank, 1985) (with Graham Abbott and K. S. Krishnaswamy), pp. vii + 51.

Money, Interest, and Banking in Economic Development (Baltimore: Johns Hopkins University Press, 1988), (Second printing, 1989; Spanish edition, 1990; third printing, 1991), pp. xx + 522.

Current Macroeconomic Policy Issues in Taiwan (Taipei: Tamkang University, 1990), pp. xiv + 74.

Foreign Direct Investment in Southeast Asia: Differential Impacts (Singapore: Institute of Southeast Asian Studies, 1993), pp. xii + 71.

Improving the Efficiency in the Financial Sector in Mauritius (Port Louis: National Economic Development Council, 1994), pp. vi + 51.

Money, Interest, and Banking in Economic Development (2nd edn) (Baltimore: Johns Hopkins University Press, 1995), pp. xxii + 570.

Central Banking in Developing Countries: Objectives, Activities and Independence (London: Routledge, 1996), pp. xii + 189 (with Charles A. E. Goodhart and Alvaro Almeida).

Emancipating the Banking System and Developing Markets for Government Debt (London: Routledge, 1997), pp. xviii + 280.

Payment Systems in Global Perspective (London: Routledge, 1999) (with I. Kilato, S. Roger, K. Senderowiez, D. Sheppard, F. Solis, J. Trundle (E)).

Journal articles

'An application of the Stone model to the Turkish financial accounts'. *Journal of Development Studies*, 7(3), April 1971, 271–83.

'Turkey's first five-year development plan: an assessment'. *Economic Journal*, 81(322), June 1971, 306–26.

'The demand for money in Pakistan: some alternative estimates'. *Pakistan Development Review*, 14(2), Summer 1975, 249–57 (with Shigeyuki Abe *et al.*).

'A monetary approach to Afghanistan's flexible exchange rate'. *Journal of Money, Credit and Banking*, 8(2), May 1976, 219–25.

'A purchasing-power-parity application to demand for money in Afghanistan'. *Journal of Political Economy*, 84(5), October 1976, 1133–8.

'Financial liberalization and domestic saying in economic development: an empirical test for six countries'. *Pakistan Development Review*, 16(3), Autumn 1977, 298–308 (with Shigeyuki Abe *et al.*).

'Alternative stabilization strategies from a model of short run price and output fluctuations in Turkey'. *METU Studies in Development*, (18), Winter 1978, 21–36.

'Further investigation into Turkey's Phillips curve'. *METU Studies in Development*, (19), Spring 1978, 22–30.

'Sectoral investment and credit policies'. *Pakistan Development Review*, 17(1), Spring 1978, 66–88.

'Deposits and deposit rates of interest'. *Economia*, 2(2), May 1978, 261–83.

'Pitfalls in partial adoption of the McKinnon-Shaw development strategy: the Nepalese experience'. *Bangladesh Development Studies*, 6(3), Monsoon 1978, 257–70.

'The money supply mechanism in Turkey'. *METU Studies in Development*, (21), Autumn 1978, 49–60.

'Money and capital or financial deepening in economic development?' *Journal of Money, Credit and Banking*, 10(4), November 1978, 464–75.

'The permanent income hypothesis in underdeveloped economies. Additional evidence'. *Journal of Development Economics*, 5(4), December 1978, 399–402.

'The failure of recent monetary policy in Portugal'. *Economia*, 3(1), January 1979, 19–35.

'The cost of financial repression in Turkey'. *Savings and Development*, 3(2), 1979, 127–35.

'Economic growth and capital shortage in Alaska, Hawaii and Puerto Rico'. *Growth and Change*, 10(2), April 1979, 17–21.

'Monetary control when demand for cash is unpredictable: a proposal for Stabilising the Money Multiplier in Portugal'. *Economic Journal*, 89(355), September 1979, 636–41.

'Saving, investment, growth and the cost of financial repression'. *World Development*, 8(4), April 1980, 317–27.

'Money, interest, inflation and growth in Turkey'. *Journal of Monetary Economics*, 6(4), October 1980, 535–45.

'Monopoly finance and Portugal's government deficit'. *Economia*, 5(2), May 1981, 315–23.

'The permanent income hypothesis in underdeveloped countries: *mea culpa*'. *Journal of Development Economics*, 8(2), June 1981, 263–8.

'Inflation and economic growth in Pacific Basin developing economies'. *Federal Reserve Bank of San Francisco Economic Review*, Fall 1981, 8–18.

'Government revenue from monopoly supply of currency and deposits'. *Journal of Monetary Economics*, 8(2), September 1981, 261–70.

'The variable rate-of-growth effect in the life-cycle saving model: children, capital inflows, interest and growth in a new specification of the life-cycle model applied to seven Asian developing countries'. *Economic Inquiry*, 20(3), July 1982, 426–42 (with Andrew Mason).

'Models of financially repressed developing economies'. *World Development*, 10(9), September 1982, 731–50.

'Analysing disequilibrium interest-rate systems in developing countries'. *World Development*, 10(12), December 1982, 1049–57.

'Saving, financial intermediation and economic growth in Asia'. *Asian Development Review*, 2(1), 1984, 82–91.

'Is land leasing a solution to unaffordable housing? An answer from fee simple versus lease-hold property price differentials in Hawaii'. *Economic Inquiry*, 22(4), October 1984, 529–49 (with James Mak).

'Terms of trade and national saving rates in Asia'. *Economics Letters*, 17(3), 1985, 271–5.

'Terms-of-trade dynamics in Asia: an analysis of national saying and domestic investment responses to terms-of-trade changes in 14 Asian LDCS'. *Journal of International Money and Finance*, 5(1), March 1986, 57–73.

'Monetary policy responses to exogenous shocks'. *American Economic Review Papers and Proceedings*, 76(2), May 1986, 79–83 (with David M. Lilien).

'Turkey's great inflation'. *METU Studies in Development*, 13(1–2), 1986, 95–116.

'Neo-classical and neo-structuralist models of financial development: theories and evidence'. *Greek Economic Review*, 9(1), 1987, 1–37.

'Foreign debt instability: an analysis of national saving and domestic investment responses to foreign debt accumulation in 28 developing countries'. *Journal of International Money and Finance*, 8(3), September 1989, 315–44.

'Financial development: theories and recent experience'. *Oxford Review of Economic Policy*, 5(4), Winter 1989, 13–28.

'Administrando o financiamento do déficit publico'. Revista Brasileira de Economia, 43(4), October–December 1989, 591–616.

'Sri Lanka's financial liberalization and trade reforms: plus ça change?' *International Economic Journal*, 4(1), Spring 1990, 71–90.

'The rate of return to Taiwan's capital stock, 1961–1987'. *Hong Kong Economic Papers*, (20), 1990, 17–30.

'Taiwan's current account surplus: incipient Dutch disease?' *International Economic Journal*, 4(3), Autumn 1990, 93–112.

'Managing deficit finance'. *Journal of Economics and Administrative Studies*, 4(1), Winter 1990, 1–23.

'Manejo del financiamiento del déficit'. *Monetaria*, 14(1), Enero–Marzo de 1991, 65–93.

'Domestic resource mobilization in developing Asia: four policy issues'. *Asian Development Review*, 9(1), 1991, 15–39.

'Choosing a money for Europe'. *Journal of Common Market Studies*, 29(5), September 1991, 481–504.

'Foreign debt reduction through improved domestic resource mobilisation and allocation'. Revue d'économic politique, 101(4), juillet-août 1991, 623–37.

'Long-run and short-run behavior of Korea's current account'. *International Economic Journal*, 5(4), Winter 1991, 93–117.

'Mobilizing external resources in Asia: structural adjustment and policy reforms'. *Asian Development Review*, 9(2), 1991, 14–39.

'The demand for money: a rational expectations approach: a comment'. *Review of Economics and Statistics*, 73(4), November 1991, 747–9 (with Wilima Wadhwa).

'Monetary and exchange rate policies during Eastern Europe's transition: lessons from further East'. *Oxford Review of Economic Policy*, 8(1), Spring 1992, 27–43 (with D. Mario Nuti).

'Monedas fuertes y monedas débiles'. *Monetaria*, 15(1), Enero-Marzo de 1992, 1–38.

'Can a Central Bank go bust?' *Manchester School of Economic and Social Studies*, 60(Suppl.), June 1992, 85–98.

'Some stabilizing and destabilizing effects of foreign debt accumulation in developing countries'. *Economics Letters*, 39(3), July 1992, 315–21.

'Saying in the Asia-Pacific Region'. *EIU Asia Pacific Regional Overview: Fourth Quarter* 1992, 2–17.

'Monetary policy reaction to foreign debt accumulation in developing countries'. *Manchester School of Economic and Social Studies*, 61(Suppl.), June 1993, 60–75.

'Foreign debt accumulation: financial and fiscal effects and monetary policy reactions in developing countries'. *Journal of International Money and Finance*, 12(4), August 1993, 347–67.

'Money-hard and soft'. *Current Politics and Economics of Europe*, 3(1), 1993, 1–32.

'Financial development in Asia: some analytical issues'. *Asian-Pacific Economic Literature*, 9(1), May 1995, 40–57.

'Pronósticos de un programa financiero para metas de crédito en China'. *CEMLA Boletin*, 42(3), mayo–junio 1996, 135–47.

'Developing voluntary domestic markets for government debt'. *Bank of England Quarterly Bulletin*, 36(4), November 1996, 449–61.

'How foreign direct investment in Pacific Asia improves the current account'. *Journal of Asian Economics*, 7(3), Fall 1996, 459–86.

'Emancipating the banking system'. *Central Banking*, 7(2), Autumn 1996, 68–82.

'Developing voluntary domestic markets for government debt'. *Bank of England Quarterly Bulletin*, 36(4), November 1996, 449–61.

'In favour of financial liberalisation'. *Economic Journal*, 107(442), May 1997, 754–70.

'Saving, investment, growth, and financial distortions in Pacific Asia and other developing areas'. *International Economic Journal*, Spring 1998, 1–24.

'Assessing Central Bank independence in developing countries: do actions speak louder than words?' *Oxford Economic Papers*, 50(3), July 1998, 512–29.

'Pitfalls and potential of financial liberalization'. *Ekonomia*, 2(1), Summer 1998, 1–28.

'International financial flows and development: editors' preface'. *World Development*, 26(7), Special Issue, July 1998, 1165–8 (with V. Murinde).

'Macroeconomic policy and economic performance in developing countries'. *Bank of England Quarterly Bulletin*, 38(1), 1998, 48–54.

Book chapters

'Manipulating demand for money' in *Essays in Modern Economics*, M Parkin (ed.) (London: Longman, 1973), pp. 371–85.

'Financial sectors in some small island developing economies' in *Problems and Policies in Small Economies*, B. Jalan (ed.) (London: Croom Helm, 1982), pp. 185–207.

'Inflation and monetary policy in Hong Kong, Indonesia, Korea, Malaysia, Singapore, Taiwan and Thailand' in *Inflation in East Asian Countries* (Taipei: Chung-hua Institution for Economic Research, Conference Series No. 2, 1984), pp. 83–137.

'Financial structure, monetary policy, and economic growth in Hong Kong, Singapore, Taiwan, and South Korea, 1960–1983' in *Export-Oriented Development Strategies: The Success of Five Newly Industrializing Countries*, V. Corbo, A. O. Krueger, and F. Osso (eds) (Boulder, CO: Westview Press, 1985), pp. 275–324.

'Financial structure, financial regulation, and financial reform in the Philippines and Thailand, 1960–1984' in *Financial Policy and Reform in Pacific Basin Countries*, H.-S. Cheng (ed.) (Lexington, MA: D. C. Heath and Company, Lexington Books, 1986), pp. 161–84.

'Summing-up: three issues of financial reform and innovation' in *Financial Innovation and Monetary Policy: Asia and the West*, Y. Suzuki and H. Yomo (eds) (Tokyo: Tokyo University Press, 1986), pp. 319–27.

'Money supply responses to exogenous shocks in Turkey' in *Liberalization and the Turkish Economy*, T. F. Nas and M. Odekon (eds) (Westport, CT: Greenwood Press. 1988), pp. 85–114.

'Monetary policy in Pacific Basin developing countries' in *Monetary Policy in Pacific Basin Countries*, H.-S. Clieng (ed.) (Boston: Kluwer Academic Publishers, 1988), pp. 153–70 (with David M. Lilien and Wilima Wadhwa).

'Monetary policy implementation during Europe's transition to a single currency' in *European Banking*, A. Mullineux (ed.) (Oxford: Basil Blackwell, 1992), pp. 44–64.

'Central banking in developing countries' in *The New Palgrave Dictionary of Money and Finance*, P. Newman, M. Milgate and J. Eatwell (eds) (London: Macmillan, 1992), vol. 1, pp. 325–7.

'Current account imbalances in Sri Lanka and Taiwan: long-run adjustment mechanisms and policy reaction' in *External Imbalances and Policy Constraints in the 1990s*, C. R. Milner and P. N. Snowden (eds) (London: Macmillan, 1992), pp. 237–61 (with Peter Burridge, Simon Sosvilla-Rivero).

'Inflation and monetary policy in Pacific Basin developing economies' in *Price Stabilisation in the 1990s: Domestic and International Policy Requirements*, K. Shigehara (ed.) (London: Macmillan, 1993), pp. 137–64.

'Unstable current account behaviour and capital flows in developing countries' in *International Finance: Contemporary Issues*, D. K. Das (ed.) (London: Routledge, 1993), pp. 54–71.

'The debt crisis: a view from the United States' in *Mexico and the United States: Neighbors in Crisis*, D. G. Aldrich and L. Meyer (eds) (San Bernardino, CA: Borgo Press, 1993), pp. 235–46.

'Financial opening and monetary control in Pacific Basin developing market economies' in *Financial Opening: Policy Issues and Experiences in Developing Countries*, H. Reisen and B. Fischer (eds) (Paris: Organisation for Economic Co-operation and Development, 1993), pp. 143–64.

'Malaysia's inverse saying-investment correlation: the role of public and foreign direct investment' in *The Economics of International Investment*, V. N. Balasubramanyam and D. Sapsford (eds) (Cheltenham: Edward Elgar, 1994), pp. 191–202.

'Foreign direct investment, financing and growth' in *Investment and Financing in Developing Countries*, B. Fischer (ed.) (Baden-Baden: Nomos Verlagsgesellschaft, 1994), pp. 181–214.

'Saving, investment and current account imbalances: a Malaysian and East Asian perspective' in *Generating a National Savings Movement*, Al' Alim Ibraffim (ed.) (Kuala Lumpur: Institute of Strategic and International Studies, 1994), pp. 11–40.

'Flexibility in finance' in *The Flexible Economy: Causes and Consequences of the Adaptability of National Economies*, T. Killick (ed.) (London: Routledge, 1995), pp. 297–324.

'Monetary and exchange rate policies during Eastern Europe's transition: lessons from Further East' in *Financial Reform in Central and Eastern Europe: Lessons from the West and Further East*, A. Mullineux (ed.) (Commack, N.Y.: Nova Science Publishers, 1995), pp. 19–45 (with D. Mario Nuti).

'Monetary integration of Central and Eastern Europe. How to proceed?' in *Monetary Policy in an Integrated World Economy*, H. Siebert (ed.) (Tübingen: J. C. B. Mohr (Paul Siebeck) for Institut für Weltwirtschaft an der Universität Kiel, 1996), pp. 239–72 (with Peter Sinclair).

'Financial opening and monetary control in the Asia-Pacific region' in *The Emerging Growth: Pole: The Asia-Pacific Region*, D. K. Das (ed.) (Singapore: Prentice Hall, 1996).

'Finance and growth in Pacific Basin developing countries' in *Financial Development and Economic Growth: Theory and Experience from Developing Countries*, N. Hermes and R. Lensink (eds) (London: Routledge, 1996), pp. 138–58.

'Saving, investment and economic growth in Laos' in *Laos' Dilemmas and Options: The Challenge of Economic Transition in the 1990s*, M. Than and J. L. H. Tan (eds) (Singapore: Institute of Southeast Asian Studies, 1997), pp. 61–83.

'Financial sector development in small economies' in *Sequencing? Financial Strategies for Developing Countries*, A. Harwood and B. L. R. Smith (eds) (Washington DC: Brookings Institution, 1997), pp. 167–87.

'Can seigniorage revenue keep China's financial system afloat?' in *Taxation in Modern China*, D. J. S. Brean (ed.) (New York and London: Routledge, 1998), pp. 93–123.

'How foreign direct investment improves the current account in Pacific Basin economies' in *Research in Asian Economic Studies, Volume 8*, R. Hooley and Z.-A. Mahani (eds) (Greenwich, CT: JAI Press, 1998), pp. 227–43.

'Foreign direct investment in a macroeconomic framework' in *Technology Diffusion in the Third World*, H. Singer, N. Haiti and R. Tandon (eds) (New Delhi: BR Publishing Corporation, 1999).

'Central banking and economic development' in *Major Issues in Central Banking, Monetary Policies and Implications for Transition Economies*, M. I. Blejer and M. Skreb (eds) (Norvell, MA: Kluwer Academic Publishers, 1999).

1 Some aspects of inflation targeting

*William A. Allen**

Introduction

This paper discusses a number of aspects of inflation targeting in the light of the experience of the United Kingdom. It is not intended to convey any recommendations, even implicitly, about how monetary policy should be conducted in other countries, but some of the issues and topics that have arisen in the United Kingdom may also be relevant to other countries.

The United Kingdom is not the only country to use inflation targeting, nor did it invent the policy. The first country to introduce it was New Zealand in 1989; other users include Canada, Australia, Israel and Sweden. The European Central Bank's monetary policy strategy incorporates an element of inflation targeting.[1]

The United Kingdom began inflation targeting in late 1992, and it may be useful to review some historical background. After the break-up of the Bretton Woods system in the early-1970s, the United Kingdom had a floating exchange rate and an unstable but increasing rate of inflation, which reached over 25 per cent in 1975 (Figure 1.1). It became clear that serious errors had been made in the conduct of monetary policy in the early-1970s, based on the mistaken belief that there was a stable trade-off between unemployment and inflation – in other words, a stable Phillips curve. It also became increasingly widely understood that the control of inflation was a necessary pre-condition for the achievement of other economic policy objectives, and therefore had to be assigned top priority among policy objectives.

During the quarter-century since then, the rate of inflation has been reduced tenfold, from over 25 per cent to below 2.5 per cent. The fall in the rate of inflation has not been steady or continuous. There have been a number of crises, and a number of different monetary policy techniques have been used. Inflation targeting is the latest of them, adopted after the United Kingdom left the European Exchange Rate Mechanism, and it has been the longest-lasting. The procedures of inflation targeting are still evolving in the light of continuous learning through experience.

*The views expressed in this chapter are those of the author alone and not the Bank of England.

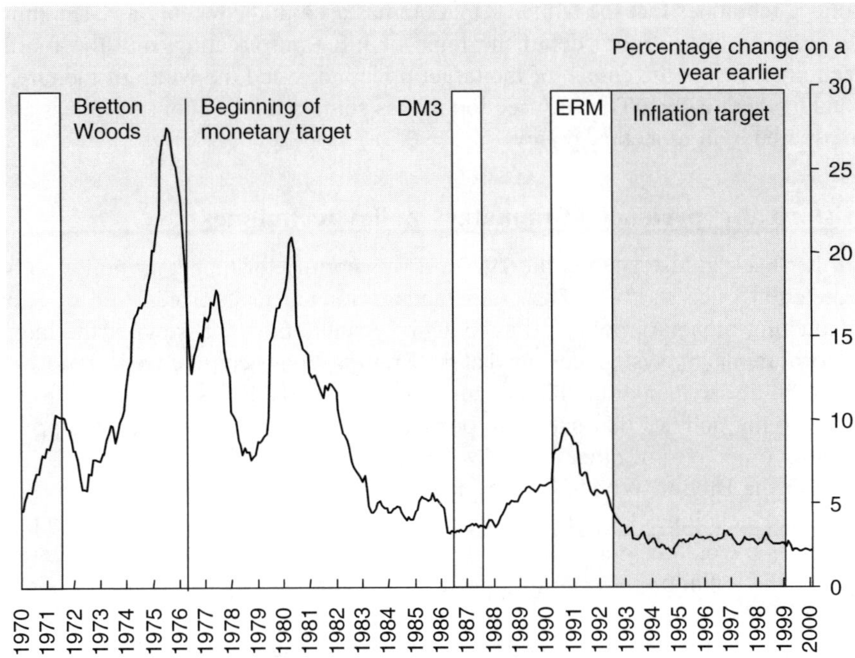

Figure 1.1 RPIX inflation from 1970.

Inflation targeting is based on the assumption that low inflation is the single proper objective of monetary policy. That assumption is based, in the United Kingdom, on the unhappy experience of trying to pursue other objectives with monetary policy. It is beyond the scope of this paper to justify the assumption that price stability should be the proper objective of monetary policy. Briault (1995) sets out the arguments: the public debate in the United Kingdom has become much less heated in the last few years, perhaps largely because low inflation has been accompanied during those years by strong economic growth and falling unemployment, so that there has been no sign of a conflict between low inflation, high growth and high employment.

Nevertheless, there have been some complaints in the United Kingdom that the fact that the central bank is pursuing an inflation target means that it is not concerned about output and employment. This is a misconception, because the inflation target is symmetrical. It is just as serious a policy error for inflation to be below target as it is for it to be above target, and if inflation is expected to be below target, it is the Bank of England's duty to ease monetary policy. Moreover, the Bank of England is required by law to support the Government's economic policy, including its objectives for growth and employment, subject to the overriding objective of maintaining price stability.

The second section of the paper reviews experience of the various monetary policy techniques that the United Kingdom has used in the recent past. The third section sets out in more detail the logic of inflation targeting, and the fourth section discusses the choice of the target price index and the width of the target band, if there is one. The fifth section makes some remarks about openness and transparency in monetary policy.

Historical experience of monetary policy techniques

Further back in history than the 1970s, it was normal for monetary policy to be directed at price stability. The gold standard amounted, in effect, to a rule for conducting monetary policy so as to achieve stable prices. Likewise, the international monetary system designed at the Bretton Woods conference in 1944 was a kind of dollar standard, which endured until the early 1970s, when the tension between the policies that had been pursued by the United States and the price-stability objectives of other countries became unsustainable.

After the Bretton Woods system broke down, industrial countries had to find their own techniques for pursuing low inflation, rather than hoping and expecting that the job would be done for them by the combination of a fixed exchange rate against the dollar and successful pursuit of low inflation by the monetary policy of the United States.

For a long time these techniques fell into three groups:

1 *Regional exchange rate arrangements.* The most important example in this category is the European Exchange Rate Mechanism, which developed into a Deutsche Mark bloc, in which the DM was the key currency (just as the dollar was in the Bretton Woods system) and the other members pursued monetary policies which were constrained to follow Germany. A necessary pre-condition for the arrangement was Germany's continued success in achieving low inflation; for the other members, their exchange rate against the DM represented an intermediate monetary policy objective, the final objective being low inflation. The Exchange Rate Mechanism was transformed at the beginning of 1999 into the European Single Currency.
2 *Monetary targets.* If there is a stable relationship between one or more monetary aggregates and the general level of prices, then monetary policy can be directed at a particular rate of growth of the monetary aggregate (the intermediate objective) compatible with low inflation.
3 *Techniques involving no specified intermediate targets.* Some countries have succeeded in managing monetary policy without reference to a specific intermediate target: perhaps the most conspicuous example is the United States in the last ten years or so.

The history of intermediate targets has been mixed. European exchange rate developments over the early to mid-1990s were turbulent, and a number of countries, including the United Kingdom, abandoned their exchange rate pegs.

As to monetary targets, the stable relationships between monetary aggregates and the price level on which they depend have in many cases broken down. The danger of managing monetary policy without an intermediate target is that with no clear and explicit objective, policy could easily become incoherent (i.e. policy actions might be mutually inconsistent) and produce poor results, though that is not an accusation that can be made against recent monetary policy in the United States.

Inflation targets

Inflation targets have in many cases been introduced when some other monetary policy technique has failed. For example, Canada introduced them after monetary targets had failed. To quote the former Governor of the Bank of Canada, Gerald Bouey, 'We didn't abandon monetary targets, they abandoned us'. Finland, Sweden and the United Kingdom introduced inflation targets after abandoning an exchange rate peg. (Finland has now, in effect, gone back to a fixed exchange rate by joining the European Single Currency.) Inflation targets are conceptually different from monetary and exchange rate targets in one important respect, namely, that monetary policy actions normally affect monetary aggregates and exchange rates more quickly than they affect inflation. Indeed, it is widely acknowledged that monetary policy actions affect inflation only after a long delay, perhaps of two years or so. As Blinder (1997) puts it, inflation targets are not really rules for monetary policy at all, but rather objectives that may require a great deal of discretion to achieve. This has two important consequences:

1 It implies that the public credibility of an inflation target policy depends not on the achievement of an intermediate target which the public can monitor continuously and which is thought to be a leading indicator of future inflation, but rather on the credibility of a promise to achieve an inflation target in the distant future. That, in turn, depends on whether the public believes that monetary policy will continue to be directed towards the objective of price stability, and that the objectives of monetary policy will not be changed. This is not just a matter of credibility of the central bank, but rather of the credibility of the political commitment to price stability. This is perhaps the reason why an inflation target was not introduced in the United Kingdom earlier than 1992 – for example in the 1970s. At that time, the public would not have believed that a monetary policy directed towards meeting an inflation target over a prolonged period would have been politically sustainable, because the belief in a long-run trade-off between inflation and unemployment was still widespread. To achieve credibility with the public and with financial markets in that environment, a continuously-monitorable target was needed.
2 It means that an additional procedure is needed to determine what monetary policy now is needed to achieve the inflation target in the future. The additional procedure in question must, as a matter of logic, involve a forecast

of inflation assuming unchanged monetary policy, and an estimate of how future inflation is likely to be affected by changes in the current setting of monetary policy instruments (e.g. interest rates). In a sense, the forecast of inflation has the same logical status in inflation targeting as the monetary aggregate has in monetary targeting and as the exchange rate has in exchange rate targeting.

Some critics have claimed that the fact that inflation targeting is logically reliant on forecasting represents a weakness of the technique, because forecasts are inherently unreliable. That is a misconception. *Any* monetary policy technique has to take account of the fact that policy changes made now do not affect inflation until some time in the future. Indeed, most economic policy instruments have their effect only after a time delay. As was mentioned above, inflation targeting requires a forecast of inflation and an estimate of how inflation is likely to be affected by changes in monetary policy instruments. Fundamentally, the pursuit of low inflation by means of any technique requires the same things. For example, the use of monetary targets has to be based on an assumption about the relationship between current monetary growth and future inflation – and, indeed, if the policy instrument is interest rates, as it usually is, a further assumption is needed about the relationship between current interest rates and future monetary growth. The difference in this respect between inflation targeting and monetary targeting is not that inflation targeting makes forecasts necessary, but rather that inflation targeting makes the need for forecasts explicit rather than implicit. The paper will say more about forecasting below.

In practical application, there has been less difference between inflation targeting and monetary targeting than might be imagined. In Germany, for example, monetary targeting was employed by the Deutsche Bundesbank for over 20 years. During that time it became evident that the assumed relationships between interest rates and the target monetary aggregate, and between the target monetary aggregate and inflation, are not completely stable and predictable. In practice the Bundesbank acknowledged this fact in the conduct of monetary policy. The result was that monetary targets were often not hit, and that actual monetary policy was perhaps not very different from what it might have been had an inflation target been pursued. Most empirical studies of German monetary policy support this view.[2]

The differences between inflation targeting and exchange rate targeting are greater, both in concept and in practice, than the differences between inflation targeting and monetary targeting. Of course, it is true that exchange rate targeting makes sense only if there is a predictable relationship between the exchange rate and future inflation, just as in the case of monetary targeting. But not every country can pursue an exchange rate target, for obvious reasons. Somewhere there has to be a so-called anchor currency country which sets a standard by using a different monetary policy technique – and in an important sense countries which target their exchange rates against the anchor currency are borrowing that country's monetary policy technique and its monetary policy credibility.

And, while it is possible to depart temporarily from monetary targets if the underlying relationships appear to have changed,[3] it is generally not possible to depart temporarily from exchange rate target bands without there being a severe loss of credibility.

Specification of the inflation target

It is easy to say that the objective of monetary policy is price stability. It is much harder to specify what that means in terms of observable quantities. A number of decisions need to be made in setting an inflation target. They include:

1 What price index, and at what level should the target be set?
2 Should there be a target band, and if so, how wide should it be?

What price index, and at what level should the target be set?

The measurement of inflation is an important subject in its own right, irrespective of the choice of monetary policy technique. The use of inflation targets merely makes its importance more obvious. Although measurement issues may appear to be matters of detail, they nevertheless raise some fundamental questions, two of which are discussed below.

Current consumption or current plus future consumption?

The first question is about asset prices and monetary policy. As a matter of principle, should the chosen index represent the prices of goods and services for immediate consumption only, or should it represent the price of goods and services for both present and future consumption? Alchian and Klein (1973) argue that the proper objective of monetary policy should be defined in terms of an index of present and future consumption, because an index confined to goods and services for current consumption fails to recognise the scope for inter-temporal substitution in consumption. In other words, according to Alchian and Klein, the price indices used for monetary policy purposes should include not only prices of goods and services for current consumption but also the prices of present claims over future goods and services.

In practice, available consumer price indices are hybrids – they are neither indices of prices of goods and services for current consumption alone, nor are they price indices of both goods and services for current consumption and present claims over future consumption. Of course, they include prices of goods and services for current consumption, but they also include prices of consumer durables, which provide services for some period in the future, until they wear out. But they do not include prices of present claims over goods and services for future consumption other than services provided by consumer durables which can be purchased now.

With few exceptions, markets for future goods and services do not exist, and there is accordingly no possibility of producing a price index of the kind that Alchian and Klein's argument indicates would be desirable. But the logic of the argument is compelling and, as Alchian and Klein note (p. 176), 'since assets are sources of future services, asset prices provide clues to prices of present claims on future consumption'. In other words, the practical implication of Alchian and Klein's argument is that monetary policy should take account of asset prices as well as conventional price indices. Even so, asset prices need to be interpreted with care, as Alchian and Klein point out. For example a change in the price of an asset may be caused simply by a re-evaluation of its likely yield – that is, a re-evaluation of the quantity or quality of goods and services that the particular asset in question is expected to produce in the future. An asset price change thus caused does not imply any significant change in the price of present claims on future consumption. However, a general change in market rates of returns on assets – for example, a fall in bond and equity yields, accompanied by rises in the prices of real assets such as land and real estate, represents a *general* change (in this example, a fall) in the price of goods and services for current consumption relative to the price of present claims over future consumption. All these problems of interpretation are analogues of problems that arise in the interpretation of conventional price indices.

It would be possible to arrive at the same conclusion for monetary policy by way of a different route, not involving Alchian and Klein's argument. Suppose that monetary policy were concerned wholly with the prices of goods and services for immediate consumption. The rate of inflation of those prices is not affected immediately by monetary policy actions: there is a time lag. So, as indicated above, monetary policy has to be concerned with managing the future rate of inflation and has to be based on a forecast of what the future rate of inflation will be. That forecast will be influenced by the current state of a wide range of economic variables, including asset prices. In other words, it is not difficult to justify the assertion that monetary policy should take account of asset prices.[4]

What does 'taking account of asset prices' mean in practice? It means that policy-makers need to analyse asset price movements carefully, and to do their best to understand them – just as they routinely analyse and try to understand developments in the main national income aggregates. For example, if equity prices have risen sharply, they need to consider whether the rise reflects:

1 an increase in expected future dividend payments (or corporate payouts of other kinds to shareholders);
2 a reduction in the discount rate (and what the reason for the reduction might be); or
3 a reduction in the equity risk premium.

They need also to consider whether the rise in prices represents a 'bubble' that will burst at some future time.

Equity price increases arising from these three different sources listed in the preceding paragraph can have different economic consequences. A rise in expected future equity returns may indicate an increase in expected future economic growth, perhaps as a result of the application of new technologies (e.g. computers). Consumer demand is likely to increase, but since productive potential will also increase, it is not obvious that monetary policy needs to react, unless it is judged that, over the time horizon relevant for monetary policy, demand (including investment as well as consumer demand) is likely to increase by more than productive potential, or unless the central bank judges that the market expectation of higher equity returns is mistaken. The central bank has no choice but to take a view on these points. A rise in equity prices that results from a fall in the discount rate could have no first-order effects on consumer demand at all, since the increase in portfolio values is broadly matched by an increase in the discounted present value of future consumption needs. There is no reason to expect any particular percentage of a 'windfall' arising in this way to be spent immediately or over a short period. Such a fall in the discount rate would be likely to influence investment demand, however. The effects of a reduction in the equity risk premium might well be to discourage saving and boost consumer spending, and perhaps also to boost investment.

Recent experience in the United States shows how difficult it can be to understand asset price developments. Nevertheless, it is an indispensable part of the monetary policy process. In particular, if the 'market forecast' of the economy, which is implicit in the constellation of financial asset prices, is substantially different from the central bank forecast on which monetary policy decisions are based, then the central bank forecast should, as a matter of logic, allow for and incorporate the changes in asset prices that will take place when the 'market forecast' is adjusted into line with the central bank forecast, as it eventually must be if the central bank forecast is correct. This means that the central bank must 'decode' the market forecast implicit in financial asset prices and estimate the behavioural effects of a shift of the market forecast into line with the central bank's own forecast.

The practical importance of asset price developments for monetary policy is illustrated by the experience of the 'bubble economy' in Japan in the late 1980s,[5] though that is by no means the only relevant historical illustration. Inflation as measured by the consumer price index was low: consumer price inflation was less than 4 per cent throughout this period 1983–90, but there were very large increases in share prices and land prices. Share prices nearly trebled between the end of 1985 and the market peak in 1989. The commercial land price index for large cities peaked at more than double its end-1985 level. In other words, the prices of goods and services for current consumption were fairly stable, but it was clear from the rises in asset prices that, although the prices of present claims over goods and services for future consumption could not be directly measured, they were nevertheless rising very fast. Monetary policy did not respond promptly to rising asset prices; indeed short-term interest rates fell in 1986 and 1987. When monetary policy was tightened in 1989 and 1990, it had extremely disruptive effects on asset markets and on the Japanese economy. Equity prices fell by more than 50 per cent between 1989 and 1992; and urban land prices have been falling continuously since the peak for seven successive years. The fall in asset prices had very serious effects on the capital position of Japanese commercial banks, which had lent heavily against the collateral of assets the value of which had fallen sharply. As everyone knows, the Japanese economy then entered a prolonged period of recession.

It is now universally acknowledged that, with the benefit of hindsight, it would have been preferable for monetary policy to have been tightened in the late 1980s as asset prices rose, even though, according to conventional indices, consumer price inflation was not excessive. Narrow-minded inflation targeting would not have been enough.

Measurement problems

On most views, the ultimate objective of all economic activity is to produce consumer satisfaction, and the ideal consumer price index would measure the money cost of achieving a particular level of consumer satisfaction, or utility (see Fisher and Shell, 1972). Such an ideal index would be called a cost of living index in the jargon. Turning the economic concept into hard numbers is fraught with difficulties, however. The Retail Price Index in the United Kingdom makes no claim to measure the cost of maintaining a particular level of consumer satisfaction. To quote the Retail Price Index Advisory Committee (1986):

> We wish to reaffirm the view taken by our predecessors that the RPI is an index of price changes and not a 'cost of living' index. It is not designed to measure the effect of changes in the kinds, amounts and quality of the goods and services people buy, or in the total amount that needs to be spent in order to live. Nor does it measure changes in the cost of maintaining a particular level of consumer satisfaction. The RPI measures the overall change in prices by reference to the cost of a 'basket' of goods and services which in turn is based on what households have actually spent their money on, the contents of the basket being brought up to date at the beginning of each year and then fixed for twelve months. We believe this to be the best practicable design for the index and see no reason to try to change it. However, we recognise that movements in retail prices must be an important factor in determining the cost of living however this is defined.

Consumer price indices are, typically, fixed-weight averages of prices of consumer goods and services. The price data are obtained by regular inquiries made by statistical offices at specified outlets (shops). The weights are based on the distribution by product of consumer expenditure and are revised at regular intervals as the distribution of consumer expenditure changes.

There are two main sources of imperfection, or bias, in measured inflation. *Substitution bias* arises because consumers can be expected to switch expenditure away from more expensive products towards cheaper products, and away from more expensive outlets towards cheaper ones. The purpose of regular reviews of the weights in the index and of the selection of outlets chosen for sampling purposes is to minimise substitution bias, but the bias is likely to remain in the periods between regular reviews. Cunningham (1996) estimates that substitution bias in the retail price index in the United Kingdom lies between 0.15 and 0.35 per cent a year. The product composition of the retail price index in the United Kingdom is reviewed every year. In other countries' where reviews are less frequent, substitution bias might be expected to be larger than in the United Kingdom. The Boskin Report (1996) estimates that, in the United States, substitution bias is 0.5 per cent a year.

Problems caused by *composition effects* are more difficult. They are of two kinds. *Quality bias* arises because the quality of goods and services within a particular category may change, but the change may not be fully allowed for in computing the price index. If quality increases over time, failure to allow for it fully will lead to overstatement of inflation.

New products raise more fundamental problems. In principle, the introduction of any new product widens consumer choice and makes it possible to achieve a given level of utility at a cost which may be lower than previously and will certainly be no higher. In other words the introduction of any new product has a neutral to negative effect on the true cost-of-living index.[6]

How large are quality bias and new product bias? Cunningham provides an estimate of 0.20–0.45 per cent for the United Kingdom, and the Boskin Report estimates 0.6 per cent for the United States. However, any estimate is likely to be ill-founded. As a matter of principle, the effect on the true cost-of-living index of the introduction of a new product depends on what the new product is. The introduction of a new brand of chocolate bar (if its price is the same as that of other brands) probably makes a negligible difference to the cost of achieving a given level of utility, because it is likely to be a very close substitute for existing products.

New products that are not close substitutes for existing products perhaps fall into two groups. New products in the first group provide the same service to the customer as the old product, but at a lower cost. The introduction of such products self-evidently reduces the cost of achieving a given level of utility. Conceptually it is straightforward to take account of this kind of technological improvement in price measurement, though in practice it is extremely difficult. Nordhaus (1997) shows how technological improvements have reduced the cost of lighting services in the nineteenth and twentieth centuries; he also reaches the remarkable conclusion that traditionally-constructed price indices would exaggerate the rate of inflation of the price of lighting services over the period since 1800 by an average of 3.6 per cent per annum. Shapiro and Wilcox (1996) examine the price of treatment for eye cataracts during a period of technological improvement.

The second group consists of new products that provide services that were previously unavailable. Treatment of such products in price indices is very difficult in concept, let alone in practice. A good example is the introduction of pharmaceutical products that can improve the quality of life of people suffering from particular diseases or ailments. The introduction of such products can make an enormous difference to the cost to those people of achieving a given level of utility: indeed, it can enable them to achieve levels of utility that would previously have been simply impossible for them. It also reassures non-sufferers that if they contract the disease or ailment, they can be treated. Such products are by no means close substitutes for existing products.

Real-life price indices make no allowance for new products in the second group. Nor could they. If they were to allow properly for such products, producers of statistics would need to know the elasticity of substitution in demand between new products and existing ones. Estimates of the elasticity could be obtained only after there had been time to analyse the demand for the new product in the light of experience, and the resulting price index would by then be well out of date. One approach to estimating the true rate of inflation – the rate of inflation of the ideal cost-of-living index – could be to estimate an average amount of bias in conventionally measured inflation, and adjust the conventional index to allow for it. The Boskin Report provides a central estimate of 1.1 per cent a year for the bias in measured consumer price inflation in the United States. Cunningham's estimate for the bias in measured inflation in the United Kingdom is 0.35–0.80 per cent. However, as indicated above (and as the authors acknowledge), the accuracy of *any* estimates is extremely doubtful; and moreover there is no reason to think that the degree of bias will be constant over time.

It seems inevitable, therefore, that monetary policy will have to continue to be conducted, and inflation targets set, by reference to estimated price indexes which fall short of the conceptual ideal. This is perhaps a disappointing conclusion, but it is not catastrophic: there have been periods in history (e.g. the period 1945–70 in most industrial countries) when monetary management was very successful, according to present-day reckoning, despite the absence of ideal cost-of-living indices. Nor does it make nonsense of inflation targeting. The objective of monetary policy is price stability. Although finding a precise numerical definition of price stability is not easy, because of the measurement problems described above, it is nevertheless possible to achieve an approximation to price stability that most people will find acceptable.

Measurement problems make it difficult to choose the level of the inflation target. If it were known with certainty that the chosen price index overstated inflation by *X* per cent a year, then it would be natural to set an inflation target of *X* per cent, so that the target for 'true cost of living inflation' was zero. In fact there is no such certainty and there is some degree of inescapable arbitrariness in the setting of inflation targets.

Should there be a target band, and if so, how wide should it be?

The purpose of an inflation target is to provide the central bank with a rule for making monetary policy decisions. For that purpose, a target band is not necessary: a single point target is sufficient. Why in that case would it be desirable to specify a band rather than a single point target, and how wide should such a band be? There are two possible reasons for specifying a band.

1 *As a promise and a monitoring device.* It is obvious that it will not be possible to hit a single point target for the rate of inflation continuously, because economic behaviour and economic developments are not completely predictable. A target band for inflation can represent an acknowledgment of that fact, and a promise that the central bank will keep inflation within the band. At the same time, it can represent a monitoring device, because the central bank will clearly be perceived to have failed if inflation strays outside the band. Obviously if a band is introduced for this purpose, its width will depend on how far the variability of the rate of inflation can be reduced.
2 *As a means of introducing flexibility into monetary policy.* A target band for monetary policy gives the central bank some discretion over which point in the band it aims for in making monetary policy decisions – for example, allowing it to accommodate some cyclical variation in the rate of inflation. The width of a band introduced for this purpose would depend on how much discretion was required.

In the United Kingdom, the target is a single point. The need for monitoring and accountability is met by a requirement that if inflation departs from the target of 2.5 per cent by 1 per cent or more, on either side, then the Governor of the Bank of England must write an open letter to the Chancellor of the Exchequer explaining why the discrepancy has occurred, how long it is likely to persist, and how the Monetary Policy Committee intends to bring inflation back to target. The inflation target makes no explicit allowance for accommodating cyclical variation in the rate of inflation. The Government can re-set the target each year and could, in principle, adjust it in parallel with business cycle developments, but such a pattern of adjustment would probably increase the amplitude of cyclical fluctuations in output and is, therefore, not very likely to be adopted.

If the initial rate of inflation is much higher than the desirable long-run target, then it may be optimal to set targets that provide for a gradual reduction in inflation to the long-run target. In setting such targets, a trade-off has to be struck between the cost of having inflation above the desirable long-run target level (which is reduced if disinflation is faster) and the cost of fluctuations in output during the disinflation process (which is increased if disinflation is faster).

If the terms of the trade-off are uncertain, there is a risk of a conflict between short-run and long-run inflation targets. A central bank might find, at some point during the adjustment process, that it was forecasting, over the time horizon relevant for current policy decisions, inflation below the short-run target but above the long-run target, with output as high or higher than previously expected. This would mean that the terms of the trade-off between the speed of disinflation and output fluctuations were more favourable than expected.

In such circumstances, the central bank might well not want to ease monetary policy in pursuit of the short-run inflation target. In order to ensure that the inflation target rule does not indicate a policy easing in such circumstances, it would make sense for short-run inflation targets, to be achieved during a process of disinflation, not to specify a lower bound for inflation – or at least, not to specify a lower bound any higher than the long-run inflation target.

Openness and transparency

During the process of disinflation, it is necessary for policy to strike trade-offs between the cost of having inflation above target (which is reduced if disinflation is faster) and the cost of output fluctuations (which is increased if disinflation is faster). The trade-off arises fundamentally because it is assumed that to reduce inflation it is necessary to reduce output temporarily. However, the extent of the necessary reduction in inflation depends crucially on the credibility of the commitment of the inflation target. The more credible the commitment, the lower the output cost of reducing inflation. Once low inflation has been achieved, a credible commitment to keep it low usefully removes one possible source of uncertainty about the future economic outlook.

Credibility can be achieved with the help of openness and transparency, which in the United Kingdom is promoted by the following five devices:

1 The Bank of England publishes each quarter an *Inflation Report*, setting out the Monetary Policy Committee's analysis of recent economic developments and a forecast of inflation and output growth over the coming two years.
2 The minutes of the monthly Monetary Policy Committee meetings are published. They give a full account of all the arguments put forward both for and against the decision actually taken, and are extensively reported and discussed in the press and in financial markets.
3 Members of the Monetary Policy Committee are frequently questioned by the Treasury Select Committee of the House of Commons.
4 If the rate of inflation strays from the target by more than 1 per cent on either side, the Governor has to write an open letter to the Chancellor of the Exchequer explaining how the discrepancy arose, how long it is expected to persist, and what the Monetary Policy Committee intends to do to correct it.
5 Members of the Monetary Policy Committee make frequent speeches about monetary policy in all parts of the country. In addition, the Bank employs regional Agents, located in different parts of the country, whose job it is to maintain contact with local businesses and business groups, gather information from them and explain the Bank's policies to audiences in their regions.

Openness and transparency are very effective means of improving credibility. First, they make it possible for those responsible for monetary policy to be publicly accountable for their decisions. That increases their incentive to achieve the inflation target, and it therefore increases the public's confidence that the inflation target will be hit. Second, the thought processes of those taking monetary policy decisions are more fully exposed to the public. That means that the public are able to comment on official thinking, so that there can be a debate which may lead to improved official thinking. It also provides reassurance to the public that the central bank is pursuing its stated objective and not some other objective that has not been announced. We have seen some of these benefits in the United Kingdom.

Concluding remarks

Advocates of other intermediate targets promise to make monetary policy easy. Just keep the money supply on track, or just keep the exchange rate pegged, they say, and all will be well. In many countries, however, experience shows that all is not always well.

Inflation targeting does not promise to make monetary policy easy. In a sense, all it does is to specify the precise objective of monetary policy. But at least it does not make any false promises, and it has the positive virtue of directing attention to the many issues that need to be resolved in conducting monetary policy.

Notes

1 For a range of case studies, see Bernanke, Laubach, Mishkin and Posen (1999). Sterne (1999), reviewing the results of a survey of 91 central banks, reports that no fewer than 54 of them said that they used inflation targets in 1998, compared with just 8 in 1990. In most cases, inflation was just one of a number of monetary policy target variables. In the countries listed above, inflation is explicitly identified as the target variable that has the highest priority.
2 See, for example, Bernanke and Mihov (1996).
3 Sterne (1999) shows that monetary targets set by central banks have typically been missed by wider margins than inflation targets.
4 Smets (1997) has explored how monetary policy should react to asset price changes in the context of a simple model.
5 I am grateful to Mr Yutaka Yamaguchi of the Bank of Japan for provoking this thought. See Yamaguchi (1999) for a description of what happened and a retrospective discussion of the policy options that were available to the Bank of Japan.
6 Equally, the withdrawal of any existing product has a neutral to positive effect on the true cost of living index. As a matter of common observation, the process of economic growth has been accompanied by proliferation of available products.

References

Alchian, A. A. and Klein, B. (1973) 'On a correct measure of inflation', *Journal of Money, Credit and Banking*, 5(1) (Part 1), pp. 173–191.

Bernanke, B. S. and Mihov, I. (1996) 'What does the Bundesbank target?' *NBER Working Paper* 5764, September.

Bernanke, B. S., Laubach, T., Mishkin, F. S. and Posen, A. (1999) *Inflation Targeting: Lessons from the International Experience*, Princeton, NJ: Princeton University Press.

Blinder, A. S. (1997) *Central Banking in Theory and Practice,* Cambridge, MA and London: MIT Press.

Boskin, M. J., Dulberger, E. R., Gordon, R. J., Griliches, Z. and Jorgenson, D. (1996) 'Towards a more accurate measure of the cost of living', Final report to the Senate Finance Committee from the Advisory Commission to Study the Consumer Price Index, December.

Briault, C. (1995) 'The costs of inflation', *Bank of England Quarterly Bulletin*, 25(1), pp. 33–45.

Cunningham, A. W. F. (1996) 'Measurement bias in price indices: an application to the UK's RPI', *Bank of England Working Paper* 47, London.

Department of the Environment Retail Price Index Advisory Committee (1986) *Methodological Issues Affecting the Retail Prices Index*, HMSO, Cmnd 9848.

Fisher, F. M. and Shell, K. (1972) *The Economic Theory of Price Indices*, New York: Academic Press.

Nordhaus, W. (1997) 'Do real output and real wage measures capture reality? The history of lighting suggests not', In T. F. Bresnahan and R. J. Gordon (eds), *The Economics of New Goods*, University of Chicago Press.

Shapiro, M. D. and Wilcox, D. W. (1996) 'Mismeasurement in the consumer price index – an evaluation', *NBER Working Paper* 5590 (May).

Smets, F. (1997) 'Financial-asset prices and monetary policy: theory and evidence', In Philip Lowe (ed.), *Monetary Policy and Inflation Targeting*, Economic Group, Reserve Bank of Australia.

Sterne, G. (1999) 'The use of explicit targets for monetary policy: practical experience of 91 economies in the 1990s', *Bank of England Quarterly Bulletin*, 39(3), London.

Yamaguchi, Y. (1999) 'Asset price and monetary policy: Japan's experience', Remarks at a symposium organised by the Federal Reserve Bank of Kansas City at Jackson Hole, Wyoming, 26–28 August 1999 (available at http://www.boj.or.jp/en/press/koen044.htm).

2 Back to the future of low global inflation

DeAnne Julius

Introduction

Conventional thinking can be deceptively dangerous when the world is changing. In such times, clinging to old paradigms is at least as risky as embracing new ones before their validity can be fully established. My thesis today is that some elements of the so-called 'new paradigm' growth theories are simply modern incarnations of the economic trends of earlier era. Other elements clearly strain credulity: none of the arguments I am about to develop could support the late 1990s stock market valuations for Internet companies in the US; nor do I suggest that economic growth is about to accelerate dramatically. But if I am right, and the decades of the 1970s and 1980s were the exceptions rather than the norm, then we must particularly guard against using the paradigms and parameters from those 20 years to shape our views about the present period and our projections for the future.

In my current role as a member of the Monetary Policy Committee (MPC), I spend most of my days thinking about the demand side of the economy. We model that using equations that have been calibrated on data going back to the mid-1970s or early 1980s. Our assigned task on the MPC is to deliver price stability. The Government has set our operational target for this as 2.5 per cent annual inflation on the Retail Price Index excluding mortgage interest payments (RPIX). To hit that target, we adjust interest rates in order to restrain or stimulate domestic demand whenever it appears that total demand, looking 1–2 years ahead, is likely to exceed or fall short of the supply capacity of the economy. Monetary policy can do very little to change the supply side. Our lever pushes on demand, and we generally take supply as given.

In this paper, however, I step out of my usual central banker's preoccupation with demand and instead examine some of the longer-term changes that affect the supply side of our economy. Some of these are international developments. Some relate to new technologies. Some stem from changes in the labour market here in the UK. They share two characteristics. First, the *direction* of their impact on UK inflation, at least over the medium-term, is downwards. But second, the *size* of their impact will be very difficult to discern until many years hence. This is because they are gradual, structural changes whose effect on economic statistics will be overlaid with, and obscured by, the cyclical surges and slowdowns to which we devote so much time and attention. In other words, if we place too much faith in econometric models calibrated from the 1970s and 1980s, we will not know what has hit us until it is too late!

Global inflation

First, the facts. Global inflation has been low in the 1990s relative to the 1970s and 1980s. Figure 2.1 shows the inflation performance of three representative countries of the G7: the US, the UK, and France. While inflation in the UK was worse than in the other two countries, all three suffered from double-digit rates of price increases for several years during that period. Inflation spikes coincided in the mid-1970s and again in the early 1980s. Britain and the US had smaller inflation bursts in 1990. But since then inflation has been well below 5 per cent, not only in these three countries, but also across the industrialised world and in most of the faster-growing developing countries.

This is largely explained by changes in the economic and policy environment in the 1990s. Some say we have been lucky. Or, perhaps more accurately, we have not been as unlucky as during the 1970s with the wars and revolutions in the Middle East that resulted in the 1973 and 1979 oil price spikes. Those reduced growth and increased inflation worldwide as central banks reacted cautiously and, with hindsight, sometimes wrongly, in response to those unfamiliar supply-side shocks. Both companies and policy-makers have learned from that experience. Firms have shifted to energy-saving production processes, governments have increased taxes on oil consumption to encourage conservation, and as a result, industrialised countries today are much less dependent on

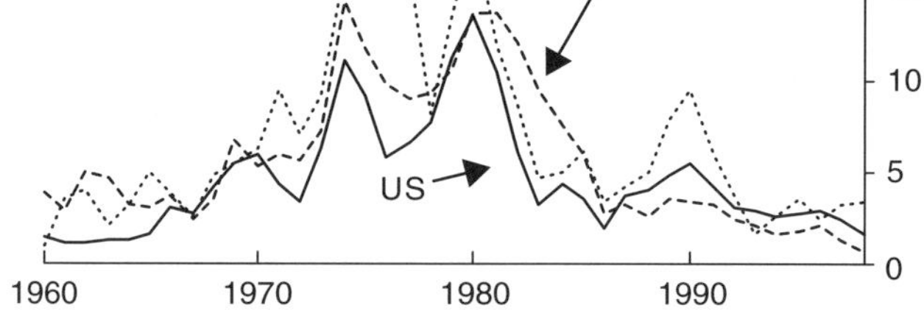

Figure 2.1 Recent inflation performance.

oil than they were 20 years ago. These shifts are largely irreversible. In 1998 the oil price, in real terms, fell below the level it had been in the early 1970s prior to the Arab–Israeli conflict. Yet oil consumption rose very little since the tax wedge paid by consumers and the energy-saving technologies used by firms were unaffected. Similarly, the current surge in crude oil prices, if it were to persist, would have much less effect on economic growth and retail price inflation than did a similar rise in earlier decades. In the UK, for example, four-fifths of the petrol price paid at the pump is actually tax. So, if the price of crude oil doubles, the retail price of petrol would rise by, at most, 15 per cent.

There have also been clear shifts in the policy environment since the inflationary failures of the 1970s and 1980s. Many governments have institutionalised their commitment to price stability with the creation of independent central banks. The UK is a prime, though certainly not the first, example of this. Our MPC has been given a clear inflation target and the instrument independence to achieve it. Our decisions on interest rates are entirely unaffected by the dates of political party conferences or upcoming elections. The same is true of the new European Central Bank (ECB). Such independence has removed a possible inflationary bias which some have blamed for the persistence of inflation during previous decades.

Thinking on fiscal policy has also evolved. In the US, the budget deficits that grew out of financing the Vietnam War and the later build-up of defense spending under President Reagan have been tamed and turned into surpluses. Public antipathy towards deficit spending is strong and support is growing for 'investing' surpluses in the social security fund for future retirement benefits rather than reducing taxes or increasing current government expenditures. The result is low government borrowing or none at all. This creates room in the financial markets for more private sector borrowing and investment. At least in the US, the combination of a tight fiscal policy and a relatively accommodating monetary policy is widely credited for the long economic upswing of the 1990s.

In Europe, fiscal deficits rather than surpluses are still the norm, but since the creation of the ECB, the relationship between fiscal and monetary policy has become more explicit. The Growth and Stability Pact sets limits on member governments' budget deficits, and the financial markets react nervously if it appears that those limits might be breached. Under the UK system as well, the Government's inflation target provides a clear fulcrum on which the balance of fiscal and monetary policy rests. Interest rates are set to achieve the inflation target, taking into account the Government's announced fiscal plans. If those plans change significantly, and the inflation target remains fixed, then the appropriate level of interest rates will also change. This interdependence of fiscal and monetary policy is as well understood by the financial markets as it is by the Treasury and the Bank of England. The decentralised decision-making that constitutes the global financial marketplace is the ultimate 'enforcer' of fiscal prudence and monetary discipline in all countries today. In that respect, it is the modern equivalent of the gold standard and fixed exchange rates.

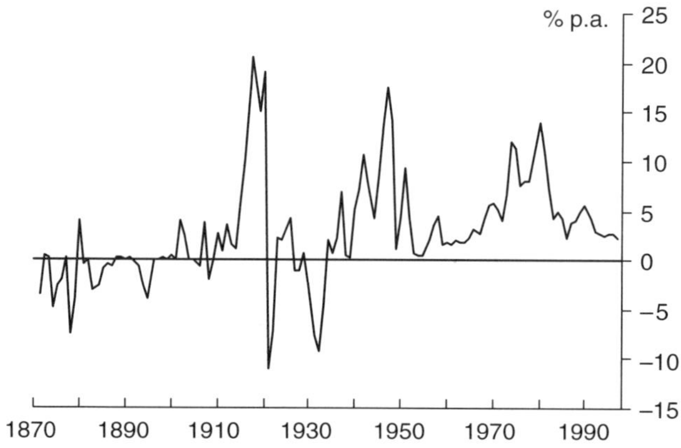

Figure 2.2 Long-term inflation performance.

Though the 1990s may seem like a new era of price stability, a longer historical comparison gives a different perspective. Before the late 1960s, low inflation was the norm rather than the exception (Figure 2.2). It took World Wars or oil price shocks or – working in the opposite direction – the Great Depression, to knock inflation off course. Throughout most of the late nineteenth century, price falls were common. This was not just because of the greater importance of commodities then; price falls occurred for manufactured goods too.

The supply-side changes in our economies today which are likely to affect inflation prospects over the next decade are broadly similar to those at work during the 50 years that ended with the World War I. Intensified international competition – which some call globalisation – and the spread of new technologies may be thought of, not as elements of a new paradigm, but rather as the current drivers towards the old norm of low global inflation. In my view, these two forces, plus greater price transparency, are the key supply-side changes that will affect global inflation outcomes. Those countries that embrace these changes actively are likely to achieve a more favourable inflation–growth combination than they managed during the 1970s and 1980s. Whether this better combination is transitory – lasting only another 5–10 years – or more permanent, will depend on whether these forces result in higher rates of productivity growth. But either way, understanding their possible effect on the inflation outlook now and for the next decade will be critical.

Globalisation

Globalisation, to an economist, means the increasing integration of global product markets. To a businessman, it means global sourcing from the lowest-cost suppliers worldwide, a global investment strategy and global competition putting downward pressure on output prices in home as well as host markets. To a consumer, it means global shopping with easy access to global products and global brands, whether on the high street or via the phone, fax or Internet.

Only the oldest and most traditional channels for globalisation – trade and foreign direct investment (FDI) – are well captured in current statistics. The importance of trade, relative to GDP, has been growing since the end of the war. For the world as a whole, the combined share of imports and exports in GDP rose from around 20 per cent in 1950 to nearly 40 per cent in 1992 and has risen further since (Figure 2.3). This reflects the success of GATT negotiations to remove trade barriers over that period, the quality improvement and cost reductions in transport and communication infrastructure, and the gains from specialisation as developing countries become important producers and exporters of many manufactured goods.

Interestingly, this trend has not been smooth, or always upward, suggesting that structural changes – to the extent that they are linked to openness – tends to occur in waves. This is even more apparent in the UK data where it is possible to look back further in history. Figure 2.4 shows that the share of trade in UK GDP rose sharply between 1850 and 1920 from 34 to 64 per cent. It then fell back to a trough of 26 per cent as a result of the Great Depression and the World Wars, before beginning the upwards march from 1950 shown on the previous global chart. But it was not until the 1980s and 1990s that the UK trade share has approached its 1920 elevation. In terms of globalisation through the trade channel, we have gone back to the future.

The FDI channel is more exciting and, particularly for the service sector that now accounts for at least two-thirds of output and jobs in most advanced economies, it is the more important vehicle for global competition. If you are in the retailing business, for example, the way to reach foreign customers is not through trade but through opening up shops in their cities. Often, this is done

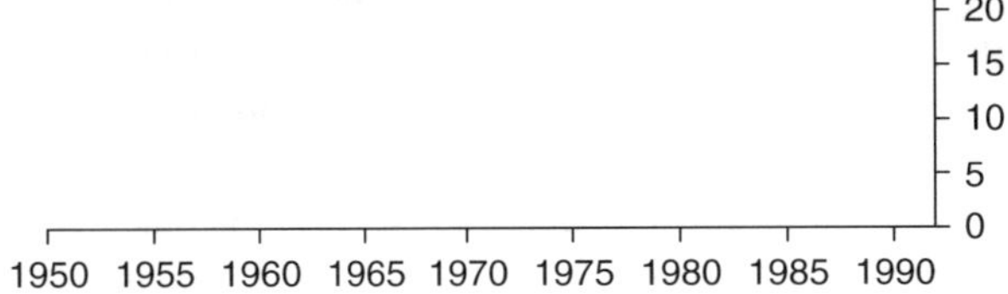

Figure 2.3 World trade relative to GDP.

Source: Penn World Tables.

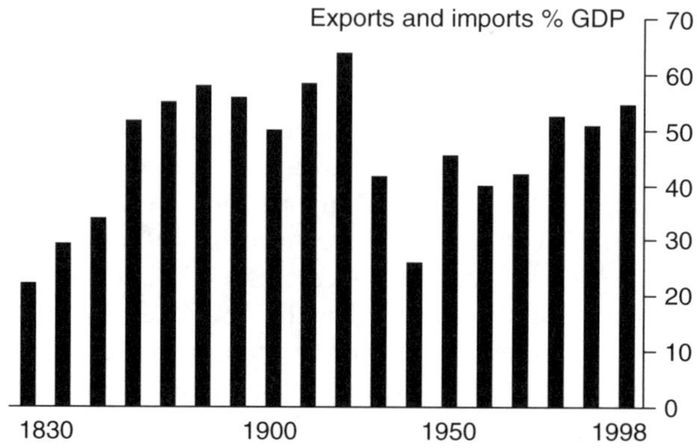

Figure 2.4 UK trade relative to GDP.

Source: Stein and National Accounts.

through the purchase of, or an investment partnership with, a domestic retail chain. The current wave of merger and acquisition activity – not only in retailing, but also in insurance, banking, telecommunications and other major service industries – is bringing international cost-cutting techniques and serious price competition directly into large parts of the economy that were formerly rather distant from such global pressures.

In the last year, the UK was the second largest recipient of inward investment after the US, and one of the most important outward investors worldwide. FDI inflows last year rose by $26 to $63 billion – accounting for over a quarter of all direct investment into Europe (Figure 2.5). Outflows rose by more, almost doubling to $114 billion, and moving close to US levels of $133 billion. British companies are clearly very active in reaching foreign markets through direct investment, and global companies headquartered elsewhere are raising the competition stakes here in Britain.

While the US and Britain lead the pack, globalisation through FDI has been one of the most striking international trends of the 1990s. World FDI flows have increased sharply, rising over threefold between 1990 and 1998. Figure 2.6 illustrates the increasing importance of this channel for global integration. FDI flows have outpaced the 30 per cent rise in world GDP and even the 65 per cent rise in world trade. By last year, the total sales of inward investors in their host-country markets were worth $11 trillion, compared with total world exports of $7 trillion.

Globalisation means different things to different people. It has many channels and its measurement will never be precise. But there is little doubt that a renewed wave of globalisation is underway which is spreading international competition into more sectors and engulfing producers in more countries. This has two important effects on the way inflationary pressures develop in any particular

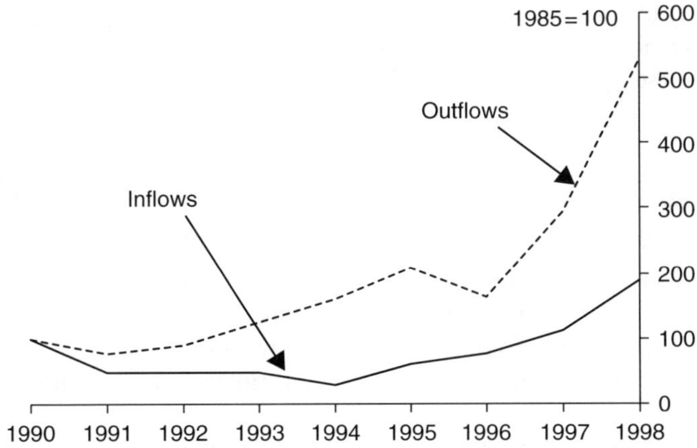

Figure 2.5 UK FDI flows.

Source: IMF Balance of Payments statistics.

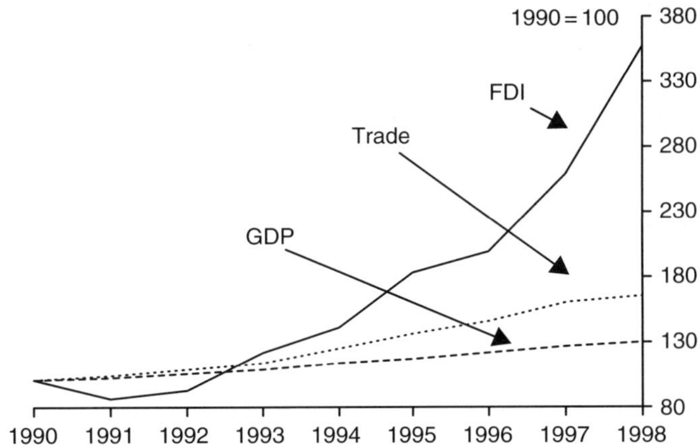

Figure 2.6 World GDP, trade and FDI.

Source: Datastream, IMF Balance of Payments statistics.

country. First, in a more integrated global economy, it is the world-output gap that matters for many prices, not domestic-supply capacity. If there is spare world capacity in goods or services that can be transmitted either actually or virtually across borders, then their prices will remain low or even fall. And supply bottlenecks at the global level are much less common than domestically, simply because of scale and the global availability of underemployed labour. Second, aside from capacity and business-cycle considerations, the faster spread of best-practice management techniques and cost-reducing technologies through FDI means that efficiency inside firms and productivity at the economy-wide level should also increase.

New technologies

The current wave of innovation in information and communications technology (ICT) is the second major supply-side development in the global economy. The effect of these technologies – which cover computing power, the development of the Internet, satellite communication, fibre optics and lasers – is to improve the speed, quality and accessibility of information flows at negligible marginal cost.

ICT has a huge potential to increase the efficiency with which capital and labour are combined in production. For many products, ICT has already reduced design times, increased quality control, and shrunk the need for precautionary stocks in the production chain. Improved information flows enable firms to respond more efficiently to shifts in consumer preferences, and to customise products and services to their needs. The speed and low cost of information transfer has led to greater outsourcing by producers to the cheapest global supplier, spurring and speeding the globalisation process. As Figure 2.7 shows, while it took 36 years to achieve 50 million users for radio, 13 years for TV, and 16 for PCs, for the Internet it has taken fewer than 5 years!

The Internet puts ICT directly at the service of the consumer. As shoppers, we can now compare the prices of standard goods and services online, and either bypass the middleman and buy them directly or use that information to extract

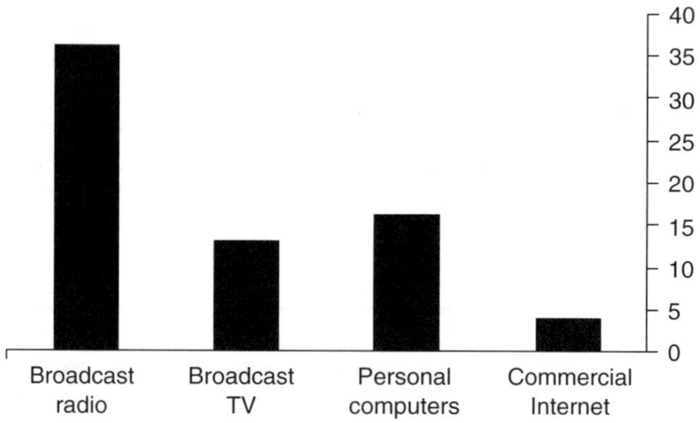

Figure 2.7 Years to achieve 50 million users.

Source: US Commerce Department.

discounts from our local supplier. While my own forays into electronic shopping are so far limited to books, airline tickets and used cars, the price reductions achieved on those items have certainly whetted my appetite for more! As both consumers and search engines become more sophisticated, competitive pressures on prices and distribution margins will intensify and affect many more items in the Retail Price Index.

Unfortunately, statisticians are lagging behind in measuring these new purchasing patterns. No country officially measures e-commerce in its national accounts yet, so estimates tend to be based on private surveys which may not be representative. With that caveat in mind, in the US, e-commerce is estimated to be worth around $35 billion or 0.4 per cent of GDP.[1] In the UK, BRMB Internet Monitor recently reported that £2 billion was spent online in the past 12 months which was a tenfold increase from a year ago. In just six months, the number of people using the Internet for shopping rose by one-third to 2.5 million and now represents about a quarter of UK Internet users. Verdict Research estimates that online shopping in the UK will rise to 2.5 per cent of retail spending in the next three years. Others have made higher forecasts. If US patterns of Internet penetration and use are followed here with a lag, then e-commerce should reach 4 per cent of GDP by 2002.

This is likely to intensify the downward pressures on retail margins, especially for goods which are easy to compare, such as books. More than 2 per cent of all books sold in Britain are already sold online. Prices are said to be 10–50 per cent below those in retail outlets. Capturing such transactions and prices in the official statistics will become increasingly important. The recent statement from the Office of National Statistics that it is examining how it can include online shopping in the Retail Price Index is to be welcomed.

However, the biggest impact of e-commerce will probably come through its effect on the ability of firms to reduce costs through outsourcing and more efficient supplier relationships. Currently, four-fifths of e-commerce is business-to-business rather than business-to-consumer use, and this share is expected to remain stable as Internet usage rises. Again the US appears to be moving faster than Europe. A recent study by Andersen Consulting found 77 per cent of US senior executives agreeing that e-commerce is 'a significant part of the way we currently operate' while only 39 per cent of European executives said so. But these percentages are growing rapidly. As Figure 2.7 showed, Internet use is spreading much faster than previous ICT innovations.

The effects are likely to be seen first on prices and margins, and then on productivity. Of this trio, only prices are measured in a reasonably accurate and timely way. Margins are estimated from input and output price series but do not take proper account of capital and labour inputs. Productivity is estimated indirectly from output and employment data, where the former is subject to large revisions years after it is first published. A recent staff research paper from the US Federal Reserve Board showed how monetary policy mistakes of the 1960s and 1970s 'could be attributed in large part to changes in the trend growth of productivity in the economy which, though clearly seen in the data with the benefit of hindsight, was virtually impossible to ascertain in real-time.' (Orphanides, 1999).[2] Our successors at the Bank of England could be saying the same thing about us in ten years' time if we rely too heavily on current productivity estimates when we have reason to believe that historical trends may be changing.

Price transparency

The third structural change exerting downward pressure on inflation, relative to the 1970s and 1980s, is increased price transparency. Part of this is interwoven with the rise of ICT and Internet shopping as just described. But there are two other contributing factors. The first is low inflation itself. Stable prices overall make it easier for consumers to spot relative-price increases by removing the background confusion of high and variable general inflation. It is also harder for producers to move off their 'price points' even when their costs are rising. The Bank of England's regional agents report ubiquitous anecdotes from their business contacts about consumers becoming more price-conscious. 'They look, they have money in their pockets, but they don't buy unless they think it's a bargain.' Even in the banking sector, low nominal-interest rates have meant more shopping around by savers and more complaints by consumer groups about the margins between banks' lending and savings rates. Margins of 2 or 3 per cent are much more noticeable when official rates are 5 or 6 per cent than when they were 15 per cent.

Price transparency in Europe is also being increased by the introduction of the euro. This will become even more apparent to consumers when euro-denominated notes and coins replace national currencies in just over two year's time. Then it will become even easier to compare prices and make purchases in neighbouring countries. For companies, the removal of foreign-exchange risk in dealing with purchasers and suppliers in other Euro-zone countries has been widely anticipated. It is beginning to feed through into increased merger activity, although it is impossible to say how much of that is driven by the euro and how much by cyclical and other factors. There are already a few instances reported of contracts negotiated in euros even where one party is outside the Euro-zone, for example, BMW with Rover suppliers in Britain. Whether Britain is in or out in the future, the consolidation of 15 per cent of world GDP into a single currency brings greater price transparency to a large share of its market.

To summarise so far, there are three powerful and partly interconnected trends in the world economy at the turn of the century that can be expected to exert downward on prices from the supply side: intensified globalisation, the rapid diffusion of ICT, and greater price transparency due, in part, to the introduction of the Internet and the euro. These certainly will not remove the necessity for monetary policy-makers to remain alert for signs of inflation and to raise interest rates whenever it appears that prospective demand growth is excessive, in relation to prospective supply. But they do imply that prospective supply will be more difficult to estimate from historical relationships, and that domestic price-setting behaviour will be more constrained than in recent decades by international competitive forces. Monetary policy can only influence nominal demand growth. The split of nominal growth between output and prices is determined by the bargaining outcomes between buyers and sellers, and employers and employees throughout the economy. If global competitive forces bear down on domestic prices more strongly, then in the short-to-medium term, domestic inflation will be lower and output growth higher. If those same forces drive improvements in domestic productivity, then a more permanent shift can be made to a higher growth path consistent with low and stable inflation.

Let us turn now to the UK. We live in an open economy, with a higher than average share of trade in GDP, where the absolute level of inward investment last year was second only to the US, and where Internet use by business ranks seventh in the world.[3] On top of that, our exchange rate has been rather strong, at least against the euro and its constituent currencies, for the past three years. We should be feeling the chills of these global competitive winds more than most. What evidence is there that they are having an effect, first, on our prices and, second, on our sustainable rate of growth?

Retail prices in the UK

Recent UK economic performance has been impressive. Output has grown for twenty-eight consecutive quarters over this recovery, the longest sustained expansion since recent records began in 1955. This has been accompanied by a fall in the unemployment rate to 4.2 per cent on the claimant-count measure – its lowest rate for nearly 20 years – or 5.9 per cent on the broader LFS measure. Since the recovery began, output growth has averaged 3 per cent per year while inflation has averaged just 2.8 per cent (Figure 2.8). Based on past experience,

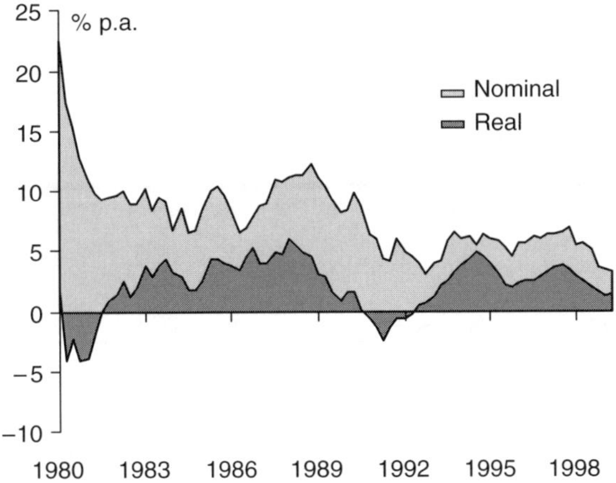

Figure 2.8 Real and nominal GDP split.

many economists would have predicted that such high rates of growth and employment would generate high wage pressure and rising inflation. On the contrary, inflation has been broadly stable over the 1990s and is currently below the Government's target at 2.1 per cent. The so-called headline rate has fallen to 1.1 per cent – its lowest rate since 1963.

While the overall inflation rate is a product of monetary policy, trends in individual price components can provide some insight into what lies behind this favourable split between growth and inflation in recent years. The degree to which policy needs to be tightened in order to keep inflation from rising depends on the strength of upward-price pressure from wages and margins when unemployment is low and the economy is growing rapidly. Offsetting these 'bottom up' cyclical pressures are the 'top down' structural forces from global competition, new technologies and greater price transparency that have been discussed. If these downward structural pressures are increasing, then they will limit or delay the rise in interest rates necessary to keep inflation from rising when domestic demand is strong.

The relative importance of cyclical and structural factors in price setting is rarely clear cut, but micro- and survey-evidence, to which we now turn, can help to establish whether particular prices rise and fall with demand or exhibit longer-term, structural behaviour.

The obvious place to look for structural pressures on margins through international competition is in the prices of goods that are both widely traded and traditionally purchased through retailers. Three examples are apparent among the major categories that make up the RPIX. Household goods, shown in Figure 2.9, exhibit a clear deflationary tendency since 1996 despite strong demand growth in that category for much of that period. Textiles, clothing and footwear demand has seen some major ups and downs over the past five years while prices have been

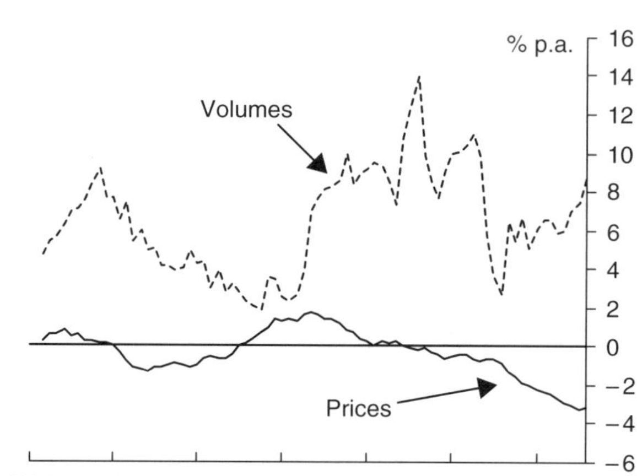

Figure 2.9 Household goods.

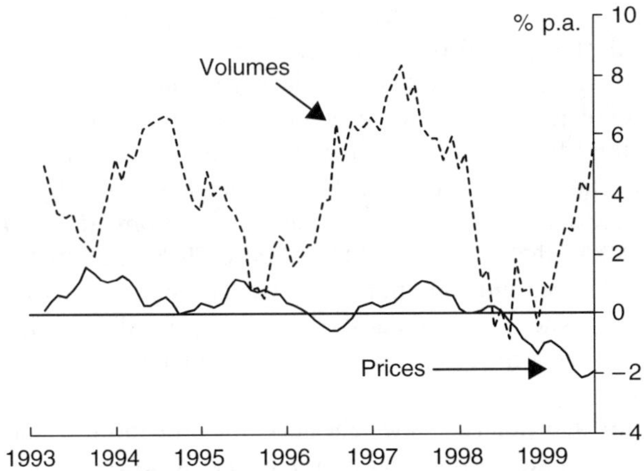

Figure 2.10 Textiles, clothing and footwear.

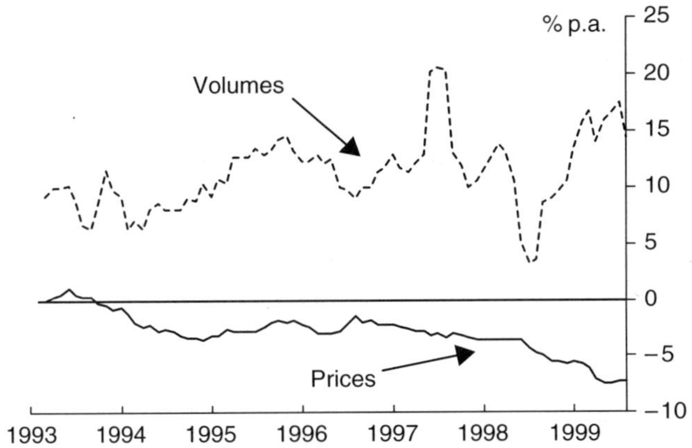

Figure 2.11 Electrical goods.

flat or falling (Figure 2.10). The picture for electrical goods is even more striking (Figure 2.11). Prices have been falling over most of the 1990s, while demand has grown very strongly. Of course, part of the fall in electrical-good prices is probably explained by technical progress, but this picture is also consistent with an increase in global capacity in these sectors and competitive pressure on retailers. Temporary factors such as the sterling's appreciation and the Asian crisis probably accelerated these deflationary trends but they do not map cleanly onto them. And despite strengthening domestic demand, new retail competitors in these and other sectors such as food may cause these price declines to accelerate.

There is also evidence from the CBI Survey of manufacturing firms on the weakening link between domestic-capacity utilisation and prices. Figure 2.12 shows the falling trend of expected output prices since the mid-1990s despite relatively high levels of capacity use at least between 1995 and 1998.

A third source of evidence on this point comes from the September-1999 survey carried out at the MPC's request by the Bank's regional agents, on the question of structural changes in retailing. This is not a statistically robust national sample but rather a reasonably diverse collection of information by those with in-depth knowledge of the respondents' businesses. The agents spoke with 102 firms covering retail goods and household services (such as insurance) across the country (Figure 2.13). They asked about the extent of price discounting and the reasons behind it. They were trying to gain an insight into whether those reasons were structural or cyclical.

Confirming the picture in official statistics, the survey results showed that most of the pickup in retail sales values over the past year had resulted from higher volumes, not higher prices. More than half of all respondents reported larger or more frequent discounting over the past 12 months compared to a year ago (Figure 2.14). Only 5 per cent of the sample reported less discounting. Discounting had increased particularly for food, cars and clothing.

Around two-thirds of respondents cited either changes in consumer behaviour or new or existing competition as reasons for greater discounting – in other words, structural rather than cyclical changes were responsible (Figure 2.15).

New competitors were particularly referred to by leisure and DIY contacts – less so by food and clothing retailers. However, the 'Walmart effect' is focusing minds in areas such as clothing, because of their global buying power, and the Internet is perceived as a growing influence driving down prices. Retail-pricing

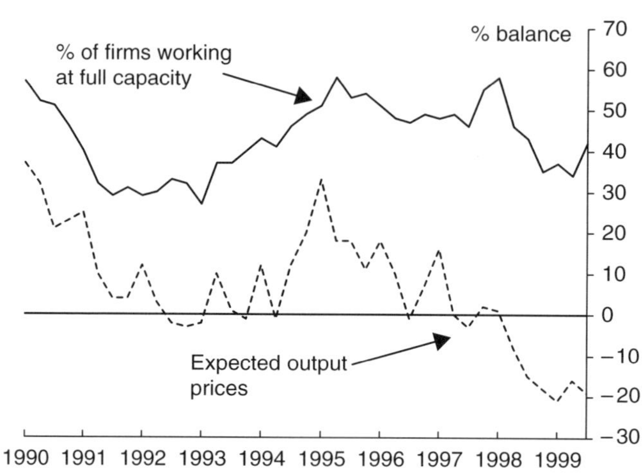

Figure 2.12 CBI capacity utilisation and prices.

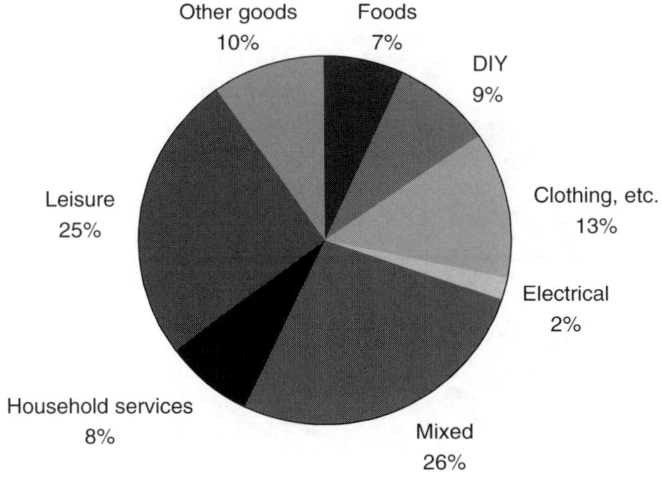

Figure 2.13 Sample coverage.

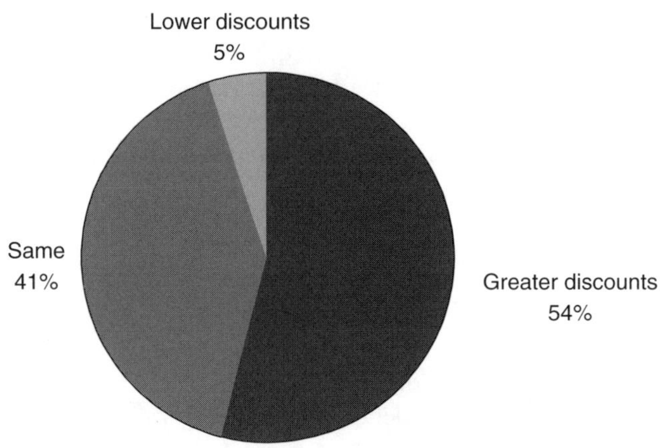

Figure 2.14 Extent of price discounting.

points are an integral feature of the market and resistance to changing them is significant, especially as the customer wants to benchmark his/her bargain against a known price. In sum, this survey showed discounting to be a widespread phenomenon which is becoming an expected feature of the market, at least in sectors such as mixed retail, food and clothing. This reflects perceptions that

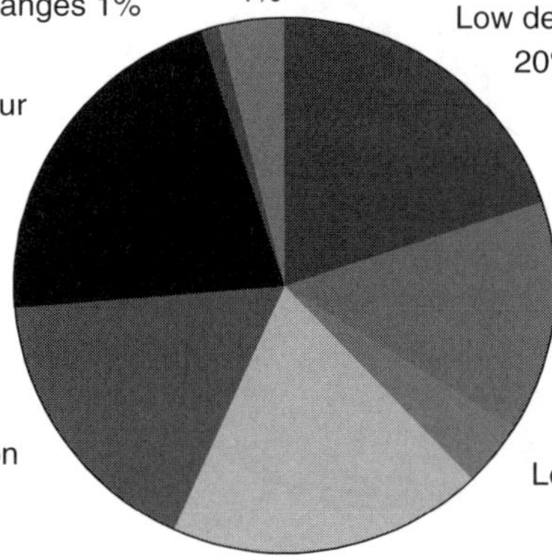

Figure 2.15 Reasons for discounting.

consumers are now accustomed to looking for bargains, and retailers say this is unlikely to change.

On the prices front, then, there is considerable evidence in the UK to suggest that long-term structural changes are bringing effective downward pressures to bear on prices and margins, even during times of relatively robust demand and high domestic capacity utilisation.

Are these competitive pressures feeding through to a supply-side improvement?

Unfortunately, the short answer to this question is 'We won't know until at least ten years hence.' Productivity improvements take time to germinate and statisticians take even longer to confirm them.

In the US, some evidence of a productivity-growth shift has begun to emerge. Since 1996, US labour productivity has risen at an annual average rate of 2.0 per cent, well above its average of 1.4 per cent since 1970. Moreover, this is more than appears to be explained by the growth of capital inputs – total factor productivity has risen also. However, there is debate about the extent to which higher productivity is concentrated in the computer sector where sharp price falls have boosted output (Gordon, 1999).[4]

In the UK, which is generally reckoned to be about three years behind the US in ICT penetration, annual labour-productivity growth has slowed since 1995, averaging around 1.5 per cent compared with a long-run average of just above

2.0 per cent. The MPC suggested in its May *Inflation Report* that this slowdown may be partly explained by firms anticipating only a temporary slowdown in demand. If so, this and other cyclical factors such as capacity utilisation, may be obscuring underlying improvements in productivity. In fact, from productivity data itself, it is difficult to discern either structural or cyclical patterns (Figure 2.16).

In any case, labour productivity provides only a partial explanation of trend growth. In a growth accounting framework, real GDP growth can be decomposed into the growth of capital inputs, labour inputs, and the efficiency with which these inputs are combined in production – or total factor productivity growth. It is more useful to analyse these determinants over longer time-horizons when cyclical influences are less predominant.

Figure 2.17 shows a decomposition of UK growth by decade since 1963. It shows how growth was affected by the oil shocks, falling from an annual average rate of almost 3 per cent between 1963 and 1970 to below 2 per cent between 1971 and 1980. Part of this fall is accounted for by capital inputs, whose contribution to growth virtually halved between the 1960s and subsequent decades. There was a sharp decline in productivity post-1973 as well, but the slower growth of investment and the capital stock mattered more. Shorter working hours and a stagnant labour force have meant that the contribution of labour inputs has been negative in three out of the last four decades, with the industrial stoppages of the 1970s particularly affecting that decade. Labour inputs have been an important swing factor in delivering higher growth. During the 1980s, higher employment and hours worked made a positive contribution to growth, more than accounting for the increase in growth rates over the 1970s. Demography and better industrial relations partly explain this, but social and economic changes which increased female participation in the labour force were also important.

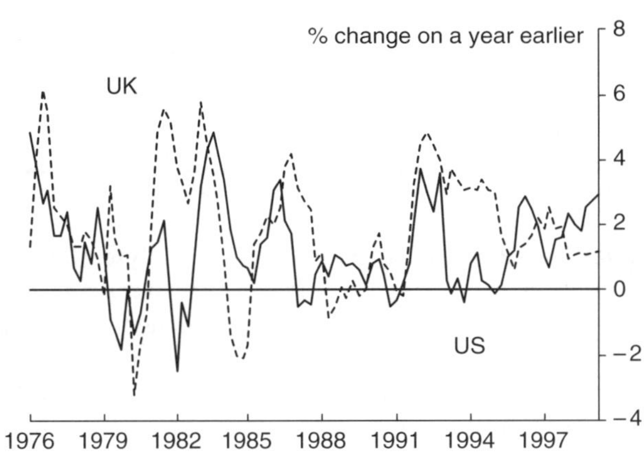

Figure 2.16 US and UK labour productivity.

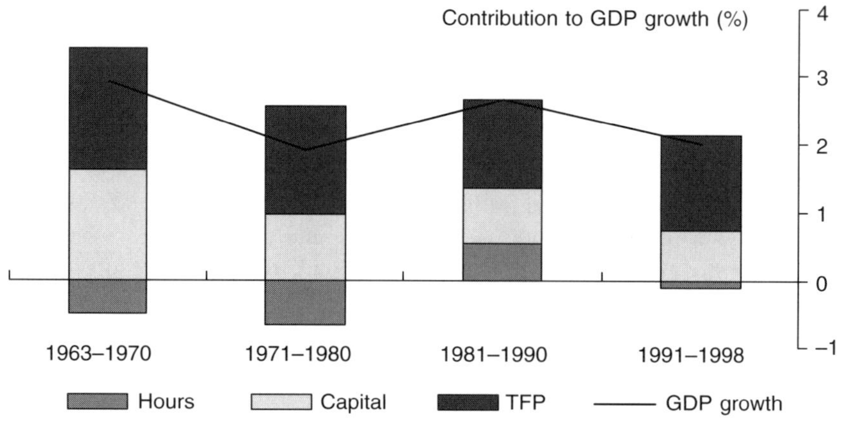

Figure 2.17 Growth accounting 1963–98.

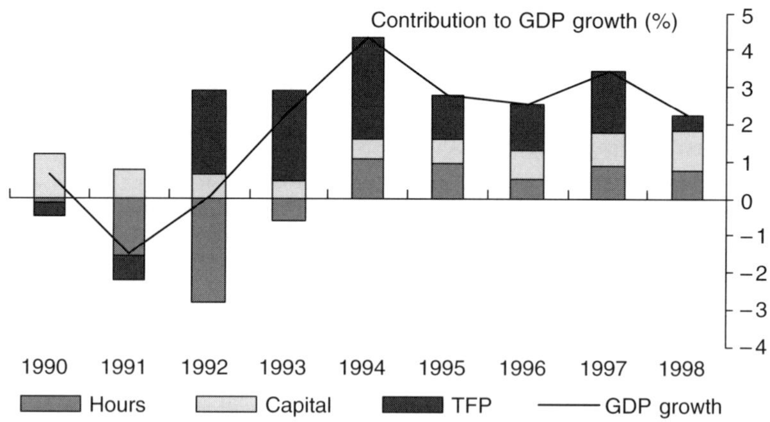

Figure 2.18 Growth accounting 1990–98.

Against this historical backdrop, it is interesting to analyse the growth patterns of the 1990s in more detail (Figure 2.18). As the upswing gathered pace, both employment and total factor productivity switched from making negative to positive contributions to growth. Employment growth has continued over the decade as unemployment has fallen and, at least until very recently, the rate of labour-force participation has risen. There is scope for a further rise if female-participation rates continue to converge with those in the US and if government programmes such as the New Deal and the Working

Families Tax Credit succeed in drawing more people into employment. Both prospects are made more likely by the current tightness in the labour market as signalled by the low unemployment rate. Once in the labour force, those formerly without a job gain experience that can make them more attractive to the next employer. Such hysteresis effects mean that prolonged periods of low unemployment can gradually reduce an economy's natural rate of unemployment that is compatible with stable inflation. Only time will tell if that is currently happening in Britain.

The other factor behind the UK's growth performance during the 1990s has been the strong increase in investment (Figure 2.19). Business investment has risen at an annual average of 6.8 per cent compared with a long-run average since 1965 of 2.7 per cent. It reached a record high in 1998 of 14 per cent of GDP, compared with a long-run average of around 10 per cent. We do not know how much of this increased investment has been in computers and related new technologies because no separate estimates are available in the UK. But investment trends in the US and UK have been similar, and we know that much of the growth in the US can be attributed to ICT investment. In the US, there was a five-year lag between the rise in investment and the eventual rise in measured, economy-wide productivity. If the UK were to follow that pattern, then evidence of an improvement in productivity would begin to emerge next year. However, recall my earlier chart showing the huge year-to-year swings in measured productivity both in the US and the UK. Even if our recent investment patterns launch us into the millennium at a higher rate of productivity growth, we probably cannot confirm that for at least another decade.

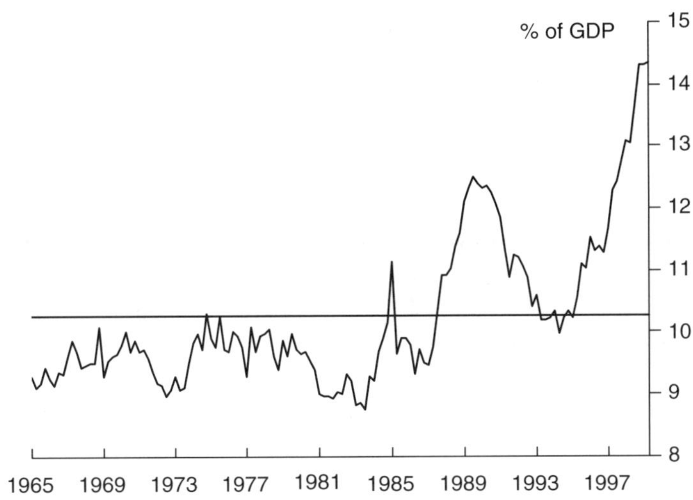

Figure 2.19 UK business investment.

Implications for policy-makers

To conclude, let me try to distil some practical advice for policy-makers out of the picture of change and inevitable uncertainty that I have been painting.

First, be sceptical of forecasts They are necessarily built upon the behavioural relationship of the past. Many of these will persist into the future. But in the case of global inflation, the 1970s and 1980s were particularly unfortunate decades. Dependence on oil and the Middle East, coupled with the abandonment of fixed exchange-rate anchors, produced inflationary tendencies in the global environment that policy-makers of the time were slow to recognise. In other decades, both past and present, the prevailing global forces have been mildly deflationary, driven by declining production costs and expanding competition. This change in 'wind direction' is too subtle, too pervasive and too recent for conventional forecasting models to incorporate.

Historically calibrated models of the UK are likely to pose particular risks in this regard because of Britain's exceptionally poor inflation performance during the 1970s and 1980s. In the forecasting work we do at the Bank of England, we try to take account of this by regularly reviewing discrepancies between our equation forecasts and actual outturns, and then imposing judgmental changes on the equations where we think they may be misleading us. We also try to illustrate the high degree of uncertainty around our forecasts by presenting them as fan charts of probability distributions rather than point-estimates. However, this does not address the bias that may be present in the model itself, and there is still a tendency by commentators to focus on the central forecast point at the two-year horizon and use the difference between that and our point-target for inflation as the central guide to policy.

Second, listen and learn from real-time experience If model-based forecasts are highly uncertain and potentially misleading, then it is especially important to seek out complementary sources of information and interpretations of economic developments from those actually in the thick of the action. The Bank's regional agents hold detailed discussions with business people around the country to provide us with such feedback. In addition, I find that first-hand meetings and visits often yield insights into puzzles in the data or provoke new ideas for our econometricians to test back in London. The many membership surveys that are carried out by organisations such as the CBI, the BCC, CIPS, EEF, etc. also help to shed light on current and future developments as revealed through orders and expectations. In changing times it pays to be eclectic.

Third, pay special attention to prices Economists are trained to think of prices as information signals. They are sensitive indicators, revealing even small shifts in supply or demand. They are readily observable, unlike output gaps, natural rates of unemployment or trend productivity. One particular set of prices is also our inflation target, and every sportsman knows the value of keeping a close eye on one's target! But the lags between changes in interest rates and inflation are such that we must also watch prices all along the supply chain. Input prices – from oil and other commodities to wages and commercial rents – will eventually influence retail prices. This 'bottom up' view of pricing is incorporated into the Bank's and most other forecasters' models. But output prices – and output-price expectations – will also influence margins, and eventually wages, rents and other negotiated input prices. In a world of stronger global competition and more price transparency, one might expect such 'top down' price-setting behaviour to become more widespread. So, as well as looking at model-based inflation forecasts, we should remember that current prices, at all levels, remain our most accurate and timely barometers of inflationary and deflationary pressures in the economy.

Fourth and finally, be pre-emptive, but delicately so If one has reason to believe that the economy is in a period of transition and that the global trends from the 1970s and 1980s no longer provide a confident grounding for forecasts, then one needs to tread carefully. It is still right, given transmission lags, to move interest rates before inflation deviates significantly from target. But we must recognise that firms and households are learning new behavioural patterns in response to the new technologies and competitive pressures facing them. Aggressive patterns of policy change, or activist attempts to fine-tune the future, carry particular risks during such junctures.

This is not a new insight in response to a new paradigm. It is another example of applying the lessons of the past. The paper by Orphanides, to which I referred earlier, concluded, after his examination of the policy mistakes in the US that led to what he calls the Great Inflation of the 1970s:

> Fundamentally, it may matter not so much whether policy is driven by rule versus discretion but whether policy reflects prudence versus over-confidence. This indicates the profound importance of appreciating the information problem for successful policy design... Activist discretionary policy as well as activist rules will fail to deliver on their promise when they are based on a false presumption of confidence about the policymaker's understanding of the economy.
>
> (Orphanides, 1999)

To avoid the policy mistakes of the past, one should be open-minded about the paradigms – new or old – that will shape our future.

Notes

1 'e-commere@its best', September 1999, Report by Performance and Innovation Unit (PIU), Cabinet Office.

2 Athanasios Orphanides, 'The quest for prosperity without inflation', Staff paper, Federal Board of Governors, May 1999.
3 As measured by Internet hosts per thousand inhabitants reported by the OECD Internet Software Consortium.
4 Gordon, R. J., 'Has the "New Economy" rendered the productivity slowdown obsolete?', June 1999.

3 Does faster inflation raise or cut the rate of growth?

Peter Sinclair

Introduction

The aim of this contribution to the volume is to examine the long-run consequences for economic growth stemming from inflation. Inflation and growth are among the major topics on which Max Fry conducted voluminous and penetrating research; this chapter is offered as a tribute to the memory of a superb economist and an excellent friend.

In traditional models, the rate of economic growth eventually settles down to the sum of the rates of population growth and Harrod-neutral technological progress. Both of these are taken to be exogenous. In such a setting, therefore, changes in monetary conditions can only exert transitional effects on the rate of growth.

With the advent of exogenous growth models, real rates of interest and growth are often solved interdependently. That opens them to a variety of influences. It is possible that the rate of inflation is one of these.

There has been recent empirical research on the relationship between growth and inflation (e.g. Barro, 1995). The cross-section evidence is that faster inflation appears to depress the rate of growth slightly. But, as yet, there is no formal theoretical model that can explain this. The paucity of research on the theory of endogenous growth and inflation stands in paradoxical contrast with the wealth of literature on other relationships. Those between money, prices and output in the short run are reviewed by Blanchard (1990). Those between inflation and growth in a traditional exogenous-growth framework are summarized by Orphanides and Solow (1990); and between growth and certain fiscal parameters by Barro (1990), and Lucas (1990). The present chapter attempts to help to fill a gap. The conclusion is that, while inflation can raise or lower growth in the long run, the latter is much the more probable outcome.

The issues

The central ideas in this paper are as follows. Endogenous growth explored here is taken to be generated by some combination of externalities and human capital formation. The first of these is first developed by Romer (1986). The second originates with Lucas (1988). These constitute the two simplest and best-known models of endogenous growth. We shall amalgamate them. Towards the end of the paper, we shall briefly review how inflation can be introduced, *inter alia*, into the later, knowledge-based model of Romer (1990).

Liquidity can be valuable for two reasons. First, it may be intrinsically desirable, entering agents' utility functions directly (as in Brock, 1974; Phelps, 1973; Sidrauski, 1967). One underlying reason for this may be that greater (real) liquid assets could act as a reserve that might stabilize consumption in the face of shocks. Second, liquidity may act as a time-saver, as for example, in the models of Braun (1994) and Guidotti and Vegh (1993). This may be thought of as a simple extension of a cash-in-advance principle. Since there is some plausibility in each of these approaches, we shall allow both avenues to operate, and see how their effects compare. One novel feature will be to introduce a possible role for claims on physical capital in the definition of liquid assets. We shall assume that a modest fraction of an agent's physical capital stock can be treated as equivalent to real money in the definition of liquid assets. This encapsulates the idea that you can always get a loan when you can prove you do not need it. Borrowing against human capital, by contrast, is much harder. Three key parameters will be shown to have a major bearing on the sign and magnitude of the long-run growth impact of inflation. These are:

1 the relative weights on the human capital and externalities variables in the production function, as captured by the parameter ϵ;
2 the weight on physical capital claims in liquid assets (η);
3 the ratio of the direct utility effect from liquidity (σ) to the constant term for liquidity in the agent's time endowment (μ).

Later in the chapter, we shall also explore the possibility that training calls for input of materials, rather than time. In other respects, the model to be deployed follows familiar lines. Homogeneous immortal agents plan optimal paths for consumption and their assets, subject to a budget constraint equating income to the sum of investment and consumption in every period. There is an exogenous, uniform and constant rate of pure time preference. Income diverted to increases in real balances, and to covering their inflation-opportunity cost, is returned as a lump sum. Attention concentrates on the steady-state solution to the optimization problem. Utility, production and transaction time functions are restricted to forms that permit steady-state solutions, where consumption, output and all assets increase in parallel.

First, optimization conditions are combined to derive an equation, linking the rate of inflation to the rate of growth. This equation is studied in various special cases, such as the 'Optimum Quantity of Money' rule where prices decline at a rate driving the nominal interest rate to zero. The equation is differentiated to obtain a general expression for the derivative of growth with respect to inflation. This general expression can then be examined to derive conclusions about the significance of the three key parameters mentioned above (ϵ, η, and σ/μ).

Analysis

Undiscounted utility at any date t depends upon the agent's consumption (c) and possibly also upon real money (m) and physical capital (k) at that date

$$U(t) = \frac{c(t)^{1-\beta} + \sigma(m(t) + \eta k(t))^{1-\beta} - 1 - \sigma}{1-\beta}, \qquad (1)$$

$$\beta > 0, \quad \eta, \sigma \geq 0, \quad 1 \gg \eta.$$

In Equation (1), β, which is positive, represents the coefficient of relative risk-aversion. Only this functional form is capable of sustaining a steady state with growth. If $\beta \to 1$, (1) reduces to

$$U(t) = \ln c(t) + \sigma \ln(m(t) + \eta k(t)). \qquad (2)$$

In Equations (1) and (2), σ reflects the relative strength of the direct utility from 'liquidity' as opposed to consumption. This parameter may be zero or positive, as may η, which captures the 'liquidity' of physical capital. Unlike σ, η is bounded above. Its maximum value is substantially less than one. Were η to equal or exceed 1, money would be a dominated asset and the rate of inflation would be meaningless.

The production function links output per head, $q(t)$, to own physical capital, and at least some of the following additional variables: capital per head elsewhere in the economy, $K(t)$; a Harrod-neutral technology parameter $B(t)$, representing human capital per head; a Hicks-neutral constant, T; net of transactions time s; and a labour endowment of 1, net of both transactions time s and training time, $x\dot{B}(t)$. The functional form is Cobb–Douglas which can sustain a steady state:

$$q(t) = Tk(t)^{\gamma}[K(t)(1-s(t))]^{\epsilon(1-\gamma)}\left[B(t)(1-s(t)) - x\dot{B}(t)\right]^{(1-\epsilon)(1-\gamma)}, \qquad (3)$$

$$1 \geq \epsilon \geq 0, \quad 1 > \gamma > 0.$$

When $\epsilon = 1$, we have a pure externalities model of endogenous growth, not unlike Romer (1986); at the opposite extreme where ϵ vanishes, Equation (3) supports a pure training model of endogenous growth, with resemblance to that pioneered by Lucas (1988).

Transactions time depends on the ratio of consumption to 'liquidity'. Only this will permit steady-state solutions. We shall assume that s is increasing in $c/(m + \eta k)$, and that $s(o)$ vanishes. There is a constant coefficient, μ, in the s function, which captures the magnitude of the time-saving benefit from holding liquidity. The simplest form for s with which we shall work, is linear:

$$s(t) = \mu\left[\frac{c(t)}{m(t) + \eta k(t)}\right], \quad \mu \geq 0. \qquad (4)$$

The budget constraint, binding at each instant, is

$$q(t) + y(t) - \pi(t)m(t) - \dot{m}(t) - c(t) - \dot{k}(t) = 0. \tag{5}$$

In Equation (5), $y(t)$ is the return of seignorage $(\pi(t)m(t) + \dot{m}(t))$ and $\pi(t)$ is the rate of inflation. As (5) reveals, we shall simplify by setting population growth and physical capital depreciation to zero.

The agent's task is to select paths for $c(t)$, $B(t)$, $k(t)$ and $m(t)$ to maximize, from date 0,

$$\phi = \int_0^{\infty} \left[\mathrm{e}^{-\alpha t} U(t) + \lambda(t)[q(t) + y(t) - \pi(t)m(t) - \dot{m}(t) - c(t) - k(\dot{t})] \right] \mathrm{d}t, \tag{6}$$

where $\alpha > 0$ and $U(t)$ and $q(t)$ are defined by Equations (1) [or (2)], (3) and (4).

In Equation (6), α represents the pure rate of impatience, and $\lambda(t)$ is the marginal utility of income at date t. The agent starts at date 0 with inherited values of assets $m(0)$, $k(0)$ and $B(0)$. There are five first-order conditions for an interior solution to this maximum problem. One, $\partial\phi/\partial\lambda(t)$, restates the budget constraint Equation (5). A second expresses the condition for optimal consumption:

$$\frac{\partial \phi}{\partial c(t)} = 0 = \mathrm{e}^{-\alpha t} c(t)^{-\beta} - \lambda(t) \left[1 + \frac{\mu F(t) q(t)}{c(t)} A(t) \right], \tag{7}$$

where

$$A(t) \equiv (1 - \gamma) \left[\frac{\epsilon}{1 - s(t)} + \frac{(1 - \epsilon)}{1 - s(t) - x\dot{B}(t)/B(t)} \right] \quad \text{and} \quad F(t) \equiv \frac{c(t)}{m(t) + \eta k(t)}.$$

The presence of the second term inside the square brackets in Equation (7) testifies to the additional drawback that consumption has in our setting; it augments transactions time, thus inhibiting output.

The remaining three first-order conditions are Euler equations on assets. These equate the marginal net benefit of *stocks* to the time derivative of the marginal net benefit of *increases* in stocks. In full:

$$\begin{aligned} \frac{\partial \phi}{\partial B(t)} &= \frac{\lambda(t)[1 - s(t)](1 - \epsilon)(1 - \gamma) q(t)}{B(t)\left[1 - s(t) - x\dot{B}(t)/B(t)\right]} \\ &= \frac{\mathrm{d}}{\mathrm{d}t} \left[\frac{-\lambda(t) x (1 - \epsilon)(1 - \gamma) q(t)}{B(t)[1 - s(t) - x\dot{B}(t)/B(t)]} \right], \end{aligned} \tag{8}$$

$$\begin{aligned}\frac{\partial\phi}{\partial m(t)} &= \mathrm{e}^{-\alpha t}\sigma(m(t)+\eta k(t))^{-\beta}+\lambda(t)\left[\frac{\mu F^2(t)q(t)A(t)}{c(t)}-\pi(t)\right]\\ &= \frac{\mathrm{d}}{\mathrm{d}t}\frac{\partial\phi}{\partial\dot{m}(t)} = -\dot{\lambda}(t),\end{aligned} \tag{9}$$

$$\begin{aligned}\frac{\partial\phi}{\partial k(t)} &= \mathrm{e}^{-\alpha t}\eta\sigma(m(t)+\eta k(t))^{-\beta}+\lambda(t)\left[\frac{\mu F^2(t)q(t)A(t)}{c(t)}+\frac{\gamma q(t)}{k(t)}\right]\\ &= \frac{\mathrm{d}}{\mathrm{d}t}\frac{\partial\phi}{\partial\dot{k}(t)} = -\dot{\lambda}(t).\end{aligned} \tag{10}$$

Equations (8), (9) and (10) describe optimum stock-flow conditions for human capital, real money and physical capital respectively. If $\epsilon = 1$, Equation (8) is deleted.

In the steady state, *F*, *A* and the ratio *q/c* (the reciprocal of the propensity to consume) are all stationary, so that

$$-\hat{\lambda}(t) = \alpha + \beta g, \tag{11}$$

where '$\wedge$' denotes a proportional rate of change, and *g* is the rate of growth of real income. With $\epsilon < 1$, so that Equation (8) applies, we must have $\hat{B}(t) = g$, with *q/B* constant in the steady state, so that Equations (8) and (11) reduce to

$$1 - s = (\alpha + \beta g)x. \tag{12}$$

This is an important result. It tells us that additional transactions time can only imply a lower rate of growth.

Together, Equations (9) and (10) imply a steady-state relation linking growth, real interest (*r*) and inflation:

$$r = (\alpha + \beta g)(1 - \eta) - \eta\pi. \tag{13}$$

This tells us that real interest and growth are positively associated, for a given inflation rate. The idea here is that a higher real-interest rate, all else equal, implies a faster rate of growth of consumption (and hence, output). It also points to a positive growth–inflation link, at least when $\eta > 0$, for a given real rate of interest. However, since higher inflation implies lower real balances and hence, presumably increased *s*, Equations (12) and (13) indicate a conflict between two inflation–growth associations. It is our main purpose in this chapter to see how this conflict is resolved.

Since Equation (4) may be written $s = \mu F$, we may now combine Equations (9), (11), (12) and (13) to write

$$\pi + \alpha + \beta g = \frac{\mu F}{x}\frac{q}{c}A\left[F + \sigma F^{\beta}\right] + \sigma F^{\beta}. \tag{14}$$

The LHS of Equation (14) is the nominal rate of interest. The RHS is an increasing function of the consumption–liquidity ratio *F*. When *F* vanishes, the nominal interest rate is zero. That special case illustrates the Optimum Quantity of Money rule, where prices decline at the real interest rate (here, $\alpha+\beta g$), and money is so high that liquidity is infinite.

In this special case, with F (and s) vanishing, Equation (12) gives us a solution for the rate of growth:

$$g = \frac{1}{\beta}\left[\frac{1}{x} - \alpha\right]. \tag{15}$$

Equation (15) applies whenever there is at least some role for human capital evolution through training. The real interest rate equals $1/x$ in that case. If endogenous growth consists exclusively of the externality mechanism, so that $\epsilon = 1$, we find that r reduces to γT (since $k = K$, s vanishes with $\pi = -\alpha - \beta g$ and the human capital term in Equation (3) drops out, so that

$$g = \frac{1}{\beta}[\gamma T - \alpha]. \tag{16}$$

To repeat: when prices decline at the real rate of interest, Equation (15) solves for the steady-state growth rate, except when human capital is excluded completely from the growth process, and, in that case, Equation (16) applies.

Outside the Optimum Quantity of Money case, inflation exceeds minus the real interest rate. The nominal interest rate, and the level of transactions time, are both positive now. A quick glance at Equation (14) suggests that inflation can be found as an explicit function of growth (recall that (12) makes F, and s, depend upon g alone). Alas, this hope is misplaced. Buried in Equation (14) is the ratio q/c. This, it transpires, also depends upon π. Let us see how.

The return of full seignorage implies $y = \pi m + \dot{m}$, so that (5) reduces to

$$q = c + \dot{k}. \tag{17}$$

Since $\hat{k} = g$, $c/q = 1 - (g\gamma)/r$, so that, using (13),

$$\frac{q}{c} = \left[1 - \frac{g\gamma}{(\alpha+\beta g)(1-\eta) - \eta\pi}\right]^{-1}. \tag{18}$$

Equation (18) reveals that whenever η is positive, a rise in the rate of inflation acts to raise q/c and hence the RHS of Equation (14). The intuition here is that faster inflation prompts agents to accumulate more capital. The ensuing fall in real balances encourages them to hold more capital, to rebuild liquidity somewhat. So the steady-state savings propensity out of income rises. This is a Tobinesque mechanism, capturing the essential argument of Tobin (1965). It operates unless η vanishes. It also underlies the positive growth–inflation link revealed by Equation (13). Our main question turns on when and whether it can ever be powerful enough to overhaul the negative growth–inflation link indicated by Equation (12) and the other elements of Equation (14).

A final refinement is to define a new parameter ζ:

$$\zeta \equiv \frac{\pi}{\alpha + \beta g}. \tag{19}$$

ζ is the ratio of inflation to the real rate of interest. When the Optimum Quantity of Money rule is obeyed, ζ is at its minimum value of -1. Otherwise, $\zeta > -1$. The algebraic analysis is somewhat lightened with ζ taken as the inflation parameter, rather than π.

We may now rewrite Equation (14) as

$$\frac{c}{q} G = H, \tag{20}$$

where $H \equiv (\mu FA)/x[F + \sigma\ F^{\beta}]$, $G \equiv (\alpha + \beta g)(1 + \zeta) - \sigma F^{\beta}$ and c/q is given by Equation (18).

At $\zeta \rightarrow -1$, so that $F \rightarrow 0$, the derivative showing the marginal effect of inflation on growth reduces to

$$\frac{\mathrm{d}g}{\mathrm{d}\zeta} \rightarrow -\frac{\mu F^{1-\beta}}{\sigma(\beta x)^2}. \tag{21}$$

This expression is non-positive under all conditions. It tells us that raising inflation infinitesimally above its Optimum Quantity of money value can never raise the growth rate, at least when human-capital development plays some role in the growth process (so that $\epsilon < 1$, and Equation (8) holds).

The derivative vanishes in two cases. If liquidity has negligible effect on transactions time, μ falls to zero and with it, $\mathrm{d}g/\mathrm{d}\zeta$. This can be observed directly from Equation (12), because F now vanishes. The result also holds with μ positive but with F zero and β less than 1.

At the other extreme, there are two circumstances when $\mathrm{d}\zeta/\mathrm{d}g$ vanishes, implying an infinitely large (negative) effect of inflation on growth. This occurs when σ, the coefficient governing the pure utility effect on liquidity vanishes, or when β exceeds unity (with $F = 0$).

At the critical intermediate case where $\beta = 1$, and both μ and σ are positive, Equation (21) shows that the marginal effect of inflation on growth is finite and strictly negative. It is proportional to the ratio of μ to σ. The greater the liquidity effect on transactions time as opposed to direct utility, the larger μ/σ will be, and the steeper the negative impact of inflation on growth at this point.

A further result – conditional on $\epsilon < 1$ and $\mu > 0$ so that human-capital evolution occurs and transactions time is non-trivial – is that the growth rate at the Optimum Quantity of Money, given by Equation (15), is higher than when inflation is at any higher rate. When $\zeta > -1$ and $\mu > 0$, it is impossible for F to be less than strictly positive. Equation (12), which always holds when $\epsilon < 1$, then tells us that the value of the growth rate whenever $\zeta > -1$ will be less than its Optimum Quantity of Money value, given by (15).

With externalities providing the sole mechanism of endogenous growth ($\epsilon = 1$), or a transactions-time reducing role for liquidity deleted ($\sigma > 0 = \mu$), these results do not apply.

If $\epsilon = 1$ and $\mu = 0$, the real rate of interest, r, reduces to γT. From Equation (13), we see that inflation can now only exert a non-negative effect on growth:

$$\frac{\mathrm{d}g}{\mathrm{d}\pi} = \frac{\eta}{(1-\eta)\beta}. \tag{22}$$

The magnitude of this effect increases with η, the liquidity component in real capital. It vanishes only when η is zero. Equation (22) holds for all values of π. This is a pure Tobin case.

With $\mu = 0$ but $\epsilon < 1$, Equation (12) now solves for the growth rate directly, with s deleted. The growth rate is given by Equation (15) at all values of π or ζ. The rate of inflation has no effect on the rate of growth here. It merely serves to reduce the real rate of interest (assuming that $\eta > 0$).

This leaves the case where $\epsilon = 1$ but $\mu > 0$, which proves to be unexpectedly complex. Equation (13) continues to apply, as always, but the deletion of the human-capital growth mechanism renders Equation (12) inapplicable. The real rate of interest is linked to s (or F) by the marginal productivity condition $r = \gamma T(1-s)^{1-\gamma}$, so that Equation (13) implies

$$\rho \equiv \frac{(\alpha + \beta g)}{\gamma} \frac{(1 - \eta(1+\zeta))}{T} = (1-s)^{1-\gamma}. \tag{23}$$

With $\beta = 1$, at the Optimum Quantity of Money ($\zeta \rightarrow -1$), the marginal effect of inflation on growth reduces to

$$\frac{\mathrm{d}g}{\mathrm{d}\zeta} = \gamma T\left[\eta - (1-\gamma)\frac{\mu}{\sigma}\right] \Big/ \left[1 - \eta + (1-\gamma)\frac{\mu}{\sigma}\right]. \tag{24}$$

This is qualitatively ambiguous. The greater the liquidity component in physical capital (η), and the stronger the direct utility effect of liquidity relative to the transactions-time effect (the higher is σ/μ), the likelier it becomes that inflation exerts a favourable effect on growth here.

Table 3.1 presents some key features of these results. It focuses on the case where $\beta = 1$ and the Optimum Quantity of Money rule holds. The main points to stress here are:

1 more inflation (less price-deflation) never raises growth if η or σ vanishes, or $\epsilon < 1$;
2 the effect becomes more strongly negative, assuming $\epsilon < 1$, as μ/σ increases;
3 the effect vanishes when $\mu = 0$ and $\epsilon < 1$;
4 the effect is positive only when $\epsilon = 1$ and η is large enough (except that when μ vanishes and $\epsilon = 1$, positive η suffices).

Table 3.1 The marginal effect of inflation on growth, evaluated at the optimum quantity of money with utility logarithmic ($\beta = 1$). Role of human-capital development in endogenous growth

		Present ($\epsilon < 1$)	*Absent* ($\epsilon = 1$)
Liquidity	Transactions time only ($\sigma = 0$)	Negative	
Transmitter	Mixed ($\sigma, \mu > 0$)	Negative	Ambiguous*
	Direct utility only ($\mu = 0$)	Zero	Non-negative; positive with $\eta > 0$

* With the sign of $\eta - \mu(1 - \gamma)/\sigma$.

Extensions

Inflation in a knowledge-driven model of endogenous growth

Romer's (1990) model of endogenous invention and growth commands attention as a very powerful contribution. It is natural to ask how inflation may affect it.

Two of the effects we have been examining can be incorporated directly. The central idea is that agents' labour is lowered by an increase in the ratio of consumption to liquid assets, in which claims on physical capital play some role. This gives rise to Equation (13), where growth is linked positively to inflation and real interest. One of Romer's two key equations, the positive growth–real-interest relationship derived from a simpler problem than the maximization of Equation (6), is now sensitive to the rate of inflation. Faster inflation raises the common steady-state growth rate of consumption and income implied by a given real rate of interest.

The second effect also turns on the labour-supply inhibiting consequence of faster inflation. What matters critically for Romer's 1990 model is the total stock of 'human capital' – talented individuals who can work either as inventors or suppliers of specialized inputs into final production. The assignment of human capital between these functions is determined by the equalization of rewards. Inflation does not erode the number of such people. But it lowers the time they can devote to either of these activities.

Growth stems from invention in this model. Inventors produce blueprints for new types of capital good. Their productivity is proportional to the stock of previous inventions. A new blueprint is auctioned to an entrepreneur who uses it to produce the new type of machine, and, since it is unique, he earns a monopoly rent from it. The capitalized value of the permanent rental stream is inversely proportional to the real rate of interest. Higher interest implies lower design auction prices, less reward for inventors, slower discoveries, and hence, slower growth. This generates a negative growth–interest link. Steady-state growth and real interest are solved by combining it with the positive link derived from the intertemporal optimization of households.

Faster inflation must detract from the output of inventors. The range of capital goods will therefore increase more slowly, implying slower growth in final output. Romer's negative growth–interest link is undermined by inflation, so that the growth rate for any rate of interest is reduced. The combination of the two effects inflation introduces must tend to lower the real rate of interest. What happens to the rate of growth is ambiguous; it depends upon the relative size of the shifts to the two relationships, and on their gradients in growth–interest space. The most favourable outcome for growth arises when the positive link is relatively sensitive to inflation (high η). If η vanishes, so that liquidity is confined to money only, the growth rate must fall.

The engine of growth in this Romer model is the stock of knowledge (new and inherited designs), which maps one-to-one into the range of physical goods in production. This range of machines (and the stock of knowledge that created it), is the only factor of production in the final output sector which advances; labour, and the human capital that works there, are stationary.

Inflation is an endogenous growth model with an exhaustible resource

Another type of endogenous growth model that relies on a third factor of production adds a role for an exhaustible resource, such as oil. In a steady state, oil inputs into production must decline at the rate at which the stock of oil is depleted; faster depletion implies slower growth; the rate of depletion is governed by portfolio equilibrium conditions that generate a Hotelling resource price path under suitable assumptions. Sinclair (1994) offers a model of this kind.

Endogenous human-capital growth and inflation can be introduced into such a setting in the following manner. Suppose we retain the general features of the initial optimization problem in Equation (6), replacing Equation (1) by Equation (2) for convenience, and modifying the production function in Equation (3) to

$$q(t) = k(t)^{\gamma}\left[B(t)(1 - s(t)) - x\dot{B}(t)\right]^{\delta}\left[-\dot{S}(t)\right]^{1-\gamma-\delta}. \tag{3'}$$

Here, $S(t)$ denotes the stock of oil (per head) at date (t), and its time derivative is the absolute rate of extraction. Oil is assumed to enter production as soon as it is extracted, and extraction costs are ignored.

To add to our first-order conditions, there is a new Euler stock-flow equation for oil. This generates the condition, given perfect competition, that the price of oil rises at the rate at which λ declines. This equals $\alpha + g$ in the steady state.

In a steady state, the real rate of interest must be stationary, so that capital and output grow in parallel. But the input of oil $-\dot{S}$, must decline. So human capital must now grow more quickly than output. Our real rate of interest Equation (13), continues to hold. A little manipulation implies that the rate of oil depletion equals the rate of impatience ($\beta = 1$ is necessary for this), and from the Euler condition on B, $1 - sx\hat{B} = \alpha x$. The resulting expression for the steady state of growth is

$$g = -\alpha + \frac{\delta}{x}\frac{1-s}{1-\gamma}. \tag{25}$$

As inflation raises transaction time s, it can only lower the long-run rate of growth, at least at the Optimum Quantity of Money; and this is where the growth rate is maximized. This result can be qualified if the value of oil is a (limited) component of liquid assets.

Inflation and the materials-cost training model of endogenous growth

The final extension we shall consider here relates to the evolution of human capital. Up to now it has been assumed that 'training' takes time, but involves no material inputs. That assumption was crucial to the idea of conflict between training time and inflation-induced transaction time; much of the argument for expecting a negative long-run growth–inflation link turned upon it. What happens if we assume that adding to human capital represents a budgetary cost rather than a sacrifice of time?

Let one unit of human capital increase carry a price of ξ. The budget constraint in Equation (5), is now amended to

$$q(t) + y(t) - \pi(t)m(t) - \dot{m}(t) - c(t) - \dot{k}(t) - \xi\dot{B}(t) = 0. \tag{5'}$$

For simplicity, we shall assume that human capital is the sole engine of endogenous growth, so that $\epsilon = 0$ and the externality term in K disappears from Equation (3) and also that μ vanishes, banishing s. The production function reduces therefore, to

$$q(t) = Tk(t)^{\gamma}B(t)^{1-\gamma}. \tag{3''}$$

The relevant first-order conditions for consumption, capital and real money are simplified versions of Equations (7), (9) and (10), shortened by the deletion of ϵ and μ. What really changes is the Euler condition on B. In place of Equation (8) we find

$$\lambda(t)(1-\gamma)[q(t)/B(t)] = \xi\dot{\lambda}(t). \tag{26}$$

In the steady state, Equation (26) and the other conditions imply

$$1-\gamma=(\alpha+\beta g)\xi(r)^{\gamma/(1-\gamma)}. \tag{27}$$

Since Equation (13) continues to hold, it is now a simple matter to find a general expression for the effect of inflation on long-run growth:

$$\frac{\mathrm{d}g}{\mathrm{d}\zeta}=\frac{\eta\gamma}{\beta}\left[\frac{a+\beta g}{1-\eta(1+\zeta)}\right]. \tag{28}$$

This shows that a liquidity role for capital ($\eta > 0$) is necessary and sufficient for inflation to exert a pro-growth effect.

The intuition here is that higher inflation, by depressing real balances of money, makes holding capital more attractive. This leads to a cut in the marginal product of capital. The resulting fall in the real rate of interest makes training 'investment' more attractive. The permanent interest-cost of financing training materials falls. As a consequence, the optimal level of training rises, and human capital advances more quickly, raising the long-run rate of growth.

Regrets

There are numerous limitations in the analysis presented in this chapter. Stochastics are banished, despite the fact that one argument for liquidity entering the utility function depends upon then. We have confined attention to steady states and to the long-run growth–inflation links. No impression of the transitional consequences for the path of output from revisions to the rate of nominal money growth is offered here. There is a single final good, and complete homogeneity of agents; much of the private benefit from money holding turns on the fact that goods and agents are heterogeneous. There is no fiscal activity by government, despite the fact that much popular discussion about the codynamics of output, money and prices betrays awareness that inflation is just one distortionary tax among many. Leisure is absent from the utility function, despite the fact that additional money holdings, by reducing transactions time, may allow agents to enjoy more of it. There are no banks. The author hopes to extend the analysis to encompass some of these points in later work. Some of the other restrictions in this paper are less important, or indeed necessary. The absence of mortality, population growth and capital depreciation for example, is trivial; their inclusion would add nothing of importance (granted that they are exogenous). Most of the isoelastic functional forms adopted are required; without them, the existence of a steady state is imperilled.

Perhaps the greatest regret is that the research behind this chapter revealed so few clear-cut results. Sometimes inflation raises growth. Sometimes it reduces it. Occasionally it has no effect. The key derivative of growth to inflation is, in general form, often ungainly, opaque and ambiguous. As Oscar Wilde observed, the truth is never pure and rarely simple.

Resolution

It has been shown that whether inflation is pro-growth or anti-growth, and how big its effects will be, depends critically on these four issues:

1. The nature of the engine driving endogenous growth (whether it is dominated by externalities or human-capital development);
2. The effect to which physical claims on capital can generate liquidity services similar to real money balances;
3. whether training calls for inputs of time, or materials;
4. whether the real effects of liquidity operate primarily through saving time allotted to transactions, or upon utility directly.

When it is only externalities that generate endogenous growth, and the transaction-time-saving aspect of liquidity is weak, inflation may well be pro-growth. This is especially likely when physical capital claims offer sizable liquidity services. If training helps to generate endogenous growth, and relies on inputs of time, inflation never raises growth, and must reduce it if the time-saving role of liquidity is at all important. When training requires inputs of materials rather than time, inflation is pro-growth. If endogenous growth turns on invention, as in Romer (1990), inflation can favour or reduce growth, and is likelier to harm it when capital provides little liquidity.

Of the two main mechanisms of endogenous growth studied here, it is hard to deny a major role for human-capital development. Training typically involves inputs of both time and materials, but of the two, time is likely to be the more substantial. The argument for liquidity transmission via transactions time-savings has more appeal than the direct utility effect. And although new technologies are increasing the collateralizability of physical capital claims, and enhancing their potential contribution to liquidity services, these points suggest that it is much more probable that we are living in a world where the net long-run impact of inflation on growth is adverse.

The answer to the question 'Does faster inflation raise or cut the rate of growth?' is this. It could do either, but the balance of arguments points unmistakably to a negative effect.

References

Barro, R. J. (1990) 'Government spending in a simple model of endogenous growth', *Journal of Political Economy*, 98, 5103–26.

Barro, R. J. (1995) 'Inflation and Economic Growth', *Bank of England Quarterly Bulletin*, 35, 166–76.

Blanchard, O. J. (1990) 'Why does money affect output? A survey', in B. Friedman and F. H. Hahn (eds), *Handbook of Monetary Economics*, North Holland, pp. 779–835.

Braun, R. J. (1994) 'How large is the optimal inflation tax?' *Journal of Monetary Economics*, 34, 201–14.

Brock, W. A. (1974) 'Money and economic growth: the case of perfect foresight', *International Economic Review*, 15, 750–77.

Guidotti, P. E. and Vegh, C. A. (1993) 'The optimal inflation tax when money reduces transaction costs: a reconsideration', *Journal of Monetary Economics*, 31, 189–205.

Lucas, R. E. (1988) 'On the mechanics of development', *Journal of Monetary Economics*, 22, 3–42.

Lucas, R. E. (1990) 'Supply-side economics: an analytical review', *Oxford Economic Papers*, 42, 293–316.

Orphanides, A. and Solow, R. M. (1990) 'Money, inflation and growth', in B. Friedman and F. H. Hann (eds), *Handbook of Monetary Economics*, North Holland, pp. 223–261.

Phelps, E. (1973) 'Inflation in the theory of public finance', *Swedish Journal of Economics*, 75, 67–82.

Romer, P. (1986) 'Increasing returns and long-run growth', *Journal of Political Economy*, 94, 1002–37.

Romer, P. (1990) 'Endogenous technological change', *Journal of Political Economy*, 98, S71–102.

Sidrauski, M. (1967) 'Inflation and economic growth', *Journal of Political Economy*, 75, 796–810.

Sinclair, P. J. N. (1994) 'On the optimal trend of fossil fuel taxation', *Oxford Economic Papers*, 46, 869–77.

Tobin, J. (1965) 'Money and economic growth', *Econometrica*, 33, 671–84.

4 Recent developments in Central Banking

Some special features of the Monetary Policy Committee and of the European System of Central Banks

Charles Goodhart

Introduction

Regime changes are always exciting, and grist for analysis by the interested commentator. There have been several such regime changes in Central Banking during the last few years, a most exciting period for someone like myself, not only in my capacity as a professional observer of Central Banking but now also as a participant. The Chancellor's initiatives in his first month in office in 1997, to give the Bank of England operational independence, and then subsequently to centralize all financial supervision, including the supervision of banks, in a Financial Services Authority (FSA), caused the most abrupt changes to the functions and structure of the Bank, probably since its foundation. But, of course, the extent and scale of this regime change, though in my view the most important economic developments of the incoming Labour government, have been dwarfed by the move to a single currency, the euro, with its associated European System of Central Banks (ESCB) within the euro area.

There are, of course, many facets of both these institutional changes that one could discuss, and one can also undertake compare-and-contrast exercises, not only for the Bank of England and the ESCB, but also, for example, with the Bank of Japan, which has again recently undergone important institutional changes, several of which are similar to those in the UK. Indeed, there has been a veritable flood of institutional change in the last decade partly carried along on a tide of academic enthusiasm for independent Central Banks and further encouraged by the apparent success of such independent Central Bankers in achieving price stability during a decade in which world growth has, I believe, recovered somewhat from previous decades, despite Asian alarums and excursions.

Perhaps the first main mile stone on this latest voyage was to be found in New Zealand, when the incoming Labour government of Lange and Roger Douglas gave the Reserve Bank under Don Brash its operational independence, with the Reserve Bank of New Zealand Act (1989), reaffirming the commitment to use monetary policy to achieve low inflation. I was an outside consultant to the Reserve Bank of New Zealand (RBNZ), and it remains now an even more personal disappointment that we failed to get my recommendation passed that those responsible for the monetary decisions should get paid largely by results. I might add that New Zealand also led the way in dismantling totally their agricultural protection system, with results that were far less damaging to the farming community than many had feared. New Zealand's emergence as a role model is a fascinating feature of political science, but why the ideas developed there were so much more successful in translation elsewhere in some areas than in others would take me well beyond my own area of competence.

Many of the innovations subsequently adopted, such as operational independence for the Central Bank, inflation targeting, monetary policy committees, structural reorganizations of supervisory systems in the financial system, have become quite widely adopted in Europe, for example, in Sweden and Spain; in America, for example, in Canada and Chile; in South Africa and in Asia, for example, in Japan and, perhaps now, in Thailand, as well as in the Antipodes, Australia and New Zealand. My colleagues in the Deutsche Bundesbank and the Swiss National Bank may, however, at this point, demur and claim that the New Zealand reforms were not so much innovations, but more amendments to their own prior practices adopted in the early 1970s. The big exception remains the USA, but the Federal Reserve System, generally known as the Fed, not only shared certain aspects of the new consensus structure, such as independence, but also has achieved under its last two Chairmen, Paul Volcker and Alan Greenspan, its greatest success and status. As they say there, 'If it ain't broke, don't fix it'.

So what I want to concentrate upon are those aspects of the Monetary Policy Committee (MPC) and then of the ESCB that are special, perhaps unique, to these particular Central Banks. It will, therefore, be a chapter of two rather separate halves. In both, I offer my personal views as an independent academic, but the opening section on the MPC is obviously informed by my personal participation, whereas my comments on the ESCB have no different status than that of any other outside, but interested, observer.

Some aspects of the Monetary Policy Committee

We regularly tend to claim during forecasting meetings at the Bank that current circumstances are uniquely difficult to interpret, but the ESCB is really unique in that it has begun to preside over a single, federal euro-currency area, wherein the vast majority of other economic, fiscal and political competences and powers remain reserved for the member nation states. Moreover, its transition, though so far remarkably smooth and successful, is complicated by the fact that it has had no organisational or statistical euro-level history on which to call as a guide to current actions and decisions.

By contrast, the features that particularly distinguish the Bank of England's MPC are less dramatic. Perhaps the most important of these is that the Inflation Forecast is not only published, but is also the signed responsibility of the Committee members of the MPC, including the fan charts with their estimates of variances and uncertainties, skews and risks, though as noted in one of the tables to the last August Report, differences of view between MPC members can, and do, occur. In virtually all other cases of which I am aware, the internal economic forecasts, whether published or not, are strictly treated as the work of that Bank's *staff*, not of its decision-making body, or staffs in the case of the USA, where the Regional Feds also publish forecasts, in some cases based on rather differing views of macro-economic inter-relationships. While such an internal staff forecast is likely to be treated much more seriously by the decision-makers than outside forecasts, it still leaves the latter free to disassociate themselves from such forecasts, and to reach their decision on the basis of whatever judgement about the future, quantitative forecast-based or intuitive, that he, or she, may prefer.

What consequences arise from this difference in operation? Let me start with what may seem to you, but not to us in the MPC, a minor matter, which is our own work schedule. During the non-forecast months, we have three regular meetings connected with the interest-rate decision itself, an all-day briefing session with the staff, and two half-day meetings for discussion on the conjuncture, and thence to the decision itself. In addition, there will be a brief meeting to clear the draft of the Minutes, and often one, or two, other meetings on an *ad hoc* basis to discuss relevant background research or procedural issues. With the associated reading, and so on, the core work of the MPC requires about one week in such a non-forecast month, or a bit more if one adds on such other duties as visiting regional agents and out-reach exercises outside the Bank.

By contrast in a forecast month, there will be approximately about another ten meetings in addition to the regular ones, with some four, or so, to discuss starting assumptions and issues already identified as needing discussion; some two, or three, to consider the evolution of the forecast; and a final couple to discuss the drafting of the Inflation Report itself. Although the staff do the bulk of the process of running the equations and drafting the results, nevertheless the actual burden on the members of the MPC during such forecast months rises by nearly a factor of three, from taking up one week in the month to approximately three weeks. Given that the meetings have to be scheduled to fit the crowded diaries of the Governor and his two Deputies, during these months all other members have to be ready to reschedule any other obligations they may have on a 'catch-as-catch-can' basis. This strictly limits the kinds of other outside activities that the so-called external members of the MPC can undertake. I am currently the only 'external' member also holding down a second outside academic job, and on the two months of the year when MPC forecasts and term coincide, this is not comfortable.

Besides the question of how many meetings, and how much prior work and involvement a Committee should have before each decision, there is also a question of how frequently a Committee should regularly meet to make its policy decision. The Bank of England Act requires us to do so once a month, including August; but there was no public discussion of the pros and cons of this choice of periodicity. One obvious advantage of a monthly meeting is that it can be fitted into the monthly cycle of the flow of economic data; one disadvantage is the burden on staff, who need to make full reports, even in August and during the Christmas/New Year season. The Federal Open Marnet Committee in the USA, commonly known as the FOMC, meets eight times a year; the Governing Council of the ESCB twice a month, but will, I believe, normally only review its interest-rate decision at its second monthly meeting. It also may be the case that the conventional minimum size of change to official rates could be a function of the frequency of meeting, with smaller step-changes accompanying more frequent decisions. The current convention around the world appears to be to have monthly meetings, (or slightly less frequently), with minimum step changes of 25 b.p., unless rates are very low, for example, below 1 per cent or very high, in double figures, when the step-change size is equivalently lowered, or raised. But I do not know of much published work seeking to address whether these conventions are optimal; they just seem to have evolved without much discussion or serious consideration.

Benefits of MPC

Our procedures make a considerably greater demand on Committee members' time than is the case, I believe, in most other countries in a roughly similar situation. What do we get in return? Do the benefits exceed the costs in effort? Let me set out five potential benefits. First, engaging personally in a forecasting exercise emphasizes and underlines to all involved how restricted is our ability to peer into the future; how little we really know and how uncertain are our estimates. The MPC is sometimes criticized for relying too much on forecasts; in my experience it is exactly those same critics without forecasting ability or experience who tend to ask for simple, single-point forecasts, and place far too much weight on them. Given then the huge range of impermeable uncertainties, how has a Committee comprised of self-confident individuals, (one unkind journalist even once described me as 'opinionated'), managed so far to agree quantitative fan projections? One partial answer is that some members have on occasions expressed reservations which have been noted in the text, and in the case of our last August forecast in a special table (6C). Perhaps another partial answer is that when the independent staff crank out certain numbers, that very same uncertainty often makes it hard to justify demanding some alternative number without sufficient analytical argumentation to sway colleagues. Such economic arguments by members of the MPC are, indeed, regularly made, some in the staff might think far too often, and by the same token cause adjustments to the forecasts.

A second possible benefit of engaging MPC members personally in the forecast is, therefore, that the resultant forecast will itself be better. Several of our members have great expertise in forecasting methods, and can probe whether the underlying equations need reconsideration. Others have practical and professional experience of macro-economic developments both at home and internationally, and can assess whether certain input assumptions and output forecast numbers do, or do not, make sense. It will probably never be possible to test the counter-factual whether the forecasts were themselves improved by the closer, direct involvement of the MPC. There is, however, a reasonable *prima facie* case for believing that this is likely to be so.

The third potential benefit is that this public process imposes a greater discipline on the MPC. The academic literature from Kydland–Prescott, via Barro–Gordon and onwards, is full of models in which the monetary decision-makers want, for a variety of reasons, to be more expansionary than would be consistent with long-term stable inflation. But if an MPC is given a primary objective to hit an inflation target, it is extremely difficult to publish an inflation forecast that shows us to be failing in this respect. Instead we would be under pressure to change interest rates now, so that, assuming constant interest rates in future, we can show publicly that the target should be approximately achieved, given our best assessment of the future evolution of all other economic factors. The cynics will say that forecasts can be manipulated. The process of interaction among numerous staff and individually accountable MPC members, however, means that the only arguments used to amend the Inflation Forecast will be purely economic ones.

How important is such a discipline? This is a matter of judgement. Personally, I have felt that attributing much of the inflation of recent decades to an in-built expansionary bias of the monetary-policy decision-makers at the time was far off the mark. There is little, or no, empirical evidence that monetary-policy follows a political business cycle; though there has been more empirical support for fiscal policies to have done so in some countries. By the same token I have no scintilla of suspicion that, simply because the Governing Council of the ESCB does not publish its own inflation forecasts, its policies would consequently be biased on the expansionary side. At present, the sudden and sharp regime change caused by the adoption of the euro and the lack of euro-area coherent time-series data would in any case make it difficult for them to construct a reasonably reliable forecasting model. Nevertheless, my own experience and conviction is that the discipline of a published forecast is useful and important.

The next potential benefit is one of greater accountability. As my erstwhile colleague, Sir Alan Budd, wrote in his excellent paper for the LBS Economic Outlook earlier in July (1999), because of lags in the transmission mechanism of monetary policy, the MPC 'is in effect targeting the expected value of future inflation'. If shocks and unanticipated events occur subsequently, then those same lags will mean that the MPC cannot offset their effects on current inflation, or only do so at the expense of unacceptable short-term fluctuations in interest rates, exchange rates and output.

I quote Sir Alan at some length.

> These issues were discussed by Bean in his evidence to the Treasury Committee (TCSC 1997). His proposed solution to the problem was to examine forecasts made at the time of the policy decisions. 'To the extent that the Bank can only really affect inflation two years or so into the future, it is in essence targeting *expected* inflation two years hence. Thus in holding the Bank accountable for its interest rate decisions, the Committee should ask whether the chosen path of interest rates is consistent with inflation being *forecast* to be $2\frac{1}{2}$ per cent (or whatever the target is) in two years time.' This

> procedure should largely overcome the problems both of lags (provided the forecasts have a sufficiently long horizon) and of subsequent shocks.
>
> He proposed that the inflation projection reported in the Bank's Quarterly *Inflation Report* and the justification behind it should be the main focus of the Treasury Committee's scrutiny of the Bank's decisions. This might imply that the Bank should use forecasts of inflation as its intermediate target – i.e. that it should set interest rates so that expected inflation is equal to the target. Apart from the problem of selecting forecasts, discussed below, Bean agreed that it is reasonable for the Bank to have its own views about the future path of inflation; but it should explain why they differ from those of the market and should expect to be criticised if the market turned out to be right.

It is possible to use published forecasts or to derive forecast expectations from the differences between interest rates on index-linked and conventional gilts. Neither is straightforward.... Finally independent forecasters tend to publish point forecasts [of future inflation]. Despite [various] difficulties, the use of contemporary forecasts remains the best way of evaluating the MPC's actions.

The Treasury Committee did not appear to be completely convinced by Professor Bean's conclusions but said 'We agree that outside forecasts may well be useful as benchmarks in probing the Bank on its inflation projections and on the interest rate decisions it takes.' It said it would also explore the usefulness of rules such as the Taylor rule in providing benchmarks.

> The Committee intends to hold the MPC accountable both *ex post* and *ex ante*. We believe that the focus for our inquiries should not lie exclusively in using the Inflation Report to examine the Bank's recent and planned monetary stance but that a degree of *past accountability* is also called for. Once the arrangements are established, we will be examining the inflation outturn in relation to the inflation target. If inflation deviates substantially from the target, we will seek a comprehensive explanation from the Bank.

As it happens, I personally think that the need to publish inflation forecasts in order to obtain accountability can be overstated. Let me again take the case of the ECB. I, and most other observers, assume that the ECB will wholeheartedly try to carry out its remit of achieving price stability, defined as achieving an outcome of between zero (or perhaps slightly more to take account of quality and other biases in the statistical price indices) and 2 per cent in the harmonised index of consumer prices (HICP). Should the external forecasts of future inflation in the euro-zone, whether market-based or by independent forecasters, suggest that this objective might not be achieved, then the European Parliament, and other commentators may probe for reasons behind the discrepancies between such forecasts and the implicit expectations of the ECB, whether, or not, these latter are published. It is the judgement of markets, and of respected independent forecasters, whether, or not, the monetary authorities have got it right that really provides the *ex ante* accountability, not so much the publication of internal forecasts. And, of course, *ex post* accountability is driven by events, not by forecasts. Finally, though I do not claim that my listing is exhaustive or complete, let me turn to the point that the publication of the Inflation Forecast adds to transparency. This enables us to explain, and to attempt to justify, our actions in the context of a comprehensive, quantitative assessment of all the determinants of output and inflation. This is particularly important because of lags in the transmission mechanism, whereby monetary policy affects output and then inflation, mean that our target has to be future, (that is, forecast) inflation, and not current, inflation. We have recently issued a short paper on the time profile of The Transmission of Monetary Policy, which includes discussion of lags. Given such lags, the optimal target has to be forecast, not current, inflation, as Professor Lars Svensson has explained in a whole series of excellent academic papers. But without published forecasts of future inflation, how could we explain coherently what we in the MPC think that we are doing?

By the same token repeated publicly-exposed relationships between forecasts and policy-reaction should allow outside commentators to come to understand more clearly our policy-reaction function, and therefore partly to do our work for us by adjusting market rates appropriately to 'news' in advance of our own actions. As Mervyn King nicely put it, we aim to be 'boring'. In order to be 'boring', you have to be predictable; and the publication of Inflation Forecasts is an essential element in making us predictable. I believe that the publication of the Inflation Forecast does make the MPC more transparent than other central banks that do not do so.

Let me conclude this first section of the paper by reminding you of the five arguments for having a published Inflation Forecast which is the responsibility of the MPC itself. These are (1) a better informed MPC, (2) a better forecast, (3) more discipline, (4) accountability and (5) greater transparency. My own purely subjective ordinal ranking of the benefits would be, (with 5 most and 1 least important):

5 Transparency
4 Discipline
3 Better informed MPC
2 Better forecasts
1 Accountability

Of course, all these putative benefits have to be weighed against the considerable costs in time and effort that goes into the process. One colleague mentioned that the labour costs of doing the forecast are tiny compared to the benefits if the forecasts should improve the resulting policy decisions by a tiny fraction. No doubt this is correct, but exactly how can one factor that thought into the administrative decisions about budgets, staffing resources and frequency of forecasts at the Bank? I cannot answer that myself. I hope that others may be able to do so. Whether it is possible to base decisions on an Inflation Forecast adopted by a Monetary Policy Committee would also depend on the make-up of the membership of such committees, if they exist at all in other countries. The membership in the UK has been chosen to facilitate such a procedure; in other central banks, the nature of membership may effectively preclude such a procedure.

European System of Central Banks

Let me turn now, as is appropriate in a Monnet lecture, from navel-gazing concern with UK monetary policy procedures to some thoughts about wider European developments, the ESCB and the Euro. Here the unique feature of such European developments is that the monetary system is federal, covering the Euro-11 countries now and prospectively an even more expanded euro-zone, whereas within the EU most other economic, fiscal and political competences and powers remain at the level of the nation state, at least for the foreseeable future.

I have already taken the opportunity to comment on certain theoretical and conceptual issues that this may cause in my paper on 'The two concepts of money' in the *European Journal of Political Economy*. Here I want to discuss three more practical, policy-oriented considerations. I should, however, first add here that whereas my comments on the forecasting process of the MPC are obviously informed by my own membership on that committee, my comments on my chosen aspects of the working of the ESCB are personal, made as an independent academic, and are in no way representative necessarily of anyone else on the MPC or in the Bank. Anyhow, the first of my considerations concerns the role of the ECB as a crisis manager and Lender of Last Resort (LOLR). Recently (July 13, 1999), I organized a Conference at LSE on the general subject of the Lender of Last Resort. One of the three sessions of this was on the topic of 'The ECB and systemic stability in the Eurozone'. There were three papers, authored by three senior expert European professors, Aglietta, Bruni and de Boissieu, and two IMF research workers, Prati and Schinasi. All three papers were unanimously of the view that the *prospective* integration of the euro-zone financial system carried with it a commensurate need for much greater centralization of the euro-zone supervisory system – though opinion was divided on whether that should be located within the ECB, or kept separate – and the speedy and conscious adoption of a central LOLR role by the ECB.

Much the same message was given by the recent CEPR monograph on *The Future of European Banking* by Danthine *et al.* (January 1999). Let me quote directly from this, pp. 98–9:

> To sum up, the advent of cross-border banking, the likely emergence of pan-European universal banks, and, more generally, the new competitive climate of European banking, confront national supervisors with delicate coordination issues. In the face of these challenges, we doubt that the simple coordination among independent national authorities – as provided for by the Second Banking Directive – will be a safe arrangement.
>
> The past European experience with national supervision has not always been satisfactory. . . . It is ironic that while the international financial

> community – precisely . . . to avoid local capture – is studying the possibility of setting up a 'world financial regulator', petty national jealousies appear to be preventing this from happening at the European level, thus putting the stability of European financial markets at risk.
>
> Building a centralized supervisory body is a possibility already foreseen in the Maastricht Treaty. Article 105(6) leaves open the possibility of a change in the assignment of responsibilities . . . . Article 105(6), however, appears only to allow centralization of supervisory responsibilities inside the ECB. While a clear improvement of the current situation, this may not be the optimal arrangement. First, the ECB is already being perceived as accumulating too much power, and issues of accountability have been raised. It seems difficult therefore to envision that the ECB might also be entrusted with regulatory and supervisory responsibilities. An independent European-wide regulatory agency, distinct from the ECB, may generate less concerns in this respect while at the same time facilitating accountability.
>
> Thinking about a new European agency would also allow one to think afresh about the desirability of combining the supervision of banks and markets . . . . [T]he likely emergence of large universal banks will make it increasingly difficult to distinguish between market risk and the risk of the bank. Moreover, while banks increase their exposure to market risk, markets have become more vulnerable to a liquidity crisis arising from the failure of a large intermediary – the role of derivatives in this process is central, as the cases of Barings and LTCM demonstrate. The argument for combining the two functions in a supranational EU independent agency seems overwhelming.

But there is a problem confronting this approach that most of these authors have missed. As I, and others, for example, Giannini (1999) have emphasized, it has become increasingly difficult for a Central Bank to distinguish between illiquidity and insolvency. With a few minor exceptions, one such being the well-known Bank of New York computer problem in 1985, the efficient, broad, interbank, wholesale, short-term money markets are able to iron out any liquidity problems that occasion no whiff of suspicion about insolvency. Normally, a commercial bank will only turn to a Central Bank for LOLR services, at a higher penalty cost in terms of both interest and reputation, if it has been effectively turned away by other banks in the inter-bank wholesale money market. This implies that there must be some doubts about solvency in such cases.

So almost any use of LOLR, in the form of lending to a particular financial institution, rather than of generalized open market operations, by a Central Bank could involve some risk of loss. It is not clear whether the ECB has the powers under its statutes to undertake such operations, see Lastra 'The Role of the ECB with regard to Financial Stability and LOLR' (1999). Moreover, if it becomes involved in direct lending to a troubled institution(s), and the scale of potential loss became at all significant, there would then be a question of who might bear that loss, as well as the issue of whether any such bail-out was consistent with EC regulations, for example, on state aid. If the ECB became financially involved in crisis management which might involve any sizeable funding, what sources could it approach? Its own capital is limited, and it might face a legal claim of *ultra vires* if it sought to use its own capital to support a commercial institution. The EU's budget is strictly limited, and whether a request for subventions to finance such a bail-out would get past the European Commission, Council and Parliament is doubtful in the extreme. Any request to the member states to divide up the fiscal cost between them would tend to run into enormous complications. Perhaps it might apply to its constituent National Central Banks (the NCBs) for an injection of additional capital, but even here there might be difficulties, for example, what would be the position of those central banks whose countries were in the EU, but not in the euro-zone, that is, the out, or to be politically correct, the pre-in countries?

In standard cases where both the key monetary and fiscal policy institutions are centralized at the national level, any major financial crisis, involving the potentiality for loss, will need to be resolved by agreement and crisis management amongst the Central Bank and Ministry of Finance. It cannot nowadays really be done otherwise, as recent examples in Asia demonstrate. But in the euro-zone the ECB has no fiscal counterpart. This is a strong argument for leaving LOLR actions at the national level, subject preferably to ECB oversight and co-ordination. This judgement is made easier currently by the fact that retail financial activities remain nationally segmented, despite the advent of the Single Market and the Euro. This may well change over time, but so also may the balance of fiscal competences between the member nation states and the federal euro centre.

Relationship between monetary and fiscal policies

There are those who argue that delegation of operational independence for setting interest rates to the Central Bank adversely affects the potentiality for appropriate co-operation between monetary and fiscal policy. I do not agree. Once the political authorities have given the objective for achieving price stability to the Central Bank, the Central Bank's reaction function is, or should be, transparent to the fiscal authorities. Given that reaction function, the fiscal authorities can then, in principle, choose any set of fiscal measures, and hence consequentially interest rates, consistent with price stability. Put more simply the fiscal authorities know that by choosing a smaller fiscal deficit, they will encourage the Central Bank to set a lower level of interest rates in its pursuit of price stability. Claims that Central Bank independence prevent policy co-operation are either analytically invalid or, more likely, represent a coded attack on the primacy to be attached by nominal demand management to the goal of price stability.

The situation is, of course, quite different in the euro-zone where the fiscal outcome is the result of separate decisions by eleven independent fiscal authorities, with the central EU budget being both too small and too inflexible to count. Despite the establishment of the Euro 11 Council, decisions will ultimately depend on national self-interest.

It is certainly arguable that the translation of monetary policy to the federal level in the EU could act to reduce the incentives to maintain prudent and tight fiscal policies at the national level, because the implications of local fiscal expansion for EU-wide interest rates and exchange rates would, most of the time, be muted. To reduce the perceived danger of the imbalance between national fiscal policies and federal monetary policies leading the EU towards a scenario of ever-expanding fiscal policies and ever-increasing interest rates, the Stability and Growth Pact adopted at the Amsterdam European Council in 1997, and drawing on the previous Waigel plan and Dublin Council meeting agreement, imposed limits on current fiscal deficits.

In several respects, these constraints are crudely designed. For example, they give no more latitude for current fiscal flexibility to nations with very low debt ratios than to countries with worryingly high ratios; they only make extremely restricted allowance for cyclical factors. Be that as it may, the constraints imposed need not have adverse effects should member countries have reached a long-run steady state equilibrium, with current deficits averaging zero. But we are not at such an equilibrium yet. We start with many countries having deficits quite close to the upper limit, and with the prospect of coping with an ageing population with currently generous, but unfunded, pensions.

The prospect is then one either of continuing tight fiscal policies, whatever the cyclical conjuncture, or of relaxations that may appear to put the Treaty agreement at some risk. The markets and the news media appeared flustered in response to the marginal easing in the Italian budget target, though the pattern of that seeming response, that is, to lower the foreign-exchange value of the euro but *not* to shift the spread between Italian and German bonds was hard for me to comprehend.

Quite what would happen if the US economy should weaken, and the euro rise sharply, is difficult to envisage. The dichotomy between international (especially US) calls for Japan to undertake ever-further fiscal expansions, with a deficit near 10 per cent of GDP and a debt ratio escalating into (what seems to me to be) dangerous territory, and the concerns expressed about a minor increase in the Italian deficit from 2.0 to 2.4 per cent are remarkable. Admittedly, the concern in the case of Italy related more to the likelihood of adherence to prior-agreed 'rules of the game' than to a few decimal points, but even so the episode highlighted for me the differences in the ground-rules that seemed appropriate in the two situations. Yet few seemed to remark on that comparison.

With European fiscal policy flexibility constrained, and the ECB focused on price stability, is nominal and real demand likely to remain on a satisfactory track in the euro-area? Yes, if the international conjuncture remains benign, as it has looked so far in 1999. The combination of continuing strength in the USA, recovery in Asia, the cut of euro-interest rates to 2.5 per cent, reduction in the euro-exchange rate and steady growth in the monetary and credit aggregates has been just about perfect. But how much room for manoeuvre remains for the policy mix if the international horizon should cloud?

My final concern relates to the issue that is usually described by the phrase 'one size fits all'. No matter how small is the area of any single monetary zone, it remains, however, unlikely that the preferred policy will be optimal for all sectors and regions. In the UK, for example, the tradeable goods, largely manufacturing, sector has been under quite severe deflationary pressure, while the non-tradeable, mostly services, sector has been buoyant. It is, at least, arguable that asymmetric, that is, differential, shocks are more likely in smaller, more open economies, especially given the wayward and volatile nature of exchange markets. The great advantage of the euro-zone is precisely that exchange rate volatility does not now impact on such a large proportion of their trade. By exactly the same token one could certainly suggest that the UK has been more affected by asymmetric (essentially exchange rate) shocks in the last few years than has the wider euro-area.

But even if it *should* be the case that the problem of such differential shocks does become somewhat worse the larger the geographic size of the monetary union (and the jury is still out on this question), the extent of any such extra disadvantage is clearly small, at least under normal circumstances. Measures of inequality tend to be less within, than between, countries, though this is not universally true, with political events such as the reunification of Germany occasionally going in the opposite direction. There have been few indications that states and provinces within vast countries such as Australia, Brazil, Canada, China, India, or the USA would do better with separate monetary institutions. Wherever there are calls for such separation, as in Quebec, Montenegro and Scotland, it is invariably driven primarily by politics, not by economics.

Within countries with their single monetary systems, there are natural defence mechanisms to contain the effects of asymmetric shocks. These equilibrating mechanisms include factor mobility, for example, labour migration, market adjustment, notably of relative wages, and fiscal transfers. Several of these are, however, effectively non-operative within the euro-area, and others may be less effective than is the case in most other country-wide monetary systems.

What may then happen if certain constituent parts of the euro-area economy should come to feel themselves disadvantaged by the combination of federal monetary policy and constrained national fiscal policy? With luck and good management, this may never happen. Within most countries such disadvantaged regions as occur generally consider the benefits of nationality sufficiently strong to resign themselves to their relative weakness. Will the perceived benefits of belonging to the euro-area continue to convince voters who may, perhaps, be led to believe, rightly or wrongly, that their current macro-economic difficulties could be resolved by a more nationalistic policy? Time will no doubt tell, but it must remain a worry.

The lesson of history has been that political moves towards unification, or separation, precede and dominate the process of currency unification or separation. There are examples all around. Perhaps, unlike some other countries whose unification was achieved by force, or by international agreements imposed by 'great powers', the process of integration in the European Union has been sufficiently more gradual, voluntary, peaceful and balanced between participants to be more enduring. Moreover the European Union is an exercise in trying to learn from history in order to change the course of history. How feasible is it then to reverse the course of history, and go for monetary unification in advance of political unification? It is what was described in the series 'Yes Minister' as a 'brave policy'.

5 Thoughts on the new financial architecture

Andrew Crockett

Introduction

I am very happy to contribute this essay to the volume that is being published in memory of Max Fry. I first came to know Max in London in the late 1960s, when we shared what has come to be a lifelong professional interest in monetary issues. Harry Johnson had just come to the London School of Economics (LSE) and taken over Richard Sayers' Monday morning seminar. He had brought with him Chicago-inspired views on money and the monetary approach to the balance of payments. It was an exciting time and place to be beginning a career as a monetary economist. My own alma mater, Cambridge, was still, under Nicky Kaldor, distinctly sceptical of the newly-revived role assigned to money. But the LSE was quietly (or under Harry Johnson, not so quietly) building its reputation as a place to explore new ideas and do solid empirical work. Harry's seminar attracted not just LSE students and faculty, but others, like Max and myself, who were anxious to hear the latest ideas and to test our own thinking. Many will have heard of Harry's legendary whittling. I can testify personally to its psychological power. One day, when presenting a paper to the seminar after a sleepless night wondering how it would be received, I heard Harry begin his usual whittling. At a certain moment the whittling stopped. Everyone knew what that meant. Rather like a V1 flying bomb whose motor would cut out seconds before the bomb hit, I feared I was in for one of Harry's devastating attacks. I was at the Bank of England at the time, and Harry was well known for his acerbic views of central bankers. Fortunately for me, however, Harry had just dropped his pen-knife and the whittling resumed before I had time to freeze up completely! In the late 1970s, I came to know Max's wife Celia as well, and from that time our families have been close. I used to visit Max and Celia in their apartment in Yenikoy, just outside Istanbul, when Max was teaching at Boazici University (the old Roberts College). It was a time when I was travelling to Egypt regularly for the IMF, and witnessing the difficulties a country had in emerging from Soviet-style economic planning. I always enjoyed coming to Istanbul (apart from the hair-raising flight on Bulgarian Airlines). Visiting Max and Celia was the main attraction. In addition, however, after the hardships of

Cairo, Istanbul seemed so green, well organised and efficient. Max and Celia used to say I was the only one of their visitors who characterised life in Turkey in those terms! It was during this period that I learned that whenever Max spent six months in one place (sometimes less) he would produce a book called, roughly, 'Money and Banking in [insert name of country]'. In this way he built not only an impressive publication record, but an encyclopaedic institutional knowledge. His natural energy and inquisitiveness always led him to apply existing models to the institutional structures he found in the out-of-the-way places to which his Graham Greene-type adventuring led him. As a keen follower of the ideas of Ron McKinnon and Ed Shaw, the topic that fascinated him most was how financial repression could retard development. By the 1980s, Celia had persuaded him to become a bit less peripatetic and they settled down in southern California. Marjorie and I visited them in their delightful house in Orange County, and got to know their young family. We wondered what life could be nicer than that of an academic in the University of California system. But Max and Celia always had a yearning to come back to Britain. In a strange way, despite all their travelling, they remained at base very British, in the best sense. I wrote numerous letters of recommendation for Max for academic posts in the UK, but not very persuasively, it seems. Most of the jobs went to people with more conventional British backgrounds. Then, finally, paydirt. Max was appointed to the position at Birmingham Business School, which he held until 1999. He continued to write copiously on monetary economics. When he accepted a position as head of the Bank of England's Centre for Central Banking Studies (CCBS), I had the sense of a wheel turning full circle. We had begun our careers with me at the Bank and him outside. It seemed we were destined to end them with him as the servant of the Old Lady, and me elsewhere. We continued to interact in this period, and I was happy to come occasionally to the CCBS to give lectures. He, in turn, occasionally visited Basle. Our families continued to see each other, both in Switzerland and in Brum. We were all saddened by the turn for the worse in Max's health in the late 1990s. Characteristically, he himself bore it with fortitude and continued working long after others would have given up. Celia and the children were a source of inspiration to him, as, in turn, he was to them and to his many friends. By the time of his death in February 2000, he was no longer able to work, and was in considerable discomfort. Nevertheless, it was a sad blow to his many friends. Marjorie and I were happy to have been able to visit him a couple of weeks earlier. He was lucid and alert, and I was happy to have been able to discuss briefly the first draft of this essay. The subject I have chosen, International financial architecture, is not one that Max worked on directly. I have chosen it, however, because many aspects of the debate on the international architecture are coming back to themes that absorbed Max throughout his professional life. The core of this concern was how to promote more stable and sustainable development through more efficient financial markets. Those of us engaged in the search for a stronger international financial system now find ourselves stressing elements that Max was writing about for years: market-oriented prudential supervision, transparency as the basis for improved market functioning, the development of securities markets, liberalisation of financial systems, and so on.

What is the financial architecture?

The international financial architecture is a term that is widely (and sometimes casually) used. It is, therefore, well to start with definitions. I take architecture to encompass two aspects: the system of rules and conventions that govern international economic and financial relations (the trade regime, exchange-rate arrangements, the adjustment process, and so on); and the network of institutions through which these rules are developed, monitored and enforced.

There have been many significant changes in the rules governing international financial relations in the half-century or more since the establishment of the post-war economic order. Still, several factors have remained constant. One is the commitment to free trade. Despite periodic upsurges in protectionist sentiment, the post-war period has seen an enormous opening of trade. Administrative restrictions have been removed and tariff barriers have come down under successive trade negotiating rounds. As a result, world trade has grown consistently faster than global output, spurring economic development in those countries that have embraced export-led growth.

Another constant has been the emphasis on a multilateral approach. Multilateralism has been sustained through such organisations as the IMF, World Bank and World Trade Organisation (WTO) (formerly General Agreement on Tariffs and Trade (GATT)). Regional organisations and trade groupings have, to be sure, grown in importance, but with relatively few exceptions, they have been compatible with global rules ('open regionalism'). The WTO now has dispute-settlement procedures to further reinforce the multilateral approach to international economic issues.

Within this broad framework of a sustained commitment to open trade and multilateral decision-making, there have, nevertheless, been major changes in the practical rules of the international financial system. The post-war economic architecture was much more 'administered' than the one that has come to prevail today. The exchange-rate system was based on pegged rates, the adjustment process and convertibility arrangements were heavily managed, and liquidity creation was, at least in theory, centrally controlled. Now, all these aspects of the system are market-driven.

There have also been changes in the allocation of responsibilities for the management of the system. The IMF remains the central body, as envisaged in the Bretton Woods arrangements. But the fact that financial markets have assumed greater importance in resource-allocation means that other bodies and groupings, such as financial supervisors, standard-setters, and so on, have to be closely integrated into the process. The private sector, too, needs to be involved, since private flows of capital have come to dwarf official flows.

In what follows, I will first discuss how the conventions governing international financial relations have evolved, and how they need to be further adapted in light of the evident deficiencies revealed by the Asian crisis. Then I will have something to say about how institutional responsibilities should develop in the new environment. At the outset, I can say that, in my view, the most fruitful approach will be to strengthen existing arrangements and correct anomalies and weaknesses, rather than to seek brand-new rules. In other words, the system needs a thorough overhaul to strengthen its foundations, not a newly-created external design.

The new architecture: the rules

A first point to make is that the international financial architecture has already evolved substantially over the past three decades. As I noted a moment ago, it has moved from being a heavily administered system, to one based on the operation of market forces. This can be demonstrated through a brief consideration of three key features of any international monetary system: the exchange-rate regime, the adjustment process and liquidity-creation arrangements.

The *exchange-rate regime* at the beginning of the 1970s was based on internationally agreed fixed parities, which, in principle, could only be changed following international agreement in the IMF. This fixed exchange-rate system broke down under the pressure of diverging inflation and growing capital flows in 1971–73. Since then, the major currencies have floated against one another. In recent years, there has been growing consensus that the integration of international capital markets has made it harder to maintain fixed-but-adjustable exchange rates.

The *balance-of-payments adjustment process* in the Bretton Woods system worked through directing domestic macro-economic policies to the objective of maintaining a sustainable current account (i.e. one that could be financed by normal long-term capital flows).

Decisions on adjustment policies were taken in a multilateral context, and in the major industrial countries were partially co-ordinated in a special working party of the OECD (Working Party 3). With the introduction of floating exchange rates and the enormous expansion in capital flows, balance-of-payments equilibrium has ceased to be a direct and explicit objective of government policy, and even the concept of equilibrium has become ambiguous. Market forces determine adjustment, with exchange rates and payment flows responding to shifts in monetary and fiscal policies and the associated movements in savings/investment balances.

Liquidity arrangements under the Bretton Woods system were likewise seen to be appropriately determined by international agreement. There was no explicit mechanism for creating primary liquidity, partly because, at the end of World War II, the gold reserves of the United States were thought to be sufficient to ensure the primary liquidity of the system for the foreseeable future. In addition, the IMF could itself supply secondary liquidity through making available its lending facilities. When concern about possible liquidity shortages began to mount in the late 1950s and 1960s, the response was to design an international facility (Special Drawing Rights) to supplement existing reserves. Nowadays, however, liquidity is generated in private markets, and the reserves held by creditworthy countries are largely endogenously determined. If countries experience a shortage of liquidity, this is generally the same thing as saying there is a loss of confidence in their currency.

What is the significance of this shift from administered arrangements to market forces in the working of the international financial system? A key conclusion is that, with the principal features of the system now market-driven, policy-makers have to pay increased attention to the efficiency and stability of private markets. The crises that have afflicted the international system in recent years have all, in one way or another, reflected market failures. Capital flows have been excessively volatile; domestic banking systems have been vulnerable; herd instinct has been prevalent; and so on. The effective management of a market-based international financial system requires putting in place a prudential and regulatory framework and providing the necessary transparency to allow markets to function efficiently and in a stabilising way. This will be the theme of the remainder of this section.

I will deal first with the issue of strengthening the financial system, so that it is less prone to crisis, and so that crises, when they occur, are less damaging. Then I will touch on the issue of crisis management and resolution. How should the international community respond when, as is inevitable, a financial crisis strikes?

Crisis prevention

There is now widespread agreement that countries can make themselves less vulnerable to crisis by adopting appropriate macro-economic policies, and by ensuring they have a well-capitalised, effectively supervised, transparent financial system. The basics of macro-economic policy are, of course, a sound fiscal position and a stability-oriented monetary policy. But the experience of the past several years has taught us that more is needed. The exchange-rate regime must be credible and defensible. If a country adopts a fixed exchange rate but cannot credibly commit to the policies needed to defend it, a crisis will sooner or later arise. And given the capacity of financial markets to crystallise future expectations in current prices, sooner is more likely than later. For many emerging market countries, a measure of flexibility in the exchange rate is now part of the defence against the risk of extreme market pressures. Only for a relatively small number will the alternative of a rigid pegging regime, backed up with institutional mechanisms to make its defence credible, be realistic.

The other lesson of recent experience is the need for transparency. In several Asian countries, as in Mexico before them, economic disequilibria were allowed to build up because private economic agents were insufficiently aware of their extent. The full and timely disclosure of relevant macro-economic information is a key element in making the international financial system more robust.

As far as domestic financial structures are concerned, the Asian crisis demonstrated that weaknesses in this domain could interact with currency problems to impart a powerful negative effect on economic activity. Any strengthening of the international financial system therefore depends on countries undertaking measures to make their financial sectors more robust to shocks. But how?

It is now recognised that an efficient and stable functioning of the financial system requires strong underpinnings in a number of dimensions. It can be helpful to think of a financial system as having three pillars: the *institutions*, (banks, securities houses, insurance companies and fund managers) that act as intermediaries; the *markets* in which financial assets are traded; and the *infrastructure* that governs financial relations among economic agents. Weaknesses in any of these pillars can undermine the stability of the system.

When institutions are not prudently run, they not only allocate resources inefficiently (inaccurately pricing risk), they also expose themselves and their clients to losses when economic circumstances turn adverse. The extreme consequence can be seen in the widespread failures that characterised Asian banking systems in 1997–98, and that led to very large resolution costs (see Table 5.1). Just as damaging as the direct losses is the fact that an impaired banking system is unable to perform its economic function of mobilising and allocating resources for productive investment.

A key element of a strengthened financial system is therefore putting in place a regulatory and supervisory regime that encourages prudent behaviour by financial intermediaries. Part of this can be achieved by improved market discipline, which in turn calls for greater disclosure and transparency, as well as the removal of unnecessary protective mechanisms shielding economic agents from the consequences of bad decisions (dealing with 'moral hazard'). In addition, the regulatory and supervisory regime must ensure that risks are properly measured and priced, and that an adequate reserve of capital is held. Space does not permit a detailed review of the specific guidelines that need to be adopted. But supervisors have now generally accepted internationally-agreed 'Core Principles' for the oversight of financial institutions. When adopted and enforced, these principles should go a long way towards reducing the number of occasions on which a financial crisis is triggered or intensified by serial collapse of financial institutions.

Markets are also a key pillar of the financial system. Increasingly, financial assets and liabilities are securitised and traded in financial markets. Intermediaries then perform the function of enabling savers and borrowers to access wholesale markets in the most efficient way. In general, markets are less vulnerable to crisis than finance intermediated through institutions. Pressures in markets are reflected in changes in price, rather than in threats to the solvency of intermediaries. But for markets to play their role effectively, they must have the necessary breadth, depth and resiliency. In many of the Asian countries, equity

Table 5.1 Cost of banking crises 1980–99

Country (time period of crisis)	*Estimate of total losses/costs (percentage of GDP)*
Latin America	
Argentina (1980–82)	55
Chile (1981–83)	41[a]
Venezuela (1994–95)	18
Mexico (1995)	12–15[b]
Africa	
Benin (1988–90)	17
Cote d'Ivoire (1988–91)	25
Mauritania (1984–93)	15
Senegal (1988–91)	17
Tanzania (1987–95)	10[c]
Middle East	
Israel (1977–83)	30[d]
Transition countries	
Bulgaria (1990s)	14
Hungary (1995)	10
Asia	
Indonesia (1997– . . .)	59
Korea (1997– . . .)	17
Malaysia (1997– . . .)	10
Thailand (1997– . . .)	24
Industrial countries	
Spain (1977–85)	17
Japan (1990s)	10[e]

a 1982–85; b Accumulated losses to date; c In 1987; d In 1983; e Estimate of potential losses.

Sources: Caprio and Klingebiel, (1996). 'Bank insolvencies: cross-country experience'. Unpublished. Washington: World Bank; World Bank, December 1999, 'Global Economic Review'.

and fixed interest markets were underdeveloped, forcing companies to finance themselves through the banking sector. In short, the economies had a critical gap in their financial structure. There was no mechanism to permit the demand for long-term investment funds in local currency to be matched by a corresponding supply. A potentially explosive mismatch was created in which long-term lending to projects with domestic currency cash flow, were financed by short-term foreign currency borrowing.

Developing financial markets requires creating the conditions in which suppliers and users of funds have the necessary incentives to come together to exchange claims in the form of securities. This brings us to the crucial role of financial infrastructure. Market development is inhibited by uncertainty, and uncertainty results when market infrastructures are underdeveloped.

It is worth reviewing some of the sources of uncertainty that have inhibited financial market functioning in the past and which can, in principle, be dealt with through efforts to improve the financial infrastructure. Perhaps the most pervasive is *diversity of accounting standards*. In order to transact with confidence in markets, economic agents must believe that they understand the characteristics of the underlying asset. Inconsistent, weak, or inadequately-enforced accounting standards undermine this confidence. They exacerbate, in other words, the asymmetrical information problem. Potential investors hold back, reducing the depth of the market. The solution is clearly to develop robust and transparent accounting standards, and to require their enforcement in any security traded in public markets.

Another widespread, and related, problem is *corporate governance*. At its most basic, good corporate governance means a framework of rules that require the managers of an enterprise to work in the interest of all shareholders. Simple enough, but often ignored. In many Asian countries, connected lending between banks and enterprises owned by the banks' managers worked to the detriment of the banks' shareholders. Companies had opaque ownership structures, variable accounting practices and no entrenched protection of the rights of minority shareholders. The result was that equity markets did not exert the necessary discipline, and allowed firms' managers to run unreasonable risks.

Insolvency procedures are another central part of the financial infrastructure that was lacking in many crisis-hit countries. In any economic enterprise, the possibility of failure has to be taken into account. The terms and conditions on which value can be recovered from a failed enterprise are essential elements in pricing the finance that launches the project. When creditor rights in the event of bankruptcy are unclear, and when judicial enforcement is uncertain, the price of finance goes up, inhibiting the growth of the market.

More generally, the formulation of a coherent structure of *contract law* and the implementation of *impartial law enforcement* are a crucial part of a stable and effective economic system. The consequences of the absence of such conditions can be seen in their extreme form in Russia. But to a lesser degree, weaknesses in legal systems and in law enforcement have plagued many emerging markets.

Lastly, *payments and settlement systems* need to be firmly based if financial systems are not to be disrupted by the failure of individual institutions. The potential for disruption was revealed by the failure of Bankhaus Herstatt in 1974, which has given its name to a particular category of settlement risk. Since then, there has not been a comparable failure, although there have been several near-misses.

It is apparent from what has just been said that building resilient financial systems requires attention to a range of factors. How can policy makers, both at the national and international level, ensure that the necessary improvements take place? The approach that is being adopted rests on two key elements, both designed to make markets work better. The first is greater transparency. This should enable internal market disciplines to function more effectively. And the second is the development of codes of good practice. Such codes, developed by international standard setters, are a necessary focal point for financial supervisors at the national level to converge on internationally agreed best-practice.

Such an approach still leaves a number of questions to be answered. Who should develop the standards? How should adherence to them be assured? Which codes should have priority for early implementation? And who should have the overarching responsibility for seeing that there are no overlaps, inconsistencies or gaps in the codes?

The answer to the first question, who should develop standards, seems to be to follow the successful experience of the Basel Committee on Banking Supervision. That is, standards should be developed by a limited number of national experts from key national authorities, who pledge to adopt the standards in their own jurisdictions. The force of their example then leads others, through peer pressure or market forces, to follow suit. Legally negotiated international agreements, embodied in treaties, are generally thought to be too inflexible to be rapidly negotiated and amended. And by involving a much wider number of participants, there is the risk that the standards that emerged would represent a lowest common denominator. Interestingly, the 'soft law' embodied in agreements such as the Basel capital requirements seems to be more robust and effective than many formal legal agreements incorporated in international treaties.

How can the international community encourage the adoption of standards across all relevant jurisdictions (i.e. in all those with the capacity to cause systemic disruptions)? The most effective mechanism is undoubtedly that of the market. If there is a reward for meeting high standards and a penalty for failing to do so, the minds of domestic supervisors and policy-makers will be powerfully concentrated. This is indeed the case for the banking standards, and by now virtually all jurisdictions have announced their desire to comply with the Basel-based standards.

However, it is probably necessary also to have a strategy for reinforcing the market, and for making sure that the market is adequately aware of what individual countries are doing. The IMF and the World Bank are developing a programme of 'Financial Sector Assessments' to help countries devise and implement plans for upgrading their financial sectors. In addition, the Financial Stability Forum (about which, more below) has established a task force to consider issues of the implementation of best-practice standards. This task force is looking at the all-important question of the prioritisation of standards – the full package will take many years to implement, and choices have to be made. It is also looking at market-based incentives and penalties, monitoring and assessment procedures, and technical assistance.

This brings me to the final question, that of who should take responsibility for seeing that financial vulnerabilities have been adequately identified and addressed. Recognising that many different authorities are responsible for different aspects of financial stability, the G7 Ministers and Governors, on the basis of a report submitted in February 1999 by the then President of the Bundesbank,

Hans Tietmeyer, decided to establish a Financial Stability Forum. The Forum is composed of deputy Finance ministers, deputy Central Bank Governors and Heads of Supervision from countries with major financial centres, as well as senior officials from the principal international financial institutions and standard-setting bodies. Its function is to promote coordination in the work of these various bodies; to identify vulnerabilities in national and international financial systems; and to see that the network of codes and standards developed to strengthen financial systems is adequately comprehensive and enforced.

The Forum has the capacity, through its membership, to manage the overall strategy of strengthening financial systems. It will not have direct executive responsibilities itself. The task of developing standards will remain with the standard-setting bodies, and responsibility for enforcement stays at the national level. The international organisations, particularly the IMF, will retain the task of surveillance and monitoring to ensure international consistency. Still, the fact that for the first time, senior officials with monetary, financial and regulatory responsibilities will be brought together in a single body holds the promise of more effective policies toward financial stability.

Crisis management and resolution

I have focused so far on issues of crisis prevention. It is appropriate that a large part of the effort of strengthening the architecture of the international monetary system should be directed to improving the functioning of financial markets to make them more efficient and resilient. But whatever is done to strengthen financial systems, crises will inevitably occur. How can they be more effectively dealt with?

The fact that international capital markets have become more open and integrated, and capital flows have become so large, has changed the parameters of crisis-response. In the traditional approach, when a crisis occurred, the IMF would agree with the country concerned an appropriate package of (mainly) macroeconomic measures, on the basis of which official financing would be provided to cover the financing gap before payments equilibrium was restored.

Now, the flows of funds have become too large for the IMF to deal with by itself, and neither payments equilibrium nor the financing gap can be easily calculated. There is no such thing as a 'normal' level of capital flows that is independent of the policy context. Moreover, it is no longer acceptable to the major creditor governments to provide finance to enable private creditors to exit more readily when they lose confidence in a country. So there is a wide consensus that private-sector lenders must share part of the responsibility of crisis resolution when a country faces liquidity or solvency problems. There is much less consensus, however, on how this should be done.

Market practice with regard to commercial enterprises does not provide a straightforward template. Bankruptcy and administration provisions cannot be easily applied to sovereign entities, partly for formal legal reasons (sovereign immunity) and partly because it is not possible to place a country in the hands of a court-appointed administrator to manage a workout or to liquidate assets. Some aspects of corporate bankruptcy procedures can be more closely replicated, however. Lending contracts could specify the circumstances in which debt service would be suspended, and could provide for collective action by creditors, with majority voting clauses to prevent 'rogue creditors' obstructing agreement.

There is as yet little agreement on how the private sector should be involved in crisis resolution in the future. There seems no doubt, however, that this is a crucial element in the new financial architecture. A balance will have to be struck between the various objectives of: maintaining the sanctity of financial contracts; providing greater certainty about what actions will be taken in the case of a crisis; avoiding unfair penalisation of private lenders (which would be counterproductive for financial flows in the longer term); and recognising the limits to official funding. It will not be easy.

Difficult, too, will be the task of designing the appropriate package of adjustment measures. The IMF was widely criticised in the Asian crisis for applying mistaken remedies for the crisis-hit countries. Much of this criticism was unfair, as reflected in the fact that many of the critics offered diametrically opposite alternatives to each other. But what the crisis did show is that a conventional package of macro-economic adjustment measures needed to restore market confidence may have serious side-effects when the basic problem is weaknesses in the financial sector, and an unsustainable exchange rate regime.

The new architecture: the institutional framework

As I noted at the outset of this chapter, the financial architecture can be thought of as comprising both the rules and conventions that govern international economic and financial relations, and the network of institutions that oversee the development and implementation of these rules. In this second aspect, too, there have been important changes in the system over the years since the Bretton Woods arrangements were introduced.

Under the Bretton Woods system, the IMF was assigned the primary responsibility for the smooth functioning of payments arrangements, liquidity provision and adjustment to payments disequilibria. The World Bank had responsibility for longer-term development assistance. And the WTO (which prior to its constitution as such in 1995 was called the GATT) had responsibility for overseeing the reduction of trade barriers.

This assignment of responsibilities remains valid and could perhaps benefit from being re-emphasised. However, in the case of both the IMF and the World Bank, it also needs to be recognised that a significant part of their original functions now take place through private financial markets. As argued above, the smooth operation of the system therefore depends less on the direct management by official bodies and much more on the efficiency and stability with which the financial sector works. Since responsibility for financial intermediaries and markets is widely shared, this implies a corresponding diffusion of responsibility for the international financial architecture.

In what follows, I will take up a few of the issues that arise. They include: (a) the relative responsibilities of national authorities and international financial organisations in developing and enforcing financial standards; (b) how to balance efficiency in rule-making with the need to have 'legitimacy' and 'buy-in' by as large as possible a number of countries; (c) who should have the primary responsibility for coordinating crisis management; (d) how to coordinate the activities of a diverse range of bodies having responsibility for different aspects of financial stability.

When it comes to the supervision of the financial sector, a number of impediments get in the way of assigning this role to a single supranational authority. Political responsibility remains at the national level, and there are no indications that this is likely to be ceded in the foreseeable future to an international body. The structure of financial systems varies considerably from country to country, and this has an inevitable bearing on supervisory approaches. For these reasons, it has been found preferable to generate certain standards of financial best-practice through committees of national experts. This facilitates acceptance by the parties concerned. Where the rules are well-conceived, and find acceptance in major financial markets, their spread is encouraged by a process of peer pressure and market forces.

Rules are, of course, easier to draft in small groups. But this leads to the second issue, that of ensuring legitimacy for the process by which the international monetary system is managed. Broad-based groupings have legitimacy, but move slowly and can often agree on less. Narrower groups (such as the G7 and G10) have greater agility, but correspondingly less legitimacy. The new financial architecture needs to find a way to balance these competing considerations. Once again, it will not be easy. One possible approach is to recognise the legitimate interest of all countries by vesting the over-arching authority in a body in which all are represented, such as the IMF. At the same time, however, more restricted groupings can be encouraged to facilitate the discussion of particular issues, or to formulate rules in areas of specialised expertise. In another context, this has been called the principle of variable geometry. It is a less tidy solution, but has the merit of reflecting a lack of tidiness in the real world.

Next comes the question of how to co-ordinate effectively the different activities being carried on by the growing number of international groupings having responsibilities for one or another aspect of the field. This was one of the key lacunae identified by the G7 when they asked Hans Tietmeyer to make a report on the issue, and subsequently called into being the Financial Stability Forum.

The Financial Stability Forum by no means replaces the functions of its constituent members (National Authorities, international financial institutions and standard-setting bodies). In particular, the IMF, with its direct relations with its 182 member countries, continues to be the main channel through which macro-economic policies are reviewed and the strength of financial systems in individual countries are assessed. The Fund is uniquely placed to analyse the interface between the regulatory and macro-economic aspects of policy.

But the Financial Stability Forum includes representatives from a range of institutions (particularly regulators and standard-setters) whose voices are heard only indirectly in the Fund. It can thus perform a coordinating function, and can supply added impetus to initiatives designed to strengthen financial systems. It is also intended to identify incipient vulnerabilities in national and international financial systems, and, where appropriate, assign responsibility for dealing with them.

This brings me to the fourth and last institutional aspect of the new architecture I want to touch on, namely, who should co-ordinate the response to financial crises. At the moment, the task is that of the IMF, though the principal creditor-countries have often provided supplementary financial resources and sometimes have pushed for adjustments in conditionality. These arrangements have, on the whole, worked well, despite criticisms levelled at particular aspects of Fund conditionality. What has been missing is a satisfactory institutional vehicle for involving the private sector. The official sector has been frustrated that private lenders have been able to exit from difficult situations in a manner that exacerbated the crisis and caused greater public sector involvement. And the private sector has been apprehensive that the official sector would mandate solutions to which private lenders were obliged to contribute without being able to influence.

This issue is complicated by the fact that capital markets are now highly integrated. Private capital flows are large and, when confidence is fragile, potentially volatile. Nothing is likely to displace the central coordinating role of the IMF. But the architecture would benefit from clearer understandings of how other players (particularly the private sector) would be involved. More work is clearly needed on this issue before a satisfactory solution is arrived at.

Conclusion

To conclude, I briefly draw the strands of the argument together.

Over the half-century of the post-war period, private financial markets have grown in importance as vehicles for effectively allocating real resources. This adds to the importance of ensuring that markets function stably and efficiently. We now understand better some of the reasons why market failures occur. They include lack of transparency, distorted incentives and insufficient or inappropriate regulation. A key focus of the financial architecture must therefore be to develop better mechanisms to avoid market failures.

To do this requires the acceptance of some need for changes of emphasis in institutional responsibilities. Financial standard-setters and regulatory authorities must be closely involved in the overall management of the system. And the fact that financial supervision is likely to remain a national responsibility must be recognised. All of this means more cooks in the kitchen, and a premium on effective coordination.

Nevertheless, a start has been made in developing new rules for the system and new institutional structures to facilitate cooperation. The objective will not be to rewrite the basic rules of international economic relations, that is, an exchange-rate regime, adjustment process and liquidity arrangements based primarily on market signals. Rather, it will be to deal with those factors that cause markets to malfunction – in other words, to make the system work better, and not to replace it with a new system. I like to think that this focus on financial market efficiency would have had the full endorsement of Max Fry.

6 Reducing the cost of bank crises

Is Basel enough?

Jerry Caprio and Patrick Honohan

Introduction

The huge fiscal cost of recent bank crises, arising when governments step in to cover some or all of the losses of depositors has underlined the importance of improved mechanisms for reducing the scale and frequency of bank failures. These losses have been disproportionately high in developing countries, for a number of reasons including higher exogenous volatility, and a greater degree of government intervention in banking. But, despite the fact that costs have also been high there, application of industrial-country prudential standards is generally – and rightly – felt to be a pre-requisite for improvements in the functioning of developing-country systems. In this paper we review these standards and their application in developing countries, and we ask: 'Are they enough?'

We begin by framing the question as one in which the State, as implicit provider of a put option on the deposits of the bank, wishes to limit its fiscal exposure, that is, the value of this option. This can be done by ensuring an adequate buffer of uninsured liabilities by reference to the volatility or risk being assumed and the duration between bank reviews. This provides a clear perspective on the traditional pre-occupation of regulators with capital, information-gathering and supervision and risk-reduction. Fiscal costs are not the only downside from banking crises, but bringing them under control has a near lexicographical status in policy-goal terms: getting this right likely ensures that the other policy concerns – whether related widely to total economic costs, or narrowly to the functioning of the payments system – are also met.

We proceed to consider the major plank of current regulatory practice – supervised capital adequacy, as promulgated by the Basel committee. Although this is a key approach to limiting the implicit exposure of Government, it has many shortcomings when applied in practice to developing countries. We report some preliminary findings of a survey of regulatory practice which provide hints that adherence to the Basel principles may be skin-deep: in several instances it seems that headline regulations – tough-sounding but hard to measure or enforce – are more likely to be in place than the detailed albeit indirect sub-regulations which might be more effective by being easier to police.[1]

Recent proposals for enhancing the Basel system have been addressed more to refining the risk-weights than to verifying that the buffer is adequate. In our view, the proposed use of rating agencies in this effort does not offer much potential for exploiting market incentives. Alternative approaches offer better prospects for limiting fiscal exposure to banking in emerging-economy banking systems. As discussed in the section on 'Harnessing incentives to reduce exposure', these include ways of economizing on direct information requirements by setting easy-to-verify rules and procedures that exploit incentive effects of different classes of agents: the supervisors themselves, the bankers and the other claimants.

Conclusions are presented in the final section.

Limiting the fiscal cost of the deposit put

As has often been noted (since Merton, 1977), the State is in a position analogous to having given away a put option on the bank's covered deposits. This perspective not only throws light on the contribution of the resulting moral hazard to failures and helps measure the State's implicit fiscal exposure, but it also serves as a way of thinking about good design of regulatory policy.

The value of this option varies depending on the net worth and the risk of the bank's portfolio; because of limited liability, it does not depend on the wealth of the banks' owners.[2] The regulator wishes to contain the value of the option through regulations, supervision and intervention. It is when this option is exercised through bank failure that the fiscal costs discussed in the introduction arise.

The duration of the option is not infinite. The regulator can intervene in the management or ownership bank, thereby limiting subsequent deterioration in its net worth. However, in practice, the wheels of regulation do not turn with infinite speed, and a bank's condition may deteriorate for some time before the regulator uncovers this, or before there is an opportunity to take pre-emptive action.

It is, therefore, convenient to see this as a rolling put option, with the rollover occurring at discrete intervals. The option will not be rolled-over if the regulator perceives its value to be too high – too costly to the State.

From this perspective, prudential regulations are designed to contain the value of the put option that the State is implicitly giving away on every rollover date. So the regulator needs to have a way of knowing the value of the option it is currently offering, as well as adjusting available regulations in order to equal the marginal reduction on option value to the marginal cost of achieving that reduction. Recent innovations in bank regulation can be analyzed within this framework.

Modeling the deposit put

For most reasonable models of the evolution of the price of the underlying asset, the value of an option depends mainly on the gap between the current and exercise price of the underlying asset (i.e. the degree to which it is out-of-the-money), on the volatility of its price and on the time left to run. The corresponding concepts here are the ratio of covered deposits to total assets (which provides a buffer against future shocks), the volatility of the value of the bank's assets, and the interval between regulatory reviews. The appendix spells out the algebra here in a simple model, where the buffer is the ratio of the current value of the bank's assets to insured deposits *A/D*, volatility is measured by the variance σ of the bank's asset value and the duration of exposure is denoted τ.

There is, thus, a distinct role for both the current value of the bank's assets and the future risks of a change in that value. Neither is easily evaluated. Although estimating the current asset value is chiefly an issue of measurement, it does have a forward-looking dimension, as does the assessment of future risk. In practice, the key element in the current value of the bank's assets corresponds to the *expected* value of future loan recoveries, with the expectation taken with regard to all information currently available, whereas future risk measures the potential for deviations from that expected value – or what is sometimes referred to as '*unexpected*' future valuation changes.

Increasingly, large banks employ probabilistic modeling of risk which follow an analogous logic.[3] The characteristics of such models include their attempt to take account of correlations between the returns of different assets, as well as matching projected mean and variance of returns to historic experience. The use of these models includes risk-based product pricing and determining the level of equity required to protect against insolvency (e.g. an AA-rated bank might wish to have sufficient equity to ensure that the calculated probability of default was no higher than that experienced by AA banks – say 0.03 per cent over a one-year horizon). In principle, therefore, the modelling used by banks could be mapped directly into this option–price framework. But because of the scale of information required to operationalize and backtest such models of portfolio risk, they remain somewhat experimental even for the banks, and are of no utility in most developing countries. Operating to some extent as black boxes, the sensitivity of these models to misspecification is very hard to judge. Indeed, one interpretation of what went wrong in the case of the LTCM incident is that they had misspecified a risk model of this general type.

Such doubts about the robustness of these methodologies, and about the accuracy and stability of parameter values being used, has meant that this probabilistic modeling approach has not yet displaced more traditional approaches to risk management, whether for the banks themselves or for the regulator.

Nevertheless, most regulations can be seen as attempting to contain the value of the deposit put that has been provided, by monitoring and controlling the buffer of uninsured liabilities (including capital) and the risk of future volatility, and doing so frequently in order to reduce the duration of exposure.

Ways of monitoring and reducing the deposit put value

Information and verifiability are at the heart of this process. Simple rules and regulatory procedures which are easily verified (and as such enforceable if the legal powers and the political will are present) may be only weakly correlated with the true value of the buffer or the volatility: but they can still be effective if the indirect behavioral response of the market to the incentives created by the rule tends reinforce the move to a higher value of the buffer and lower risk. Other rules or procedures designed to come closer in principle to the theoretical measures of buffer and volatility may, because of their complexity or because they demand so much information, be largely unverifiable and, as such, largely unenforceable.

The search for procedures that will improve the incentive compatibility of simple, verifiable and enforceable rules and procedures is, thus, one way forward for the regulator. Increased sophistication can also be helpful, but not if it is bought at the price of reduced enforceability. In emerging economies particularly, the allure of the sophisticated must be resisted, especially if it creates incentives for behavioral responses that bring hidden increases in risk or reductions in the buffer. Unfortunately, as we will see, LDCs have been quicker to adopt the less verifiable – albeit high-profile – regulations and procedures while neglecting the practical and enforceable.

It is for such reasons that the core of the standard regulatory model for the past two decades has not been built on an explicit and theoretically-coherent probabilistic modeling framework as discussed above, but by the older approach of simply assigning minimum capital percentages to the bank's assets classified into risk-classes, and verifying that this capital is in place through external supervision.

There is some congruence between this Basel-supervised capital adequacy paradigm and the main elements of the option–price approach. In place of a fully-consistent probabilistic model of risk, the Basel approach introduces an explicit mapping from the bank's accounts to obtain a ratio of capital to risk-weighted assets which must be kept above a regulated minimum (the famous 8 per cent). Although the mapping is not fully consistent with the theory, it does provide a rough-and-ready feasible rule-of-thumb for operationalizing the key parameters. The minimum capital ratio is analogous to the buffer; the risk-weighting bears some relation to the volatility. And the duration of the exposure is reduced by the frequency and quality and frequency of supervision stressed by the Basel approach – indeed, the whole approach fails if the information system tolerates seriously-biased estimates.

These issues are constantly kept in view by the Basel Committee, including recent initiatives aiming at an extensive overhaul of the system. But, we argue in the next section that practical difficulties remain, and that, at least for the developing countries, recent initiatives, which emphasize the volatility more than the buffer, do not offer much prospect of a better containment of fiscal exposure.

As discussed in the section on 'Harnessing incentives to reduce exposure', more indirect approaches to limiting fiscal exposure seek to economize on direct information requirements by setting easy-to-verify rules and procedures that exploit incentive effects of different classes of agents: the supervisors themselves, the bankers and the other claimants.

The Basel system and its limitations

A major early goal of the Basel Committee on Banking Supervision[4] was to establish a level playing-field for international banks in the face of intensified but un-harmonized national regulatory regimes, and to avoid the danger of regulatory competition. Its imposition of a common risk-weighted minimum capital percentage – albeit a compromise – has surely contributed to an increase in average bank capitalization over the past decade.

The centerpiece of the industrial country ('Basel') approach has been the requirement that each bank should maintain a minimum of accounting capital in relation to its risks, a requirement that is supported by a supervisory procedure akin to, but going well beyond, the audits to which non-financial firms are subjected. Notwithstanding this conceptual simplicity, the Basel committee, and regulators generally, have had to work almost continuously to refine and redefine the measure of risks, as well as having to cope with ever-increasing difficulties of verification of the value of capital. Part of the problem has been the evolving complexity of financial market instruments, and the fact that a bank's position in such instruments can change from moment to moment. For this reason the recent trend has been for industrial country supervisors to supplement the ratio approach by auditing of the bank's risk management systems, rather than simply assessing the state of the balance sheet at a moment in time. Additionally, one must note the endogeneity: as authorities try to force bankers to hold more capital than they deem optimal, their response is to innovate, such as by shedding or appearing to shed risks, as through the securitization process. As supervisors catch up in their understanding of more complex instruments and tighten the rules accordingly for risks still affecting banks, the bankers can be expected to innovate again.

But there are other limitations to the 'supervised capital adequacy' paradigm, some related to the question of capital adequacy itself, others to the inherent shortcomings of administrative supervision, even where the 'Core Principles of Effective Banking Supervision' are in place. Many of these problems have been identified in the theoretical literature,[5] which began to evolve rapidly once microeconomists interested in regulation began to realize not only the points of common ground with other principal-agent incentive structures, but also the challenging differences that arise in the regulation of bank-like financial institutions. Many have been confirmed in the field, not least in developing countries.

In practice, the Basel system is being rapidly adopted by developing economies. Over 100 countries have now formally adopted the system. Indeed, a survey of regulatory practices now being carried out by the World Bank reveals that, for each sub-group of low-, lower-middle, upper-middle and high-income countries, the *median* value of the regulatory floor on capital as a percentage of risk-weighted assets is exactly 8 for each (Figure 6.1). The rulebook in some countries does tolerate a lower percentage, but even the *average* floor for low-income countries is 7 per cent. But it is one thing formally to adopt the rules; quite another to implement them adequately.

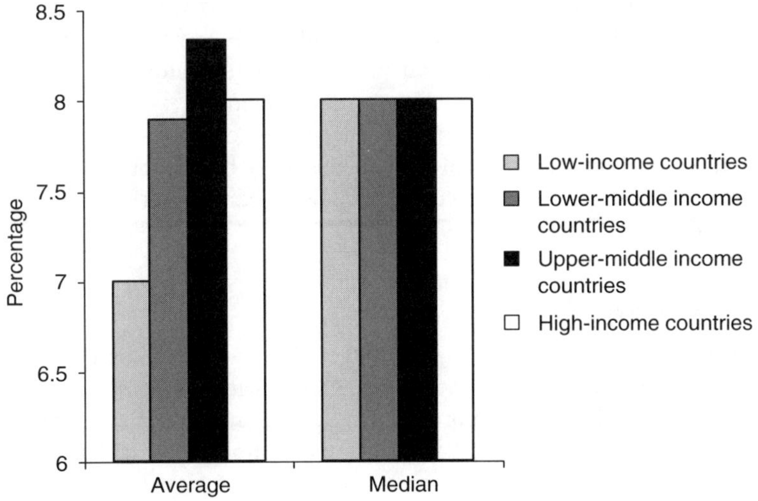

Figure 6.1 Minimum capital ratios.

Note: Except where noted, the data in all figures is based on preliminary results (covering 44 countries) of a World Bank survey[6] of regulatory practices, 1998–99.

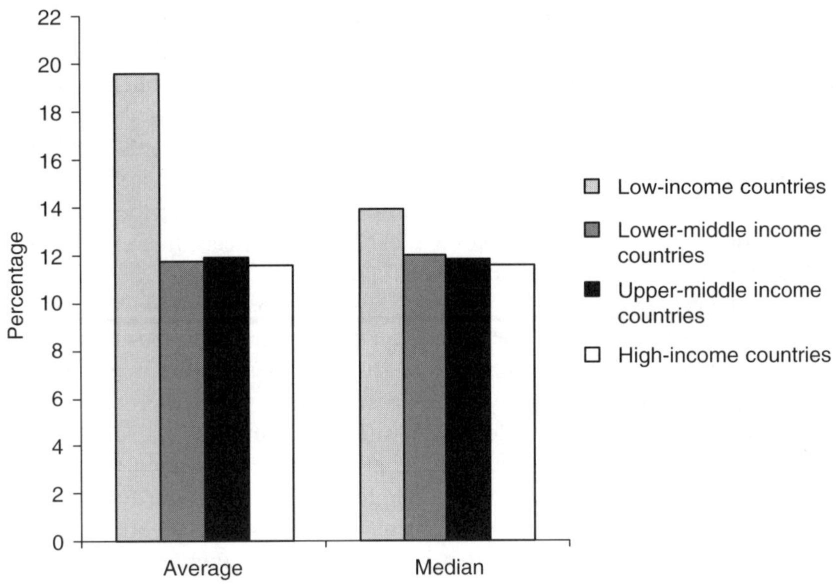

Figure 6.2 Actual capital ratios (risk-adjusted – December 1998).

To be sure, average *reported* capital of banks in the surveyed countries does exceed the 8 per cent threshold. However, the fact that reported excess capital is highest in the low-income countries should cause us pause (Figure 6.2): do banks really hold substantial capital in excess of regulatory minima in these countries, or is the verification of capital problematic, with a less rigorous application of accounting principles in the poorer countries? The latter interpretation would imply that initial appearances may be deceptive in the case of developing countries, and that compliance with hard-to-verify standards may often be cosmetic.

Measuring capital

In order to calculate capital as a percentage of risk-weighted assets, measuring capital – which entails valuing the assets (i.e. with allowance for expected losses) – is arguably more important than the risk-weighting (i.e. making provision for the unexpected). In terms of the option-value discussion of the previous section, we need to ensure an adequate buffer as well as limiting the volatility. Yet, recent attention has focused almost entirely on the matter of risk-weights. This is understandable insofar as the principles underlying asset-valuation have been extensively discussed in the past, and inasmuch as recent pressure on the Basel system from international banks in the Industrial Countries has reflected attempts to arbitrage the very simple structure of risk-weights that was introduced in 1988. But all too often a bank is truly insolvent long before its accounts tell us so. If capital is actually negative, no amount of risk-adjustment will alter that fact.

All accounting authorities agree on the importance of loan-loss provisions (allowances) in arriving at a fair value of loans, which remain the major item in most banks' balance sheets. Although not always explicitly couched in probabilistic terms, we may say that the provisions are supposed to take account of expected loan-losses. Unlike the situation with marketable assets, this cannot often be approximated by a market price. After all, it is its private information about credit quality that allows a bank to profit from lending; the asymmetric information thus underlying much of the loan portfolio means that it could not be sold without encountering severe 'lemons' problems.

Bank supervisors do try to classify loans into forward-looking categories such as 'normal', 'especially mentioned', 'sub-standard', 'doubtful' and 'loss', and regulations implicitly attach loss probabilities to each of the last three categories by requiring a certain percentage (typically 20, 50 and 100 respectively) of the value of loans classified as sub-standard, doubtful and loss to be provisioned in the bank's accounts (usually in addition to a required general loan-loss provision of about 1 per cent of the entire portfolio). Indeed, here too our survey shows that requirements are on average slightly tougher on paper in low-income countries. What is important here, though is that the provisioning requirements should actually correspond to subsequent loan-loss experience.[7]

But ensuring an adequate forward-looking classification of loans is not straightforward. Especially when economic conditions move out of the normal, or for the large or unusual loans that are often the weak point of a reckless bank, past experience may be a poor guide, even to the banker. The high-risk environment and rapidly evolving economic structure of most developing countries obviously exacerbates the severity of this problem. Realistically, in the face of a resistant bank management and being on the light end of the asymmetric information scales, supervisors often can do little more than insist on a backward-looking measure: insisting on provisions being made when the loan goes into arrears. And in this respect the accounting rules or standards vary widely. In particular, we have found, in regard to the standard delays before provisioning is required, that the median low-income country is more lenient than the upper-middle-income group, with loans being allowed to run 90 (180) days before being classified as sub-standard (doubtful) (Figure 6.3a,b). This is a further concrete indication that application of the Basel principles may often be little more than skin-deep.

Another telling finding is that one in three low-income countries allow banks to treat interest that is in arrears as earned income, at least for a time. In Thailand, interest accrual on non-performing loans was allowed for up to 360 days in 1997. And, in most countries, it is still more difficult to prevent a bank from concealing a non-performing loan simply by 'evergreening' that is, making a new loan to cover the repayment.

Our conclusion is that measuring the size of the buffer is a challenge which is far from being under control. Headline regulations are promulgated without having the information needed for verification or putting in place the incentives that might help reveal it.

The risk-weights

As mentioned, recent discussion of reforms to the Basel agreement has focused on the risk-weights to be used in the ratio. Evidently this does bear some relationship to the role of the risk factor σ in our discussion of option-value above. But it is not a very close relationship. Indeed, the gap between the Basel Committee's approach to risk and that of standard finance theory is very striking. Their idea can be thought of as essentially requiring that each class of assets should have a certain percentage capital buffer, and that capital covering one class of assets could not be used to cover others (thereby neglecting possible correlations between different asset classes).[8,9] The choice of weights has not explicitly been justified in terms of actual default experience, and the initial weights that have been in effect for over a decade now seem rather simplistic (e.g. residential mortgages = half the risk-weight of commercial loans).

More recently, the Basel Committee has proposed extensive revisions to the system, including an increase in the number of risk categories, and the use of assessments by private credit-rating agencies to establish appropriate

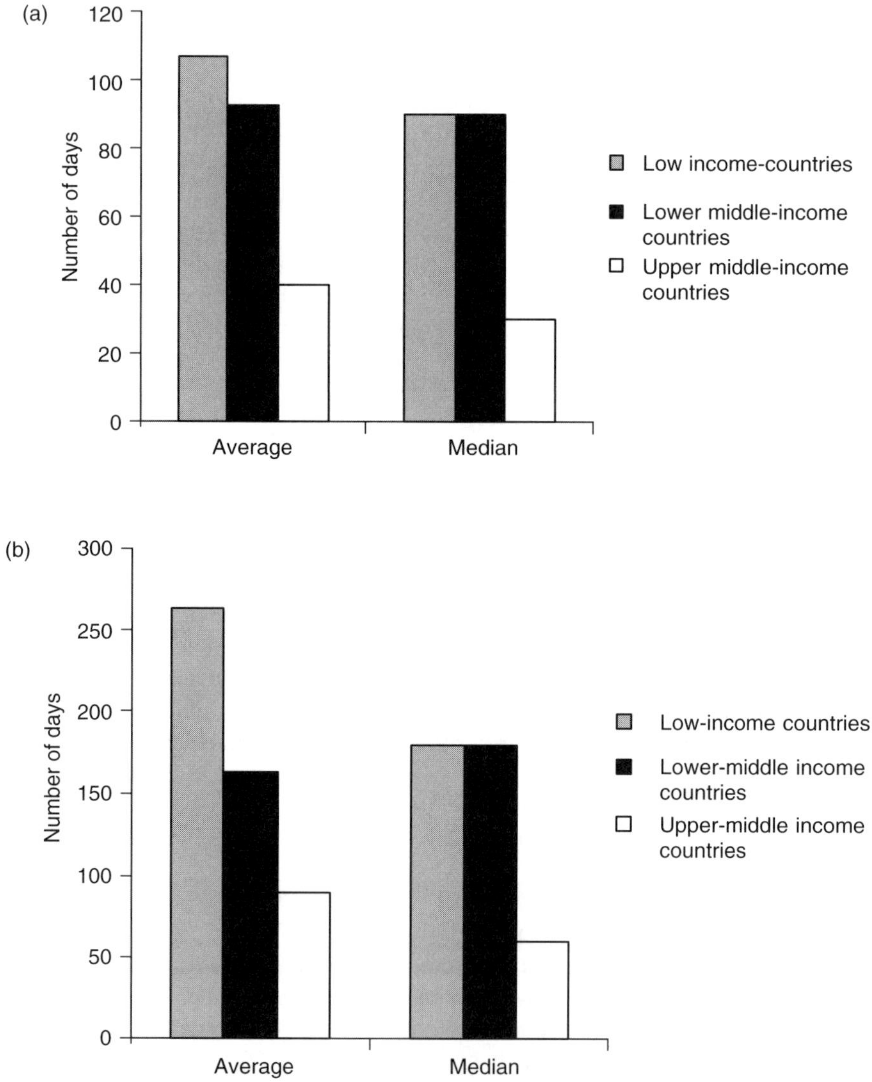

Figure 6.3 No. of days before loans are compulsorily classified (surveyed countries). (a) Classification of sub-standard loans and (b) Classification of doubtful loans.

risk-weightings to be attatched to different loans for the purpose of computing risk-weighted capital adequacy. While these new ideas are still evolving, and the final shecme will likely have a better alignment of risk-weightings with default experience.[10]

It is worth recalling that, in choosing risk-weights, we are here concerned with the risk of the *unexpected*; expected loan-losses being a matter to be dealt with by the loan-loss provisions. While the expected recovery rate from a portfolio composed of loans to borrowers with low credit-ratings is undoubtedly lower than that from a portfolio composed of loans to those with higher credit-ratings, it is not inevitable that the *risk* of the latter portfolio is lower. Yes, historical experience from defaults of US securities since the 1920s shows that a *standard deviation* of default rates from individual B rated securities 3.8 times higher than those of AA rated securities; but the *mean* default rate of B rated securities is fully 11.7 times higher than that of the AA rated (Figure 6.4). The relatively small increase in standard deviation as rating declines suggests that the standard deviation of a low-rated portfolio composed of a large number of uncorrelated risks could be *lower* than that of a high-rated portfolio comprising a small number of correlated risks. But the 1999 proposals had capital weights 5 times higher for those elements of the loan portfolio not rates AA- or better.

The proposed use of ratings thus tends to blur the distinction which we have been here stressing between the buffer and the volatility; between provisioning for expected or predictable loan-losses and taking account of vulnerability to variance. It could also have the practical implication of requiring higher-than-necessary capital from a large retail-oriented bank, while giving spurious comfort

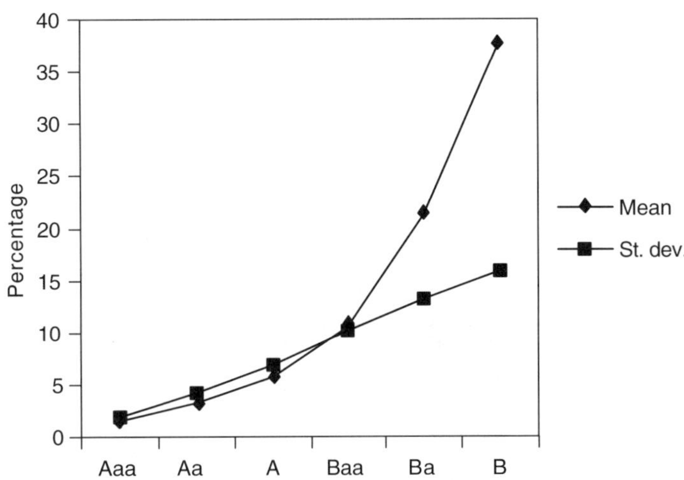

Figure 6.4 Default percentages by rating.

Source: Adams *et al.* (1999).

Note: Shows mean and standard deviation of 10-year cumulative default rates by US bonds rated by Moody's 1920–50 and 1965–98.

to a small investment bank dependent on a small number of sectorally concentrated loans to high-rated companies. Of course, the market does not stand still, and it is easy to foresee such discrepancies being arbitraged for example by rebundling what are individually low-grade loans into securitized packages, some tranches of which can receive high ratings. More work for lawyers and accountants.

Evidently, nobody expects the ratings approach to provide a very accurate risk assignment. It is essentially a way of refining what had been seen as too coarse a partition of obligors into risk classes. Even if each borrower is assigned the correct risk-class, a coarse partition is more prone to being arbitraged, with banks lending to the highest-yield borrowers in each risk-class, regardless of the impact on portfolio risk. Refining the partition could, therefore, be an improvement.

Some other drawbacks of the use of agency ratings have already been noted by the Basel Committee itself. Specifically, credit-rating agencies have had a limited and mixed record in respect both of country risk and the credit-worthiness of corporate borrowers in the developing world. The limited scope of their experience is illustrated by our survey's finding that, while nine of the top ten banks is rated in the typical high-income country, only about a half of the top ten banks in middle-income countries have ratings, and none in the low-income countries (Figure 6.5). Evidently this will change as the ratings industry responds to the new incentives.

One specific concern for emerging economies relates not to the use of rating agencies for influencing local banks' capital requirements, but rather to the

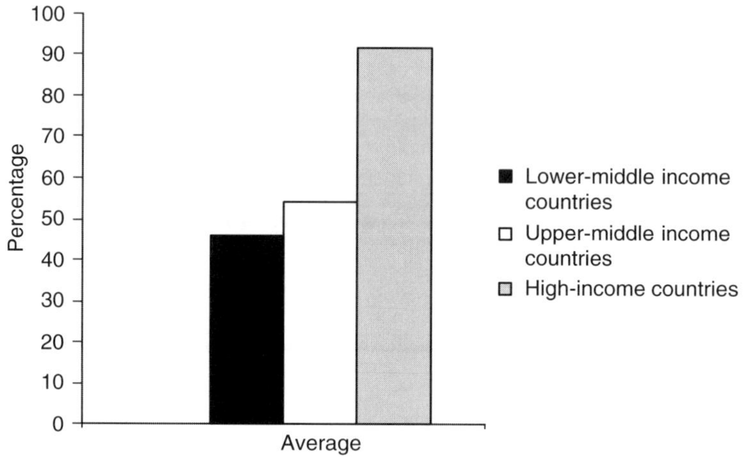

Figure 6.5 Percentage of top ten banks that are rated by international credit rating agencies.

possible impact on the availability of international bank credit to emerging economy borrowers. Specifically, there is the suggestion that the agencies may over-react to news about country credit-worthiness, and as such their use for determining capital requirements may exacerbate the pro-cyclicality of lending.[11] Already fluctuations in the availability of external credit have had an important impact on macro-economic instability in developing countries. These credit cycles entail substantial economic externalities: these should not be exacerbated by unwarranted regulations, and so there is a case for damping the fluctuations in required capital for international bank lending to LDCs that might result from mechanical reliance on rating agencies.

But what of the likely impact in practice on bank behavior in developing economies? It would be a mistake to over-emphasize the imperfections of the weighting scheme, and of the performance of ratings in the past. After all, the whole approach of the Basel rules is to employ feasible rules-of-thumb for reducing risk on an internationally harmonized basis. In adopting this approach, the Basel Committee has been following an older tradition of banking whereby risk-control was exercised in a decentralized manner by imposing rules-of-thumb on lending officers and branches. Such rules were expressed in terms such as exposure limits to individual clients and limits on risk-concentration by sector, geographical area and other convenient, though crude, measures. This approach offered a degree of risk-control while retaining the advantages that delegated authority offered in terms of the local or sectoral knowledge and judgement.

Nowadays banks can achieve better risk-control by the centralized assembly and computerized analysis of large bodies of data, and reliance on rules-of-thumb has lessened. Clearly, controlling social risk (as measured by the value of the deposit put) could also benefit from the systematic application of better information than has been brought to bear in the existing Basel risk-weightings. Not that there is anything novel about using agency ratings as a prudential criterion – indeed it represents an old-fashioned approach with a long pedigree. Over the years, regulators have also used the ratings of private agencies as a similar rule-of-thumb tool for limiting risk. Starting in the 1930s in the US, the achievement of an 'investment-grade'-rating has been the pre-requisite for regulatory approval of bonds as acceptable instruments in a variety of regulated investment intermediaries and fiduciaries (cf. Adams *et al.*, 1999). From this perspective, the introduction of ratings might seem to be just a further elaboration of the rule-of-thumb approach, but employing more data.

It might also be held to represent a way of bringing market information to bear on banking risk. But in this respect, it is less likely to be much of a success. Indeed, a major potential weakness of the proposed approach of using rating agencies as a means of bringing additional information into play lies in the problematic incentives that this may introduce. Rating agencies are mostly paid by the issuers of securities; this alone might induce them to over-rate securities, but continued business requires their ratings to achieve credibility (a favorable rating from a non-credible agency will not help to sell bonds). For bank loans, the incentives are quite different. Both borrower and lender want to see a favorable rating, the former for obvious reasons, the latter in order to reduce the regulatory capital bringing it closer to what the bank would prefer. Market forces are thus against realistic ratings; the market has not been effectively harnessed. Instead, the incentives of agencies may be subverted, potentially giving rise to the need to regulate these too.

In economies where bank lending is still far more important than bond issue, the potential business from bank borrowers could easily dominate the turnover of rating agencies. By introducing the possibility of lowering regulatory capital requirements for some high-quality borrowers, the introduction of these new proposals would evidently elicit a market response in the form of the emergence or expansion of the rating agency business in all countries. But to what end? What degree of independence can be expected from these agencies? How would integrity be rewarded when both borrower and lender stood to gain from an optimistic rating?[12]

Already supervisors can often benefit from some independent opinions in the form of report from the auditors. Indeed, it is in low-income countries that supervisors are most likely to have access to audit reports. But here again, the substance may fall short of appearance, in that regulators' in low-income countries are the least likely to have the power to take legal action against auditors for negligence, a potentially fatal neglect of enforcement powers (Figure 6.6a,b). This again is consistent with a model in which only the high-profile aspects of 'good practice' are adopted. The necessary support from tough detailed measures that would give real bite is not forthcoming. One must fear that this would apply also to the use of agency ratings. Regulatory design should be enhancing incentives for market participants; not co-opting them in a way that is not incentive compatible.

Harnessing incentives to reduce exposure

If we wish to promote bank-soundness effectively in emerging economies, we will need to go beyond the bare bones of the supervised capital-adequacy paradigm. In particular, we will need to marshal the incentive effects of market behavior so that they are working on behalf of the regulator, making the job of limiting the value of the free deposit put easier both by reducing risk and easing measurement. The Basel Committee does, of course, acknowledge the value of market discipline, and is going some way towards mandating disclosure of information about banks to the market. But there are several other dimensions to the incentive issue. As we will see below, these include the need to enhance incentives for outside investors, for the bankers and for the supervisors themselves. By multiplying the watchful eyes in this way, not only is the likelihood of early problem detection increased, but (especially where public opinion can also be mobilized) the political pressures are side-tracked. (Caprio, 1997; World Bank, 2001).

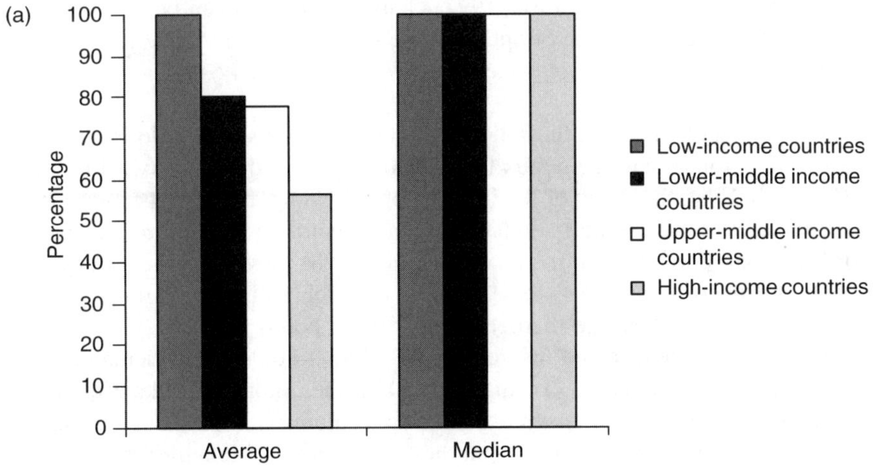

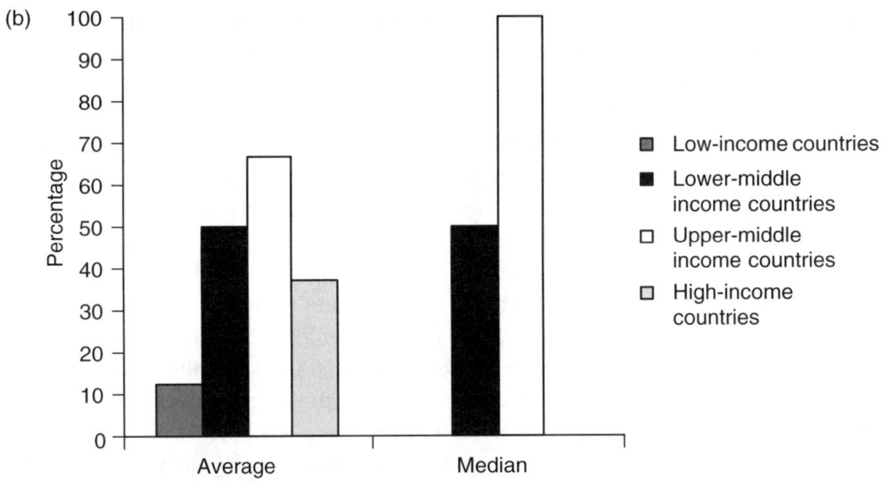

Figure 6.6 Relationship between auditors and regulators. (a) Do supervisors get a copy of the auditor's report? and (b) Can supervisors take legal action against external auditors for negligence?

Incentives for outside investors

Even with some deposit insurance, there is evidence that depositors do monitor banks, perhaps because the credibility of the deposit guarantee falls into question (Demirgüç-Kunt and Huizinga, 1999; Martinez-Peria *et al.*, 2001). One interesting idea to exploit this natural market tendency is already in place on an experimental basis in Argentina. This imposes a requirement that banks should frequently issue a certain minimum of uninsured marketable subordinated bonds to unrelated investors (Calomiris, 1997). This requirement can be interpreted in the context of our discussion of option-value above as creating, in effect, another issuer of derivatives with put-like characteristics, namely the holders of the uninsured debt.

Like the deposit insurer, the subordinated debt-holders have sold a derivative with payoff somewhat analogous to a put option. But there are two important differences. First, the value of the implicit option which these debt-holders have issued increases much more quickly with a declining quality of the bank's portfolio than does the deposit insurer's put. It will move into the money well before the deposit insurer's does. Second, the debt-holder will not offer this option for free.[13] Thus, the market price of these bonds provides a generalized early-warning system to the insurer. And the bond-holders will demand better information and disclosure. (To make sure that they monitor banks effectively, effort has to be devoted to ensure – such as by Calomiris' (1997) suggestion that they be required to issue abroad – that they are at an arm's length from the banks who issue the paper.)

The possibility has been raised that the incentive effects of the subordinated-debt scheme could be undermined if the holders of the subordinated debt were to use credit derivatives to hedge their risk.[14] Undoubtedly the subordinated debt-holder is exposed to loss in the event that the issuing bank defaults, and credit derivatives[15] could be used to offset or hedge this exposure. While this would would reduce the incentive for the sub-debt holder to monitor the bank, it is less clear that this would undermine the incentive effects of the scheme overall? After all, the provider of the protection in the derivative market would in turn have an incentive to monitor, unless he/she too offset the exposure. And if that offset were effective, then the monitoring would pass on to the ultimate provider of protection. Only if that ultimate provider were the State, or, as suggested by Garber, the original issuing bank of the subordinated debt, would the incentive to monitor lapse. It seems unlikely that that original issuing bank would be a credible counterparty in offering protection against its own failure. Unless this protection was fully collateralized and highly liquid (e.g. the issuing bank puts up US Treasuries), it would not truly offer protection.

In other words, even if there is some use of credit derivatives to hedge the exposure arising for holders of subordinated debt, anyone selling such protection – that is coverage in the event that the bank issuing subordinate debt fails – would either be unhedged or would need to be receiving funds in the default event, which could only occur if some other entity is providing them, and that entity will become the monitor. And if a bank issuing subordinated debt has to back it by high-quality securities, then this itself induces that bank to hold a more conservative portfolio.

Though it requires a certain market infrastructure to be workable, this kind of regulation, thus, has great attractions in terms of verifiability and the likely indirect-incentive effects. Verifying that the subordinated debt is in place should be *relatively* easy, and the regulation creates incentives likely to elicit a risk-reducing behavioral response.

Not only can subordinated debt help by forming a core of well-motivated and presumably informed monitors, who in effect can become the next generation of bank owners for institutions whose current generation fails, but it also provides a better balance between official and market monitoring. Correcting this imbalance is particularly important in developing countries due to the greater concentration of power, and therefore, higher likelihood of political interference with the supervision process.

Incentives for the bankers

Capital may not be only a buffer: the idea that banks in which owners have more funds at risk would behave in a more prudent fashion has some plausibility. However, we cannot be sure of this. Gaining nothing from the up-side risks, the regulator is more concerned than the shareholder with risk of failure: accordingly, regulatory capital will tend to be higher than that which would be chosen by the bank, whose response may well (as stressed by Calomiris, 1997) be to increase the risk of its portfolio. Only when staying in business is the best option does the bank stand much chance of survival.

The franchise value of the bank (which could be measured as the difference between the value of the bank as a going concern and its liquidation value) is not fully captured by the usual accounting, but it is key to bankers' incentive. Damaged by taxation and quasi-taxation and enhanced by restrictions on entry, increasing franchise value is an objective that has to be tempered by other considerations, including consumer welfare and budgetary needs, but achieving an adequate franchise is a pre-requisite for reducing risk in banking.

Sticks may be involved as well as carrots.

Nostalgic folk note that limited shareholder liability is one thing that has encouraged banks to assume excessive risk-taking, as bank owners face unlimited upside gains with limited losses. In addition to theoretical support for this notion (Stiglitz), historical evidence has emerged that US banks that faced enhanced liability in the nineteenth and early twentieth century behaved more conservatively than those with limited liability (Esty, 1996). Indeed, the deposit put option may be said to exist because of limited-liability provisions.[16] If bank owners are not forced to cover the downside associated with their actions, then regardless of the existence of a deposit-insurance fund, or other explicit or implicit guarantees deposits, they have the option to put losses to someone else; deposit insurance, in addition to facilitating the raising of funds, merely tells the banker where to send the bill for excessive risk-taking.

Increased liability for bank directors (as for other company directors) has been a legislative trend in several countries, among which New Zealand, where it applies under specific circumstances (e.g. disclosure of incomplete or erroneous information).

One promising idea is a pre-commitment approach toward regulation (Kupiec and O'Brien, 1997), according to which bankers agree with supervisors on the models, procedures and performance criteria they will use to evaluate their risks, and are subject to penalties for violation or under-performance relative to the agreed criteria. More generally, the approach that is adopted by the authorities to resolving one crisis sets the scene and signals the incentives to bankers for avoiding future incidents – if, that is, the models are reliable and the penalties reliably applied.

Incentives for the supervisors

Although many may scoff at the ability of government supervision to be effective, the empirical evidence on this score is divided. Some (Berger *et al.*, 1998) find that supervisory assessments in the US appear to add value regarding the current condition of banks, but in predicting future performance are less accurate than bond and equity market assessments. However, a recent study, also for the US (Flannery *et al.*, 2001) shows that current bank-examiner ratings, which are supposed to remain secret, help predict subsequent assessments in the subordinated debt market. Improving supervisory capacity is thus, potentially an important way of increasing the precision of measures of the State's exposure and also reducing the effective duration of exposure.

But supervisors are faced with information problems and pressures to forbear from enforcement. Often they are underpaid and demoralized, and this needs to be met with an incentive structure for supervisors more likely to elicit the kind of performance which the paradigm of supervised capital adequacy took for granted.

Bank supervisors are generally paid less than bankers (our survey suggests a premium of about a quarter after 10 years' experience) and – though here, we do not yet have sufficient firm data – the gap seems often to be much larger in emerging markets, where financial liberalization and the arrival of high-wage foreign banks have often had the effect of greatly increasing remuneration in the private financial sector. Indeed, in some cases, private bank compensation might exceed supervisory levels by 10 : 100 : 1; with such a wide gap, effective supervision is simply implausible. As a result not only do developing-country supervisory agencies have greater difficulty in retaining skilled supervisors, but the opportunity for outright bribery is greater, as well as the possibility of a nice deferred bonus, in the form of a future job, for light supervision. Bonding regulators (Kane, 1995) through deferred bonuses, with losses deducted, would improve their incentives, but is likely to be infeasible, at least for the present; significantly raising supervisory compensation, where it is a mere fraction of market salaries, is likely to be a necessary condition for improvements here.

Working both to upgrade skills and improve compensation are important initiatives, and the latter, in particular, meets political resistance in many countries; even the costly banking crisis in Japan has not yet clearly produced a change in the *amakudari*, or 'descent from heaven' system, according to which regulators move to senior posts in banking. Authorities may attempt to ban future employment in the banking sector by supervisors, at least for a number of years, to reduce the likelihood of deferred compensation with poor incentive properties.[17] However, without higher compensation for supervisors, this will be more likely to make it even more difficult to attract capable staff, and merely increase the pressure for corruption during an official's career.

Supervisors' incentives to enforce the regulations can perhaps also be enhanced by reducing the discretion to forbear.[18] This mandated 'prompt corrective action' is a potentially powerful tool against political pressures, though it remains somewhat controversial inasmuch as it removes a flexibility to circumstances that could be useful.[19] Moreover, prompt corrective actions, like US accounting standards as the S&L crisis was becoming evident, can easily be shelved, all the more so when ownership of banks and corporations is concentrated. A crucial element here is to ensure that regulators have adequate legal protection against law suits brought, for example, by aggrieved owners of intervened banks. The risk for a regulator of incurring personal liability even in the performance of official duties is a real one in many emerging markets, and has a chilling effect on regulatory intervention.

Enforcement of regulations can, for obvious reasons, be particularly tricky in the case of Government-owned banks, which have been the source of some of the costliest bank failures in developing countries. The share of government-owned banks in the total financial system tends to increase as we go down the income scale (Figure 6.7).

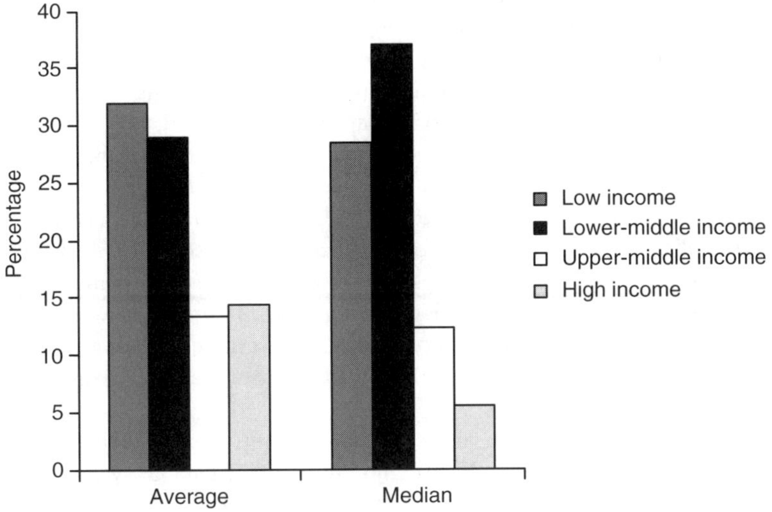

Figure 6.7 Fraction of banking system's assets in banks that are 50 per cent or more government owned.

If informed public opinion is intolerant of bad banking and critical of undue regulatory forbearance, the political pressures that inhibit enforcement will abate. Some progress is being made on this front, including at the international level, but there is still much scope for enhancing the flow of reliable information and public awareness.

This does not exhaust the potential for novel approaches to reducing fiscal exposure. In Caprio and Honohan (1999) we discuss how opening the domestic banking market to ownership by reputable foreign banks can also serve to lay-off the risks of the domestic banking environment (thereby reducing the volatility in the option-price formula). Other ways of enlarging the market through regionalization can also help in the same dimension. A reversal of the trend of the past two decades away from liquidity requirements might also help contain risk, especially where information is poor, as can other blunter instruments of regulation (Honohan and Stiglitz, 2001).

Concluding remarks

Intermediaries in an ideal financial system will allocate funds shrewdly to a well-diversified mix of projects yielding high private (and social) returns without exposing the intermediary to a disproportionate risk of failure. Such a financial system serves as an absorber, rather than a magnifier of economic disturbances.

It is impractical to think in terms of an unregulated system for delivering this result, but recent regulatory failures certainly suggest that we are well below optimum performance in this regard. The sources of heightened regulatory failure in recent years: volatility of real and nominal shocks, the difficulty of operating in uncharted territory following regime changes such as financial liberalization, and the political pressures that can inhibit enforcement of prudential regulation, are all present in a heightened form in developing countries, and it is there that the most recent wave of collapses has occurred.

Emerging market authorities have to cope, at least for the time being, with the current system in which large real and financial disturbances – either from domestic or foreign sources – threaten with some regularity. Tightening the regulation of domestic financial systems appears warranted, a course that already has been followed by some countries that experienced severe financial crises in the 1980s. Problems that loom particularly large in emerging markets both argue for a re-thinking of conventional approaches to government interventions in this key sector and point the way to specific paths to follow in adjusting the regulatory environment.

The pendulum must not be allowed to swing too far; the benefits of rapid economic growth supported by liberal and innovative financial systems must not be neglected, nor the costs of a heavy repressive regulatory hand. Prevention is not costless. Yet, we believe that governments can do better: that a richer regulatory pallet can be used to protect the financial system more successfully against crisis while still preserving its growth-enhancing effectiveness.

Some well-worn messages remain valid and are respected more in theory than in practice. Thus, problems would be fewer if there were: more diversification, more balanced financial structures (e.g., as between debt and equity), the presence of foreign banks and, above all, better enforcement of both regulations and contracts.

Because financial-sector participants will constantly attempt to get around rules that limit their profitability, regulation must be seen as an evolutionary struggle. Some of the new approaches that are only now beginning to be applied will have a limited life before the regulated entities find ways of nullifying their effect. Regulatory innovation will remain a constant challenge.

It would be absurd to deny that ensuring adequate capital is a central goal for bank supervision – and in high-risk environments a margin of safety is even more critical. But all too often, neither bank capital, nor the risks it supports, can be reliably measured. In developing countries, the situation is worsened by severe information asymmetries, shading into concealment and worse, often by politically powerful bank-insiders, combined with the heightened risk-environment and uncharted conditions that prevail. Survey evidence suggests that low and middle-income countries adhere to the form more than to the substance of the Basel approach of supervised capital adequacy.

The new Basel initiatives focus on refining the risk-weights rather than verifying that there really is a capital buffer. The attempt by new initiatives to co-opt the rating agencies is unlikely to ensure incentive compatibility. For emerging economies, a shift in emphasis in favor of simple but enforceable rules and procedures that have favorable indirect incentive effects would seem to offer better prospects.

Acknowledgments

We are grateful to Iffath Sharif for assistance with the regulatory data, and to Jim Barth, Stijn Claessens, Asli Demirgüç-Kunt, Ross Levine, Millard Long, Sole Martinez-Peria, Rick Mishkin, Larry Promisel, Joseph Stiglitz, Dimitri Vittas and participants at the AEA Meetings in Boston, January 2000 for helpful suggestions on our ongoing research in this area. Nevertheless, the findings, interpretations, and conclusions expressed in this paper are entirely those of the authors and do not necessarily represent the views of the World Bank, its Executive Directors, or the countries they represent.

Appendix

Modeling the deposit put

This Appendix elaborates the assertion in the section an 'Limiting the fiscal cost of the deposit put' that the value of the implicit put offered by the deposit-insurer depends on the buffer of uninsured liabilities, the volatility of the value of the bank's assets and the rollover frequency.

Let us simplify by assuming that the typical bank's balance sheet can be summarized as $A = B + C + D$, where A is the present value of the bank's existing risk-assets, B stands for the face value of uninsured subordinated liabilities of the bank (think of 'B for bonds'), C is the residual true value of capital and D is insured deposits.[20] As long as C remains positive, the bank should be in a position to meet all claims, both to insured depositors and uninsured subordinated creditors.[21] Indeed, as long as the value of C remains greater than *minus* B, the implicit put sold by the deposit-insurer remains unexercised.

Thus, in the current application of option-price theory, the price of the underlying asset is effectively the true current value of the bank's risk assets A, and the exercise (strike) price is the face value of the deposits D. If $D > A$, then the market has an incentive to exercise the option in the sense that the deposit-insurer has to pay (the depositors) D and receive the assets A.

We picture the regulator as reviewing the situation from time to time. After each review, the regulator can choose to intervene in the bank, or to rollover the deposit put for a further τ months. As it is the dynamic of the value of the banks' assets that is the key source of uncertainty, let us ignore interest, as well as any time-variation in D between reviews. But the time-variation in the value of the assets $A(t)$ leaves the insurer vulnerable to loss if $A(t) < D$ while the deposit put is still in place. With the volatility of the stochastic process governing $A(t)$ measured by σ, the prospective scale of this vulnerability can be measured at the time t_0 of the review as the value $G(A(t_0), \sigma, \tau;\ D)$, of the option being offered.

There are, thus, two sources of uncertainty: one concerns estimating the current value of the bank's assets $A(t_0)$; the other concerns the future shocks that may occur.[22] The first can be seen as chiefly an issue of measurement, the second is an issue of assessing future risk σ. Alternatively, as indicated in the previous note, it may be useful to see the current value as corresponding to an expected value of future loan recoveries, with the expectation taken with regard to all information currently available, whereas future risk measures the potential for deviations from that expected value – or what is sometimes referred to as 'unexpected' future valuation changes.

There are several contrasts with the standard option pricing problem. First, the underlying asset is not regularly traded (though the bank's equity capital may be) hence not only invalidating the underlying assumptions of much conventional option-pricing theory, but making the underlying asset's price itself opaque. We are used to the problem of having to estimate the variance of the underlying asset, but not knowing what its current price is presents a novel problem, and elevates the question of accuracy of the parameter estimates being used in valuation. To the extent that the true value is based on an expected value-concept, the regulator may need to work hard to assemble the information required to estimate this expected value, let alone the risk.[23]

Even though the conditions under which the Black–Scholes formula is derived may not hold, nevertheless it may provide a reasonable approximation to the value/cost of the deposit put option $G(A, \sigma, \tau; D)$ where s is the variance of A and τ is the time horizon. If so, we can regard the ratio A/D – which is larger the more uninsured liabilities there are to absorb losses before the insurer is called upon – as the size of the *buffer* against future shocks. Specifically, G will be a decreasing, convex function of A (i.e. the 'delta' of the option-value is negative and its 'gamma' is positive). Furthermore, the option-value is increasing in the *volatility* (risk) σ and in the *duration of exposure* or time to maturity τ ('vega' and 'theta'). In order to estimate the option value, the regulator needs to estimate the values of the parameters shown, of which only τ and D can normally be taken as known.

The higher the variance σ of A, the higher the option-value G, which is not only higher, but also generally more uncertain: as shown by Campbell *et al.* (1997) for the Black–Scholes case, the maximum likelihood estimate of the option-value G obtained from a time-series of observations of the asset-price, while consistent, has asymptotic variance

$$\frac{\sigma^2}{n} Y^2,$$

where Y is the vega of the option,

$$Y = A\sqrt{\tau}\phi(d_1),$$

r is the riskless rate of interest and ϕ is the ordinate of the standard normal density at

$$d_1 = \frac{\ln A/D + (r + \frac{1}{2}\sigma^2)\tau}{\sigma\sqrt{\tau}}$$

An additional more subtle point arises in the present context, where even the underlying asset-value A is not known. Because option-value is generally a convex function of the underlying asset-price, even if the regulator's estimate $\hat{A}$ of the asset-price A is unbiased, uncertainty about the asset-price raises the mean of the estimated option value above its value calculated at the true asset-price. This can be shown for the Black–Scholes case by a Taylor's series expansion of the option-value formula around the true value A:

$$G(\hat{A}) = G(A) + \Delta(\hat{A} - A) + \frac{1}{2}\Gamma(\hat{A} - A)^2,$$

where Δ and Γ are the 'delta' and 'gamma' of the option respectively:

$$\Delta = \Phi(d_1) - 1 < 0 \quad \text{and} \quad \Gamma = \phi(d_1)/(A\sigma\sqrt{\tau}) > 0.$$

Accordingly, for an unbiased estimate of the option-value, option-value calculated at the estimated price should be reduced by an amount that is proportional to the variance of the asset-price estimate.

$$G(A) = E[G(\hat{A}] - \frac{1}{2}\Gamma Var(\hat{A})$$

In many real-world cases, unbiasedness of the asset-value estimate cannot be assured. Indeed many recent regulatory failures can be attributed to over-optimism in the estimate $\hat{A}$. As is evident from the above formula, the downward bias in the estimate of G is an increasing convex function of any unsuspected upward bias in the asset-value estimate.

This discussion thus identifies essentially four dimensions[24] along which steps can be taken to limit the cost of the deposit put.

(a) Increase the *buffer*, i.e., the ratio of the 'true asset-value' to insured deposits *A/D*.
(b) Reduce the *volatility* (risk) σ.
(c) Reduce the *duration* of exposure τ, i.e., increase the rollover frequency.
(d) Improve *precision* (reduce bias and variance) of the estimate of A and σ.

This provides a framework for interpreting the channels through which recent and proposed approaches to regulation operate.

Notes

1 For example, in some countries, there has been a limit on the amount of the equity ownership of commercial banks by individuals and families, but it is routinely evaded through a variety of simple and complex ownership structures, and, in one case, the enforcement was in the domain of the Finance Minister, a member of the family controlling one of the largest banks in the country.
2 Even though they benefit from the upside of the risks the bank takes. We discuss the link with limited liability in the section on 'Harnessing incentives to reduce exposure'.
3 The recent review by a task force of the Basel Committee (1999), and based on a survey of practice at twenty major banks, is most informative on the methodologies that are being used.
4 The Basel Committee comprises senior bank regulators from twelve industrial countries. Their landmark 1988 agreement on capital adequacy requirements for international banks was only the first in a series of accords governing common banking standards. In 1997, the Basel committee published a document setting out 'Core principles for effective banking supervision'. This was much less detailed, but of broader scope, and is intended to present guidelines for developing and transition economies, many of which have indeed subscribed to the Principles.
5 Extensive reviews of the formal theoretical literature are in Bhattacharya *et al.* (1998), Dewatripont and Tirole (1994); and Freixas and Rochet (1997).
6 This survey covers how authorities regulate and supervise their commercial banking systems, and includes information on the powers available, when they have been

utilized, the independence and funding of supervisory agencies, supervisory compensation relative to that in the private sector, etc.

7 It is not only emerging economies that under-provision. A recent Bank of Japan study (1998) found that 75.3 per cent of loans classified in 1993–94 as doubtful at a sample of eighteen banks became write-offs over the following three years – but required provisioning for such loans is only 52 per cent; and that 16.7 per cent of 'category 2' loans, for which only a 2 per cent provision is required, were written-off.

8 Up to now risky assets required 8 per cent capital; with less required for less risky assets such as residential mortgages (4 per cent) and OECD treasury bills (no requirement at all). The new June 1999 proposals will include a high-risk category requiring 12 per cent capital.

9 Additional capital loading is required for market risk, recognizing, e.g., that, although long-term government bonds attract a zero credit-risk weighting in the Basel scheme, fluctuations in their market price can, in reality, make them highly risky for banks.

10 For example, the 1999 proposal would have required, for corporates rated A, five times the capital required for those rated AA, whereas historical experience indicates a mean default rate only 75 per cent higher and a standard deviation only 60 per cent higher (Figure 6.4). The rough-and-ready nature of the weights is suggested by another example: according to the proposals, credit risk for sovereign debt from AA-issuers would still require no capital, whereas debt from a BB + country would require 8 per cent capital.

11 Indeed, according to the Report of the Task Force on Risk Assessment set up by the Steering Committee on Emerging Markets Finance of the Institute of International Finance (IIF) in 1999, developments in the global economy have outpaced improvements in the analytical capacity of the country risk profession.

12 Cho (2001) describes the lenient ratings provided by agencies in Korea during the 1990s. The top 2 ratings (corresponding to loans that would require only a 1.6 per cent capital charge instead of 8 per cent) accounted for over a quarter of rated Korean firms in 1995–97, compared with 1 in 16 in the US.

13 A more technical difference is that this option is accompanied by a cap.

14 This possibility was raised by Peter Garber at the Federal Reserve Bank of Chicago–BIS conference on the Lessons from Recent Global Financial Crises, October 1, 1999.

15 See J.P. Morgan, The J.P. Morgan Guide to Credit Derivatives, 1999.

16 With unlimited liability, bankers are forced to absorb their own losses; with double liability, and no government intervention (the case of some US banks, pre-1930s), owners first lost their capital, then were liable for a 'post-closure' assessment, and only then could 'put' the losses to depositors. Note that with unlimited liability – for example, capital punishment for bankers who make losses – even a generously-funded deposit-insurance scheme is not likely to engender any moral hazard, as the cost of exercising the option would be rather severe!

17 Some senior supervisory officials in the US are banned from banking jobs for one year.

18 The US Federal Deposit Insurance Corporation Improvement Act (FDICIA) of 1991 embodied prompt corrective action and structured early intervention, mandating certain supervisory actions as banks' net worth deteriorates, and was the response to the regulatory forbearance that characterized the S&L debacle (see Barth, 1991, Kane, 1989).

19 The abrupt closure of sixteen small banks in Indonesia in the middle of the crisis in October 1997 intensified the panic and prompted bank runs. Some see this as an excuse for forbearance; but it has equally been argued that there was still too much forbearance, and that there would have been less panic had the closures been more widespread and credibly final.

20 One of the complications that is thus being avoided is that many deposit insurance schemes only partly insure deposits: thus, in addition to subordinated creditors, there are uninsured depositors over whom the insurer may not have priority.

21 Note that we are, thus, abstracting here from the important issue of losses arising from enforced early liquidation of assets, as might result from a depositor panic, such as is discussed by Chang and Velasco (1998).

22 We may think of this as a rolling version of the two-period model of Dewatripont and Tirole (1994). In their notation, the bank has a portfolio of loans with starting value $\eta_0 + \mu_0$. In the first period, some of the bank's loans mature with total value μ. There is also a signal ν received at time 1 about the likely range of value of the remainder of the loans, which are not due to mature until the next time-period. This could be a signal about macro-economic conditions, or about the conduct and performance of the bank management and the risk-profile of its portfolio. At time 2, the remainder of the loans mature, with realized value η. The interesting date here is time 1: at this date, we can hope to have some information about the portfolio, both in terms of realization to date (μ) and prospects for next period (ν). They assume that μ is known; and that knowledge of ν gives a probability density for $\eta : h(\eta \mid \nu)$. This probability density tells us both the expected value of η, given ν – which they denote $\eta(\nu)$ – and its conditional variance. The conditional expected value of the total portfolio after receipt of the signal at time 1, namely $\mu + \eta(\nu)$ is close to our concept of the true current-value of the portfolio A_t as measured by the regulator.

23 Thus, whereas Dewatripont and Tirole (1994) picture the regulator at time 1 as observing both μ and ν, and knowing the stochastic mapping $\eta(\nu)$ (see previous note), the accuracy of the regulator's information about μ and the degree to which the signal ν is informative depends in practice on regulatory structures and procedures. Whether deliberately or due to inadvertent measurement error, the bank may report, in lieu of the true μ, a biased value $\mu^* = \mu + u$; the scope for such biased reporting may be reduced at some cost by regulatory action or structures. The signal ν that is observed, and the precision of stochastic mapping $\eta(\nu)$ is partly a consequence of regulatory decisions.

24 It is because it assumes that a continuously-adjusted hedge portfolio in the underlying asset is possible that the Black–Scholes formula does not depend on another parameter, namely the trend-change in the asset-price. This could also be relevant in our application to bank regulation.

References

Adams, C., Mathieson, D. J. and Schinasi, G. (1999) *International Capital Markets: Developments, Prospects, and Key Policy Issues* (Washington DC: IMF).

Bank of Japan (1998) 'Utilization of financial institutions' self-assessment in enhancing credit risk management', *Bank of Japan Quarterly Bulletin*, 6(February), 19–32.

Barth, J. (1991) *The Great Savings and Loan Debacle* (Washington DC: American Enterprise Institute).

Basel Committee On Banking Supervision (1999) 'Credit risk modeling: current practices and applications', BCBS Discussion Paper 49, Basel.

Berger, A. N., Davies, S. M. and Flannery, M. J. (1998) 'Comparing market and supervisory assessments of bank performance: who knows what when', Discussion paper, Board of Governors of the Federal Reserve System, March (Washington DC).

Bhattacharya, S., Boot, A. and Thakor, A. (1998) 'The economics of bank regulation', *Journal of Money Credit and Banking*, 30.

Calomiris, C. (1997) *The Postmodern Bank Safety Net* (Washington DC: The American Enterprise Institute).

Campbell, J. Y., Lo, A. W. and McKinlay, A. C. (1997) *The Econometrics of Financial Markets* (Princeton NJ: Princeton University Press).

Caprio, G. (1997) 'Safe and sound banking in developing countries: we're not in Kansas anymore', in G. G. Kaufman (ed.), *Research in Financial Services: Public and Private Policy*, 9 (Greenwich, Conn.: JAI Press).

Caprio, G. (1998) 'Banking on crises: expensive lessons', World Bank Policy Research Working Paper 1979 and in G. G. Kaufman (ed.), *Research in Financial Services: Public and Private Policy*, 10 (Greenwich, Conn.: JAI Press).

Caprio, G. and Honohan, P. (1999) 'Restoring banking stability: beyond supervised capital requirements', *Journal of Economics Perspectives*, 13(4), 43–64.

Chang, R. and Velasco, A. (1998) 'Financial fragility and the exchange rate regime', NBER Working Paper 6469 (Cambridge MA).

Cho, Y. J. (2001) 'Korea's financial crisis: a consequence of unbalanced liberalization', in Gerard Caprio, Patrick Honohan and Joseph E. Stiglitz (eds), *Financial Liberalization: How Far, How Fast?* (Cambridge: Cambridge University Press).

Claessens, C. A., Djankov, S., Fan, J. and Lang, L. (1999) 'Corporate diversification in East Asia: the role of ultimate ownership structure and group affiliation', Policy Research Working Paper 2089 (*The World Bank, Washington DC*).

Demirgüç-Kunt, A. and Huizinga, H. (1999) 'Market discipline and financial safety net design', World Bank Policy Research Working Paper 2183, September (Washington DC).

Dewatripont, M. and Tirole, J. (1994) *The Prudential Regulation of Banks* (Cambridge MA: MIT Press).

Esty, B. C. (1996). 'The impact of contingent liability on commercial bank risk taking', *Journal of Financial Economics*, 47(2), 189–218.

Flannery, M. J., DeYoung, R., Lang, W. and Sorescu, S. (2001) 'The informational advantage of specialized monitors: the case of bank examiners', *Journal of Money, Credit and Banking*, forthcoming.

Freixas, X. and Rochet, J.-C. (1997) *Microeconomics of Banking* (Cambridge MA: MIT Press).

Honohan, P. and Stiglitz, J. E. (2001) 'Robust financial restraint', in Gerard Caprio, Patrick Honohan and Joseph E. Stiglitz (eds), *Financial Liberalization: How Far, How Fast?* (Cambridge: Cambridge University Press).

Morgan, J. P. (1999) *The J.P. Morgan Guide to Credit Derivatives* (London: Risk Publications).

Kane, E. J. (1989) *The S&L Insurance Mess: How Did It Happen*? (Washington DC: Urban Institute Press).

Kane, E. J. (1995) 'Three paradigms for the role of capitalization requirements in insured financial institutions', *Journal of Banking and Finance*, 19, 431–59.

Kupiec, P. H. and O'Brien, J. M. (1997) 'The pre-commitment approach: using incentives to set market risk capital requirements', Federal Reserve Board, FEDS Working Paper, 97–14 (Washington DC).

Levine, R., Loayza, N. and Beck, T. (2000) 'Financial intermediation and growth: causality and causes', *Journal of Monetary Economics*, 46(1), 31–77.

Martinez-Peria, Soledad, M. and Schmukler, S. (2001) 'Do depositors punish banks for "Bad" behavior?: examining market discipline in Argentina, Chile, and Mexico', *Journal of Finance*, 56(3), 1029–51.

Merton, R. C. (1977) 'An analytic derivation of the cost of deposit insurance using option-pricing estimates', *Journal of Banking and Finance*, 1, 3–11.

Mishkin, F. S. (1997) 'Understanding financial crises: a developing country perspective', in M. Bruno and B. Pleskovic (eds), World Bank Annual Conference on Development Economics, 1996 (*Washington DC: The World Bank*).
World Bank (2001) *Finance for growth: Policy choices in a volatile world* (New York: Oxford University Press).

7 A world without money and banking?

Andrew Mullineux

What is money?

One of the problems with 'monetarism' was that money itself had never been properly defined. Milton Friedman (1969) basically argued that 'money is what money does'. In his view, what money (i.e. monetary growth) does is cause inflation and *thus*, we could simply define money as the sum of the monetary assets that best correlate ('explain') inflation (measured as the rate of increase of some price index e.g. the Retail Price Index in the UK). Clearly there are a number of problems with this approach (not least that correlation does not imply causality) and, to be fair, Friedman and Schwartz (1963), in their impressive monetary history of the US, did suggest that a monetary index of some sort might be more appropriate than a measure of money formed by simply adding together, or summing, various monetary components.

In order to answer the question, 'What is money?', let me outline some of the economic fundamentals relating to money. There are a number of ways of proceeding towards the definition of money, but perhaps the most influential has been what Hicks (1967) called 'The Two Triads' in his 'Critical Essays', which explores the relationships between them. 'The Two Triads' are listed in Box 7.1.

To get to grips with Triad 1, it may help to pause and reflect on the euro. It will not be circulating as a currency (notes and coin or cash) for use in day-to-day transactions until January 2002, but is already used for large electronic and cheque-based transactions, involving transfers between bank accounts. It should be noted that the cheques and electronic signals, are not themselves money. They are merely instructions to move 'money' from one bank account to another. The euro is, however, fulfilling a unit-of-account function in mainland Europe, if not in the UK. French supermarkets have for some time now been quoting prices in both French francs and euros and this has become the practice in the other countries participating in EMU.

On 1 January 2002, the existing currencies will cease to be legal tender in 'Euroland' (the Euro Zone) and will be replaced by the euro as a means of payment, or cash. It is important to note that currency (or cash) is widely accepted as a means of payment in part because it has legal backing, that is, it is 'fiat money' or 'legal tender'.

Box 7.1 What is money? The Two Triads

Triad 1: The functions of money

- Means of payment (settlement)
  (Medium of exchange)
  (credit vs money)
- Unit of account (measure of value)
- Store of value
  - Money and time
  - Intertemporal consumption
  - Savings and future consumption
  - Wealth as accumulated annual savings

Triad 2: Motives for holding money

- Transactions
- Precautionary
- Speculative (risk aversion)

(Precautionary and Speculative: } Liquidity Demand)

Cash needs to have certain attributes to be useful. In my day, 'A' level textbooks used to provide long lists – portability, divisibility, durability, etc. This, of course, still holds true (the £1 coins are too heavy in my view) and divisibility remains important, as pre-millennium problems in Mexico demonstrated. The Central Bank of Mexico issued large numbers of 500-peso (approximately £30) notes in autumn 1999 to avert a shortage of cash over the millennium holiday period. Unfortunately, they failed to issue sufficient lower-denomination notes and coins and people found it difficult to use the 500-peso notes because few vendors of goods and services could give change – taxi drivers, for example, refused to accept them.

The 'Keynesian' approach has been to come at the definition of money from the point of view of motives for holding money. A transactionous (payments) demand is readily identified and linked to the means of payment function. Money is needed to effect planned day-to-day transactions. A precautionary motive is also identified, money is held to effect transactions that cannot be readily identified in advance, for example, the need to buy a new inner-tube for my bike. Finally, a risk aversion or speculative motive is identified. Keynes (1936) emphasised the holding of wealth in a liquid form, as money, to enable opportunities to make a profit to be taken. In contrast, the Nobel Prize winners Hicks (1935) and Tobin (1958), emphasised the holding of money in a wealth portfolio as a means of reducing risk-exposure. The net result is that money is in demand because it provides transactions or payments services, and liquidity. The more liquid an asset, the lower the cost of converting it into transaction balances (i.e. currency and bank current-account balances). There may be a penalty in terms of lost interest when savings-account balances are liquidated, for example, and to achieve a quick sale of a house (the assets in which most people hold most of their wealth) a steep price discount normally has to be accepted.

In sum, the 'moneyness' of a financial asset is related to its provision of payment services, and thus, its ability to communicate and store value, and also to its liquidity.

Measuring money

How then can we measure moneyness? Which assets should be included in an index number representing money, and what weights should be attached to these assets? To this day, most central banks concentrate on monitoring, and, now less commonly, targeting, simple sum aggregates.

Many of the 'broad' monetary aggregates, which are the most commonly employed by the monetary authorities, include savings balances held at banks and other liquid financial assets on the grounds that they can be easily converted to the components m_1 (notes and coins, i.e. cash) and m_2 (bank current-account balances). Indeed, as financial innovation has progressed over recent decades, the array of liquid assets has expanded. Which assets should be included? When does an asset become too illiquid to be included? There is no simple answer. It is, however, clear that cash and current-account balances have more moneyness than many of the other components of the broad money aggregates M_3 and M_4. And yet, these other assets are treated as having the same amount of moneyness when they are simply summed in an unweighted manner (see Box 7.2).

Following the seminal work by Barnett (1980), an alternative approach is to construct Divisia monetary indices in which the weights are determined by moneyness as measured by interest foregone by holding monetary assets (see Box 7.2). Non-interest-bearing cash and current accounts receive the highest weights because they receive the lowest interest rate. Employing this approach, the issue of which assets to exclude becomes less important since assets with less moneyness simply receive lower weights. Recent work done in collaboration with my colleagues (Drake *et al.*, 1999*a*,*b*) indicates that, due to their increased liquidity, which continues to increase as a result of the Internet revolution, mutual funds (money market and investment and unit trusts, etc.) and bonds and shares should also be included (albeit with relatively low weights).

It is important to remember that money, especially cash, is fundamentally a social construct. Its usefulness arises because it normally helps transactions to be effected much more cheaply and efficiently than under barter (in Russia in recent years, normality has been suspended!). It does so largely through the information about the market value of a product conveyed by its price (the 'unit-of-account' role). It remains useful as long as it holds its value and thus allows payments to be deferred until some future date. Hence, inflation makes the holding of money less desirable because it erodes its value. When inflation is very rapid, cash loses its usefulness and substitutes are sought (often other currencies, for example, the US dollar, which circulates as a parallel currency in many countries, legally or illegally). Where normal use of the legal tender is not permitted, for example, in

Box 7.2 Measuring money

'Simple sum' money

$$M_{\rm t} = m_{1\rm t} + m_{2\rm t} + m_{3\rm t} + m_{4\rm t} + \cdots$$
$$= \sum_{i=1}^{n} m_{it}$$

when

m_{1t} = notes and coins (at time t),

m_{2t} = current account balances (at time t),

$m_{3t} = \cdots$

'Divisia' money (Quantity index)
where

$$Q_t = Q_{t-1} \prod_{i=1}^{n} \left[\frac{m_{it}}{m_{it-1}} \right]^{\bar{S}_{it}}$$
$$\bar{S}_{it} = \frac{1}{2}(S_{it} + S_{it-1}) \tag{1}$$

and

$$S_{it} = \frac{\pi_{it}(m_{it}/p_t)}{\sum_{i=1}^{n} \pi_{it}(m_{it}/p_{it})}$$

is the value share of asset i at time t in the index
and

$$\pi_{it} = \frac{p_t \cdot (R_t - r_{it})}{1 + R_t}$$

is the user cost (price) of monetary asset i at time t (see Equation (2) below). p_t is the general price level (measured using a suitable price index), R_t is a 'benchmark' interest rate (ideally on a 'riskless' asset) e.g. UK government bonds, and r_{it} is the 'own rate' of interest of i at time t.

We normally work with Equation (1) in log difference form as follows:

$$DQ_t = \sum_{i=1}^{n} \bar{S}_{it} D\left(\frac{m_{it}}{p_t}\right), \tag{2}$$

where D is the log difference operator.

prison, then alternative monies are substituted, for example, cigarettes. Something similar has occurred recently in areas of high unemployment, where access to cash and bank accounts (due to 'financial and social exclusion') is restricted. Local Enterprise Trading Schemes (LETS) have emerged. Under these schemes, hours of work are traded for 'points', which can be used to purchase services from other members of the scheme. The popularity of such schemes, often related to baby-sitting circles in middle-class neighbourhoods, suggests, however, that some of the attraction may lie in tax avoidance. This, of course, is why the Inland Revenue is taking an interest, and why the state provides legal tender.

We have already referred to the existence of another sort of money, 'bank money', that is, current account balances held at banks on which cheques can be drawn and which can receive electronic instructions to make payments to third parties. This money is not legal tender and yet is (normally, i.e. in the absence of a banking crisis) widely accepted as a means of payment.

The future of money

It has long been anticipated that cash will eventually disappear from use (see e.g. Black, 1970), but in most countries, the 'cashless society' is some way off yet, since the bulk of transactions (in both volume and value) are still made using cash, the more so the smaller the transaction; but 'plastic-card' usage has increased rapidly and debit-card usage is now increasing faster than credit-card usage. Iceland is a notable exception and is probably the closest to a cashless society (see Financial Times, 2000). Only 14 per cent of all transactions are now made using notes or coins compared with 80 per cent in many other parts of Western Europe. Iceland is a small homogenous society with little fraud and no black market to speak of – there is little or no financial exclusion, and virtually everyone has a credit rating. There is no deep-seated attachment to the domestic currency, unlike Germany, and seemingly the UK, which are also much larger, more complex societies. However, a process of 'electronification' (to use a phrase Professor Ford (1994) and I (see Mullineux, 1997) 'coined', if you'll excuse the pun) of money is underway. Debit or payments cards serve as the equivalent of cheques in electronic-funds transfers but, like cheques, they are not money.

Electronic wallets or purses are, however, a replacement for cash. These plastic cards have memory chips which can 'store' money withdrawn from ATMs. Instead of withdrawing notes and putting them in a nice leather wallet or purse, you will simply charge the memory of your card and then swipe it to effect payments. When the wallet is empty you simply re-charge it. Further, e-money is already being used for Internet transactions and there is a chance that Microsoft or some other Internet firm may come to dominate the payments system, displacing traditional banks; which Bill Gates has already declared to be dinosaurs on their way to extinction.

Will money disappear altogether? The world without money would still need a unit of account, but we can envisage more and more transactions involving electronic transfers of wealth between portfolios held at financial institutions, perhaps including Microsoft, in Web space; many of these will be effected from mobile terminals, such as the new web-enabled mobile phones and hand-held PCs.

Mervyn King (1999), Deputy Governor of the Bank of England and a former Professor in the Department of Economics at this University, speculated at Jackson Hole in August 1999 that, as a result of this technology-driven financial revolution, central banks in their present form would cease to exist, and base money (i.e. cash and bank reserves held with the central bank) would disappear. The demise of 'base money' would lead to the demise of the central banks because it is the fulcrum of monetary control. Without it, central banks would have no lever on the instrument of modern monetary-control, the rate of interest. The argument thus runs that the demise of base money eliminates the need for central banks, whose function has increasingly concentrated on monetary control (rather than supervision, etc. – see also Ben Friedman, 1999). But surely banks can create money and liquidity all by themselves, you may ask? We have no time here to explore this debate, which is as old as the study of monetary policy (see, for example, Davies (1994) on the Currency School vs Banking School). But if the central bank is to disappear, what about the other banks? Economists have long speculated about what banking would look like in a world without money and Bill Gates has predicted that banks too will disappear. Will I then soon be out of a job? Will it be necessary to appoint a successor? This leads me into the final part of the lecture.

What is a bank?

Legal definitions of banks and the scope of banking varies widely from country to country. There was no easy answer to the question 'What is a bank?' It is commonly argued that what distinguishes banks from other financial intermediaries is that the banks alone have liabilities which are money. This, in turn, means that they are treated differently from other financial intermediaries, so long as governments try to influence monetary creation directly, rather than indirectly through manipulation of interest rates. Remember, however, it is increasingly evident that, due to the financial innovation, there is no clear cut definition of what money is either. Indeed, financial liberalisation around the world has led to the transformation of the larger banks into financial conglomerates engaged in banking, securities-related business (broking and underwriting etc.), and insurance. Indeed, one could argue that the big banks are gradually abandoning banking. Meanwhile, specialist insurance companies are moving into 'banking' in a big way (e.g. Prudential's 'Egg'). As a result 'bankassurance' firms are springing up all over Europe and are also beginning to emerge in the US (Citygroup) and Japan. Supermarkets (e.g. Tesco and Sainsburys) and even football teams and pop stars (Man Utd and David Bowie) are also getting banking licences. In other words, financial innovation and liberalisation have fundamentally changed the face of so called 'banking' and increased the moneyness (liquidity) of financial assets previously not regarded as money. We have a moving target, but is 'banking' itself moving towards extinction? This, of course, depends on how you define banks and banking.

To provide an answer to the question of whether 'banking' faces extinction, we need to consider the question: Why do banks exist? The economists' answer is that they exist because they are able to reduce transaction costs, that is, for the same reason that money exists. The most important transaction costs relate to the costs of collecting and processing information, especially information about credit worthiness. One reason people prefer to be paid in cash, rather than being granted credit, is that they are uncertain about the credit worthiness of the counterparty to the transactions. In addition, to avoid taxes, many people prefer to transact in cash simply because other forms of transaction reveal information and can thus be traced. If we were able instantly to verify the credit worthiness of counterparties, then we would have no need for money, as Mervyn King (1999) argued. Similarly, banks extend credit in the form of loans and overdrafts knowing that there is a 'credit risk', a risk of non-repayment on time and in full. A business to which they are lending may simply fail or may act fraudently. The problem for banks is that borrowers tend to know more about their own credit worthiness (chances or intentions to repay) than the banks, as lenders, do (economists call this asymmetric information). The banks do, however, gain expertise by making a large number of similar loans and specialise in collecting information to enable them to gauge the credit standing of potential borrowers. Further, they are becoming increasingly able to do so as they gain access to larger data bases through mergers and conglomeration. In economic parlance, they lower transaction costs by exploiting economies of scale. In this information age, it is economies of scale in collecting and processing information that really matters, but these developments also facilitate 'cherry picking'. It has often been said that banking is about money and information. Banking without money is all about making the best use of information to sell financial services. Will traditional banks turn out to be best at utilising financial innovation to sell financial services, or will Microsoft, or some other telecommunications or information technology firm? If it is Microsoft, will it not simply have to become a bank, especially as the ECB intends to regulate issuers of e-money in the same way as other issuers of money (i.e. banks) by setting reserve requirements. My guess is that 'clicks and mortar' or 'clicks and bricks' will prove to be the winning strategy for retail banking, at least in the medium term. Further, whilst cash remains important, access to ATMs is crucial for new entrants, hence the attempt to raise the costs of withdrawal by customers of the new banks which have not invested in the build up of the ATM networks.

There is, however, a real risk that the big banks will progressively abandon traditional retail commercial banking in favour of securities business (or investment banking) and insurance (see Box 7.3). They are already closing branches in rural and deprived areas (exacerbating financial exclusion) in order to cut costs. Under the watchful eye of the Bank of England (since the early 1990s recession) they have (so far) continued to service the needs of small- and

Box 7.3 Banks and banking

- **Retail (Commercial) banking**

  – Provision of payments and related services
  – Lending to customers excluded from capital markets (loans too small/asymmetric information) i.e. personal loans and loans to SMEs
  – A by-product is liquidity (and thus, money) creation as a result of financial intermediation to better meet the needs of depositors and borrowers.

- **Investment banking**

  – Provision of wholesale banking services
  – Securities (capital market) orientated business
  – The main clients are large firms, governments, and international organisations etc., who can tap the capital markets (large enough issues of bonds and shares, well known).

- **Private banking**

  – The provision of financial services to wealthy individuals.

- The terms 'bank' and 'banking' have usually been associated with retail banking.
- Modern big 'banks' are increasingly concentrating on investment banking or capital-market orientated business.

It is thus likely that 'banks' will increasingly ignore all but the most profitable retail banking business ('cherry picking'). Branch closures enhance this. The results are:

  – Increased financial exclusion (*pace* telephone and Internet banking)
  – A risk of increased credit rationing for smaller firms.

In sum, many big 'banks' (financial conglomerates) are progressively withdrawing from (retail) banking whilst building up their private and investment banking and insurance businesses.

medium-sized enterprises (SMEs), but it is notable that the remaining building societies have not taken much advantage of their new freedom to lend to SMEs and those of their number that have converted to banks have not rushed into the market either. Under current trends in banking, small firms thus face the possibility of enhanced credit rationing, or financial exclusion. Following the Cruickshank report (see Cruickshank, 2000), the provision of banking services to small businesses was referred to the UK's Competition Commission.

Conclusions

So, is the end of money and banking nigh? Information (or lack of it) remains the key. We can only get rid of money if we have instant verification of credit worthiness and everyone is creditworthy (i.e. everyone has an acceptably low credit risk *and* has access to the financial system (no financial or social exclusion) *and* there is no tendency towards tax evasion). In such a world, all finance might well be direct from lender to borrower and probably negotiated over the Internet because stock exchanges themselves are also looking increasingly dodo-like. 'Borrowers' would simply receive transfers of assets from 'lenders' portfolios.

However, once we acknowledge the existence of credit-risk, it is clear that lenders will need to seek a higher return to cover the risk, and it is less clear that we do not need money (unless risks can be accurately measured). Sellers can however, be reasonably sure that they will be paid if real time payments can be made (now technologically possible) and the payments intermediaries ('bank' or Visa) are willing to underwrite the transactions. But not everyone can yet get bank accounts or credit cards.

Both money and banks have a clear purpose once the credit-risk cannot be measured with certainty and instantly verified (see also Goodhart, 1989; Chapter II). This, I conjecture, is the real world. It is a world of uncertainty in which risks are not perfectly measurable. At the moment, banks can only estimate average credit-risks for classes of lending. They cannot accurately and instantly verify individual credit-risks, anymore than a shopkeeper can when one of us walks into a shop. Shopkeepers normally still demand cash, or payment guaranteed by a bank or credit-card company (whose credit-worthiness is better known), and many people, perhaps an increasing number, are financially excluded, whilst others are seeking to evade taxes.

Thus, until we have full information on credit-worthiness, money and banking will continue to exist, even if Microsoft (or others) become banks, issuing e-money! If, however, big banks withdraw further from retail commercial banking services then there will be a major crisis in SME financing. This will inevitably provoke a policy response since the SME sector is the engine for job creation in a world where continuous industrial-restructuring leads to job losses in many bigger firms – Rover being the notable local example. The government is already tackling the personal financial exclusion issue. An increased role for the Post Office and credit unions is anticipated. I have not had time to address such issues at length, but have been working with colleagues at Birmingham (John Doling) and the New Economics Foundation in London on Rowntree sponsored projects in this field. Our 'Small is Bankable' Rowntree Report (Mayo *et al.*, 1998) has proved to be influential over the past 18 months or so.

Postscript

So what advice might Max Fry have given me in writing my Inaugural Lecture (I delivered on 1 May 2001 and upon which this chapter is based) and how does the foregoing analysis inform monetary and financial policy formation for economic development, which was a major focus of Max's work (see Fry, 1995). A colleague, Andrew Hawker (School of Business, University of Birmingham) sent me comments on my lecture which confirmed just how much Max's energy was being missed in the Business School, and the members of the Department of Economics (and others in the School of Social Sciences) certainly feel the same loss. Andrew also informed me that on one occasion he had discussed e-money with Max, who, fairly brusquely, dismissed it as unimportant in the wider scheme of things. I must confess that I too have my doubts about its importance, but what of the impact of the ongoing monetary and financial innovation (or 'electronification of banking') on monetary and financial policies in developing (and transition) economies?

Plastic cards, particularly those with memory chips ('smart cards') provide a number of opportunities for developing payment and credit systems. They can be used in conjunction with telephones, the Internet, or with mobile banking units or remote networked ATMs. They can serve as credit or debit cards in paper-based or electronic funds-transfer system and, importantly for those unable to get credit-ratings, serve as pre-payment cards. The latter could be sophisticated rechargeable electronic wallets or simply purchased in the same way as landline and mobile telephone pre-payment cards are. One advantage of rapid adoption of such technology is that it saves on the costly processing of paper (banknotes and cheques etc.) and is relatively secure (and likely to become more so). Developing countries thus have the opportunity to replace creaking paper-based systems with cheaper, more efficient and secure payments systems. Further, access to such systems (apart, perhaps, from the non-rechargeable pre-payment cards) will probably require the opening of bank accounts with consequent beneficial effects on bank intermediation levels.

As regards monetary control, this is notoriously difficult in periods of financial innovation. However, if developing and transition economies adopt policies of financial liberalisation in order to improve lending practices and corporate governance, and thus efficiency in the allocation of credit and capital, then they must live with the consequent financial innovation. Participation in the WTO and adherence to the GATT in a world of increasingly freer international capital flows will reinforce the restructuring process; in part by stimulating entry by foreign financial institutions, leading to increased competition.

In such an environment, the measurement of money becomes even more problematic than under financial restructuring and innovation at the *relatively* leisurely pace experienced in developing countries. The establishment of market-based mechanisms for controlling the level of short-term interest rates thus becomes a priority. The debate over the appropriate level for real-interest rates in developing, transition and emerging market economies is one in which Max actively engaged in (see Fry, 1995, Chapter 18). There can be little doubt that his significant contribution to this debate will be quoted for many years to come.

In the final chapter of his career, Max served as Director of the Bank of England's Centre for Central Banking Studies. Not only did he focus on payments systems towards the end, (Fry, 2000*a*), but he also became a strong advocate of the need for an effective bank regulatory and supervisory system to ensure that financial stability was not undermined by financial liberalisation (Fry, 2000*b*).

References

Barnett, W. A. (1980) 'Economic monetary aggregates: an application of index number theory and aggregation theory', *Journal of Econometrics*, 14(1), 11–48.

Black, F. (1970) 'Banking and interest in a world without money', *Journal of Bank Research*, Vol. 1, Autumn, 9–20. (reprinted in Black, F. 1987).

Black, F. (1987) *Business Cycles and Equilibrium*, Oxford: Basil Blackwell.

Cruickshank, D. (2000) 'Guest editorial on the Cruickshank report: the review of banking services in the UK', *Journal of Financial Regulation and Compliance*, 8(2), 102–8.

Davies, G. (1994) *The History of Money: From Ancient Times to Present Day*, Cardiff: University of Wales Press, pp. 310–13.

Drake, L., Fleissig, A. R. and Mullineux, A. W. (1999*a*) 'Are "risky assets" substitutes for "monetary assets" ', *Economic Inquiry*, 37(3), 510–26.

Drake, L., Mullineux, A. W. and Agung, J. (1999*b*) 'Incorporating risky assets in divisia monetary aggregates', *Working Paper*, December.

Financial Times (2000) 'Land of ice and plastic', Inside Track, (*IT*): the cashless society, Wednesday May 3, p. 18.

Friedman, B. M. (1999) 'The future of monetary policy: the central bank as an army with only a signal corps', *International Finance*, 2(3), 321–8.

Friedman, M. (1969) *The Optimum Quantity of Money*, London: Macmillan.

Friedman, M. and Schwartz, A. J. (1963) *The Monetary History of the United States, 1867–1960*. National Bureau of Economic Research, Princeton, NJ.

Ford, J. L. (1994), 'Financial evolution and innovation', *Advances in Austrian Economics*, 1, 175–96.

Fry, M. J. (1995) *Money, Interest and Banking in Economic Development*, 2nd edn, London, Maryland: Johns Hopkins.

Fry, M. J. (2000*a*) 'Payments systems and economic development in transitional economies', in D. G. Dickinson and A. W. Mullineux (eds) *Financial and Monetary Integration in the New Europe – Convergence between the EU and Central and Eastern Europe*, Chapter 13, Cheltenham: Edward Elgar (forthcoming).

Fry, M. J. (2000*b*) 'Financial stability and economic development in transitional economies', in *Financial and Monetary Integration in the New Europe – Convergence between the EU and Central and Eastern Europe*, Chapter 12, Cheltenham: Edward Elgar (forthcoming).

Goodhart, C. A. E. (1989) *Money, Information and Uncertainty*, 2nd edn, London: Macmillan.

Hicks, J. R. (1935) 'A suggestion for simplifying the theory of money', *Economica* (February), 2, 1–19.

Hicks, J. R. (1967) 'The two triads: lectures I to III', in *Critical Essays in Monetary Theory*, Oxford: Clarendon Press, pp. 1–60.

Keynes, J. M. (1936) *The General Theory of Employment, Interest and Money*, London: Macmillan.

King, M. A. (1999) 'Challenges for monetary policy: new and old', *Bank of England Quarterly Bulletin*, 39(4), 397–415 (especially Section 5 entitled 'The Future of Central Banks', speech given at the Symposium (organised by the Federal Reserve Bank of Kansas) on 'New Challenges for Monetary Policy' at Jackson Hole, Wyoming on 27 August 1999).

Mayo, E., Fisher, T., Conaty, P., Doling, J. and Mullineux, A. W. (1998) *Small is Bankable*, York: Rowntree Foundation.

Mullineux, A. W. (1997) 'Financial innovation, money, banking and financial fragility in the UK', in B. Schachter (ed.), *Derivatives, Regulation and Banking*, Chapter 11, Amsterdam: North Holland, pp. 263–85.

Tobin, J. (1958) 'Liquidity – preference as a behaviour towards risk', *Review of Economic Studies*, 25(1), 65–86.

8 Money and finance on the periphery of the international dollar standard

Ronald McKinnon

> In most developing countries, neither corporate nor government bonds are traded on open markets. Indeed, corporate bonds simply do not exist in many developing countries. Typically, the commercial banks are captive buyers of low yielding domestic government bonds by virtue of liquidity ratio requirements. Government deficits are financed almost entirely by loans from the central and commercial banks.
>
> (Maxwell Fry (1995) p. 236)

Introduction

The problem of excessively short-term finance in developing countries was long one of Maxwell Fry's principal concerns. Indeed, his 1997 book is provocatively titled *Emancipating the Banking System and Developing Markets for Government Debt*. Together with developing institutions that would better allow capital markets to thrive, Fry focused on domestic monetary stabilization with financial liberalization as the key to more robust longer-term bond markets.

This paper does not approach Fry's ingenuity in econometrically testing the ideas it contains, but it is written in the spirit of his work on emerging-market economies. Why is monetary and financial management so much more difficult on the periphery of the industrial world than at the center? In particular, why is the term to maturity of finance in emerging markets so short, with external liabilities all denominated in foreign exchange, largely dollars? This paper's focus, an overview on how the world dollar standard works, is a vehicle for throwing light on problems faced by central banks and regulatory authorities in Asia, Latin America, and elsewhere.

The dollar as facilitator of international exchange

Apart from the large size of the American economy, why should the US dollar now be so important in international finance?

The reasons are partly historical. In the aftermath of World War II, the United States provided the essential funding for the International Monetary Fund, the Marshall Plan, and the Dodge Plan, which jointly restored exchange and price-level stability among the industrial countries while replenishing official exchange reserves. The world's only capital market without exchange controls was the American. Thus, the US dollar, under the legal cover of the IMF's requirement that member countries declare a par value for their currencies, became the official *reserve* and *intervention* currency to which governments in other industrial, as well as developing, economies pegged their exchange rates. As long as the US kept its own price level stable (as was more or less true in the 1950s and 1960s), these dollar pegs served to anchor the domestic price levels of participating countries (McKinnon, 1996).

Even when the America's money manager, the Federal Reserve System, was controlling inflation rather badly – through the 1970s into the early 1980s – the dollar-based modes of international exchange proved surprisingly resilient. Although many other industrial countries had by then opened their financial markets and floated their exchange rates, the dollar was not significantly displaced as the international vehicle, invoice, and reserve currency in the foreign exchange markets. Let us go into more depth on the dollar's benign role of facilitating international exchange.

If postwar history had not been biased in favor of dollar supremacy, a 'natural' asymmetry across different countries' currencies would have developed anyway. First consider a world of N national currencies without official interventions or foreign exchange targeting by governments. In organizing *private* interbank markets for foreign exchange, great savings in transactions costs can be had if just one national currency, the Nth, is chosen as the vehicle-currency. Then, all foreign exchange quotations – bids and offers – at all terms to maturity, can take place against this one vehicle-currency. The number of active markets can be reduced from $N(N-1)/2$ to just $N-1$. In a world of more than 150 national currencies, this is a tremendous economy of markets for the large commercial banks that make the foreign exchange market. The dollar's interbank role as the *vehicle*-currency (being on one side of almost 90 per cent of interbank transactions outside of Europe) allows banks to cover both their forward exchange and options exposures in much more liquid markets.

At longer term, international bond markets gain liquidity if just one, or no more than a small number, of fully convertible currencies denominate private or sovereign bond issues. Here, the US dollar remains the most important currency, but with diminished status because America is a net borrower with ongoing current-account deficits. In contrast, the European Union as a whole is a large net creditor to the world economy, with ongoing current-account surpluses. Thus, without diminishing the dollar's role in short-term international finance, the euro could become more important for new issues of international bonds.

However, trade in primary commodities shows a stronger pattern of using one national money as the main currency of *invoice*. Exports of homogeneous primary products such as oil, wheat, and copper all tend to be invoiced in dollars, with worldwide price-formation in a centralized exchange. Spot trading, but particularly forward contracting, is concentrated at these centralized exchanges – which are usually in American cities such as Chicago and New York, although dollar-denominated commodity exchanges do exist in London and elsewhere. In periods of reasonable confidence in American monetary policy, these dollar commodity prices are relatively invariant to fluctuations in the dollar's exchange rate. In contrast, if any other country allows its exchange rate to fluctuate against the dollar, its domestic currency prices of primary commodities will vary in proportion – unless its trade is restricted.

Invoicing patterns for exports of manufactured goods are more complex. Major industrial countries with strong currencies tend to invoice their exports in their home currencies (Grasssman, 1973; McKinnon, 1979). Before European Monetary Union, more than 75 per cent of German exports had been invoiced in marks, more than 50 per cent of French exports invoiced in francs, and so on. But these illustrative ratios were dominated by intra-European trade. With the advent of the European Monetary Union, continental European countries will begin invoicing much of their net exports outside the EU in euros. However, because intra-Latin American and intra-East Asian trade is mainly invoiced in US dollars, a substantial but as yet unknown fraction of EU industrial exports to these areas will also be dollar invoiced.

Latin American exports to Europe are dollar invoiced if only because such a high proportion is primary products. Countries like Canada and Australia also find that the great bulk of their imports and exports are invoiced in US dollars. In East Asia, another strong dollar area, the great bulk of foreign trade is invoiced in US dollars even though Japan is the principal exporter to the region (McKinnon, 2000). (The central role of the euro for trade on the European periphery is similarly dominant.)

So, in the absence of a purely international medium of exchange – such as gold in the nineteenth century – to facilitate a region's trade, one national money or regional one (if it exists) naturally tends to intermediate among a multitude of national monies. If the US dollar was not already playing this role, another (major) currency would replace it. But once established, the economies of scale for reducing transactions costs are so great in having most participants in international commerce using the same intermediary currency that only some cataclysmic financial event could displace it (Krugman, 1984).

The upper panel in Table 8.1 summarizes our paradigm of the dollar's central role as the benign facilitator of international exchange in the absence of single world money. For both the private sector and for governments, the upper panel classifies how the dollar performs as medium of exchange, store of value, unit of account, and standard of deferred payment for purely international transacting on current and capital account. It is a slight generalization of a similar table presented in Kenen (1983), and applies as much to countries like Canada and Australia (with the European exception to be discussed), as to most of the Third World.

As long as the rules of the game, that is, the conventions of international exchange for using the dollar as the facilitating currency (see McKinnon (1996) for a deeper discussion of the evolution of these rules) are well understood by all the participating countries, then international trade can be monetized and multilateral. However, if the rules and conventions for converting one national

Table 8.1 The US dollar's role as international money

1. *Facilitates international exchange: all countries*	*Private*	*Official*
Medium of exchange	Vehicle	Intervention
Store of value	Banking	Reserve
Unit of account	Invoice	Peg or target
Standard of deferred payment	Private bonds	Sovereign bonds

2. *Encroaches on national money in domestic uses: strongly in Latin America, less so in other LDCs*

Medium of exchange: dollar circulates domestically in parallel with national money.

Safe haven (Store of value): domestic-currency assets only held at higher real-interest rates than those on dollar assets.

Unit of account: money-wage and other short-term domestic contracts linked to dollar exchange rate.

Standard of deferred payment: longer-term domestic private debt contracts in dollars. But finance is generally short term.

Nominal anchor: Fiscal conditions permitting, the national central bank naturally gears monetary policy toward stabilizing its dollar exchange rate – if only on a downward crawl. Directly targeting domestic-price inflation is not feasible.

money into another break down, as they did in the 1930s, international trade becomes more bartered and bilateral.

Dollar encroachment on national monies

However, this central role of the dollar in international finance today also has a darker side: the potential displacement of national monies for domestic uses – displacement that is particularly marked in the Latin American context. The lower panel of Table 8.1 displays the various textbook roles of *domestic* money – medium of exchange, safe haven (store of value), unit of account, and standard of deferred payment – and summarizes how the US dollar might encroach (has encroached, in the Latin American case) in each of these dimensions.

To be sure this dollar encroachment is not now a problem in the industrial economies, although it was a potential problem in the aftermath of World War II when European and Japanese currencies suffered from a complete loss of confidence. Most countries in Western Europe, as well as Japan, retained capital controls well into the 1970s – in large part to protect the domains of their domestic currencies. But step-by-step European unification, culminating in the late 1990s with the adoption of the euro, ended any lingering problem of dollar encroachment in Europe. This huge new, but highly credible, euro-based regime can operate on a stand-alone basis with perhaps the world's largest market for long-term bonds.

However, for those developing economies without effective controls on inflows and outflows of short-term financial capital and where domestic finance is naturally very short term, encroachment is present in greater or lesser degrees. In

Latin America, we see widespread encroachment on all the functions of domestic money listed in the lower panel of Table 8.1. Let us consider each in turn.

Medium of exchange

As medium of exchange, the dollar now circulates widely as hand-to-hand currency throughout Latin America – and dollar bank accounts (interest-bearing and some checking) have been legalized within several countries. This parallel circulation means that comprehensive capital controls, designed to prevent switching between the domestic money and dollars, are impossible to enforce. (But mild reserve requirements or taxes on foreign borrowing, as in Chile until recently, may still be feasible.)

Why have Latin American monetary authorities allowed such invasive parallel circulation in dollars, where the demand for the domestic monetary base erodes and becomes quite unstable, to develop? First, many governments, with short time-horizons of their own, want to attract emigrant remittances to the home country. So they offer domestic dollar deposits to nationals returning money to the country. (Even if Mexico's banking system does not now offer dollar-linked bank accounts, Mexico's long border with the US with heavy two-way migration makes holding of interest-bearing dollar bank accounts just across the border very easy.) Second, where records of illegal export earnings do not exist for very important export products, such as narcotics, the national government can neither tax them nor force conversion of dollar export proceeds back into its domestic currency. It is better to keep at least some of the dollar proceeds in banks within the country by offering attractive domestic deposit facilities in dollars.

Last, but not least, is the long history in almost all Latin American countries of persistent financial instability: high inflation, temporary stabilizations, currency crashes, renewed inflation, and so on. Holders of naked cash balances in the domestic currency have been heavily taxed in the past. Thus, the precautionary motive for holding at least some dollar balances, at home or abroad, is strong. Similar relatively large dollar holdings are commonplace in much of Africa and in the disintegrated fragments of the old Soviet Union – including Russia itself.

However, the internal circulation of dollars in parallel to domestic currencies is not a general phenomenon. Virtually all the economies of East Asia provide counter examples. Even in those economies – Indonesia, Korea, Malaysia, Philippines, and Thailand – whose currencies were attacked in the great crisis of 1997–98, the internal circulation of US dollars was negligible before the attacks began. These crisis economies – as well as the non-crisis ones of China, Hong Kong, Singapore, and Taiwan – all had what looked like sustainable, if informal, fixes for their dollar exchange rates before 1997 (McKinnon, 2000). By and large, they did not have the same turbulent history of inflation and currency attacks so common in Latin America in the postwar period. Indeed, with the possible exception of Indonesia, after the 1997–98 crisis, all the emerging markets of East Asia appear to be returning to informal dollar pegging (McKinnon, 2001*a*). Their domestic rates of inflation remain surprisingly muted.

Store of value

However, as a *safe haven* store of value, interest-bearing dollar assets dominate domestic assets of the same term to maturity in Asia and Latin America as well as in other developing countries – all those parts of the world not dominated by the subsystem of European trade based on the euro. In the 1990s, the Federal Reserve System again succeeded in stabilizing the American price level (as measured by the US producer price index). A political or economic crisis in any one of the developing countries on this periphery of the dollar standard generates pressure from domestic nationals to fly into dollars (unless restrained by capital controls) – including interest-bearing dollar assets.

Even on the East Asian periphery of the world dollar standard, US Treasury bonds and certificates of deposit in American banks are viewed as the 'risk-free' asset in the international bond markets. In the absence of exchange controls, domestic-currency bonds will only be willingly held if they bear a real rate of return higher than those on dollar bonds at an equivalent term to maturity. In effect, a substantial risk premium must be paid on term deposits (or bonds) in domestic currency compared to term deposits (or bonds) denominated in dollars – and this risk premium is typically much greater at long term than at short term. Indeed, the risk premium on long-term bonds denominated in domestic currency may be so great that an open market at the long-end of the maturity spectrum usually does not exist.

How to measure this risk premium, that is, distinguish it from the expected annualized depreciation (or appreciation) of the domestic currency, is a tricky econometric problem. Moreover, within developing economies, interest rates are highly variable – both in time-series and across countries. Before the 1997 currency attacks began in Thailand, the relevant risk premia on three-month deposits in the East Asian debtor economies averaged about 4 percentage points, whereas in Latin America they averaged closer to 5 to 6 percentage points, above those on benchmark dollar assets.[1]

When finance is very short term, having such marked asymmetry between the center's and the periphery's interest rates, poses severe problems for regulating banks and other domestic financial institutions – particularly in the peripheral countries themselves. Because of deposit insurance, whether formal or informal, and other bail out provisions for the banking system in a general crisis, there is always latent moral hazard. Thus, if interest spreads between accepting domestic-currency and dollar deposits are high, domestic banks may prefer to gamble by accepting low-interest dollar deposits to finance high-interest loans in the domestic currency and not hedge the foreign exchange risk. The resulting 'over-borrowing' syndrome has been analyzed by McKinnon and Pill (1999).

This interest rate gap between the center and the periphery, coupled with weak regulation of domestic banks, helps explain excessive capital inflows into Chile in the late 1970s, into Mexico in the early 1990s, into the East Asian crisis economies before 1997. Even when the US dollar does not encroach directly on domestic monetary circulation, the problem of regulating banks to hedge their foreign exchange risks is more difficult for debtor countries on the periphery of the dollar standard. Importers and banks see the cost of forward cover, that is, the interest differential, to be too high. In contrast, in the US itself, virtually all short-term claims on, and liabilities to, foreigners are dollar denominated – so that chronic foreign-exchange exposure is generally not a problem for the world's biggest debtor economy. In this important respect, the regulation of banks at the center is much easier than it is on the periphery.

Unit of account

Unit of account and standard of deferred payment are closely related concepts, and refer to money's role as a numéraire in domestic contracts: the former is more of a short-term concept whereas the latter is longer term. For longer-term private debt contracts within Latin American countries, the dollar is commonly used as the standard of deferred payment even when the domestic currency is used as the means of settlement. The presumption is that dollar keeps its real purchasing value through time better, and that one can get instantaneous exchange-rate quotes on the value of the dollar in domestic currency when the contract matures. Correspondingly, private debt contracts are seldom linked to domestic price indexes – such as the WPI or CPI – in part because of doubts over the statistical reliability of such indexes and because of lags in collecting price data. Even with the dollar as numéraire for domestic-bond issues, such contracts are usually short term – or have a floating interest rate set according to the yield on short-term (30-day) assets.

More subtle is the dollar's role as a unit of account in other short-term contracts – such as the setting of money wages, and on its impact on the flexibility of real wages. In Latin America, it seems that real wages may be more rigid under flexible exchange rates than if the exchange rate is fixed.

> Consider the problem faced by a trade union representative of the widget industry that is negotiating a collective contract. He is asked to sign a contract which is implicitly denominated in dollars in the fixed exchange rate regime but is denominated in an erratic and unpredictable unit in a flexible regime. It is reasonable to assume that under the flexible rate regime the representative would bargain for a shorter life to the contract (to provide more rapid renegotiations), or for some form of indexation (to denominate the contract in a more stable unit). Under these conditions, nominal wages tend to react more swiftly to price shocks under flexible regimes than under fixed, leading to more *defacto* indexation.
>
> (Hausmann *et al.* (1999) p. 13)

The authors go on to provide empirical evidence that real wages are more rigid in response to, say, terms of trade shocks for Latin American countries with flexible exchange rates than for those with fixed rates. This finding is quite contrary to what had been the accepted theory (Friedman, 1953; Mundell, 1961) of flexible exchange rates leading to greater real-wage flexibility for easing adjustment to real economic shocks. These problems in domestic labor and capital markets, with the very short-term of both domestic and international payments, help explain why we do not observe 'pure' floats in emerging-market economies (Calvo and Reinhart, forthcoming).

To see this better, suppose ongoing inflation requires some downward drift in the dollar value of the domestic currency measured at low frequencies, that is, monthly or quarterly, as with the fairly predictable downward crawl of 4–5 per cent per year in the Indonesian rupiah before 1997. This predictable crawl is then reflected in commensurately higher domestic nominal (but not real) interest rates and in ongoing nominal wage adjustments – perhaps built into longish domestic wage contracts – of 4–5 per cent per year. Even then, governments find it optimal to peg closely to the dollar at high frequencies, that is, on a daily basis or even weekly basis, in order to reduce (short-term) payments risk – thus, further reducing the risk premium in the short-term interest differential.

Before the 1997–98 crisis, *all* the emerging-market economies in East Asia pegged remarkably tightly to the dollar on a daily basis in comparison to the much greater daily fluctuations in the yen–dollar or euro–dollar rates (McKinnon, 2001*a*). Like the US itself, Europe and Japan have robust longer-term bond markets. Their better developed capital markets without exchange controls make hedging short-term exchange risk by importers and banks relatively easy. Thus, the euro and the yen float 'freely' against the dollar on a daily or weekly basis. In contrast, after the 1997–98 crisis, all the emerging markets in East Asia have returned to very tight high-frequency pegging against the dollar into the year 2000 (McKinnon, 2001*a*). In Latin America, the same kind of high-frequency exchange rate pegging is observed in non-crisis periods.

Exchange rate policy and bank regulation

Can we relate this general tendency for high-frequency exchange-rate pegging to different bank and foreign-exchange regulatory regimes in the peripheral countries? If the regulatory authorities strictly limit any net direct or indirect foreign-exchange exposure on the part of banks, this would drive them out of the business of accepting low-cost foreign exchange deposits to finance higher-yield domestic-currency loans. The inflow of *short-term* foreign capital into the economy would be reduced. But such strict regulation would not impair the banks' role of servicing and facilitating foreign-exchange transactions by domestic merchants and manufacturers.

However, strict regulation against foreign-exchange exposure could severely limit the ability of the banks to act collectively as dealer-speculators to 'make' the foreign-exchange market. 'Stabilizing' speculation by banks, the most natural foreign-exchange traders and dealers, would not be possible.

Consider the implications for optimal short-term foreign-exchange management, first when capital controls are absent, and second, when they are effectively applied.

Case 1: No capital controls, imperfect bank regulation Either because regulatory weakness leaves too many banks (and possibly importers) with exposed foreign-exchange positions, or because the government does not want to impose draconian rules against institutions assuming *any* open foreign-exchange position, an informal hedge is provided by keeping the exchange rate steady in the short term. The short time-frame over which foreign-currency debts – largely in dollars – are incurred, and then repaid on a day-to-day or even a week-to-week basis, defines the same time-frame over which the dollar exchange rate is (and should be) kept stable in non-crisis periods.

Case 2: Direct capital controls Suppose the government prevents banks, other financial institutions, and individuals from holding any foreign-exchange assets or liabilities. Non-bank firms engaged in foreign trade cannot take positions in foreign exchange except for the minimum necessary in their particular trade. Importers are prevented from building up undue foreign-currency debts except for ordinary trade credit, and exporters are required to repatriate their dollar earnings quickly. In particular, banks cannot accept foreign-currency deposits or hold foreign-currency deposits abroad, or make foreign-currency loans. Then, private agents in general, and banks in particular, cannot act as dealer-speculators to determine the level of the exchange rate (McKinnon, 1979, Chapter 6). The exchange rate will become indeterminate (highly volatile) unless the government steps in as a dealer to clear international transactions. Thus, the government must take open positions, which determine the level of the exchange rate, and assume the exchange risk. So if the government is determining the exchange rate day-to-day anyway, why not keep it stable?

China and Malaysia more or less correspond to Case 2 in imposing capital controls (although not as rigidly as described above) Thus, their governments have wisely fixed their dollar exchange rates – certainly in the short run and maybe longer. Because Korea and Thailand have now pretty well rid themselves of the last vestiges of the capital controls they once had, they correspond more to Case 1. And the Korean and Thai governments are indeed reducing exchange risk in their economies by keeping their rates virtually pegged in the short run, even if they cannot prevent some medium- and longer-term movement – particularly in the unsettled aftermath of the 1997–98 crisis.

However, while such soft short-term pegs reduce foreign exchange risk for 'well-behaved' merchant traders and financial institutions, this regime may be exploited by financial institutions (and some traders) with moral hazard. Poorly regulated and under-capitalized banks with deposit insurance may be more willing to gamble by accepting short-term foreign currency deposits to finance their domestic loan portfolios if they know the exchange is stable in the short run.

What might we conclude? *With* or *without* capital controls, high-frequency pegging is optimal when the term-structure of finance is very short and domestic capital markets are underdeveloped. Beyond the nominal anchor argument for stabilizing exchange rates in the medium and longer terms, there is a risk-reducing argument for very short-term pegging.

But, except in a crisis, pervasive direct capital controls on the gross foreign-exchange positions of banks (as under Case 2) are unlikely to be the best way of controlling exchange risk when private financial markets are incomplete.

First, preventing banks from accepting any foreign-currency deposits, or making any foreign-currency loan, disrupts banks' traditional role of clearing foreign payments and settling accounts. On any trading day, the enormous flow of foreign payments would have to be cleared directly by the central bank.

Second, such capital controls make it impossible for banks to do the covered interest arbitrage necessary to make the forward market in foreign exchange, that is, determine the forward rate relative to the spot rate (McKinnon, 1979, Chapter 5). Either the private sector is left with no mechanism for hedging international transactions, or the government (central bank) is dragged willy-nilly into writing forward-exchange contracts for private traders – a process which has been open to abuse around the world.

So, on the periphery, the best way of controlling risk in the foreign exchanges is Case 3.

Case 3: Net foreign-exchange exposure of banks is regulated to be zero The domestic banking authorities let authorized commercial banks acquire foreign-exchange assets and liabilities gross, but their net position, perhaps defined at the end of each trading day, must be zero. Further, in making this calculation, the regulators also consider indirect as well as direct foreign-exchange liabilities. For example, if a bank accepts dollar deposits to lend to domestic firms in dollars, its balance sheet may look square. But the non-bank domestic borrower may now be exposed to currency risk and could default if the domestic currency is devalued. Exchange risk is translated into default risk into banking risk. Similarly, banks may undertake off balance-sheet transactions in derivatives, which increase their foreign exchange exposure, and which are hard to detect.

While necessarily only approximate in practice, forcing banks to (near) zero net foreign-exchange exposure is nevertheless a valuable regulatory principle. It counters the various margins of temptation not to hedge – as described above. In particular, it prevents banks from accepting foreign-currency deposits to make domestic-currency loans. But even if applied quite strictly, this regulatory principle leaves enough flexibility for the commercial banking system as a whole to perform its normal facilitating role in the foreign exchanges. For any given spot-exchange rate, the clearing of international payments and settling accounts can devolve from the central bank. The commercial banks can still undertake covered interest arbitrage and so create a market in forward exchange to service the hedging needs of their non-bank 'retail' customers.

That said, however, imposing the rule of no net foreign-exchange exposure (Case 3) means that the banks still cannot act as (stabilizing) speculators to determine the level of the exchange rate. In this one important respect, Case 3 is similar to Case 2. With either capital controls or a rule of no net foreign-exchange exposure, the exchange rate would be indeterminate, that is, highly volatile, unless the government itself enters the market to act as a stabilizing speculator. So even with 'first-best' bank regulation for controlling risk in place, that is, Case 3, the government is still forced to determine the equilibrium exchange rate.

With these cases, we have examined three quite different foreign-exchange regimes. All three were found to be consistent with the high-frequency pegging to the dollar observed in East Asia. But the argument applies quite generally to other peripheral countries in Latin America, South Asia, and so on.

Lengthening the term structure of finance: a concluding note

I now return more explicitly to Maxwell Fry's concern. For the peripheral countries, how can the regulatory and foreign-exchange regimes be reformed so as to encourage the development of longer-term bond markets, both domestically and for foreign-capital inflows?

First, in the face of fiscal deficits, inflation, and ongoing depreciations, the term-structure of domestic finance cannot be lengthened. Domestic finance will remain short-term – with the risks somewhat ameliorated by the high-frequency exchange-rate pegging described above. But measured on a low-frequency basis, that is, monthly or quarterly, the domestic currency inevitably depreciates – whether by a comparatively gentle downward crawl or by a series of discrete devaluations. The result is that nobody will willingly hold longer-term unindexed financial instruments denominated in the domestic currency.

Because Latin America has been associated the most strongly with this syndrome, many see the solution to be one of eliminating domestic monetary independence altogether. Currency boards based on the dollar – as in Argentina and Panama – or outright dollarization, as in Ecuador, are draconian schemes for reducing the monetary distinction between the periphery and the center. At the same time, they solve the time-consistency problem in domestic macroeconomic decision-making. And the net loss of seigniorage is minimal because many of these economies start from a position of being largely dollarized anyway.

However, out-of-control fiscal policies remain a serious loose end so that the interest-rate differential in Argentina and Panama with the US remains surprisingly large at various terms to maturity. Moreover, capital inflows into these dollar-based countries remain ultrasensitive to shocks in the world capital market as with the 1998 Russian crisis and the 1999 Brazilian crisis of 1999 (Hausmann, 2000). Indeed, the depreciation of the Brazilian real against the dollar created a double whammy for Argentina: a sudden loss of competitiveness against a major trading partner and the increased spread over LIBOR of all dollar-based borrowing in the area. Clearly, it is risky for one country to adopt a currency board when close trading partners do not.

Nevertheless, because of the tumultuous financial history of countries such as Argentina and Ecuador, using a currency board to become part of the monetary regime of the center country may still be worthwhile in the longer term. Macroeconomic stability is more easily maintained, and greater credibility in the international capital markets may eventually allow lengthening the term to maturity of both domestic finance and foreign borrowing. The key is to give investors long-term assurance that 10–20 years from now the peripheral country's nominal exchange rate will be the same as it is today. Then both private firms and the government can issue 10- to 20-year fixed interest rate bonds on terms not too much less favorable terms than those on 'risk-free' US Treasury bonds of the same maturities.

But what may be best for Latin America's already largely dollarized economies need not be a good choice for East Asian debtor economies. In East Asia, dollars do not impinge on domestic monetary circulation, and ongoing inflation has not been a problem (except for Indonesia) as government budgets often showed surpluses. During their 'miracle' growth phases before 1997, the East Asian economies successfully pegged to the dollar as the nominal anchor for their domestic price levels (McKinnon, 2000). With the benefit of hindsight, however, we now know that this policy was seriously incomplete. First, and most obviously, was the failure to properly regulate the financial system – including the central bank itself in some cases – against undue risk taking including short-term foreign-exchange exposure.

Second, and more subtly, the East Asian debtor economies had not committed themselves to a long-term exchange-rate parity in the mode of the nineteenth century gold standard (Goodhart and Delargy, 1998) – even though they seemed to be securely pegged in the short and medium terms. Because of the short-term structure of finance, each was vulnerable to a speculative attack on its currency; but none had a long-run exchange-rate strategy in place to mitigate the worst consequences any such attack. Post-crisis, there was no well-defined tradition of returning to the pre-crisis exchange rate. In contrast, under the classical gold standard, if a government was forced to suspend its gold parity in a crisis, it was obligated to return to its pre-crisis parity (McKinnon, 1996, Chapters 2 and 4). This restoration rule kept exchange-rate expectations regressive.

The problem was aggravated because the pre-1997 East Asian dollar standard was informal rather than formal. With the exception of Hong Kong, none of the countries involved had formally declared a dollar parity – and each had been classified by the IMF as following some variety of managed floating rather than being pegged to the dollar. Thus, with the forced suspension of these dollar pegs in the 1997–98 crisis, there was no traditional dollar parity (gold parity in the nineteenth-century sense) to which the government was bound to return. In the crisis, the absence of regressive expectations led to a very inefficient tradeoff: the East Asian five suffered from both deep (albeit temporary) devaluations and very high (short-term) interest rates (McKinnon, 2000).

Thus, emerging economies whose macroeconomic fundamentals are sound so as to permit a 'good fix' for their exchange rates (McKinnon and Pill, 1999), should extend the maturity of that commitment to the distant future. If the East Asian five had, before the 1997 crisis, adopted a restoration rule explicitly – and, ideally, collectively – they could have moderated the high-interest rates and deep devaluations, which bankrupted so much of their economies, once the attacks began. (Of course, countries that must rely on the inflation tax, and cannot credibly commit to long-run exchange-rate stability, should not try it.) The benefits from having the exchange rate pinned down in the long run exceed those from having a hard short-term fix.

Only with long-term confidence in the purchasing power of domestic money (against the center country's) would exchange-rate expectations be naturally regressive, and are long-term bond and mortgage markets possible to organize – both domestically and for commercial (non sovereign) international borrowing. An appropriate accounting framework with full disclosure for bond issuers, and a legal framework to secure the rights of bond holders, and so on, now become more relevant.

Barry Eichengreen and Ricardo Hausmann (1999) discuss, very perceptively, the need to lengthen the term to maturity of domestic markets for bonds and bank loans. However, their approach is the inverse of what I am suggesting here. They want to start encouraging longer-term bond finance by domestic institutional and legal changes and hope that this would lead to greater (long-term) exchange-rate stability. I would start with a long-run exchange rate commitment, that is, the restoration rule, to create a friendlier environment for strengthening the institutions governing bond markets. The emphasis of the two approaches is different, but they are not in conflict.

There is a virtuous circle. When long-term bond issues in the nineteenth-century mode begin to displace short-term bank finance, the government's commitment to long-term exchange rate stability is naturally reinforced. On the one hand, lengthening the term-structure of finance makes the economy less vulnerable to currency attacks in the foreign exchanges; but, on the other hand, the domestic banking system becomes less vulnerable to internal runs. And the empirical evidence suggests that currency attacks and commercial bank runs are strongly correlated (Kaminsky and Reinhart, 1999). Finally with a more vigorous domestic bond market, the central bank can better conduct domestic open-market operations to defend the currency and secure the domestic-price level over the longer run – a key point that Maxwell Fry (1995, 1997) argued so persuasively.

Note

1 Measured against the absurdly low nominal-interest rates on yen assets in the 1990s, these spreads would have been much higher. But one can show that the low-interest rate trap in Japan in the 1990s was also an indirect effect of the operation of the world dollar standard. See McKinnon and Ohno (1997) and McKinnon and Ohno (2001*b*).

References

Calvo, G. and Reinhart, C. 'Fear of floating', Quarterly Journal of Economics (forthcoming)

Eichengreen, B. and Hausmann, R. (1999) 'Exchange rates and financial fragility', 1999 Pacific Basin Conference: 'Financial Crises in Emerging Markets', San Francisco (September).

Friedman, M. (1953) 'The case for flexible exchange rates', in *Essays in Positive Economics*, pp. 157–203. Chicago: University of Chicago Press.

Fry, M. (1995) *Money Interest and Banking in Economic Development*, 2nd edn, Baltimore and London: The Johns Hopkins University Press.

Fry, M. (1997) *Emancipating the Banking System and Developing Markets for Government Debt*, London: Routledge.

Goodhart, C. and Delargy, P. J. R. (1998) 'Financial crises: plus ça change, plus c'est la même chose', *International Finance*, 1(2), 261–88.

Grassman, S. (1973) *Exchange Reserves and the Financial Structure of Foreign Trade*, Saxon House: Westmeade, England.

Hausmann, R. (2000) 'Latin America: No fireworks, no crisis?' in J. Bisignano, W. Hunter and G. Kaufman (eds), *Global Financial Crises: Lessons from Recent Events*, pp. 27–48. Boston: Kluwer Academic Publishers.

Hausmann, R., Gavin, G., Pages-Serra, C. and Stein, E. (1999) 'Financial turmoil and the choice of an exchange rate regime', Working Paper 400, Inter-American Development Bank, Washington.

Kaminsky, G. and Reinhart, C. (1999) 'The twin crises: balance of payments and banking crises in developing countries', *American Economic Review*, 89(3), pp. 473–500.

Kenen, P. (1983) 'The role of the dollar as international currency', *Occasional Paper*, 13, Group of Thirty, New York.

Krugman, P. (1984) 'The international role of the dollar: theory and prospect', in J. Bilson and R. Marston (eds), *Exchange Rate Theory and Practice*, pp. 261–78. Chicago: University of Chicago Press.

McKinnon, R. I. (2000) 'The East Asian dollar standard, life after death?', World Bank Workshop on Rethinking the East Asian Miracle, published in *Economic Notes*, 29(1) (earlier version available at http://www-econ.stanford.edu/faculty/workp/index.html).

McKinnon, R. I. (2001*a*) 'After the crisis, the East Asian dollar standard resurrected: an interpretation of high frequency pegging', in S. Stiglitz and S. Yusuf (eds), *The East Asian Miracle Reconsidered*, World Bank and Oxford Press, New York, pp. 197–246.

McKinnon, R. I. (1996) *The Rules of the Game: International Money and Exchange Rates*, Cambridge, MA: MIT Press.

McKinnon, R. I. (1993) *The Order of Economic Liberalization: Financial Control in the Transition to a Market Economy*, Baltimore: Johns Hopkins University.

McKinnon, R. I. (1979) *Money in International Exchange: The Convertible Currency System*, New York: Oxford University Press.

McKinnon, R. I. and Ohno, K. (1997) *Dollar and Yen: Resolving Economic Conflict Between the United States and Japan*, Cambridge, MA: MIT Press (Japanese Translation, Nihon Keizai Shimbun, 1998).

McKinnon, R. I. and Ohno, K. (2001*b*) 'The foreign exchange origins of Japan's economic slump and low interest liquidity trap', *The World Economy*, 24(5) (March).

McKinnon, R. I. and Pill, H. (1999) 'Exchange rate regimes for emerging markets: moral hazard, and international overborrowing', *Oxford Review of Economic Policy*, 15(3), 19–38 (earlier version available at http://www-econ.stanford.edu/faculty/workp/index.html).

Mundell, R. A. (1961) 'A theory of optimum currency areas', *American Economic Review*, 51(2), 509–17.

9 Survey data on exchange-rate expectations

More currencies, more horizons, more tests

Menzie Chinn and Jeffrey Frankel

Introduction

A new literature uses surveys of market participants to measure their expectations of exchange rates.[1] This paper extends earlier tests, based on a broader sample of survey expectations. More currencies are studied than in the early literature, many of them in newly-important emerging markets. (The countries and currencies are listed in the first appendix to the paper.) More importantly, tentative assessments are made regarding the characteristics of long horizon forecasts, whereas all prior research has focused on short to medium horizons (one week to one year). Finally, we investigate the improvement in fit for a structural exchange rate model using survey-based measures of the exchange risk premium.

The empirical results presented in this paper are based on a data set derived from *Currency Forecasters' Digest* (hereafter *CFD*). The chief advantage of exploiting this data set is that it covers over twenty-five exchange rates, and includes several for newly-industrializing countries in Asia, and smaller developed countries in Europe and elsewhere. With a broader and more heterogeneous set of currencies, interesting patterns, not readily apparent in more narrow sets of currencies, can be identified.[2]

This paper is organized in the following fashion. In the section entitled 'Updating the standard results', we re-evaluate the predictive ability of both the survey-based measure of expected exchange rates and the forward rate. In the section on the 'Forward discount and the exchange risk premium', the nature of the risk premium is investigated in a setting where we have direct observations on the expected depreciation, that is, the survey measure. In the section on 'Long horizon forecasts', the characteristics of long run forecasts are evaluated. The section on 'Survey data and structural models of exchange rates' is composed of an investigation of the empirical usefulness of exchange rate models incorporating information about the exchange risk premium derived from survey data. Concluding remarks follow.

Updating the standard results: expectations and forward rate bias

Overview

In these two sections we extend some of the most standard tests.[3] The exchange-rate forecasts were usually compiled on the fourth Thursday of each month from February 1988 to June 1994.[4] The survey respondents were reported to number approximately forty-five, of whom two-thirds were multinational firms and the remainder forecasting firms or the economics departments of banks. We use as the measure of expectations the 'consensus forecast' that CFD emphasizes. This measure is the geometric mean:[5]

$$\bar{X} \equiv \prod_{i=1}^{n} (X_i)^{w_i},$$

where, in this case, $w_i = 1/n$, $n =$ number of forecasts, and X_i represents the individual forecast responses.

The regressions are run on a pooled time-series/cross-section.[6] In this portion of the paper, we investigate the nature of the 3- and 12-month-horizon forecasts. Since the data are sampled at intervals finer than the forecast horizon, the regression residuals will exhibit a moving average process of order $k-1$ (where k is the forecast horizon). Hence, we use an estimate of the parameter covariance matrix that is robust with respect to heteroskedasticity and serial correlation.[7]

This new sample considerably expands the number of observations and time span investigated in previous papers. For 3-month horizons, the number of observations is essentially doubled, and for 12-month, tripled. Further, the 6-plus years covered by this data set encompass the 1992–93 bouts of turmoil in the EMS (European Monetary System), the depreciation of the dollar against the yen in the early 1990s (see Figures 9.1 and 9.2), and the acceleration in capital

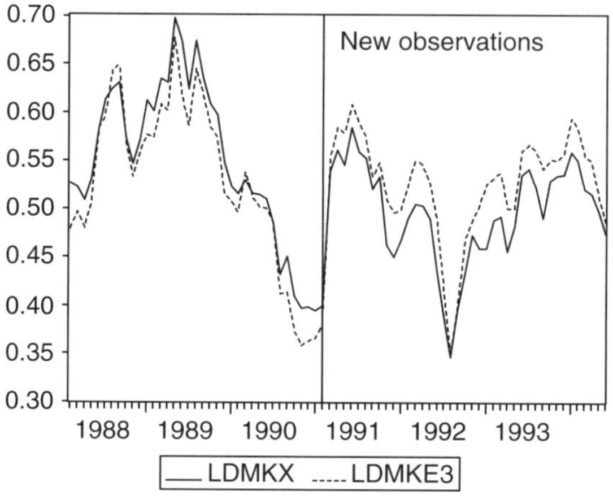

Figure 9.1 DM/US$ log exchange rate and 3-month expected rate.

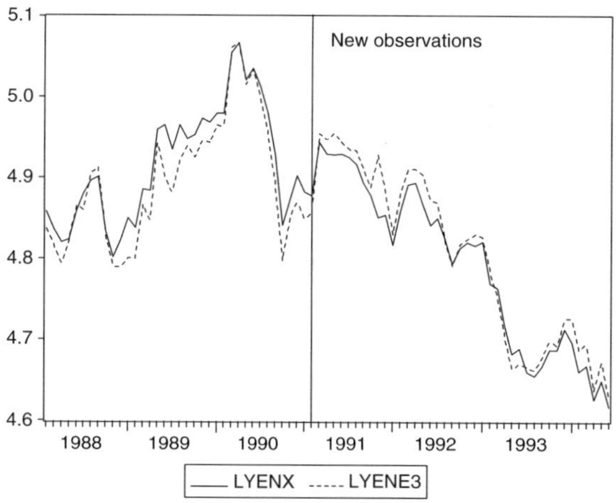

Figure 9.2 Yen/US$ log exchange rate and 3-month expected rate.

flows to emerging markets preceding the Mexican-peso crisis of December 1994 and the East Asia crisis of 1997–98.

Conditional bias in expectations

We now explicitly evaluate of the forecasting characteristics of our expectations measures. A common procedure is to regress the *ex-post* depreciation on the survey measure of expected depreciation. In that case, the unbiasedness proposition is represented by the null hypothesis that the coefficient on expected depreciation equals unity.

$$\Delta s_{t+k} = \alpha_1 + \beta_1 \; \Delta\hat{s}^e_{t,t+k} + u_{1,t}, \tag{1}$$

where Δs_{t+k} is the *ex-post* depreciation between periods t and $t+k$, and $\Delta\hat{s}^e_{t,t+k}$ is the period t survey-based expected depreciation from time period t to $t+k$ (all variables are annualized). The unbiasedness hypothesis is represented by the null hypothesis that $\beta_1 = 1$, and the alternative, by $\beta_1 < 1$. If the alternative is accepted, then investors could make better guesses by betting against the consensus forecast. These regressions were run on both the entire sample, and a sample excluding the three countries that historically had had high inflation rates, Argentina, Brazil and Mexico. Estimates for this equation are presented in Table 9.1.

Results for six regressions are reported. Two constrain the intercept for all currencies to be the same. Since such constraints are usually rejected statistically, the constrained-regression results are provided only for purposes of comparison. Focusing attention on the full sample-unconstrained regressions, one finds that the estimate of β_1 is usually positive and large in economic terms. One can reject the null hypothesis that the coefficient is zero at the 3-month horizon, and can

Table 9.1 Regression of actual depreciation on expected depreciation (February 1988 to June 1994)

$$\Delta s_{t+k} = \alpha_1 + \beta_1 \Delta \hat{s}^e_{t,t+k} + u_{1,t} \quad (1)$$

Term (k)	*3-month (intercept constrained)*	*3 month*	*3-month (No Arg., Brz., Mex.)*	*12-month (intercept constrained)*	*12 month*	*12-month (No Arg., Brz., Mex)*
β_1	0.740	0.461	−0.163	1.411	0.828	0.003
SE	(0.017)	(0.029)	(0.058)	(0.025)	(0.045)	(0.057)
GMM SE	(0.077)	(0.123)	(0.096)	(0.303)	(0.453)	(0.115)
t: $\beta_1 = 1$	3.377[c]	4.382[c]	12.115[c]	1.356	0.380	8.670[c]
t: $\beta_1 = 0$	9.610[c]	3.748[c]	1.698[a]	4.657[c]	1.828[a]	0.026
d.f.	1639	1616	1409	1458	1435	1287
$\bar{R}^2$	0.54	0.58	0.02	0.68	0.74	0.14
DW	0.514	0.456	0.566	0.143	0.105	0.248

Notes: 'Intercept constrained' indicates that all the exchange rates are constrained to have the same intercept term. OLS β is the point estimate from the OLS regression. SE is the OLS asymptotic standard error. GMM is a heteroskedasticity and serial correlation consistent-Generalized Method of Moments standard error. GMM SE is from regressions with de-meaned data. a, b and c indicate significance at 10%, 5% and 1% level.

reject it at the 10 per cent level at the 12-month horizon. In the 3-month case the null of a unit coefficient is strongly rejected, indicating bias in expectations. On the other hand, when the intercepts are unconstrained at the 12-month horizon, unbiasedness is not rejected.

It appears here (as in our previous papers) that the results, particularly the finding of some predictive ability, are being driven by the inclusion of currencies for high-inflation countries. When the sample excludes the currencies of Argentina, Brazil and Mexico, coefficient estimates become either negative (at the 3-month horizon) or insignificantly different from zero. In these cases, the null of unbiasedness is resoundingly rejected.

This finding of conditional bias over the 1988–94 period corroborates results in Frankel and Froot (1987), which pertained to a turbulent period in the 1980s encompassing a large rise and fall in the value of the dollar. Here, the results obtain over a period of relative dollar stability against the European currencies, combined with uncertainty within the EMS.

The finding of parameter estimates substantially below unity may be due to the presence of measurement error in the survey forecasts. Even if such measurement error is randomly distributed, the coefficient estimate in Equation (1) is biased downward.[8]

Forward rate bias

Many studies have concluded that the forward discount is a biased predictor of the future spot rate. We replicate the conventional test for forward rate bias using our data sample as given:

$$\Delta s_{t+k} = \alpha_2 + \beta_2 fd_{t,t+k} + u_{2,t}, \qquad (2)$$

where $fd_{t,t+k}$ is the forward discount at time t for a trade k periods hence.

The results of estimating this equation are reported in Table 9.2 (only seventeen of the twenty-four currencies are covered since not all currencies have forward markets). One can view this regression as an explicit test of the unbiasedness properties of the forward discount. In contrast to some estimates in this literature, as well as in our own earlier findings, we find that the point estimates for the forward discount are positive. Moreover, the null of unbiasedness cannot be rejected in the cross section regressions.

These surprising findings are apparently being driven by the behavior of those European currencies that were forced to devalue in the crises of 1992 and 1993 in the Exchange Rate Mechanism (ERM). A regression using only EMS currencies yields point estimates (GMM standard errors) of 1.214 (0.553) and 1.606 (0.461) for the 3-month and 12-month-horizon regressions.[9] This difference in slope parameters implies that the non-EMS currencies have lower coefficients. In fact, a cross-section regression for non-European currencies yields estimates of −1.483 (0.594) and −1.524 (0.763).

Moreover, inspection of the time series regressions bears out the assertion (see Appendix B). The currencies with coefficients of 1.0 or greater are the Swedish krone, Irish punt, Italian lira, Norwegian krona, and Spanish peseta. Hence, the forward discount appears during this period in some degree to have correctly anticipated the subsequent movements in the European currencies. This could

Table 9.2 Bias in the forward discount (February 1988 to June 1994)

$$\Delta s_{t+k} = \alpha_2 + \beta_2 fd_{t,t+k} + u_{2,t} \qquad (2)$$

Term (k)	*3-month constr.*	*3 month*	*3-month EMS*	*12-month constr.*	*12 month*	*12-month EMS*
OLS β_3	0.883	0.805	1.214	1.142	1.113	1.606
OLS SE	(0.169)	(0.209)	(0.311)	(0.101)	(0.140)	(0.190)
GMM SE	(0.327)	(0.382)	(0.346)	(0.346)	(0.410)	(0.461)
t: $\beta_2=0$	2.700[c]	2.107[c]	2.195[b]	3.301[c]	2.715[c]	3.484[c]
t: $\beta_2=0.5$	1.171	0.798	1.291	1.855[b]	1.226	2.399[b]
t: $\beta_2=1$	0.358	0.301	0.387	0.410	0.268	1.315
d.f.	1246	1230	680	1127	1111	609
$\bar{R}^2$	0.02	0.01	0.01	0.10	0.10	0.12
DW	0.548	0.559	0.550	0.259	0.224	0.230

Notes: OLS β is the point estimate from the OLS regression. SE is the standard error. OLS Het. SE is the White heteroskedasticity consistent SE. GMM SE is a heteroskedasticity-consistent Generalized Method of Moments standard error. GMM SE is from regressions with de-meaned data. t is the absolute value of the t-statistic using the OLS point estimate and GMM standard error. a, b and c indicate significance at 10%, 5% and 1% level.

be an instance of the much-discussed 'peso problem.'[10] It could also be evidence that, after twenty years of observed bias in the forward discount, market participants began to adjust their behavior. The 'convergence play' of the early 1990s, when speculators went long in those European currencies that were paying high interest rates, would be an example. A further-updated test confirms that the coefficients on two major European currencies that showed a large bias during the period 1976I–1989IV, showed a smaller bias during the period 1990I–1998I.[11]

Most other currencies in our sample show the familiar pattern of small or negative coefficients. The yen, Australian dollar (12-month), Singapore dollar, South African Rand and Canadian Dollar all show statistically significant deviations from unbiasedness. The reason that the deviations for other currencies are not significant is presumably the large standard errors attendant with these pure time series regressions.

The forward discount and the exchange risk premium

The forward rate bias found for certain currencies could be due either to variation in the risk premium or to within-sample bias in expectations. Recall Equation (2):

$$\Delta s_{t+k} = \alpha_2 + \beta_2\, fd_{t,t+k} + u_{2,t}. \tag{2}$$

The null hypothesis of unbiasedness is represented as $\beta_2 = 1$. (A constant is allowed to account either for a constant risk premium, or for the convexity term arising from Jensen's Inequality.) A common finding in the literature is rejection of the null, where β_2 is usually estimated to be closer to zero than to unity. This finding is taken to be evidence that most of the variation in the forward discount constitutes a time-varying risk premium (defined by $rp_{t,t+k} \equiv fd_{t,t+k} - \Delta s^e_{t,t+k}$).

As discussed above, the forward rate appears to be a biased predictor of the spot rate for particular currencies, and not for others. While the null of unbiasedness cannot be rejected for all currencies in general, in part because the standard errors are quite large, we have seen that unbiasedness is clearly rejected for non-European currencies. The question is what is the source of the bias in the forward discount.

To assess whether the bias is due to expectational errors or a time-varying risk premium, one can regress the expected depreciation, $\Delta\hat{s}^e$ as estimated by the *CFD* survey, on the forward discount, as suggested by Froot and Frankel (1989). That is,

$$\Delta\hat{s}^e_{t,t+k} = \alpha_3 + \beta_3\, fd_{t,t+k} + u_{3,t}. \tag{3}$$

The results are reported in Table 9.3. The null hypothesis that the slope coefficient is zero is strongly rejected.[12] Thus, at least some of the variation in the forward discount must be due to expected depreciation. In other words, one can

Table 9.3 Test for time-varying risk premium (February 1988 to June 1994)

$$\Delta \hat{s}^{e}_{t,t+k} = \alpha_3 + \beta_3 fd_{t,t+k} + u_{3,t} \quad (3)$$

Term (k)	*3-month constr.*	*3 month*	*3-month constr., non-Europe*	*12-month constr.*	*12 month*	*12-month constr., non-Europe*
OLS β_3	1.403	1.820	0.956	0.736	1.126	0.445
SE	(0.069)	(0.081)	(0.095)	(0.042)	(0.050)	(0.062)
GMM SE	(0.111)	(0.165)	(0.171)	(0.068)	(0.084)	(0.105)
t: $\beta_3=0$	12.640^c	11.030^c	5.591^c	10.824^c	13.405^c	4.238^c
t: $\beta_3=0.5$	8.135^c	9.212^c	2.667^c	3.471^c	7.452^c	0.524
t: $\beta_3=1$	3.631^c	4.976^c	0.257	3.882^c	1.500	5.286^c
d.f.	1230	1212	315	1231	1213	316
$\bar{R}^2$	0.25	0.30	0.24	0.20	0.38	0.14
DW	0.574	0.707	0.852	0.516	0.715	0.375

Notes: OLS β is the point estimate from the OLS regression. SE is the standard error. OLS Het. SE is a White heteroskedasticity-consistent standard error. GMM is a heteroskedasticity consistent-Generalized Method of Moments standard error, assuming MA processes of order two. Assuming higher order lags implies only slightly different results. t is the absolute value of the t-statistic using the OLS point estimate and either the White heteroskedasticity-consistent or the GMM standard error. a, b and c indicate significance at 10%, 5% and 1% level.

reject the hypothesis that all of the variation in the forward discount is due to a time-varying risk premium.[13] This finding also supports the validity of the survey data as a measure of expected depreciation, as opposed to the null hypothesis that the survey responses are random noise.

The next question is whether *any* of the variation in the forward discount can be attributed to a risk premium or, in other words, whether we can reject the hypothesis of a unit coefficient. Here we get somewhat different answers depending on whether we look at the 3-month results or the 12-month results. Overall, there is more evidence to support the existence of a risk premium in this cross-section of seventeen currencies than there was in the earlier studies of five major currencies. The coefficient estimate of 0.736 is significantly different from 1, for example, in the case where the 12-month horizon is used and the intercept terms are constrained to be equal across currencies.[14]

At the 3-month horizon one can reject the null hypothesis that $\beta_3 = 1$. The rejection however is in the direction $\beta_3 > 1$, which is inconsistent with the usual view that some positive share of the variation in the forward discount constitutes variation in the risk premium.[15]

The regression is also capable of shedding light on a claim set forth by Fama (1984) and Hodrick and Srivastava (1986) (FHS) that expected depreciation is less variable than the exchange risk premium. The FHS claim is:

$$\text{var}(\Delta s^{e}_{t,t+k}) < \text{var}(rp_{t,t+k}). \quad (4)$$

To see the relevance of the regression results for this claim, note that Equation (4) can be re-written (dropping subscripts) as:

$$\text{var}(\Delta s^e) < \text{var}(fd) + \text{var}(\Delta s^e) - 2 \times \text{cov}(fd, \Delta s^e).$$

Rearranging,

$$\frac{1}{2} \geq \frac{\text{cov}(fd, \Delta s^e)}{\text{var}(fd)}. \tag{5}$$

As Froot and Frankel (1989) observe, the probability limit of the β coefficient in Equation (3) is:

$$\text{plim}\,\hat{\beta}_3 = \frac{\text{cov}(u_3, fd) + \text{cov}(\Delta\hat{s}^e, fd)}{\text{var}(fd)}. \tag{6}$$

Assuming the measurement error is uncorrelated with the forward discount, then the probability limit of the regression estimate is the same as the expression in the RHS of Equation (5). Hence, if one can reject the null hypothesis that $\beta_3 \leq 0.5$, then one is rejecting the FHS hypothesis that the variation in the expectation of depreciation is less than the variation in the risk premium.

In almost all cases, one can reject the hypothesis $\beta_3 \leq 0.5$, indicating there is less evidence of a time-varying risk premium than in the previous results reported in Frankel and Chinn (1993). However, at the 12-month horizon for the non-European currencies, the null hypothesis $\beta_3 \leq 0.5$ is not rejected, implying some role for a risk premium.

Long-horizon forecasts

Extrapolative and adaptive expectations

In this section, we evaluate the characteristics of multi-year forecasts provided by *CFD*. Previous studies used, at the longest horizon, 12-month-ahead forecasts. In contrast, we examine the behavior of 5-year-ahead forecasts. We evaluate the evidence in favor of extrapolative, adaptive and regressive expectations in a variety of cross-section regressions.

CFD reports the exchange rate expected 4–5 years into the future. For instance, the March 1993 issue reports forecasts for the end of 1993, 1994, 1995, 1996, and 1997; the June, September and December 1993 issues, also report forecasts for the end of these same years. Hence the forecasts are not precisely 5 years ahead, except in the case of the March 1993 issue. To be safe, we interpret only data for the first observation of the year as a 5-year-ahead forecast. This produces six observations per currency, or a total of approximately 150 observations in the cross-section sample.

Table 9.4a Extrapolative expectations in long horizon forecasts (February 1988 to June 1994)

$$\Delta \hat{s}^{e}_{t,t+60} = \alpha_4 + \beta_4 \Delta s_{t,t-k} + u_{4,t} \tag{7}$$

Term (k)	*1-month lagged depreciation*			*3-month lagged depreciation*		
	Constrained		*No ABM*	*Constrained*		*No ABM*
OLS β_4	0.044	0.040^{b}	−0.006			
SE	(0.040)	(0.016)	(0.009)			
OLS β_4				0.206^{c}	0.176^{c}	0.026
SE				(0.045)	(0.040)	(0.028)
d.f.	129	106	98	129	106	121
$\bar{R}^2$	0.02	0.86	0.52	0.06	0.56	0.52

Notes: OLS β is the point estimate from the OLS regression. SE is the OLS standard error, assuming $T/3$ observations. t is the absolute value of the t-statistic using the OLS point estimate and adjusted standard error. a, b and c indicate significance at 10%, 5%, and 1% level.

In Table 9.4a, results are reported for regressions of the form:

$$\Delta \hat{s}^{e}_{t,t+60} = \alpha_4 + \beta_4 \Delta s_{t,t-k} + u_{4,t}, \tag{7}$$

where k is either 1 or 3. If there are bandwagon effects, then the coefficient estimate should be positive. On the other hand, if expectations are stabilizing, the coefficient estimate should be negative. With static expectations (which would be consistent with the stylized fact of random walk exchange rates), the coefficient should be zero.

The point estimate is significant and positive, which is indicative of bandwagon effects. At the end of a month when the currency has depreciated at a rate of 1 per cent, the expectation is for a further depreciation over the next 5 years at a rate of about 0.05 per cent. (All variables are at annualized rates.[16]) However the standard errors are sufficiently large to make these estimates statistically insignificant, except when the intercept is unconstrained. Moreover, this point estimate seems to be driven by the inclusion of the three currencies that during the sample period were coming off of very high inflation rates – Argentina, Brazil and Mexico. Omitting these observations leads to a negative estimate. Slightly more evidence for bandwagon effects is found when using 3-month-lagged depreciation. However the significance of these findings is again not robust to the omission of the high-inflation currencies.

Another possible expectations-formation scheme is adaptive. We model adaptive expectations according to the following equation:

$$\Delta \hat{s}^{e}_{t,t+60} = \alpha_5 + \beta_5 (\hat{s}^{e}_{t-12,t} - s_t) + u_{5,t}. \tag{8}$$

Table 9.4b Adaptive expectations in long horizon forecasts (February 1988 to June 1994)

$$\Delta\hat{s}^e_{t,t+60} = \alpha_5 + \beta_5(\hat{s}^e_{t-12,t} - s_t) + u_{5,t} \tag{8}$$

Term (k)	*12-month forecast error*		
	Constrained		*No ABM*
OLS β_5	−0.100	−0.091	−0.090[b]
SE	(0.102)	(0.086)	(0.040)
d.f.	132	120	103
$\bar{R}^2$	0.27	0.45	0.48

Notes: 'constrained' indicates that all the exchange rates are constrained to have the same intercept term; 'No ABM' indicates Argentine, Brazilian, and Mexican observations omitted. OLS β is the point estimate from the OLS regression. SE is the OLS standard error, assuming *T*/3 observations. *t* is the absolute value of the *t*-statistic using the OLS point estimate and adjusted standard error. a, b and c indicate significance at 10%, 5% and 1% level for the null hypothesis of zero coefficient.

The results of running this regression, using 12-month expectations, are reported in Table 9.4b. Surprisingly, regardless of the specification, the estimated coefficient is *negative*. A negative coefficient implies that agents heavily discount year-old forecasts of the current exchange rate in forming their expectations regarding the exchange rate 5 years hence, and rely instead on the most recent spot rate. Once again, much of the result appears driven by the inclusion of the high-inflation currencies. Nonetheless, the estimate is statistically negative even in the low-inflation sample (although it too is economically small).

These two sets of results suggest that even for horizons far in the future, expectations may not be stabilizing. Rather, it appears that agents place a great deal of weight on the current spot rate in formulating their expectations regarding even the very remote future. One cannot make strong conclusions regarding the stabilizing attributes of expectations, however, without regard to some sort of fundamentals.

Regressive expectations

In certain cases, regressive expectations may be the same as rational expectations, as in Dornbusch (1976). A reasonable interpretation of regressive expectations is:

$$\Delta s^e_{t,t+k} = -\upsilon(s_t - \bar{s}_t), \tag{9}$$

where the over-bar indicates the long-run equilibrium value. One can investigate whether the long-run value of the nominal exchange rate is constant, or whether it varies with price levels according to PPP. This suggests two regressions:

$$\Delta\hat{s}^{e}_{t,t+60} = \alpha_6 + \beta_6 s_t + u_{6,t}; \tag{10}$$

and

$$\Delta\hat{s}^{e}_{t,t+60} = \alpha_7 + \beta_7(s_t - \bar{s}_t) + u_{7,t}, \tag{11}$$

where $\bar{s}_t \equiv \log(\text{CPI}^{\ell}_t/\text{CPI}^{\text{US}}_t)$, for the case of a constant long-run real exchange rate. (The currency dummies pick up the base-year effects.) In both cases, the slope coefficient should be negative under the hypothesis that the exchange rate is expected to regress back toward equilibrium. Note that if inflation rates are always the same in the two countries, then $\beta_6 = \beta_7$.

The results of these regressions are reported in Table 9.4c. The estimates of the slope coefficient in Equation (10) are positive, but the standard errors are sufficiently large that the 90 per cent confidence bounds easily encompass negative values.

The assumption of a constant long-run nominal exchange rate is implausible for currencies experiencing very different price trends. The regression for Equation (11) over the entire sample, allowing for a long-run exchange rate moving with PPP, yields a negative, but statistically insignificant estimate of -0.029.

Some of the currencies included in this sample experienced fairly rapid inflation. As Frankel (1979) points out, in the presence of secular inflation, Equation (9) is no longer appropriate, and should be rewritten as:

$$\Delta\hat{s}^{e}_{t,t+k} = -\upsilon(s_t - \bar{s}_t) + \pi^{\ell}_t - \pi^{\text{US}}_t, \tag{12}$$

where the inflation rates are the expected rates over the next 5 years. In the absence of expectations data regarding inflation rates, we proxy them by using 3-month and 12-month lagged *ex post* inflation. Re-estimating Equation (11) over the same sample, allowing for inflation differentials:

$$\Delta\hat{s}^{e}_{t,t+60} = \alpha_7 + \beta_7(s_t - \bar{s}_t) + \gamma_7(\pi^{\ell}_t - \pi^{\text{US}}_t) + u_{7,t} \tag{13}$$

produces a slightly more negative point estimate, but results that are still not statistically significant. (Results using 3-month inflation rates are reported in Table 9.4c, but the results using 12-month rates do not differ substantially.)

This particular specification relies upon PPP holding in the long run. If the PPP condition fails to hold even in the long run, perhaps due to the presence of non-tradables and differential productivity growth rates, then one might expect a better fit for a sample that excludes currencies associated with Asian countries that are thought to have experienced high productivity growth. We report results for a sample including only the European currencies, in the

Table 9.4c Regressive expectations in long horizon forecasts (February 1988 to June 1994)

Term (k)	*Constant LR exchange rate*	*PPP varying long run exchange rate*		
	No ABM	*No ABM*	*No ABM*	*Europe*
OLS β_6	0.0098			
SE	(0.045)			
OLS β_7		−0.0126	−0.0285	−0.0590
SE		(0.037)	(0.044)	(0.046)
OLS $\hat{\gamma}_7$			0.124[c]	−0.006
			(0.054)	(0.063)
d.f.	120	110	100	64
SER	2.762	3.111	2.758	2.078
$\bar{R}^2$	0.52	−0.01	0.04	−0.01

Notes: Regression estimates from equations 10, 11 and 13. In this table, depreciation rates are expressed in decimal form (i.e., 10% is 0.10) so that coefficients are interpretable as elasticities. SE is the OLS standard error. t is the absolute value of the t-statistic using the OLS point estimate and adjusted standard error. a, b and c indicate significance at 10%, 5% and 1% level for the null hypothesis of zero coefficient. In regressions involving PPP, the following currencies were omitted: IRE, SFR, AUS and BOL.

right-most column of Table 9.4c. In this sample, we do obtain an economically significant negative-coefficient estimate, as hypothesized (although statistically significant only at the 20 per cent significance level). The point estimate, −0.059, implies that if the currency today is overvalued by 10 per cent according to the PPP criterion, market participants expect it to depreciate at an annual rate of 0.59 per cent over the next 5 years, or 3.0 per cent cumulatively, a plausible estimate.

Survey data and structural models of exchange rates

One of the most resilient stylized facts of international finance is the failure of structural models of exchange rate determination to fit the data well, particularly out of sample (e.g. Meese and Rogoff, 1983). Instead of looking to new econometric techniques to gain insight into exchange rate dynamics, we investigate here whether including a time-varying risk premium, as measured by the survey data, improves in-sample fit.

Assume in a conventional monetary model (perhaps with sticky prices) covered interest parity holds as usual,

$$i^{\ell}_{t,t+k} - i^{\text{US}}_{t,t+k} = f_{t,t+k} - s^{e}_{t,t+k},$$

but the uncovered interest parity condition is modified by the addition of a risk premium:

$$i^{\ell}_{t,t+k} - i^{\text{US}}_{t,t+k} - \Delta s^{e}_{t,t+k} = rp_t.$$

This leads to an expression for the exchange rate of the form:

$$s_t = \gamma_0 + \gamma_1 \hat{m}_t + \gamma_2 \hat{y}_t + \gamma_3 \hat{i}_t + \gamma_4 \hat{\pi}_t + \gamma_5 rp_t, \tag{14}$$

where $rp_t \equiv f_{t,t+k} - \hat{s}^e_{t,t+k}$, where the carats '∧' indicate relative differences (local minus US). The coefficients on money and inflation should be positive, and those on income and interest rates negative. The coefficient on the risk premium should be positive, and equal in magnitude to the negative of the interest rate coefficient.[17]

Monthly data on money (M1), income (industrial production), interest rates (usually interbank), and 3-month CPI inflation rates were drawn from the IMF's *International Financial Statistics* database. All these macroeconomic series are seasonally adjusted. The risk premium was calculated using the forward rate and survey data on expectations at the 3- and 12-month horizon, used in the previous analyses. Of course, we do not observe the true risk premium, merely the risk premium implied by the survey data.

The regressions were run on the pooled time-series/cross-section for the period April 1988 to June 1994. Some currencies were omitted, either because they lacked forward markets or because certain macro-data were unavailable. In total, thirteen of the possible seventeen currencies were included in the regressions.

The results of estimating Equation (14) in first differences are reported in Table 9.5.[18] In the first column are the estimates for the standard specification, without country dummies. The proportion of variance explained is very low, and only income shows up significantly, and in the correct direction. In the second

Table 9.5 Structural models of the exchange rate (April 1988 to June 1994)

Coefficient	[*1*]	[2]	[*3*]	[*4*]
m	−0.0019	−0.0011	−0.0005	0.0006
	(0.020)	(0.025)	(0.025)	(0.025)
y	−0.0662[a]	−0.0653[a]	−0.0818[b]	−0.0789[a]
	(0.039)	(0.039)	(0.042)	(0.042)
i	0.0088	0.0091	0.0244	0.0127
(×100)	(0.034)	(0.034)	(0.035)	(0.035)
π	0.0058	0.0595	0.0709	0.0763
(×100)	(0.049)	(0.050)	(0.052)	(0.052)
$rp3$			−0.0717[c]	
(×100)			(0.017)	
$rp12$				−0.0528
(×100)				(0.038)
Currency dummies	No	Yes	Yes	Yes
d.f.	903	881	823	825
$\bar{R}^2$	0.00	−0.01	0.01	−0.01
DW	1.789	1.799	1.879	1.829

Notes: Estimates from first difference regressions. OLS standard errors in parentheses. Interest and inflation rate, risk premia coefficients multiplied by 100. Currencies covered: DMK, FFR, DKR, UKM, NTH, SKR, BFR, LIR, NKR, SPN, YEN, SAF, CAN. a, b and c indicate significance at 10%, 5% and 1% level for the null hypothesis of zero coefficient.

column, each currency is allowed a separate intercept, with no appreciable change in the results. In the next column, the 3-month risk premium is included. It enters in negatively and with statistical significance. The 12-month risk premium is included in the last column, and enters without statistical significance. The results using long-term interest rates instead of short term are not appreciably different.

The sign on the risk premium (or, equivalently, on expected depreciation) is the opposite from that hypothesized. It is possible that the problem is simultaneity bias; after all, in the section on 'Long horizon forecasts' we estimated equations in which expectations depended on the spot rate rather than the other way around. Further research could use news reports of central-bank intervention as an instrumental variable. For the time being, we must conclude that our approach to entering expectations as an explanatory factor is no more encouraging than other typical equations of exchange rate determination.

Conclusions

We have applied a comprehensive data set, consisting of forecasts for twenty-four currencies against the dollar, to four topics: (1) the ability to predict the spot rate, (2) evidence of a time-varying risk premium, (3) the formation of expectations, and (4) exchange rate determination.

On the first topic, we have found some predictive power in the survey data (and in the right direction!).[19] As in past tests, the forecasts are nevertheless biased: variability of expected depreciation is excessive (in the sense of Bilson, 1981), especially at the 3-month horizon.

On the second topic, we have found some evidence of time-varying risk premium,[20] especially at the 12-month horizon. But the coefficient on the forward discount is usually significantly greater than 1/2, implying that the $\text{var}(rp) < \text{var}(\Delta s^e)$.[21]

On the third topic, we examined new data on forecasts at the 5-year horizon, and found weak evidence of regressive expectations. The estimate implies that if a European currency today is overvalued by 10 per cent according to the PPP criterion, market participants expect it to depreciate 3 per cent cumulatively over the next 5 years. The result is consistent with past findings that, as the horizon lengthens from 1 week to 3 months to 1 year, expectations become increasingly regressive.[22]

On the fourth topic, we have so far had no more success than anyone else. Simultaneity is a likely culprit.

Acknowledgements

We thank Data Resources, Inc. for providing exchange rate data. James Hirakawa provided assistance in collecting data. We acknowledge the financial support of UCSC faculty research funds. An early version of this paper was presented at the 1995 American Economics Association meetings.

Data appendix

Currency Forecasters' Digest (*CFD*) is published monthly. The publication indicates that the forecasts apply to a specific date, usually either the third or fourth Thursday in the month. The forecasts include 1, 3, 6 and 12-month horizon forecasts, with the following measures: Geometric mean, arithmetic mean and modal mean. Contemporaneously dated spot-rate data are also provided. All rates are converted to domestic currency units per US dollar.

The following currencies are surveyed:

Mnemonic	*Currency*	*FR*	*A*	*T/I*	*E*
DM	West German DM	F			E
FFR	French Franc	F			E
DKR	Danish Krone	F			E
UK	UK Pound Sterling	F			E
NTH	Netherlands Guilder	F			E
SFR	Swiss Franc	F			
SKR	Swedish Krone	F			
IRE	Irish Punt	F			E
BFR	Belgian Franc	F			E
LIR	Italian Lire	F			E
NKR	Norwegian Krone	F			
SP	Spanish Peseta	F			
YEN	Japanese Yen	F			
TAI	Taiwanese Dollar				
AUS	Australian Dollar	F			
SNG	Singapore Dollar	F	A		
PHL	Philippine Peso		A		
KOR	Korean Won				
SAR	South African Rand	F	A		
CAN	Canadian Dollar	F			
ARG	Argentine Austral			I	
MEX	Mexican Peso			I	
CHL	Chilean Peso			T	
BRZ	Brazilian Cruzeiro/ado			I	
BOL	Venezuelan Bolivar		A		

Key: F: Forward rate available; A: Alternating monthly; T: series terminates before June 1994; I: Many missing values due to currency change; E: EMS currency categorization, for this paper.

Forward rates are the arithmetic average of bid and ask rates at London close, as reported by DRIFACS.

To minimize the number of missing observations, a recursive Chow-Lin (1976) procedure for interpolation was used for the expectations series. The missing observations are November 1989, February 1990 and April 1990. The related series used in the interpolation procedure is the contemporaneous (log) spot rate.

Appendix

Table 9.A1 Tests of bias in survey expectations (February 1988 to June 1994)

Exch. rate	*Term (k)*	*Const.*	β_1	$\bar{R}^2$	*SER*	*DW*	*d.f.*
DMK	3	−0.989	−0.307	0.01	24.679	0.553	75
		[5.261]	[0.384]				
DMK	12	−1.231	−0.043	−0.01	10.318	0.238	67
		[4.400]	[0.461]				
FFR	3	−0.459	−0.222	−0.00	24.202	0.508	75
		[5.703]	[0.415]				
FFR	12	−0.063	−0.184	−0.01	11.002	0.213	67
		[5.416]	[0.554]				
DKR	3	−0.387	−0.226	−0.00	25.054	0.513	75
		[5.751]	[0.438]				
DKR	12	−0.086	−0.156	−0.01	11.636	0.211	67
		[5.562]	[0.545]				
UK	3	3.478	−0.309	0.00	27.455	0.613	75
		[5.367]	[0.348]				
UK	12	3.885	−0.198	−0.01	11.657	0.257	67
		[2.341]	[0.556]				
NTH	3	−0.872	−0.287	−0.01	24.842	0.548	75
		[5.391]	[0.401]				
NTH	12	−1.297	−0.041	−0.01	10.355	0.238	67
		[4.390]	[0.449]				
SFR	3	−0.104	−0.497	0.03	26.881	0.542	75
		[5.723]	[0.437]				
SFR	12	1.074	−0.429	0.02	12.091	0.226	67
		[5.749]	[0.540]				
SKR	3	3.448	0.0346	−0.01	29.463	0.465	75
		[5.760]	[0.321]				
SKR	12	0.795	0.544	0.03	14.192	0.173	67
		[2.554]	[0.506]				
IRE	3	−0.258	0.105	−0.03	21.870	0.460	75
		[5.552]	[0.385]				
IRE	12	−0.583	0.132	−0.01	12.286	0.182	69
		[6.444]	[0.411]				
BFR	3	−1.262	−0.125	−0.01	25.371	0.514	75
		[5.657]	[0.402]				
BFR	12	−0.532	−0.159	−0.01	11.310	0.219	69
		[5.248]	[0.526]				
LIR	3	2.503	0.125	−0.01	28.335	0.550	75
		[5.828]	[0.417]				
LIR	12	−0.471	0.529	0.02	13.254	0.185	67
		[4.475]	[0.686]				
NKR	3	2.162	−0.055	−0.01	24.330	0.581	66
		[5.189]	[0.253]				
NKR	12	0.930	0.159	−0.01	10.243	0.250	62
		[3.013]	[0.354]				
SP	3	1.158	0.107	−0.01	27.481	0.568	75
		[5.450]	[0.384]				
SP	12	−0.721	0.604	0.04	13.901	0.197	67
		[3.792]	[0.461]				

(Continued)

Table 9.A1 (Continued)

Exch. rate	*Term (k)*	*Const.*	β_1	$\bar{R}^2$	*SER*	*DW*	*d.f.*
YEN	12	0.367	−1.352	0.39	7.475	0.610	67
		[3.090]	[0.269]				
TAI	3	−2.184	−0.070	−0.01	9.837	0.578	54
		[2.341]	[0.229]				
TAI	12	−2.537	−0.239	0.07	5.829	0.153	52
		[1.786]	[0.181]				
AUS	3	1.443	−0.270	−0.00	18.612	0.621	75
		[4.636]	[0.473]				
AUS	12	0.720	0.411	0.07	6.435	0.311	67
		[2.183]	[0.264]				
SNG	3	−4.543	0.000	−0.03	8.344	1.340	36
		[1.988]	[0.353]				
SNG	12	−4.369	0.050	−0.03	2.804	0.554	32
		[0.589]	[0.257]				
PHL	3	6.058	−0.259	−0.02	17.070	1.014	37
		[4.050]	[0.320]				
PHL	12	12.983	−1.058	0.17	8.350	0.641	33
		[4.314]	[0.332]				
KOR	3	1.882	0.493	0.22	6.198	0.348	66
		[1.298]	[0.217]				
KOR	12	2.751	0.341	0.23	4.191	0.084	62
		[1.230]	[0.181]				
SAF	3	15.554	−1.111	0.18	16.459	1.227	50
		[4.227]	[0.373]				
SAF	12	15.375	−1.534	0.29	6.185	0.781	47
		[1.719]	[0.128]				
CAN	3	1.160	0.005	−0.01	8.818	0.765	75
		[1.638]	[0.457]				
CAN	12	1.833	0.042	−0.01	4.796	0.167	69
		[2.377]	[0.598]				
ARG	3	44.730	0.628	0.18	203.529	0.354	69
		[37.446]	[0.327]				
ARG	12	55.975	0.912	0.17	149.843	0.074	51
		[74.193]	[0.682]				
MEX	3	5.194	0.065	0.04	7.107	0.446	69
		[1.636]	[0.051]				
MEX	12	4.966	0.091	0.19	4.215	0.129	51
		[1.914]	[0.046]				
BRZ	3	129.752	0.423	0.38	87.301	0.900	63
		[32.745]	[0.086]				
BRZ	12	91.164	1.061	0.61	40.601	0.431	40
		[23.321]	[0.064]				
BOL	3	26.344	−0.330	−0.01	23.800	0.772	34
		[10.205]	[0.290]				
BOL	12	20.155	0.019	−0.02	10.202	0.272	44
		[4.934]	[0.116]				

Notes: Term (k) is the forecast horizon in months. Figures in brackets [.] are Newey-West robust standard errors, using equal-weight windows for lag length k-1. a, b and c denote significance at 10%, 5% and 1% levels.

Table 9.A2 Bias in the forward discount (February 1988 to June 1994)

$$\Delta s_{t+k} = \alpha_2 + \beta_2 fd_{t,t+k} + u_{2,t} \tag{2}$$

Exch. rate	*Term (k)*	*Const.*	β_2	$\bar{R}^2$	*SER*	*DW*	*d.f.*
DMK	3	−1.445	−0.221	−0.01	24.944	0.544	75
		[5.150]	[1.393]				
DMK	12	−1.939	0.514	0.01	10.205	0.240	67
		[2.916]	[0.902]				
FFR	3	−2.411	0.364	−0.01	24.302	0.502	75
		[6.008]	[1.207]				
FFR	12	−5.399	1.733	0.10	10.413	0.238	67
		[4.065]	[0.912]				
DKR	3	−3.736	0.695	−0.00	25.062	0.513	75
		[6.881]	[1.074]				
DKR	12	−5.793	1.623	0.09	11.028	0.239	67
		[4.109]	[0.670]				
UKM	3	1.712	0.164	−0.01	27.674	0.608	75
		[7.349]	[2.457]				
UKM	12	1.515	0.276	−0.01	11.688	0.254	67
		[7.498]	[2.526]				
NTH	3	−1.226	−0.236	−0.01	25.072	0.538	75
		[5.474]	[1.563]				
NTH	12	−1.911	0.360	−0.01	1.622	0.239	67
		[3.060]	[0.914]				
SFR	3	−1.199	0.019	−0.01	27.480	0.528	75
		[5.516]	[1.512]				
SFR	12	−1.286	0.029	−0.01	12.275	0.218	67
		[3.205]	[0.828]				
SKR	3	−20.890	4.803	0.17	26.640	0.563	75
		[12.333]	[2.883]				
SKR	12	−14.724	4.416	0.40	11.204	0.290	67
		[6.107]	[1.373]				
IRE	3	−4.235	1.273	0.02	24.978	0.560	75
		[6.285]	[1.139]				
IRE	12	−4.831	1.700	0.13	11.422	0.229	67
		[4.437]	[0.954]				
BFR	3	−0.060	−0.324	−0.01	25.497	0.519	73
		[7.506]	[1.625]				
BFR	12	−4.394	1.379	0.05	11.087	0.221	65
		[4.556]	[1.337]				
LIR	3	−17.825	3.743	0.18	25.545	0.684	75
		[8.107]	[1.480]				
LIR	12	−13.773	3.488	0.39	10.417	0.373	67
		[3.989]	[0.667]				
NKR	3	−2.281	0.811	0.03	23.918	0.525	66
		[5.085]	[0.368]				
NKR	12	−5.990	1.923	0.17	9.355	0.394	62
		[4.662]	[1.183]				
SPN	3	−22.712	3.673	0.21	24.265	0.589	75
		[9.039]	[1.133]				
SPN	12	−19.438	3.777	0.35	11.433	0.310	67
		[8.677]	[1.331]				

Table 9.A2 (Continued)

Exch. rate	*Term (k)*	*Const.*	β_1	$\bar{R}^2$	*SER*	*DW*	*d.f.*
YEN	3	−6.967 [4.166]	−2.905 [1.608]	0.07	20.813	0.652	75
YEN	12	−8.978 [2.367]	−4.016 [0.940]	0.59	6.121	0.515	67
AUS	3	−1.199 [6.245]	0.333 [1.175]	−0.01	18.677	0.621	75
AUS	12	2.993 [5.888]	−0.260 [1.025]	−0.01	6.694	0.294	67
SNG	3	−6.916 [2.100]	−1.425 [0.835]	0.06	8.496	0.710	48
SNG	12	−4.598 [2.290]	0.113 [0.848]	−0.02	3.214	0.296	48
SAF	3	23.519 [9.229]	−2.042 [0.923]	0.13	16.931	0.710	53
SAF	12	16.409 [3.728]	−1.437 [0.556]	0.12	6.734	0.321	69
CAN	3	6.057 [3.648]	−1.856 [0.960]	0.06	8.473	0.711	75
CAN	12	3.392 [5.535]	−0.626 [1.726]	−0.00	4.768	0.158	67

Notes: SER is standard error of regression. DW is Durbin–Watson statistic. d.f. is number of degrees of freedom. Figures in the parentheses are standard errors.

Table 9.A3 Test for time-varying risk premium (February 1988 to June 1994)

$$\Delta\hat{s}^{e}_{t,t+k} = \alpha_3 + \beta_3 fd_{t,t+k} + u_{3,t} \qquad (3)$$

Exch. rate	*Term (k)*	*Const.*	β_3	$\bar{R}^2$	*SER*	*DW*	*d.f.*
DM	3	−0.966 [1.920]	2.581 [0.420]	0.51	8.356	0.663	75
DM	12	4.476 [0.881]	1.166 [0.270]	0.45	3.595	0.686	75
FFR	3	−1.830 [2.608]	2.133 [0.645]	0.33	9.025	0.964	75
FFR	12	4.142 [1.169]	1.100 [0.303]	0.27	3.620	0.795	75
DKR	3	−3.749 [2.375]	1.939 [0.337]	0.36	8.603	0.787	75
DKR	12	3.524 [1.295]	1.049 [0.308]	0.27	3.807	0.715	75
UKM	3	5.469 [4.579]	−0.469 [0.985]	−0.00	11.262	0.323	75
UKM	12	3.086 [1.888]	1.042 [0.434]	0.15	4.180	0.514	75
NTH	3	−1.637 [2.070]	2.7082 [0.468]	0.47	8.782	0.735	75

(Continued)

Table 9.A3 (Continued)

Exch. rate	*Term (k)*	*Const.*	β_1	$\bar{R}^2$	*SER*	*DW*	*d.f.*
NTH	12	4.342 [0.894]	1.121 [0.264]	0.39	3.717	0.7303	75
SFR	3	1.099 [1.950]	1.871 [0.421]	0.35	9.195	0.736	75
SFR	12	5.434 [0.698]	0.910 [0.232]	0.35	3.758	1.036	75
SKR	3	−6.783 [5.093]	2.013 [0.860]	0.18	11.039	0.542	75
SKR	12	0.720 [2.760]	1.347 [0.520]	0.25	4.719	0.469	75
IRE	3	−4.296 [2.571]	2.445 [0.500]	0.43	10.312	0.834	75
IRE	12	3.145 [1.334]	1.208 [0.271]	0.35	4.158	0.908	75
BFR	3	−6.853 [2.985]	3.071 [0.774]	0.46	8.538	1.124	73
BFR	12	3.706 [1.035]	1.442 [0.283]	0.37	3.591	0.843	73
LIR	3	−5.373 [3.487]	1.921 [0.487]	0.34	8.717	0.767	75
LIR	12	3.155 [1.715]	0.920 [0.257]	0.25	3.725	0.720	75
NKR	3	−5.238 [3.118]	1.404 [0.213]	0.41	11.049	0.581	66
NKR	12	0.719 [2.247]	1.267 [0.422]	0.24	5.073	0.535	66
SPN	3	−8.904 [3.958]	1.758 [0.442]	0.23	11.063	0.632	75
SPN	12	−0.389 [2.681]	1.049 [0.365]	0.18	4.970	0.693	75
YEN	3	0.641 [1.985]	1.946 [0.759]	0.18	8.866	0.796	75
YEN	12	4.915 [0.808]	1.072 [0.439]	0.18	3.912	0.618	75
AUS	3	−1.450 [2.425]	1.430 [0.401]	0.30	5.478	0.854	75
AUS	12	−4.454 [1.410]	1.769 [0.292]	0.64	2.887	0.605	75
SNG	3	4.398 [0.777]	1.743 [0.370]	0.43	3.534	1.234	32
SNG	12	3.856 [0.527]	1.220 [0.309]	0.50	1.658	0.812	32
SAF	3	1.268 [3.130]	0.690 [0.357]	0.09	6.919	1.461	50
SAF	12	4.400 [1.704]	0.204 [0.235]	0.00	2.554	0.883	51
CAN	3	−1.423 [1.289]	0.750 [0.426]	0.07	3.222	0.853	75
CAN	12	−2.079 [1.332]	1.300 [0.513]	0.21	2.235	0.347	75

Notes: SER is standard error of regression. DW is Durbin–Watson statistic. d.f. is number of degrees of freedom. Figures in the parentheses are standard errors.

Notes

1 Early contributions were Dominguez (1986), Frankel and Froot (1987), and Froot and Frankel (1989). Takagi (1991) reviewed the early literature.
2 As was also evident in Chinn and Frankel (1994), and Frankel and Chinn (1993).
3 This is an updating results that we obtained using the *CFD* data set described in Chinn and Frankel (1994) and Frankel and Chinn (1993).
4 These data are proprietary with *CFD* (acquired by the *Financial Times Group* of Alexandria, VA, toward the end of the data set) and obtained by subscription by the Institute for International Economics. The survey has apparently been conducted for some years, but the subscription of the IIE did not begin until 1988.
5 The *CFD* originally described the consensus forecast as the harmonic mean. Later publications identified the consensus forecast as the geometric mean. The mode and mean responses are available, but they are very highly correlated with the geometric mean, so that the choice of measure is less likely to make much difference.
6 We also ran regressions on individual time series (reported in the Appendix Tables 9.A1–3). The results are consistent in a qualitative sense with those reported in the text, although there is much variation in the estimated slope coefficients, as one would expect from the relatively small number of observations in each time series.
7 The robust standard errors take into account the moving-average serial correlation induced by overlapping horizons, but do not adjust for cross-currency correlation. In tests on the entire sample, regression residuals do not exhibit substantial cross-currency correlation. (The correlation for regression (1) residuals is about 0.13.)
8 Attempts to address this problem by application of two-stage least squares, using lagged values of expected depreciation as instrumental variables, usually reinforce the results obtained above. When two-stage least squares is applied to a regression of *ex post* depreciation on expected depreciation, the coefficients become even more negative. Because the standard errors become larger, however, rejection of the null hypothesis of unity becomes more difficult.
9 Flood and Rose (1994) also find that the forward discount puzzle does not hold for EMS currencies. In other words, the forward rate correctly predicts the direction of change in the spot rate in these cases.
10 The peso problem is usually invoked (often *ex post*) to explain forecasts of changes in the exchange rate that did not materialize, or materialized to a smaller extent than forecast. The crude explanation is that 'the feared devaluation did not happen to occur during the sample period.' More correctly, the non-normality of the distribution produces biased standard errors by which to evaluate the significance. If peso problems abound, however, *some* studies should catch a sample period when the devaluation *did* happen to occur, and thus when the change in the exchange rate materialized to a greater extent than forecast. This appears to describe the European currencies in our sample.
11 Not reported in the tables. The estimated coefficient changes from −2.7 to −0.5 for Germany, and from −2.2 to 1.2 for the United Kingdom. For France and Italy, there was less bias in the 1970s and 1980s to begin with. The tests use the 3-month offshore-interest differential and heteroskedasticity-consistent standard errors. But the data are quarterly, so the standard errors are fairly large (2.1 and 1.7 for Germany; 0.9 and 1.2 for the UK).
12 Results of these regressions report GMM standard errors since there is some evidence of serial correlation. Although the correlation is not due to overlapping observations, empirically, the assumption of MA(2) errors in calculating robust standard errors appears adequate. The assumption of higher-order MAs yielded similar estimates of the standard errors.
13 The same is true for most of the currencies considered individually (Appendix Table 9.A3), despite the much-reduced degrees of freedom.

14 This can be considered a more powerful test of the no-risk-premium hypothesis than the unconstrained case, because under that null hypothesis all intercept terms are zero. The rejection is even stronger when the sample is restricted to non-European currencies.
15 When the European currencies are excluded, the coefficient is very close to 1, suggesting no time-varying risk premium, in line with the results from the narrower five-currency sample of Froot and Frankel (1989).
16 In absolute terms, the estimated effect of a 1 per cent depreciation is an expected cumulative 3 per cent further depreciation [$=0.05 \times 5 \times 12$].
17 This equation was derived and tested, for example, as a synthesis of the monetary and portfolio-balance models (Equation 25), in Frankel (1983).
18 The regressions are implemented in first differences because the levels regressions exhibited extreme serial correlation.
19 Results in Chinn and Frankel (1994, p. 762) show some predictive power, but usually in the wrong direction (especially if Argentina, Brazil, and Mexico are excluded).
20 As in Frankel and Chinn (1993).
21 As in Froot and Frankel (1989).
22 E.g., Frankel and Froot (1987).

References

Bilson, J. (1981) 'The speculative efficiency hypothesis', *Journal of Business* 54(3), 435–51.

Chinn, M. and Frankel, J. (1994) 'Patterns in exchange rates for 25 currencies', *Journal of Money, Credit and Banking* 26(4), 759–70.

Chow, G. and Lin, A.-L. (1976) 'Best linear unbiased estimation of missing observations in an economic time series', *Journal of the American Statistical Association* 71(355), 719–21.

Dominguez, K. (1986) 'Are foreign exchange forecasts rational? New evidence from survey data?' *Economics Letters* 21(3), 277–82.

Dornbusch, R. (1976) 'Expectations and exchange rate dynamics', *Journal of Political Economy* 84(6), 1161–76.

Fama, E. (1984) 'Forward and spot exchange rates', *Journal of Monetary Economics* 14(3), 319–38.

Flood, R. and Rose, A. (1994) 'Fixes: of the forward discount puzzle', *NBER Working Paper* 4928 (November).

Frankel, J. (1983) 'Monetary and portfolio-balance models of exchange rate determination', J. Bhandari and B. Putnam (eds) *Economic Interdependence and Flexible Exchange Rates*, Cambridge MA: MIT Press, (Revised in *On Exchange Rates*, J. Frankel, Cambridge, MA: MIT Press, 1993.)

Frankel, J. (1979) 'On the Mark: a theory of floating exchange rates based on real interest differentials', *American Economic Review* 69(4), 601–22.

Frankel, J. and Chinn, M. (1993) 'Exchange rate expectations and the risk premium: tests for a cross section of 17 currencies', *Review of International Economics* 1(2), 136–44.

Frankel, J. and Froot, K. (1987) 'Using survey data to test standard propositions regarding exchange rate expectations', *American Economic Review* 77(1), 133–53. (Reprinted in J. Frankel, *On Exchange Rates*, Cambridge, MA: MIT Press, 1993.)

Froot, K. and Frankel, J. (1989) 'Forward discount bias: is it an exchange risk premium?' *Quarterly Journal of Economics* 104(1), 139–61.

Hodrick, R. J. and Srivastava, S. (1986) 'The covariation of risk premiums and expected future spot exchange rates', *Journal of International Money and Finance* 5(suppl.), S5–S22.

Meese, R. and Rogoff, K. (1983) 'Empirical exchange rates of the seventies: Do they fit out of sample?' *Journal of International Economics* 14(1–2), 3–24.

Takagi, S. (1991) 'Exchange rate expectations: a survey of survey studies', *IMF Staff Papers* 38(1) (March) 153–83.

10 Alternative monetary targets and policy transmission and adjustments

The case of Taiwan

James Ford and Katherine Hsu

Introduction

The economic performance of Taiwan since the 1960s is reflected in its high economic growth rate and low inflation. The only exception to the low inflation being a sudden jump in the rate to 20 per cent (in respect of the CPI) 1974 in the wake of the first oil crisis. The attainment simultaneously of the twin objectives of economic policy can be attributed to government economic policies, based on sound industrial strategy,[1] a tight control of wages, judicious monetary and exchange-rate policies, including only a slow introduction of promised deregulation of the monetary/financial system. These fashioned a healthy external position in respect of the balance of payments and foreign reserves which, however, put upward pressure on the domestic currency. Instead of a once-and-for-all adjustment of the exchange rate, a policy of gradual appreciation generates an expectation that the money supply will grow at an accelerated rate.[2] Thereby, such a policy can spread over into other financial markets and result in an increase in the financial transactions in the stock market (Chiu and Hou, 1992, 1995; Wenninger and Radecki, 1986; Wu and Hwung, 1990).

In fact, the growth rates of the three monetary aggregates (M1A, M1B and M2) that the Central Bank of China (CBC) publishes do tend to move together.[3] Their turning points are similar and they all show a higher-growth rate on average in the 1980s than in the 1970s and the 1990s. Yet some differences are evident. The growth rate of broad money M2 did not accelerate in the second part of the 1980s. In the same period, M1A and M1B depict a different picture; they show a noticeable acceleration to a double-digit figure of growth rate. The CPI and its inflation rate are portrayed in Figure 10.A1 of Appendix A. The level and rate of growth of GNP (in 1996 prices) are depicted in Figure 10.A2; whilst Figures 10.A3 and 10.A5 graph the nominal monetary aggregates and their rates of growth. Figure 10.A4 gives the time profile of the monetary base. The exchange rate (units of domestic currency per US dollar) and the balance of payments on the current account are graphed in Figure 10.A6. Interest rates are illustrated in Figure 10.A7.

In regard to the behaviour of the levels of the monetary variables and the stock price index we note that the correlations between them are: 0.924, 0.905 and 0.859, respectively for M1A, M1B and M2. Compared with the fluctuations of the M1B (or the M1A) growth rate, the behaviour of the M2 growth rate seems more stable and, therefore, does not produce such close movements with the stock-market index as M1A or M1B do.

This conflicting picture might make it hard for the monetary authority to decide on the right course of policy action (Hwung, 1996). Recent studies of the CBC's monetary policy favour the adoption of the broadest monetary aggregate (M2) as the intermediate target variable, to provide a link with the real sector and with inflation (Hsu, 1996; Hwung, 1996; Lin, 1996; Lin and Lee, 1989; Shih, 1994). In their empirical study of selection of an intermediate target, for instance, Shen and Wai (1993) conclude that M2 outperforms the other candidates for the monetary variable with regard to controllability by the CBC and the determination of income velocity. However, we observe that Agung and Ford (1999) show by means of cointegration and ECM modelling that the Divisia monetary aggregate dominates M2 and other narrower monetary aggregates, M1A and M1B. We will refer to that aggregate in the section on 'Data description, policy instruments and targets'.

We note now, however, that the Divisia monetary aggregate might be able to embody the financial innovation and liberalisation that the CBC and the Ministry of Finance instituted from the 1980s onwards (ostensibly such changes were meant to have been effected at an earlier date but they only became operational later than the authorities announced).[4] Such a programme could affect the behaviour of real 'money' balances and, thus, raises the difficulty of achieving the objectives of monetary policy through a measure of aggregate money that might not capture such effects, such as the simple sum monetary aggregates, M1A, M1B and M2. Those monetary aggregates are based on the implicit assumption that all their constituents are perfect substitutes for each other: in effect, they are 'money' as is the 'cash in circulation with the public' which is the core element of every monetary aggregate. The Divisia monetary aggregate permits the degree of substitution to vary across the potential components of the aggregate.

Our empirical study concerns the three ingredients of monetary policy: final targets, or objectives; intermediate targets; and direct targets or policy instruments. It considers, therefore, the variables that seems as though they can be included in each class; the interdependency between these three classes of variables; the impact of innovations to each of the variables in each category on all other variables; by implication, the effect of the economic system to innovations in policy instruments; and the role of different monetary aggregates as intermediate targets.

The rest of the paper is organised as follows: the section on 'Empirical methodology' covers some elemental, even if elementary and familiar, observations about the autoregression methodology that forms the basis of our empirical enquiry into central bank's policy reaction function and the impact of monetary policy. Vector autoregressions (VARs) provide a means of making minimal theoretical demands on the structure of a model. Their impulse response functions permit us to trace out the responses of the endogenous variables to the shocks (innovations) mentioned above. Further, of course, the forecast-variance decomposition provides information on the contribution that each innovation makes to the subsequent variance over time of each variable in the system. The third section focuses on data description, the selection of variables in the VARs as policy instruments or targets, as well as the order of integration of the variables. The fourth section comments further on the policy transmission process and presents our findings.

Empirical methodology

One obvious means of conducting a comprehensive evaluation of monetary policy is to construct a large-scale econometric of the economic-financial system, and to accommodate within it, policy targets, instruments and potential reaction functions. However, such a construct requires large resources, especially of time and of data. Ultimately, such paradigms can suffer from being over-elaborate and too disaggregated. It has been argued that the methodology of estimating a set of structural equations at a time and then aggregating all equations to construct overall macroeconomic forecasts seems unreasonable in the sense of ignoring the feedback effects between variables under consideration (Sims, 1980, 1986, 1992). This 'dilemma' is usually resolved in the area of policy debate by adopting Sims' view and utilising as standard an n-variable semi-structural vector autoregression (VAR) of order p, so that each equation contains p lags of all n variables in the system:

$$By_t = A_1 y_{t-1} + A_2 y_{t-2} + \cdots + A_p y_{t-p} + \eta_t = \sum_{i=1}^{p} A_i L^i y_t + \eta_t \tag{1}$$

here y_i is an $n \times 1$ vector of endogenous variables; the matrices A_i being conformable with the y-vector; L^i is the lag operator; and p, of course, defines the order of the VAR. We can, naturally, convert this equation into a structural VAR in the true sense by adding a vector of exogenous variables and their associated coefficients' matrix to the right-hand side. We have written the VAR in the level of the variables; in essence, we know that in the VAR the variables should be stationary, so that if they are not and are I(1) for example, they should be entered in first differences. We come to that issue shortly.

The VAR (in whatever form the variables are entered) will be estimated in its reduced form:

$$y_t = K(\boldsymbol{L})y_t + \epsilon_t; \quad K(\boldsymbol{L}) = \sum_{i=1}^{p} K_i L^i = \sum_{i=1}^{p} B^{-1} A_i L^i; \quad \epsilon_t = B^{-1}\eta_t. \tag{2}$$

This gives the MA (moving average) representation (assuming that the process is invertible):

$$y_t = [I - K(\boldsymbol{L})]^{-1}\epsilon_t \equiv C(\boldsymbol{L})\epsilon_t. \tag{3}$$

From the estimated VAR we seek the impulse response and variance-decomposition functions for the *structural* system. Consequently, we must identify the structural disturbances, the (one standard deviation) change in which generates the impulse those functions for the structural system.

The MA representation of the structural equation, Equation (1), is

$$y_t = \left[B - \sum_{i=1}^{p} A_i L^i\right]^{-1} \eta_t \equiv \Gamma(\boldsymbol{L})\eta_t; \quad \Gamma(0) \equiv B^{-1} = K(0). \tag{4}$$

From Equation (2)

$$\epsilon_t = B^{-1}\eta_t. \tag{5}$$

The identification of η_t and its covariance matrix can be effected by uncovering the matrix B, since ϵ_t are clearly known from the estimation of the reduced-form equation. The 'orthodox' fashion in which this is accomplished is that of Sims (1980) who decomposes the covariance matrix of the reduced form residuals invoking the Cholesky decomposition; on the assumption that the covariance matrix of the structural disturbances is diagonal, and which is taken to be an identity matrix. Thus, to repeat that approach, from Equation (5)

$$E(\epsilon_t\epsilon_t') = B^{-1}E[\eta_t\eta_t'](B^{-1})' = B^{-1}(B^{-1})'; \quad E(\eta_t\eta_t') = I. \tag{6}$$

The matrix B^{-1} is the decomposition of the known reduced-form covariance matrix. However, it has to be restricted to enable us to deduce the structural disturbances because, being symmetric, the reduced-form covariance matrix is not sufficient to enable us to identify the elements of B^{-1}, providing us with $n \times (n+1)/2$ restrictions, so that $n \times (n-1)/2$ additional restrictions are required to identify B^{-1}. Those additional restrictions are obtained by assuming that the latter matrix is the Cholesky decomposition of the reduced-form covariance matrix.[5]

That decomposition, since it is lower triangular (with the standard deviations of the reduced-form residuals on its leading diagonal), means that the reduced-form residuals follow a Wold causal chain. A *ceteris paribus* unit (one standard deviation) change in the innovation in a variable affects its own variables and those subsequent to it in the ordering. It is clear then, that the ordering of the variables can be important. A rule-of-thumb that is frequently applied is that if the correlation between the reduced-form errors is less than 0.20 in absolute value, the ordering does not matter. Using economic intuition as an alternative to determining the order of the variables, the argument is that if, for example, one of the variables is a policy variable, then that variable should be placed first if we can assume that there is no contemporaneous feedback onto it from non-policy, for example, target, variables in the VAR. This amounts to assuming that the policy decisions are made without considering the simultaneous evolution of the system; and this is a plausible assumption, naturally, when current data on non-policy variables are not readily available. By contrast, if we assume that the policy variable responds to contemporaneous feedback from non-policy variables, and that there is a one-period lag of the policy shock on those variables, then we should place the policy variable last in the system (see also, Chinn and Dooley, 1997; Clarida and Gertler, 1996; Clarida *et al*., 1997, for recent work).

We refer to that issue again in our results' section. For now, we also note that as is conventional, we shall also report the variance decompositions for the variables. These, we recall, indicate the proportion of the variance in a variable after a defined period of time that is attributable to the innovations in each of the variables in the system.

It will have been noticed that we have referred above to the levels of the variables. The modern research on integration and cointegration informs us that unless variables in a regression are stationary, any such regression will be spurious, unless the variables exhibit evidence of cointegration in their I(1) format. Self-evidently, all that we had written above holds when we estimate the VAR in first difference form. However, it has been claimed, for example, by Sims (1980, and this is followed in his 1992 paper) and by Doan (1992) that even if the endogenous variables in a VAR are not stationary, the VAR should be estimated with the variables in their levels. The justification for such a view is that in running a VAR, our interest does not lie in the estimates of the coefficients, which are almost impossible to interpret anyway, but only in the predictive value of the system and its impulse-response functions therefore; and in taking first differences we are discarding potential information on the movement of the variables. The recent work on integration and cointegration informs us, of course, that we can incorporate both short-run and long-run dynamics in the VARs by running, as appropriate, VEC equations.

Accordingly, we have used both the levels of the endogenous variables and then VEC systems, since for all our systems there is evidence of cointegration. As we shall note later, all variables in our VARs are I(1). Use of the error (or equilibrium)-correction equations, however, presents its own difficulties; and needs to be the subject of further work (along lines similar to those described in note 5). Nevertheless we report the results from VECs in the section on 'Empirical results'.

Data description, policy instruments and targets

Our sample period is 1970(1)–2000(2) on a quarterly basis. In our modelling, of course, the aims of monetary policy have to be imagined. In Taiwan, they seem not to have altered over the years, embracing both internal and external objectives. In regard to internal objectives, price stability (represented here by the consumer price index, CPI) seems to have been paramount as a legacy from the problems inherited by the Nationalists after the Japanese occupation, so too does economic development in the form of economic growth (or the level of real income as used here, in the form of GNP96, being GNP in 1996 prices). The external objectives appear to have embraced the trade balance (denoted as BOPCA), the level of foreign reserves and the nominal exchange rate (FOREX here). Generally speaking, internal objectives are more important than external objectives.[6] However, though the latter cannot be ignored given the importance of the trade sector in a small open economy, we were unable to find any role for the balance of payments in our VARs.

These objectives have, of course, been pursued, indirectly if not directly as it were, by other policy initiatives other than monetary policy (or monetary and the related exchange-rate policy) which is (are) the focus of this paper. Those other policies have included industrial policy, aimed at promoting a transfer of resources from agriculture to industry and to services, as well as policies designed directly and indirectly to attract foreign direct investment. In addition, there was a wages policy until the late 1980s. Obviously, in this study we have to take those strategies as given.

In accord with the standard literature on 'targets and instruments' we suppose that the authorities have determined a set of intermediate targets, or intermediate instruments we might call them, which appear to affect directly their objectives, but which themselves cannot be controlled directly. In the case of monetary policy, our concern here, the range of such possible intermediate targets cover one measure or another of 'money' or monetary aggregate, and some one representative interest rate or a vector of interest rates. In selecting the potential set of intermediate targets, we immediately think of the monetary variables, M1A, M1B and M2, going from narrowest to broadest that the Central Bank of China calculates and publishes. One of these, or all of them, might be supposed to have a strong and 'predictable' relationship with the final policy goals of real national income and the price level.

In respect of interest rates, the central bank can quickly influence those payable on the various types of deposits in monetary institutions. A wide set of interest controls has existed over the years on rates (set as limits) including the rate of passbook savings deposits (RPSD) and rates of six-month and one-year time-deposits (RTD6 and RTD1Y).[7] The other 'price' variable that the central bank will want to influence is the exchange rate (FOREX). We have suggested above that this might be regarded as a final target variable. In addition to the conventional intermediate target variables, here we also take into account the effect of financial activities in the stock market, measured as *SP* (Hsu, 1996; Sellin, 1998).

Apart from the importance its controllability, it is suggested that the operating target be directly monitored by central bank and also to be easily observed by the private sectors with no confusion as to the intent of policy actions (McCallum 1984, 1987, 1988, 1993*a,b*, 1994*a,b*). In this regard, we have adopted the monetary base (MB) as the operating variable since it can be monitored and adjusted directly by the monetary authority; this is also partly as the consequence of extensive experimentation with a range, and indeed, a package, of direct monetary instruments in including the central bank discount rate and the required ratio on the reserve holdings of the banks.[8]

Zero-order correlations To obtain some possible (though of course only superficial) indication about the likely of our final selection of final, intermediate and direct target (instrument) of monetary policy we catalogue in Tables 10.B1–10.B3 of Appendix B the zero-order correlations in the postulated 'causal chain'. These are for the real values of the variables except for the exchange, since again after extensive experimentation, we could discern no difference between the VARs run in nominal and real terms. We did experiment with the real exchange rate but that was a problematic procedure given that the domestic price level, a constituent of the real exchange rate, was included in the systems, and given that an element of the real exchange rate, in the form of the US price level (as a surrogate for the world price level) was exogenous.

The information revealed lends support to the general view of the specification of monetary policy transmission mechanism. Let us take the objectives in the order in which they appear in Table 10.B1 (here, in Tables 10.B2 and 10.B3, and in the presentation of our results, we have appended R to the notation for each relevant variable where applicable, and we have included the three interest rates and BOPCA for illustration). The links between real income and four monetary aggregates are high with the broader aggregates just dominating, and positive. The correlation between real income and the real stock price index is substantial and also positive. As expected intuitively, the boom in the stock market is indicative of a situation where firms increase the amount of their outstanding debt in order to finance real investment, thereby raising aggregate output. The *ceteris paribus* impact of interest rates is to reduce real income probably in Keynesian fashion by putting a brake on investment spending and hence on aggregate output. Given the definition of exchange rate, a reduction of the rate means appreciation of the domestic currency against the US dollar, in reflection to the existence of negative relation between aggregate output and exchange rate.

Correlations of consumer price index with alternative-monetary aggregates, a vector of rates of interest on various types of deposits, real stock-price index and the exchange rate have the same signs but lower magnitudes as they have with real output. The rationales for the signs are identical with those offered in the case of real income. An increase in the real stock-market index, with its impact on wealth and consumer spending would result in a higher aggregate-price level. The negative impacts of interest rates on prices could be taken to arise through the adverse impact on consumer demand for loans, and hence, on aggregate demand.

When we come to the external balance, we are, indeed, confronted by the limitations of such simple correlations. For example, those with the monetary aggregates could be rationalised by merely linking their movements to what is happening to the balance of payments through some expansion at least of the monetary base; otherwise, a complex set of interrelationships have to be imagined to justify the sign of the zero-order correlation coefficient. If that were to be the link, the effects of gradually increasing the domestic currency supply would spill over into the stock market, giving the positive link between the balance of payments on the current account and the stock market. Again, the negative impact upon the current account of an increase in interest rate has to be rationalised by drawing in cross links with other variables, especially (the appreciation in) the exchange rate.

We turn to the zero-order correlation matrices between intermediate targets and policy instruments. The monetary base shows (a not-too-surprising) near-perfect positive correlation with the monetary aggregates. Again the negative relationship between the exchange rate and the monetary base has to be viewed in a multi-variable system if it is to be rationalised; and this could be done, though less circuitously, through the impact of the exchange rate on the balance of payments and of the latter on the monetary base.

In regard to the policy-reaction function, Table 10.B3 records the simple correlation matrix for the objectives and, in the models that we present here, our one operating variable. The relations between monetary base and both the internal and external objectives are of positive sign and also of similar magnitudes. These can be rationalised along the lines used for the links between the monetary aggregates (intermediate targets) and the final goals.

Unit root tests We mentioned earlier on the approaches that can be adopted, and have been adopted, to estimate VARs. One of these is to ignore the order of integration of the endogenous variables. The other two are based upon using the order of integration to estimate VARs that are stationary, either in some transformation of the data, usually the first since most series that are not stationary are I(1), or in VEC format. The results of conducting standard unit root tests, Dickey–Fuller, augmented Dickey–Fuller test and Phillips–Perron, making allowance for the possible presence of seasonal variables, all confirm that the variables we use in our systems are I(1).[9] Before we proceed we should make some further comment about the Divisia monetary aggregate to which we have referred earlier and in the zero-order correlation tables. This index has become fairly commonplace in the monetary economics literature (thanks to the pioneering work of Barnett, for example, Barnett (1978, 1980), so that we shall not provide a detailed discussion of its derivation.[10] We note again that it is a monetary aggregate that attempts to circumvent the main potential deficiency of the simple sum monetary aggregates in that they are simple sums, so allocating to every component of the aggregate the same weight as 'pure money'. That weighting system means in effect that all monies are perfect substitutes. The Divisia aggregate accommodates the possibility that such an assumption is incorrect, permitting variable degrees of substitutability between the competing monies at a point and over time. The weights, roughly speaking, encapsulate the monetary services, the 'overall moneyness' that is embodied in each of the monies or near monies. It is possible that such a construct can assimilate the effects of deregulation and liberalisation in financial markets, giving it a further potential advantage over simple sum monetary aggregates. However, it can also be developed so that such forces are incorporated separately, to see if they need to be so. We have done this for Taiwan adjusting the elements of the standard Divisia to reflect those forces, especially over the later years of the 1980s and of the early 1990s. That index is not used here, since its properties are similar enough to those of the Divisia not to alter the findings of this study.[11] We referred to the time profiles of some of the variables in the introduction, having depicted them in Appendix A. The graph of the Divisia index appears there as Figure 10.A8.

Empirical results

We have already found it necessary to mention the extensive experimentation that we have undertaken, and that as a consequence we have omitted interest rates and the balance of payments from our systems. This experimentation embraced several considerations: (a) selection of the lag length for the VAR bearing in mind several criteria; (b) whether the VAR is robust to the seasonal dummies; (c) whether the dynamic behaviour of monetary policy should be evaluated with real term or in nominal variables; and, (d) whether the dynamic performance of monetary policy is sensitive to the ordering of the variables in the VAR.

In addition, in respect of the tests for cointegration, and hence, for the structure of the VECs, the role of the seasonal factors was investigated by means of the seasonal centring suggested by Johansen (1995). Furthermore, the role of the time trend in the tests had to be determined.[12]

In regard to the ordering of the variables, which was yet an additional factor to take into account in the experimentation, we finally settled on GNPR, CPI, SPR, FOREX, M1AR/M1BR/M2R, MBR. To reiterate, in all systems, the lag-length was four, and we found no role for seasonal factors, even that is in the test equations for cointegration; and so they were excluded from the final models.[13]

Dynamic policy responses to various shocks and variance decompositions

Figures 10.C1–10.C4, in Appendix C, are the graphs of the estimated impulse responses (to a one standard deviation innovation in the particular variable) for the six variables under the four alternative definitions of the intermediate monetary aggregate policy targets, where the variables enter the VARs in their original form. The impulse response functions are drawn here for only sixteen periods ahead for reasons of clarity of presentation. In all cases, we note that these innovation-multiplier effects are stable; that is, they eventually reach zero, in most instances after about 5 years, but in others a much longer period. The graphs in a given row have identical scales, so providing a visual measure of the relative contributions of innovations listed in the columns to the explanation of the variance in the variable listed in a specific row. Those contributions are catalogued in the first set of tables, for the VARs in their levels, in Appendix C.

Obviously, there is a vast amount of information that is contained in the impulse response functions and in the variance decompositions and it is not possible to analyse every item. We will focus on the forces that appear to operate on the monetary base and on the likely link between that base, the particular monetary aggregate and the macro-variables, output and the price level. That will permit us to offer some view as to whether or not the monetary aggregates can be taken as intermediate targets, and whether the policy targets appear to be policy targets and how they then appear to be influenced by the policy intermediate targets and direct instruments.

We begin with the innovations that affect the monetary base, taking the four monetary aggregates in turn. For the M1A regime, the monetary base responds positively, after a lag, to the changes to output, but to a much lesser extent, of course; with the maximum proportion of the variance of the monetary base that is attributable to output being just under 11 per cent, which is after one year. Output itself continues for some time to respond positively, but in cycles, to its own innovation. The monetary base reacts negatively to an innovation in the price level; and doing so for several years; since the shock to the price level itself generates a higher-price level, the increase in which only declines after a year and a half, and which only tails off gradually. After 4 years, for example, variation in the price level causes 24 per cent of the variation in the monetary base. Initially, after the innovation to the monetary base itself, the greatest proportion of its variance emanates from the innovation to M1A; and this increases steadily so that after 4 years its percentage impact has risen to just over 62 per cent. Consequently, linking this back to the impact of the price level on the monetary base, we note that M1A falls by a more or less constant amount for several years after the shock to the price level. Concomitantly, therefore, the monetary base falls consistently for many years. All of these observations are suggestive of a system in which inflation, and probably output, are policy targets of the central bank; and that M1A mirrors with a lag what is happening to both of those targets, so that it can serve as, or is used as (bearing in mind the Lucas critique), an intermediate target. The behaviour of the monetary base is such that it could be taken as the direct instrument of policy.

What though of the stock-market index and the foreign-exchange rate? The stock-market index has some influence in the first year, but overall seems to impact very little on the monetary base. The monetary base, however, tracks the index. The foreign-exchange rate never exercises an influence much above 1 per cent of the variation in the monetary base; but the response of the monetary base accords with the notion that the central bank has attempted to pull back the exchange rate and to stop it appreciating too much at any one time. So that the exchange rate can be seen as an intermediate target of policy. Thus, if we consider the shock to the exchange rate itself, this raises it for some considerable time though the increases approach zero after 4 years. This change means that, as we have defined the exchange rate, NT dollars per US dollar, the currency is depreciating, so that, *ceteris paribus*, exports would rise, imports would fall (note that the positive impact on output of the exchange rate shock is small), so that foreign reserves would increase. Sterilisation would be exercised to reduce the monetary base, and thereby M1A. That too is in line with perceived central bank and general economic policy.

It is apparent that the (alleged) intermediate monetary target has significant impacts upon the other (claimed-to-be) policy objectives, output, the price level, the stock market and the foreign-exchange rate. However, the M1A monetary aggregate responds negatively to innovations in the monetary base and then not substantially. This, if anything, could lead us to conclude since that the decline in the nominal value of M1A over a 4-year period consequent upon a sudden expansion of the monetary base, is due to there is an intervening variable, in the form of 'the rate of interest', which is increased consequent upon the expansion of high-powered money. Thus, if we consider the final column of Table 10.D1 in Appendix D for the M1A system in levels, the shock to the monetary base depreciates the nominal exchange rate; and to counter that tendency the interest rate could be increased. That would explain the fall in the stock-market index, the fall in M1A (with substitution out of the narrower monies into the less-liquid monetary assets that constitute part of M2), the slight fall (rise) in the price level (output). However, as we have mentioned earlier on, in this particular framework we have been unable to find a role for interest rates, not even the central-bank discount rate. This is the case whether we have let that rate be set on the basis of targets and instruments or be exogenous.

We turn now to the VAR in levels using M1B as the intermediate monetary aggregate target. It is not that surprising M1A and M1B exhibit fairly similar impulse responses and variance decompositions. Nevertheless, the patterns do differ and so too, therefore, do the decompositions. In regard to the response of the monetary base to the other innovations we find that over time it is dominated by M1B and the foreign-exchange rate; where in the preceding table these were M1A and the price level. It could be that the authorities see control of the foreign exchange rate as their indirect means of controlling the domestic price level. The impulse responses of output, the price level, the stock market, the foreign-exchange rate and M1B to the monetary base barely diverge from those for M1A. They differ sufficiently, though, to provide different variance decompositions. After 4 years, for example, the monetary base in the M1A model accounts for around 13.5 per cent of the variance of the stock market index compared with a figure of about 9.5 per cent for the M1B system; and, the figures for the price level are, respectively, roughly 6 per cent and approximately 0 per cent.

The picture begins to alter when we move to the broader simple sum monetary aggregate, M2 and the broad variable-weight aggregate, the Divisia. Further, these two monetary aggregates produce different impulse responses and variance decompositions from each other. Consider then M2: in respect of the impact of the innovations upon the monetary base we find that the striking differences between the regimes that include this as the intermediate monetary target, compared with that based on its narrower cousins, occurs in the response to innovations in the monetary aggregate and in the monetary base itself. Thus, a sudden increase in M2, after one and a half years of slight expansion also in the monetary base, will lead to a reduction, increasing for about 3 years, in the stock of (real) M2. If we were to imagine that the response of the monetary base were the reflection of changes of policy, this adjustment would make sound economic sense. However, it would need to be supported by evidence that M2 could be an intermediate monetary target, by considering the impact of innovations of the latter on the alleged final targets of policy, output and the price level, in particular, and maybe the exchange rate.

So, let us examine the sixth column of the impulse responses for the M2 VAR system. The stock of M2 continues to increase, albeit at a lower level after one and a half years, for many years. Output increases for two quarters, then falls, to increase again, and then cycle in this fashion around a very small change, for about 4 years. For a year, the price level increases, but at a decreasing rate; and then it begins to fall steadily for another 5 years or so. For a year and a half the stock market is more or less immune from the innovation to M2; then it begins to fall for another such period of time, before reaching a low. Meanwhile, the nominal value of the exchange rate has been increasing steadily quarter-by-quarter for 2 years, until its rise lessens. Can all these time-paths be reconciled, and in terms of our 'null hypotheses' about which variables fall into the different categories of final target, intermediate target and direct instrument? The answer is only a partial, yes!

What seems to be revealed is the key role of the exchange rate. The impacts of the innovation to M2 suggest that the rate could be an intermediate policy target and that to counteract the devaluation that its generated by the shock to the broad monetary aggregate, the monetary base is reduced after a lag in order to counter the continuing increase in the monetary aggregate and in the devaluation. The importance of output and of the price level is not so clear cut. The sudden expansion in the broad monetary aggregate prompts, as noted a cycle of small increases and declines in output. This could mean that there is, in effect, in a full structural model of the Taiwanese economy, no real wealth effect in consumption. The slight fall in the price level would have been expected to enhance those effects on consumption, and with the devaluation of the currency to have led to more pronounced increases in output. Intervening variables such as the stock-market index cannot provide a connection with output response; since we would have expected it to fall consequent upon a monetary expansion (which since M2 is measured in real terms and the price level falls for several years, means that there is a continued expansion in nominal money balances increasingly in excess of the rate of inflation) in the wake of likely inflationary pressures. Monetary expansion, in this framework at least does not seem to spill-over into the stock market, despite the intimations to the contrary in our introduction based on the opinions of other researchers.

Let us consider now the impulse responses of the monetary base to the variables in the M2 VAR. Those for output, the price level and the foreign-exchange rate reveal responses consistent with the view that the monetary base is a direct instrument of policy and that the three variables listed are final targets of policy. The role of the stock market, naturally, is as problematic as before. The expansion in the monetary base is initially explainable in terms of the increased demand for broad money as the stock market improves. This can simply be a reflection of an altered placement of portfolio wealth. The increased demand is accommodated by the increase in high-powered money to maintain the interest-rate levels; which levels could be intervening variables, but whose influence, as we have noted, we have been unable to capture in these VAR models. The pattern of dynamic responses of the monetary base to a disturbance in the stock market, working through the demand for M2 is difficult to interpret after about a year and a half has elapsed. We note from the variance decompositions that for the monetary base, after 4 years, apart from its own disturbance, its variance is explained by output (nearly 24 per cent), the price level (nearly 18 per cent) and the foreign exchange rate (10 per cent). Over the first one and a half years, however, the stock-market index explained over 10 per cent of the variation.

We now move on to what is in effect the broad monetary-services index, the Divisia aggregate. The impulse responses are given in Figure 10.C4 of Appendix C; and the variance decompositions in Table 10.D4 of Appendix D. We begin with the impacts on the monetary base. Consider first, output. There is a cyclical, but always positive, relationship with output, to sustain it as in the case of the simple sum monetary aggregates, in line with policy objectives. The response pattern is very close to that for the narrow simple sum aggregates. With regard now to the price level, we observe that the response of the monetary base is very close to those for M1A and M2. Turning now to the stock-market index, its impact on the monetary base in the Divisia regime is closest to that for M1A and differs considerably from those for M1B and for M2. In fact, the impact of the innovation to the stock-market index is virtually zero until two years have elapsed. Again, in respect of the foreign-exchange rate, the response of the monetary base is closest to that for M1A and, indeed, diverges little from it, being very marginal.

When we examine the responses of the monetary base to its own innovation we again see that it mirrors the impulse-response function for the M1A regime. The reaction to the shock to the Divisia monetary aggregate differs from that for every other regime, being smaller, persistently positive, though declining over time, for approximately 5 years.

The commonality of the findings for the greater part for the Divisia and the M1A regimes, taken in conjunction with the slight differences between them, point to the conclusion that the Divisia is, indeed, capturing monetary services or 'moneyness' or liquidity, however we care to interpret this, and doing so 'more comprehensively' than does the narrowest simple sum monetary aggregate. This should have similar implications, therefore, for the responsiveness of the alleged final objectives of policy and the intermediate targets to the monetary base. This is the case as can be seen by comparing the sixth column of Figures 10.C1 and 10.C4 in Appendix C. Consequently, we need make no comments about the sixth column of Figure 10.C4.

Instead, we turn to column five of Figure 10.C4. Here we see that the price level and the foreign-exchange rate react in ways similar to the outcome in the narrow money regimes. The response of output in a qualitative sense is also the same in the two narrow money regimes as it is in the Divisia regime. However, the response in the latter is what we would expect it to be if the Divisia were to be seen as an intermediate monetary target: to be precise, output responds consistently and positively to the innovation to the Divisia monetary aggregate. The response in the stock market is more like that in the narrow money regimes than it is in the M2 regime. However, it is far more pronounced an impact in the first 2 years; and demonstrates the strong link (hinted at in our preamble) that others have said exists between monetary expansion and the stock market.

For the Divisia-based VAR, we gather from Table 10.D4 in Appendix D that, in summary, the variance decompositions are as follows. The variance of the monetary base is dominated by the variances to the price level and to output; and to a much lesser extent as time proceeds, to the Divisia index. After 4 years the variance proportion explained by the price level and output being, respectively, nearly 15 per cent and 62 per cent. Even then 11 per cent of the variance is stilled explained by the Divisia index. As for the target output and the price level themselves, most of their variance can be attributable to their own innovations; though output is affected by disturbances to the price level, the stock market, and the exchange rate, as we would expect. The dominant influence on the price level is its own innovation; with little part being left for any other innovation, and this pattern persists over time. The stock market is affected by every innovation, the most important being that to the price level and its own. However, both the Divisia index and the monetary base each explain around 13 per cent of the variance after 4 years. The strongest influence on the Divisia index turns out fairly quickly to be the price level; other substantial factors, leaving aside the Divisia itself and the monetary base, are the innovations to output and the stock market. These findings suggest that we have been encapsulating a dynamic demand for this monetary aggregate in the VAR.

Cointegration and VECs

Alternative systems which are stationary are presented in Appendices E and F. These are VECs which contain the number of cointegrating vectors listed at the top of each table.[14] The graphs in Appendix E reveal a picture that appears not to differ that radically from that obtained for the VARs in the levels of the variables, especially for M1A, M1B and Divisia. There are, however, even in these cases one or two significant differences, which are, naturally, reflected in the variance decompositions. For M2, for example, we find many (about eight out of the thirty-six) impulse responses differ rather markedly from their counterparts in the VARs in the levels of the variables.

Taking M1A, the picture is essentially unchanged for output and the monetary base. For the price level, there are marginal changes from the previous findings: the response to the own-shock and to that emanating from the stock market. These result in the contribution of own-variance falling by around 10 per cent and to that of the stock market increasing by around that percentage. Likewise there are minor changes for the stock market index itself: its own-variance response is reduced by about 9 per cent which goes to the variance from M1A; and for M1A itself. The only substantial changes relate to the exchange rate, where the own-rate influence increases fourfold mainly as a consequence of a halving of the impact of the variance of M1A.

For M1B the significant changes relate to the foreign-exchange rate, but also to the stock market, M1B and the monetary base. With regard to the foreign-exchange rate, the switch of comparative variances is identical with that for the M1A regime. For the stock market, M1B and the monetary base, the overwhelming factor is the alteration in the relative importance of the M1B, though not to the extent that arises with the exchange rate.

When we consider the impulse responses and the variance decompositions for M2, two general findings emerge: the role of the intermediate monetary aggregate is not altered much; but, that of the monetary base is altered, being reduced substantially for the exchange rate, M2 and the monetary base itself. The latter consequences are reflected in: the substantially increased own-response of the exchange rate; the increased impact of the innovation to the stock market on M2; and, an increase in the importance of the price level to variations in the monetary base.

In contrast, the results for the Divisia show little change with regard to the impact of the monetary base on any of the variables, and significant changes in respect of the impact of the Divisia itself. In the latter case, there is a large upward revaluation of the impact on all variables. For output, the stock market, Divisia, and the monetary base, that has largely been accommodated by reductions in the role of the price level. For the exchange rate, the impact of innovations to the price level has been enhanced, as has that to output. The accommodating innovation here is the own-innovation.

The impulse-responses of the variables to the innovations in the Divisia regime as we noted are very similar to those obtained from the VARs in levels. What is happening in the VECs is that the impulse-response graphs are being stretched as it were: the upward or downward impacts are occasionally slightly larger, and they last longer before converging to zero. However, those slight divergences are sufficient to alter the relative importance of the variances in some instances.[15]

One question that can be considered in this framework is that of *Granger-causality*, through the evaluation of the statistical significance of the error correction terms in the VECs.[16] This, of course, is here a test of *weak exogeneity*. In the VECs that underlie the impulse responses and variance decompositions given in Appendices E and F we find the following in respect of the influence of the error correction terms. For all regimes, both the price level and the foreign-exchange rate are weakly exogenous: so that changes in those variables prompt changes in the others. For the M1A regime these are the only two weakly exogenous variables. M1B, M2 and Divisia are each accompanied by one other variable, respectively, the stock-market index, the monetary base and the Divisia index itself. This confirms the important role of the price level, and of the exchange rate (possibly because of its potential impact on the price level itself) in causing policy reactions.

Conclusions

We have considered the transmission of monetary policy through a set of intermediate and direct targets, as well as the reverse links between those targets and monetary policy. In our pilot studies with our systems of semi-structural VARs, we were unable to discern any role for the balance of payments (and as it happens, for foreign-exchange reserves) in the pattern of responses of monetary policy, no matter how we constructed the set of possible direct instruments. For example, in the latter we included the central-bank discount rate, other short-term that in partly determines (at least, we could say 'partly' in the sense of, 'for part of', our sample period) direct controls on the banking institutions balance sheets on their own, either separately or in combination, with or without the monetary base. This finding was general across the four simple sum and the Divisia monetary aggregates.

The concern with external factors and their impact on the domestic goals of high output (or of high growth) and of stable prices (or inflation) was encapsulated through the role of the exchange rate in the VARs. This manifested itself by the link between innovations to the exchange rate and the monetary base, and vice-versa; a link that partly-operated through the intermediation of the monetary aggregate. Those connections were probably conditioned by the level and structure of interest rates that the central bank controlled, through the bands that it announced for those rates certainly before and to some extent consequent upon the financial liberalization of more recent years. The attempt to keep interest rates (certainly interest-rate bands) stable, naturally meant that any innovation to the (demand for) monetary aggregate had to be accommodated, and by means, therefore, of changes to the monetary base. Those interest rates, and concomitantly, their bands, as we have said, do not appear to be determined (at least directly) by reference to the macro-variables included in our VARs, or in the broader ones that we used in our pilot studies.[17]

In the narrow money regimes, the evidence confirms, or at least we should probably say is not inconsistent with, our choice of final and intermediate targets and direct instrument. The pattern of impulse responses is very similar across M1A and M1B. However, there is one difference in that, over time, whilst the impulse response to the monetary base depends increasingly on the monetary aggregate in both regimes, in the M1A regime, the price level becomes an increasing influence, but in the M1B regime it is the foreign-exchange rate that provides this secondary impact. The slight differences in the impulse responses are also sufficient to impart some dissimilar variance decompositions to the monetary base. In particular, over time as well as the price level, the stock market influences the variance of the monetary base in the M1A regime to a greater extent than is the case in the M1B regime. However, the influence of the stock-market innovations on all the other variables in the system tends to be invariant to choice of M1A or M1B.

When we turn to the broader monetary aggregates the picture changes somewhat, and it also differs as we move from the M2 regime to that of Divisia. Take, as a follow-on from the above, the innovations to the stock-market index. For the M2 regime, the impulse responses of both output and the price level to the innovations to the wider financial market differ from their counterparts in the narrow monetary aggregates' regimes. Initially output and the price level are largely unaffected, then falls; whilst in the Divisia regime output falls immediately. Likewise, the impact of M2 on the stock is only marginal; whereas for Divisia it is substantial, and similar to the impact of M1B. The responses of output, the price level and the foreign-exchange rate for the M2 system also suggest that our categorisation of targets is not wholly corroborated. However, this is not the case for the Divisia which, apart from the response it engenders from the monetary base, produces impulse responses that come close to matching those arising from the M1A regime. This finding is bolstered by the fact that, apart from some small differences in respect of output, the responses of variables to the innovation in the monetary base are very similar in the case of Divisia and M1A.

The overarching conclusions that we can draw seem to be these. When the narrowest monetary aggregate M1A or the widest Divisia index are employed as the intermediate targets of monetary policy, they are likely to be useful in that capacity. The final targets of that policy can then be seen to be output, price level, stock-market conditions and the foreign-exchange rate. It is revealed that there is an overriding preoccupation with the price level, and thereby, with inflation, and to a lesser extent with output.[18] That is reflected, in its turn, with the concern about the state of activity in the stock and foreign-exchange markets.

The narrow monetary aggregate M1B comes close, as it were, to meeting the requirements of policy as we have conceived of them here (leaving aside the Lucas critique), whilst the broad simple sum has some potential defects. The similarity between the narrowest aggregate and the Divisia can perhaps permit us to speculate that it is the narrow concept of measure of money and of the demand for money (for transactions purposes) that still dominates in an economy with a high level of economic development and of financial sophistication. This concept is arguably best measured by a Divisia index.

Appendices

Appendix A

Graphs of the time series of the variables

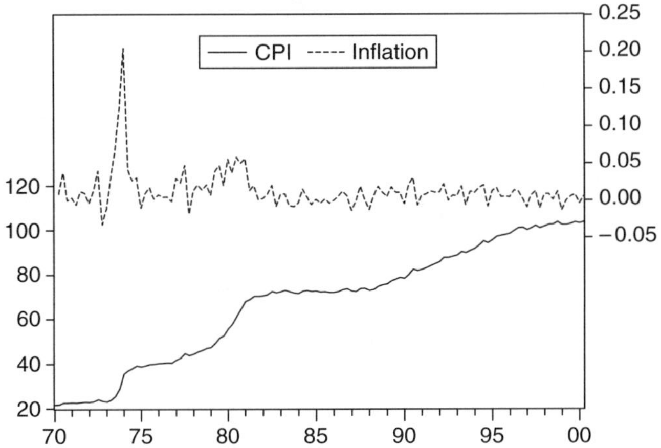

Figure 10.A1 The price level and inflation.

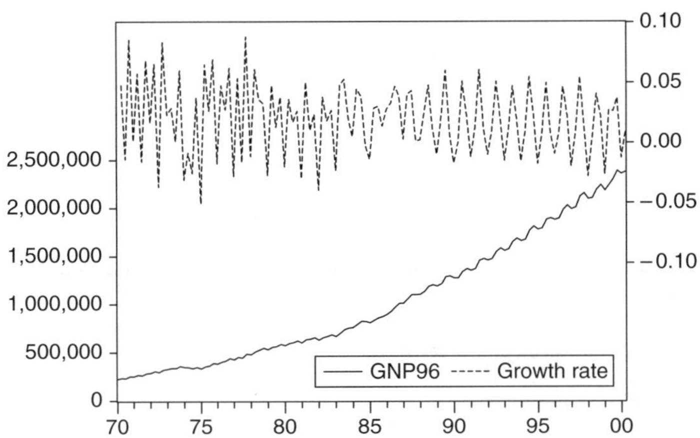

Figure 10.A2 The level of output and its growth rate.

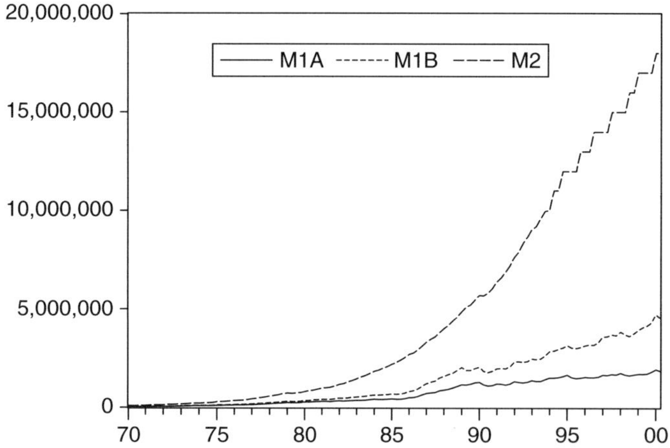

Figure 10.A3 The levels of the simple sum monetary aggregates.

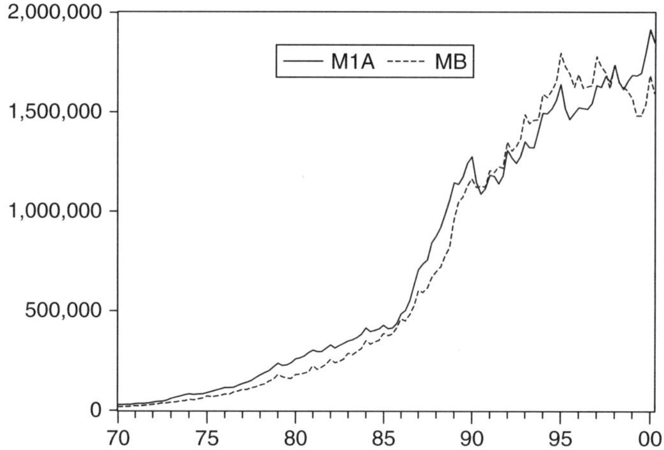

Figure 10.A4 M1A and the monetary base (MB) in nominal values.

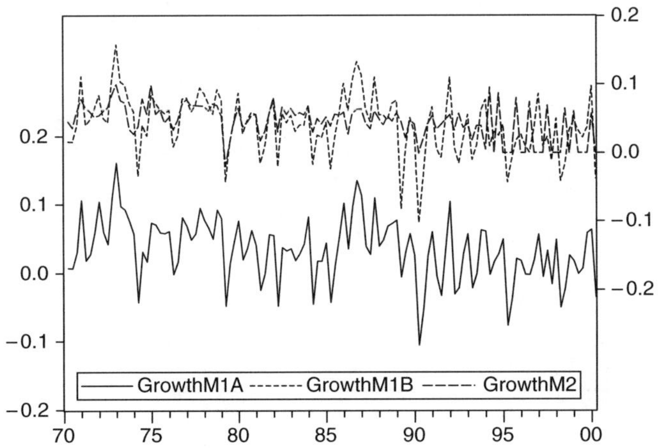

Figure 10.A5 The growth of the simple sum monetary aggregates.

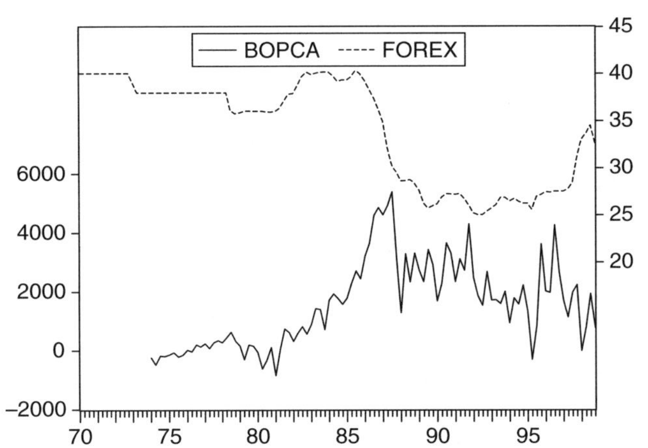

Figure 10.A6 The current account and the exchange rate.

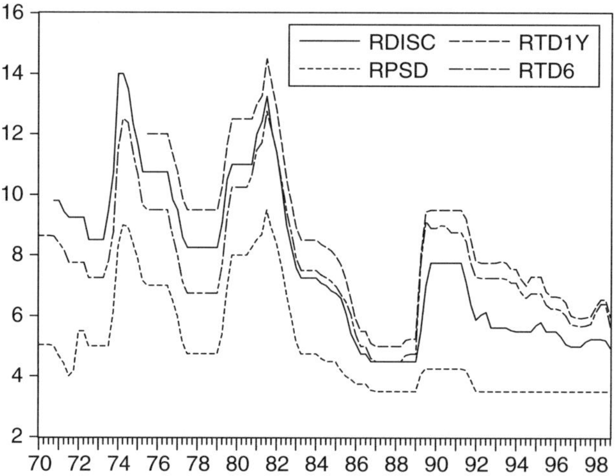

Figure 10.A7 Interest rates (Rdisc is the central bank discount rate).

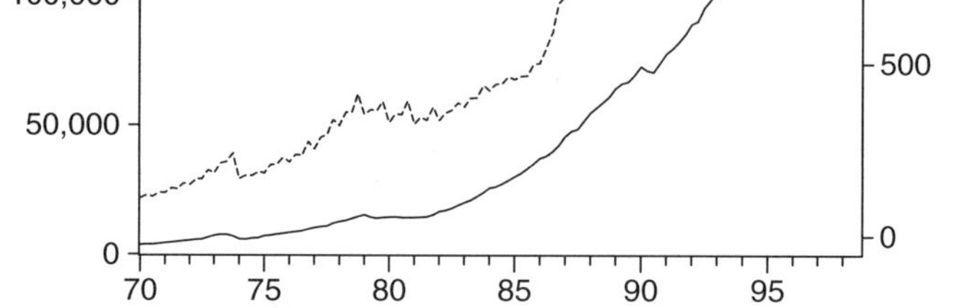

Figure 10.A8 Divisia and real M2.

Appendix B

Table 10.B1 The zero-order correlations between the Objectives (OBJ) and the Intermediate Targets (INT)

	GNPR	*CPI*	*BOPCA*
SPR	0.7197	0.5577	0.4361
M1AR	0.9617	0.8125	0.5965
M1BR	0.9763	0.8297	0.5934
M2R	0.9877	0.8411	0.5246
DIVISIA	0.9700	0.8181	0.6013
RPSD	−0.6804	−0.5269	−0.7033
RTD6	−0.3304	−0.2074	−0.7634
RTD1Y	−0.5551	−0.4945	−0.6013
FOREX	−0.8722	−0.6506	−0.4350

Table 10.B2 The zero-order correlations between the Intermediate Targets (INT) and the Policy Variable (PIS)

	MBR
SPR	0.800
M1AR	0.985
M1BR	0.985
M2R	0.983
DIVISIA	0.983
RPSD	−0.667
RTD6	−0.282
RTD1Y	−0.491
FOREX	−0.928

Table 10.B3 The zero-order correlations between the Objectives (OBJ) and the Policy Variables (PIS)

	GNPR	*CPI*	*BOPCA*
MBR	0.9796	0.8268	0.5518

Appendix C

Graphs for impulse responses: levels

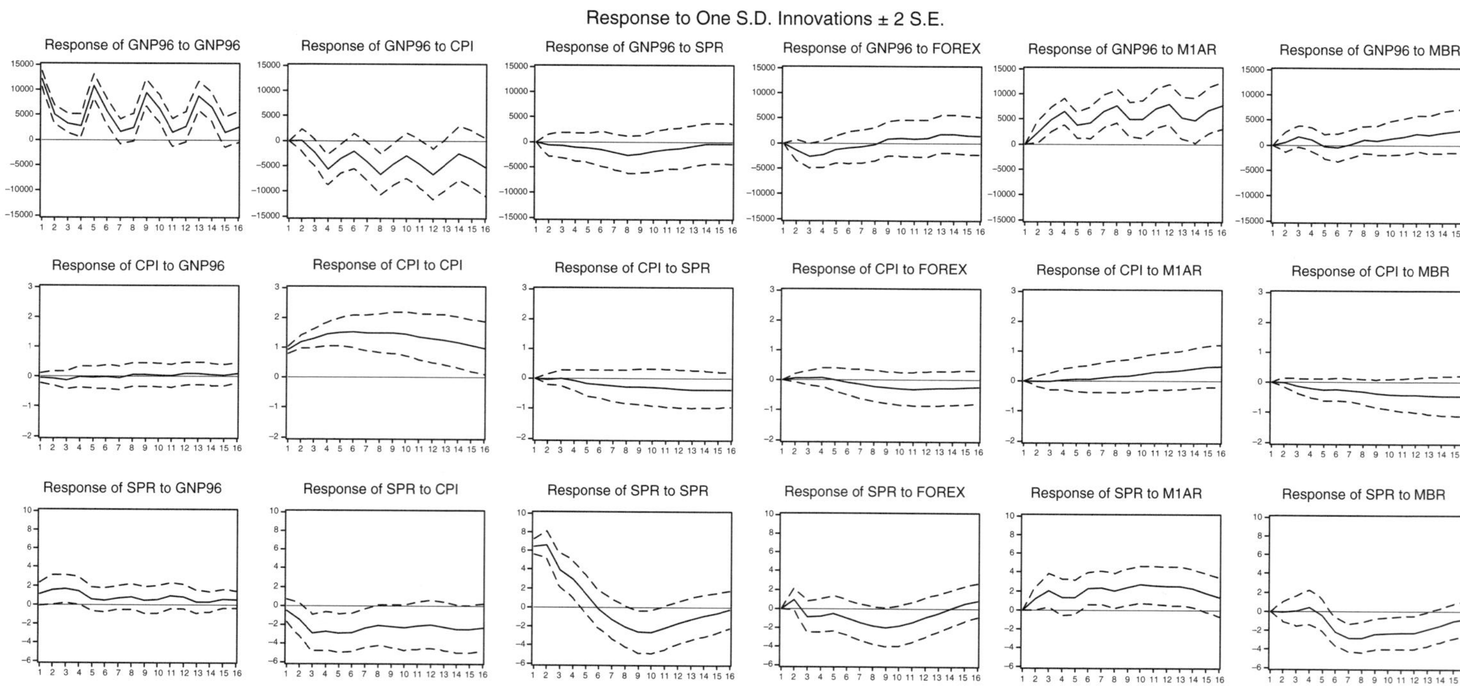

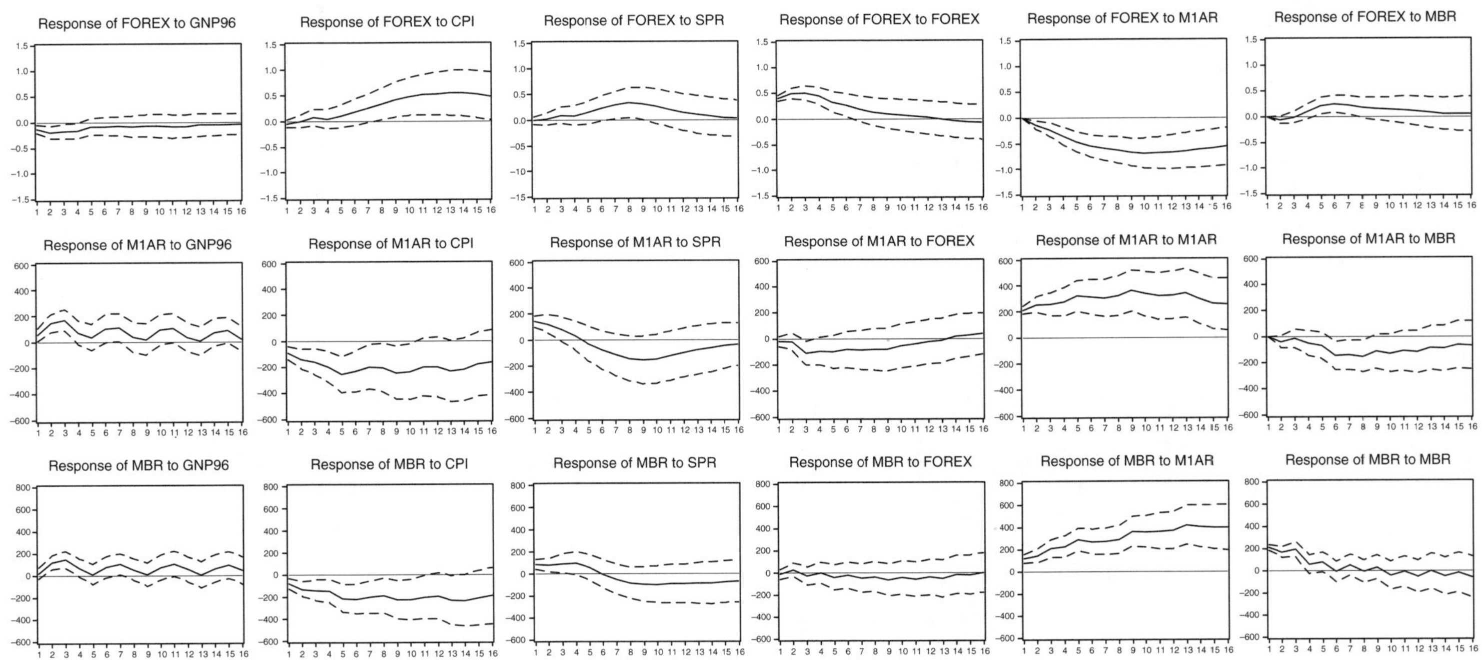

Figure 10.C1 M1A.

Response to One S.D. Innovations ± 2 S.E.

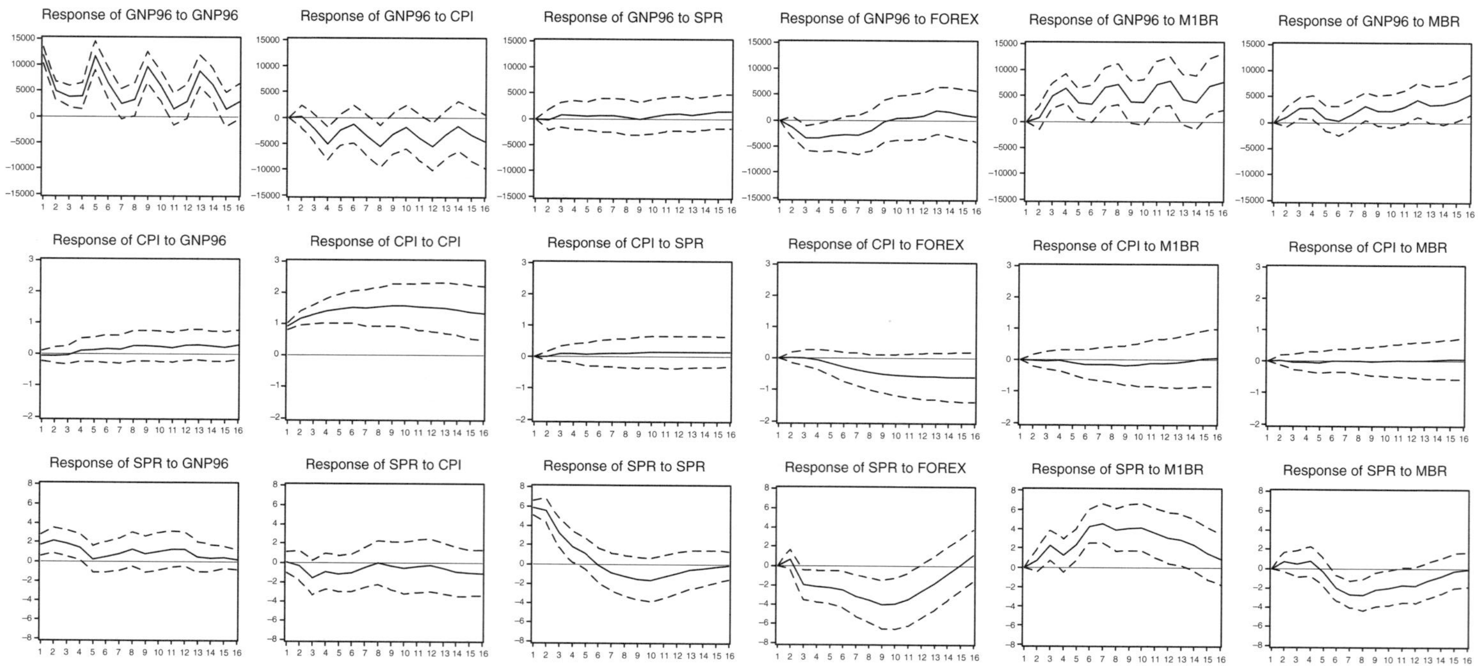

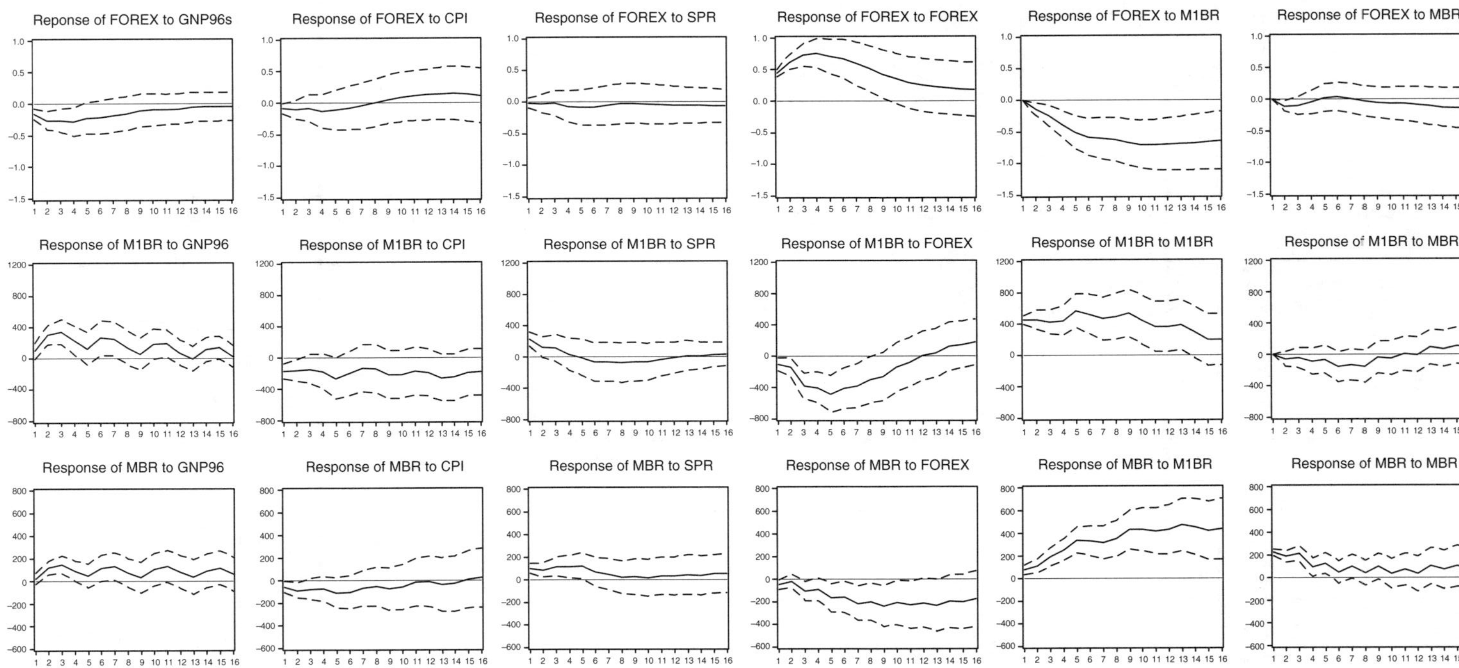

Figure 10.C2 M1B.

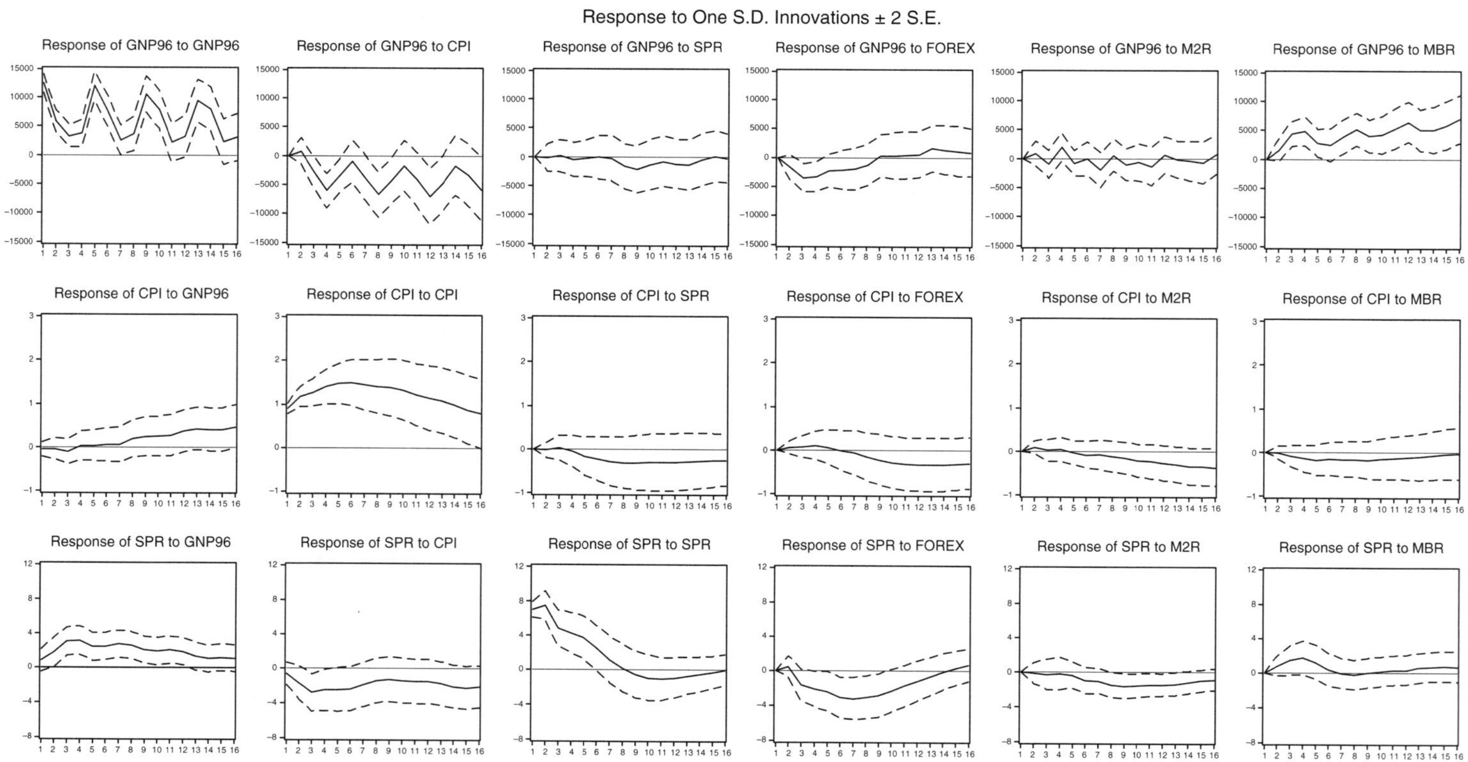
Response to One S.D. Innovations ± 2 S.E.
Response of GNP96 to GNP96
Response of GNP96 to CPI
Response of GNP96 to SPR
Response of GNP96 to FOREX
Response of GNP96 to M2R
Response of GNP96 to MBR
Response of CPI to GNP96
Response of CPI to CPI
Response of CPI to SPR
Response of CPI to FOREX
Rsponse of CPI to M2R
Response of CPI to MBR
Response of SPR to GNP96
Response of SPR to CPI
Response of SPR to SPR
Response of SPR to FOREX
Response of SPR to M2R
Response of SPR to MBR

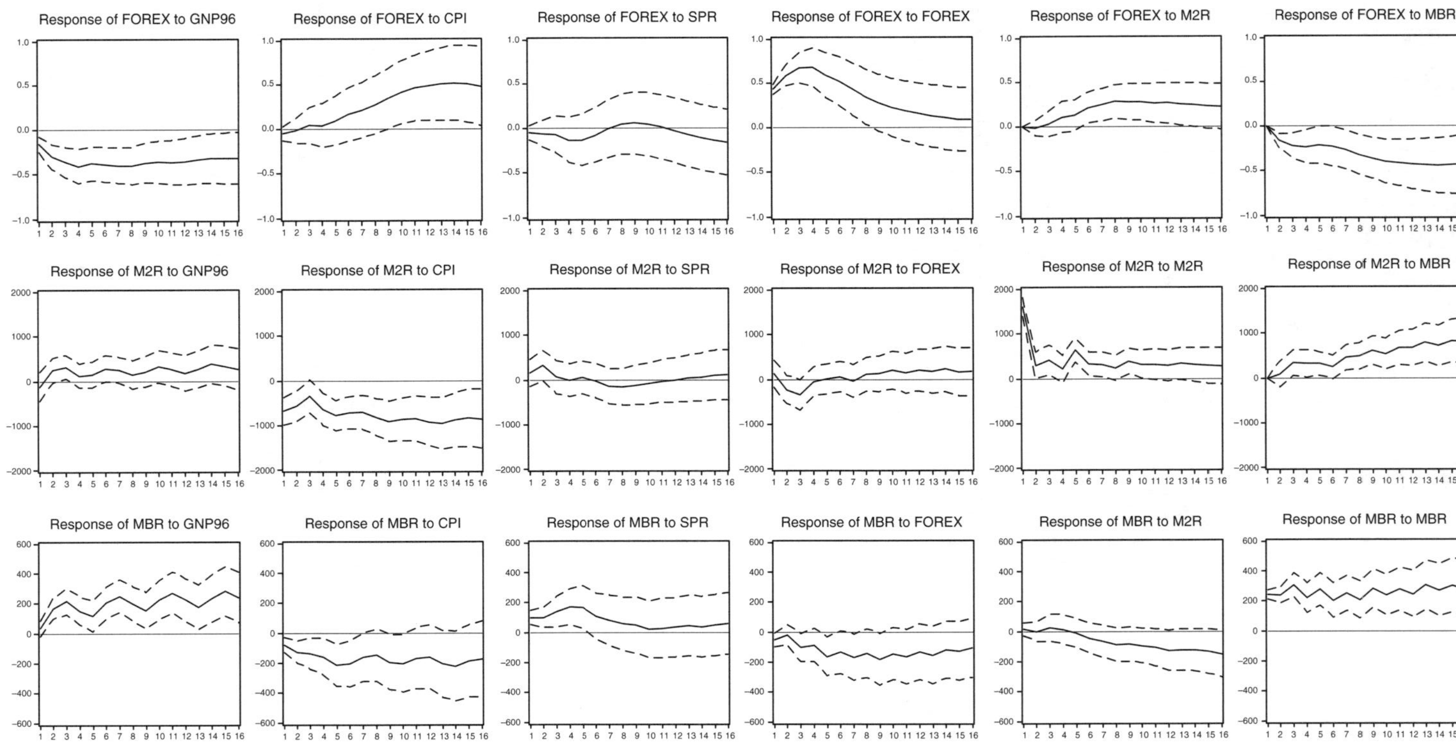

Figure 10.C3 M2.

Response to One S.D. Innovations ± 2 S.E.

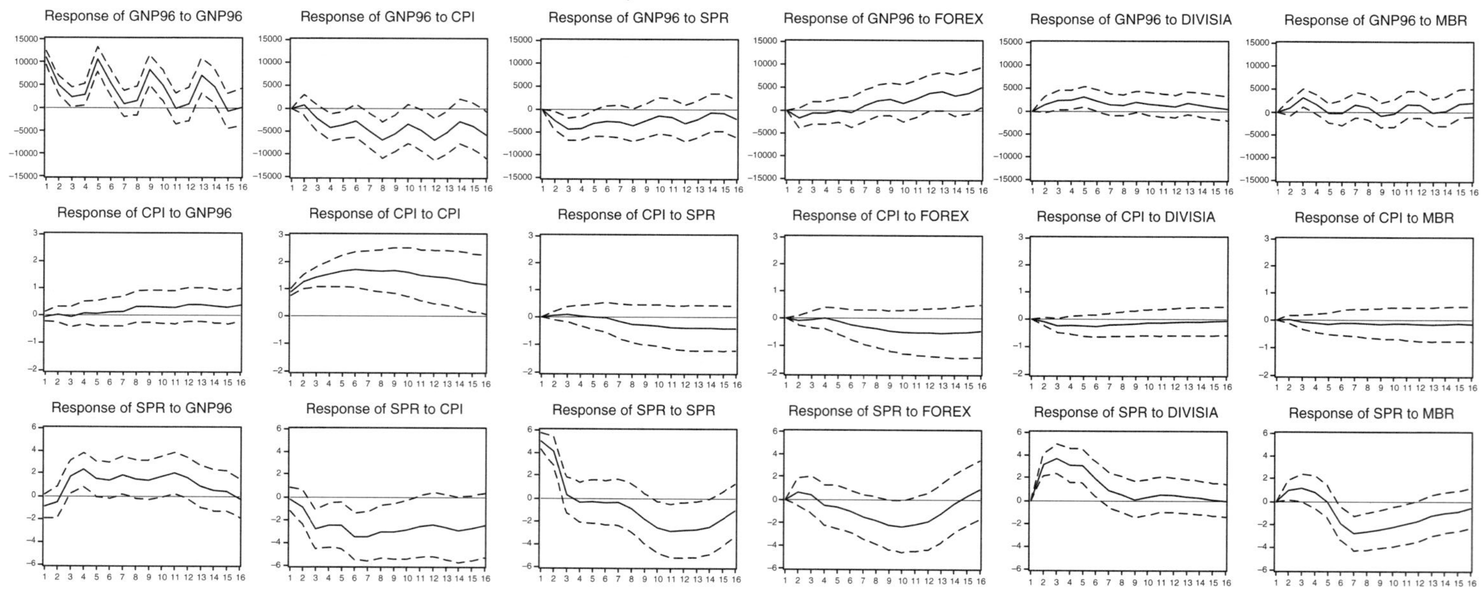

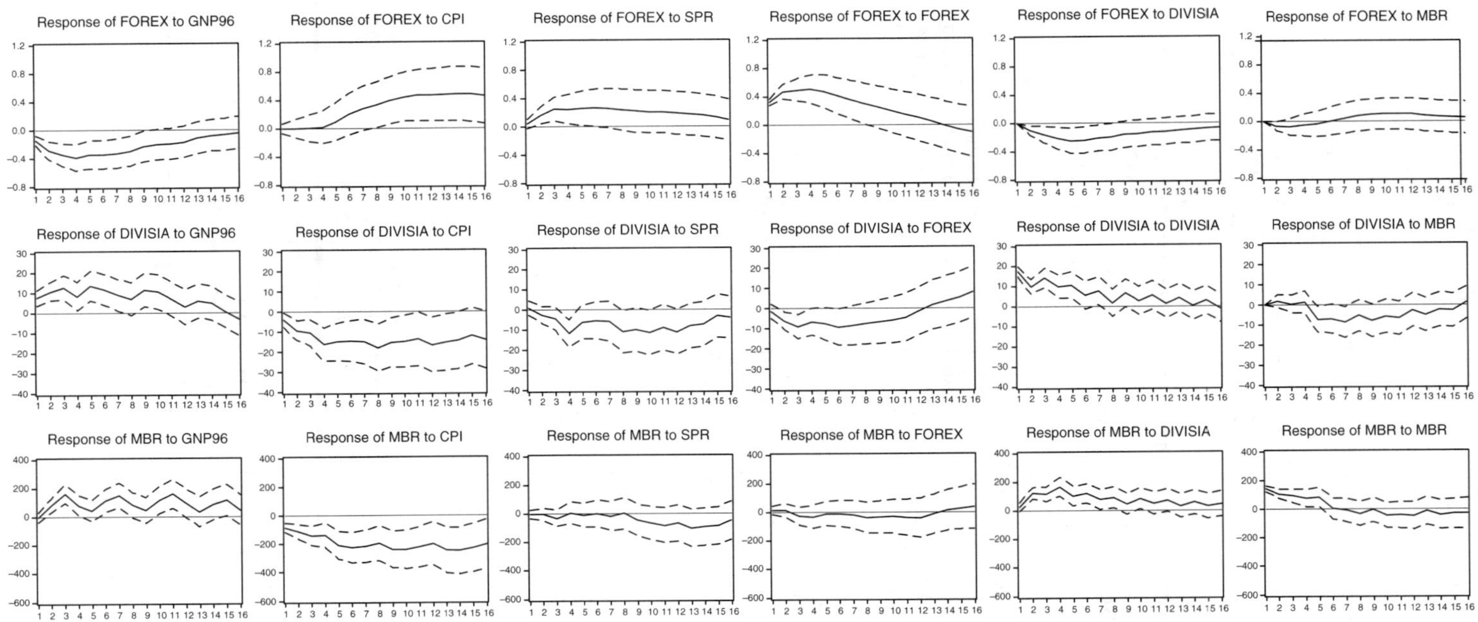

Figure 10.C4 Divisia.

Appendix D

Variance decompositions: Levels of the variables

Table 10.D1 M1A

Period	*S.E.*	*GNP96*	*CPI*	*SPR*	*FOREX*	*M1AR*	*MBR*
Variance decomposition of GNP96							
1	12120.44	100	0	0	0	0	0
4	17873.58	59.54581	12.074	0.674563	4.448222	21.94852	1.308885
8	26584.93	49.03577	16.77953	2.399183	2.443798	28.54218	0.79953
12	33581.9	42.78049	19.13929	2.68964	1.831157	32.15051	1.408915
16	38904.41	40.25454	18.83777	2.081884	2.043643	33.93101	2.851153
Variance decomposition of CPI							
1	0.920971	0.276933	99.72307	0	0	0	0
4	2.477064	0.401118	98.2701	0.091251	0.213375	0.046768	0.977384
8	3.975197	0.203621	95.30153	1.351467	0.55415	0.290514	2.29872
12	5.034233	0.17929	90.25334	2.416431	1.692435	1.308004	4.150497
16	5.735901	0.219283	84.86789	3.557153	2.188032	3.338856	5.828785
Variance decomposition of SPR							
1	6.547208	2.947706	0.561435	96.49086	0	0	0
4	12.05435	5.845909	12.41359	75.0642	1.554469	5.007118	0.114709
8	15.02892	4.546613	19.72227	51.81318	3.960148	10.5447	9.413095
12	18.05431	3.768603	19.35283	42.48082	5.923674	15.19967	13.2744
16	19.43708	3.457507	22.65533	37.43822	5.435347	17.48545	13.52815
Variance decomposition of FOREX							
1	0.422793	9.20466	1.17799	0.038884	89.57847	0	0
4	1.093175	9.643124	0.727085	1.047654	70.95778	16.59805	1.026308
8	1.83662	4.249227	6.557864	7.943481	31.91667	43.73328	5.599473
12	2.548325	2.564728	17.71532	7.659546	16.84716	51.18343	4.029815
16	3.016472	1.94088	24.64388	5.658064	12.12565	52.60065	3.030879
Variance decomposition of M1AR							
1	277.7757	4.103993	11.18391	25.93234	0.655688	58.12407	0
4	684.6461	12.26826	20.03409	8.933528	4.789937	52.97961	0.994574
8	1109.524	6.69805	24.04092	6.80387	4.450231	51.89002	6.116913
12	1426.691	5.094765	24.16105	7.665747	3.322785	53.23304	6.522607
16	1608.567	4.526615	25.23666	6.593134	2.713536	54.84968	6.080369
Variance decomposition of MBR							
1	265.723	0.549292	9.247024	10.01472	0.349196	19.05706	60.78271
4	610.9439	10.66487	18.10274	7.561874	0.495104	33.80494	29.37047
8	952.1808	6.51988	26.72925	4.623936	0.960798	48.1279	13.03824
12	1301.99	4.614856	25.32931	4.631517	1.253111	56.84101	7.330197
16	1611.473	3.550737	24.02956	4.043312	0.962528	62.37805	5.035813

Ordering: GNP96 CPI SPR FOREX M1AR MBR.

Table 10.D2 M1B

Period	*S.E.*	*GNP96*	*CPI*	*SPR*	*FOREX*	*M1BR*	*MBR*
Variance decomposition of GNP96							
1	11784.32	100	0	0	0	0	0
4	18205.88	58.11178	9.234525	0.31042	7.870249	19.69118	4.781849
8	27198.24	52.43369	11.08888	0.292645	7.433796	24.87792	3.873072
12	33434.29	46.99372	12.74957	0.361682	5.023014	28.95742	5.91459
16	38817.31	43.25945	12.47474	0.63542	4.251697	30.50097	8.877731
Variance decomposition of CPI							
1	0.922877	0.364521	99.63548	0	0	0	0
4	2.435464	0.366656	99.24156	0.274549	0.044235	0.036481	0.036519
8	3.973674	0.988467	95.32354	0.34313	2.847615	0.468925	0.02832
12	5.205218	1.539129	91.27029	0.485701	6.095587	0.58809	0.021205
16	6.08455	1.929465	88.68584	0.61363	8.259884	0.473829	0.037354
Variance decomposition of SPR							
1	6.085588	7.67427	0.000208	92.32552	0	0	0
4	10.60441	11.40208	3.075107	70.19058	7.953534	6.321692	1.057007
8	15.27112	6.515426	2.646282	35.31479	18.27485	28.63791	8.610744
12	19.15566	5.41782	1.857018	24.50196	25.32863	33.34414	9.550434
16	19.88624	5.15334	2.616265	22.88984	24.85778	35.03755	9.445217
Variance decomposition of FOREX							
1	0.474423	10.98335	3.45723	0.125482	85.43394	0	0
4	1.484016	11.00622	1.971146	0.301748	75.33682	10.21544	1.168619
8	2.301788	7.571226	1.269884	0.47766	60.44273	29.69852	0.539981
12	2.788108	5.619675	1.363583	0.413314	46.9851	44.98415	0.63418
16	3.141852	4.52194	1.82237	0.487494	38.59571	53.38721	1.18527
Variance decomposition of M1BR							
1	549.3414	3.051748	9.810511	16.50629	3.665847	66.96561	0
4	1259.206	16.73643	6.957158	4.884567	21.54472	49.03412	0.842997
8	1917.472	11.67249	7.141486	2.525639	26.73195	49.59571	2.332716
12	2186.846	10.56362	8.908017	2.174641	22.59069	53.89147	1.871558
16	2329.355	9.891046	11.54568	1.945165	21.11783	53.23485	2.265431
Variance decomposition of MBR							
1	267.6473	0.544905	4.737396	13.84059	3.559433	8.102689	69.21499
4	621.3696	11.10606	6.199644	10.68938	5.9991	30.44706	35.55876
8	1041.852	7.347632	5.212921	5.674001	15.24594	51.2184	15.30111
12	1440.12	5.495588	3.230799	3.095095	17.67224	61.67218	8.834096
16	1759.351	4.515211	2.262434	2.324128	17.2393	66.79338	6.865553

Ordering: GNP96 CPI SPR FOREX M1BR MBR.

Table 10.D3 M2

Period	*S.E.*	*GNP96*	*CPI*	*SPR*	*FOREX*	*M2R*	*MBR*
Variance decomposition of GNP96							
1	12425.2	100	0	0	0	0	0
4	18307.43	63.63794	13.47482	0.09007	8.015433	1.636132	13.1456
8	26609.46	61.31666	16.81279	0.465343	5.97184	1.481423	13.95194
12	33168.5	56.52062	18.906	1.11513	3.899205	1.294322	18.26472
16	38478.87	53.25231	18.91802	0.989249	3.318329	1.046925	22.47517
Variance decomposition of CPI							
1	0.907795	0.289414	99.71059	0	0	0	0
4	2.41319	0.258474	98.67525	0.051225	0.382681	0.167433	0.464935
8	3.831639	0.41397	96.31708	1.708826	0.365372	0.272377	0.922372
12	4.74354	1.803772	91.63684	2.767221	1.755676	1.045531	0.990954
16	5.290653	4.073943	86.45251	3.223556	2.871908	2.504784	0.8733
Variance decomposition of SPR							
1	7.075944	1.435022	0.713641	97.85134	0	0	0
4	14.10661	11.32039	8.71468	73.33498	3.749391	0.070322	2.810237
8	17.43132	15.82718	11.43947	54.90477	13.92513	1.50394	2.399509
12	18.91442	17.66025	11.98519	47.53811	16.76852	3.953499	2.094441
16	19.71597	17.57606	15.35643	43.99226	15.69496	4.961107	2.419186
Variance decomposition of FOREX							
1	0.466052	12.54046	1.226956	1.170532	85.06206	0	0
4	1.432551	20.84696	0.296643	1.499539	70.25982	0.582854	6.514179
8	2.064945	24.86768	3.679346	1.363761	55.57266	4.897179	9.619372
12	2.583024	24.12401	13.33376	0.951348	38.2666	7.412593	15.91169
16	3.036523	22.17131	20.62917	1.372312	28.14421	7.776741	19.90625
Variance decomposition of M2R							
1	1753.115	0.473959	14.88622	0.83765	0.537593	83.26458	0
4	2213.913	3.794035	26.70656	2.72367	3.80696	58.43655	4.532226
8	2948.392	4.219881	41.36962	2.108837	2.343268	40.49205	9.466344
12	3770.072	4.309091	47.51293	1.449724	2.253243	27.78749	16.68752
16	4553.819	4.835582	47.74424	1.123764	2.213185	20.80802	23.27521
Variance decomposition of MBR							
1	279.4057	1.279014	7.905142	12.17045	3.426998	0.236621	74.98177
4	711.4716	18.77141	13.34135	13.1356	4.139247	0.200993	50.41141
8	1084.835	21.15952	17.40738	9.751494	9.675854	1.367547	40.6382
12	1387.672	23.09537	17.5663	6.168726	11.08178	3.133869	38.95395
16	1666.794	23.89447	17.86402	4.590237	10.0801	4.708238	38.86293

Ordering: GNP96 CPI SPR FOREX M2R MBR.

Table 10.D4 Divisia

Period	*S.E.*	*GNP96*	*CPI*	*SPR*	*FOREX*	*DIVISIA*	*MBR*
Variance decomposition of GNP96							
1	10830.38	100	0	0	0	0	0
4	15828.48	61.64589	9.132415	17.37316	1.504742	5.351246	4.992551
8	23482.93	53.88558	21.22413	14.57449	1.651369	5.818495	2.845945
12	28691.07	47.36281	28.03553	12.35609	4.611692	5.011734	2.622144
16	32695.33	43.11894	29.44321	10.48283	9.853596	4.421671	2.67975
Variance decomposition of CPI							
1	0.88992	0.27427	99.72573	0	0	0	0
4	2.64239	0.193208	97.52242	0.183697	0.172045	1.643782	0.284851
8	4.359146	0.780525	94.84833	0.537316	1.747612	1.667045	0.419168
12	5.558107	1.938255	90.02948	1.838217	4.421779	1.257195	0.515077
16	6.308467	2.760426	86.50158	3.024687	6.047432	1.039089	0.626784
Variance decomposition of SPR							
1	5.093389	3.025881	0.144363	96.82976	0	0	0
4	10.13306	8.953107	14.37931	41.39746	0.766094	31.73129	2.772738
8	13.8701	9.75733	28.18175	22.67734	4.170967	24.1066	11.10601
12	17.22365	10.17959	28.26814	23.37267	9.143135	15.82506	13.21141
16	18.74187	8.953866	32.1276	24.84593	8.447416	13.41995	12.20523
Variance decomposition of FOREX							
1	0.356201	16.25608	5.70E-05	1.431385	82.31248	0	0
4	1.198855	26.10797	0.028027	10.20133	57.23867	5.503367	0.920634
8	1.786063	25.49198	7.515442	12.63441	44.9579	8.706568	0.693694
12	2.133898	21.41814	22.38461	12.48995	34.49896	7.815593	1.392758
16	2.370987	17.79193	34.15815	11.52713	28.23044	6.834761	1.457582
Variance decomposition of LEVDIV1							
1	19.21025	14.7263	4.681533	0.157247	0.69542	79.7395	0
4	43.68935	20.25152	25.68161	9.051076	9.274601	35.50118	0.240022
8	65.52145	18.99854	34.95783	9.495346	10.9847	20.42361	5.139975
12	79.53799	17.42423	38.75986	13.5787	9.2324	15.10586	5.898948
16	86.77064	15.51366	43.40308	13.47454	9.058535	13.04987	5.500316
Variance decomposition of MBR							
1	168.6529	0.041219	26.02294	0.094573	0.687723	2.459509	70.69403
4	452.1682	18.89382	29.75497	0.56823	1.105447	27.61963	22.0579
8	691.4917	17.17033	50.62792	0.340927	0.883568	19.85598	11.12127
12	883.1674	16.88637	57.34976	2.602065	1.207088	14.31597	7.638748
16	1031.505	14.62004	62.39637	4.72938	1.128713	11.18063	5.944869

Ordering: GNP96 CPI SPR FOREX DIVISIA MBR.

Appendix E

Cointegration models: impulse responses

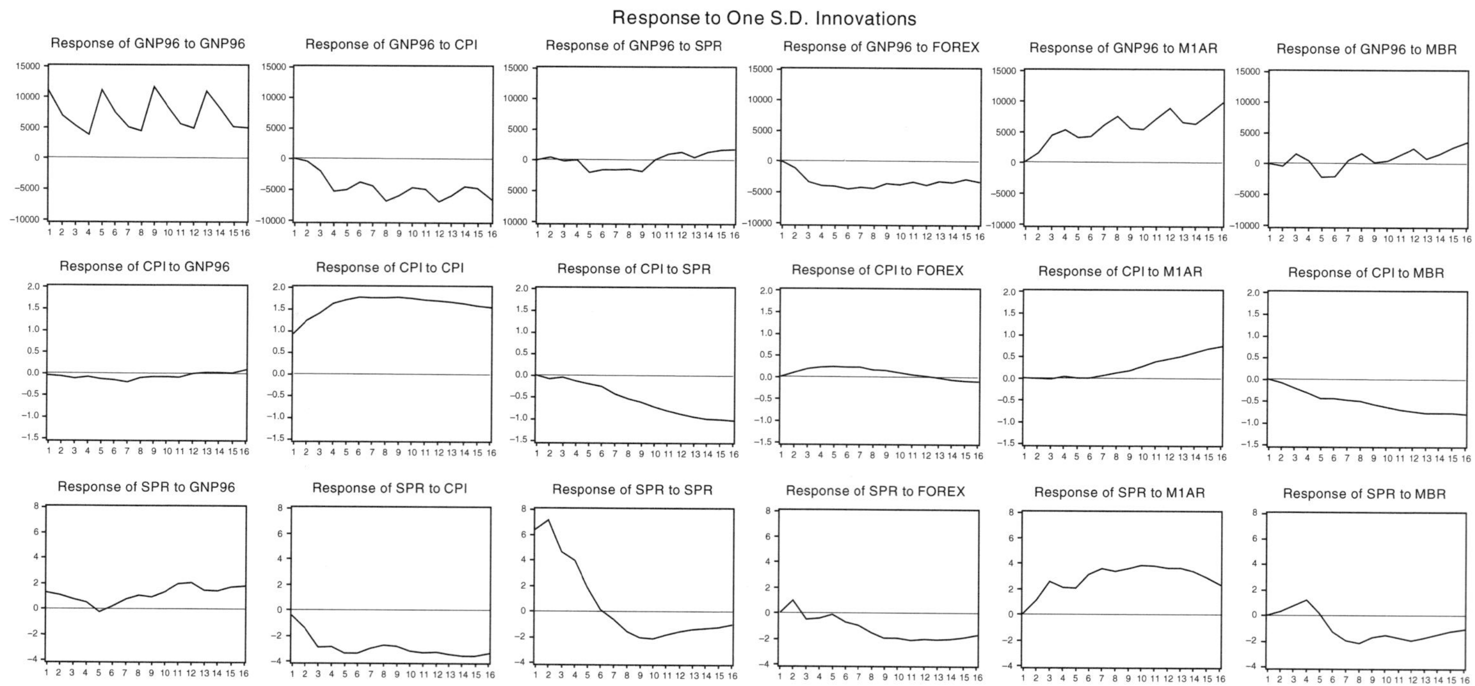

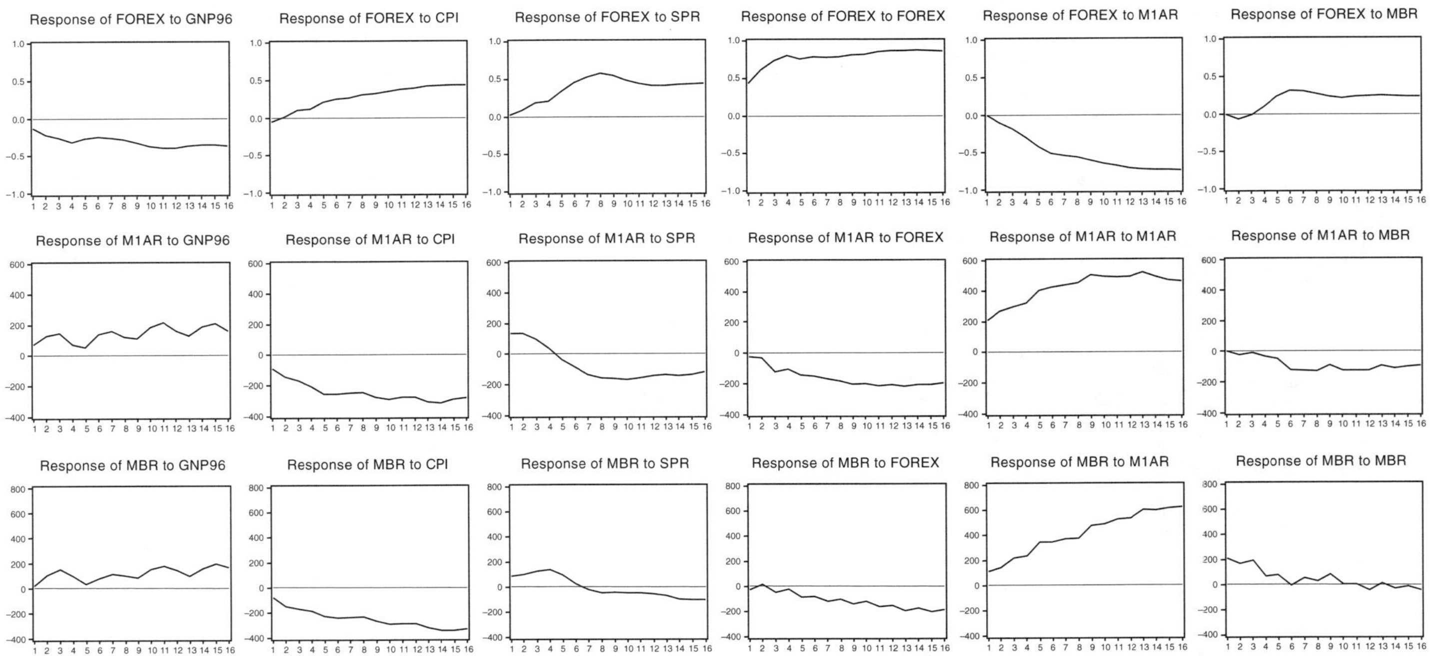

Figure 10.E1 M1A (3 cointegrating vectors).

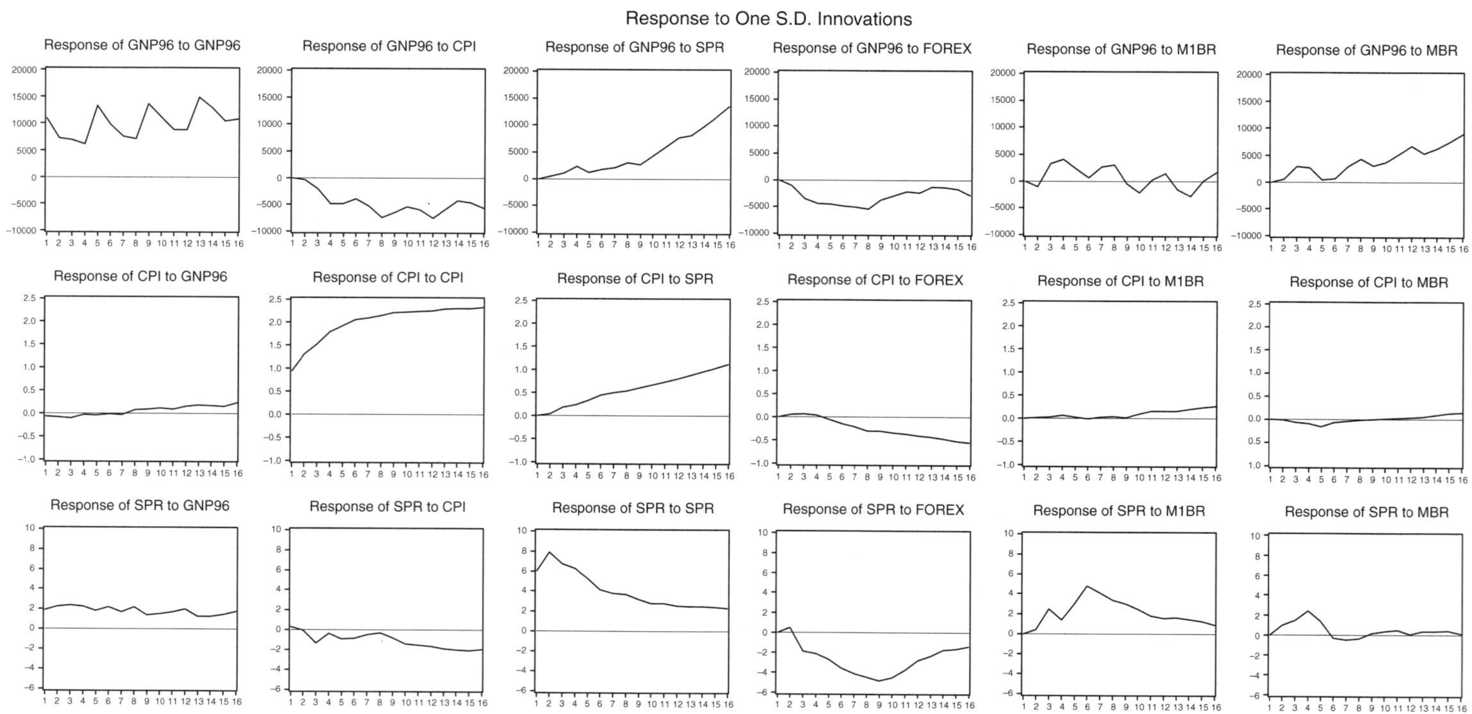
Response to One S.D. Innovations
Response of GNP96 to GNP96
Response of GNP96 to CPI
Response of GNP96 to SPR
Response of GNP96 to FOREX
Response of GNP96 to M1BR
Response of GNP96 to MBR
Response of CPI to GNP96
Response of CPI to CPI
Response of CPI to SPR
Response of CPI to FOREX
Response of CPI to M1BR
Response of CPI to MBR
Response of SPR to GNP96
Response of SPR to CPI
Response of SPR to SPR
Response of SPR to FOREX
Response of SPR to M1BR
Response of SPR to MBR

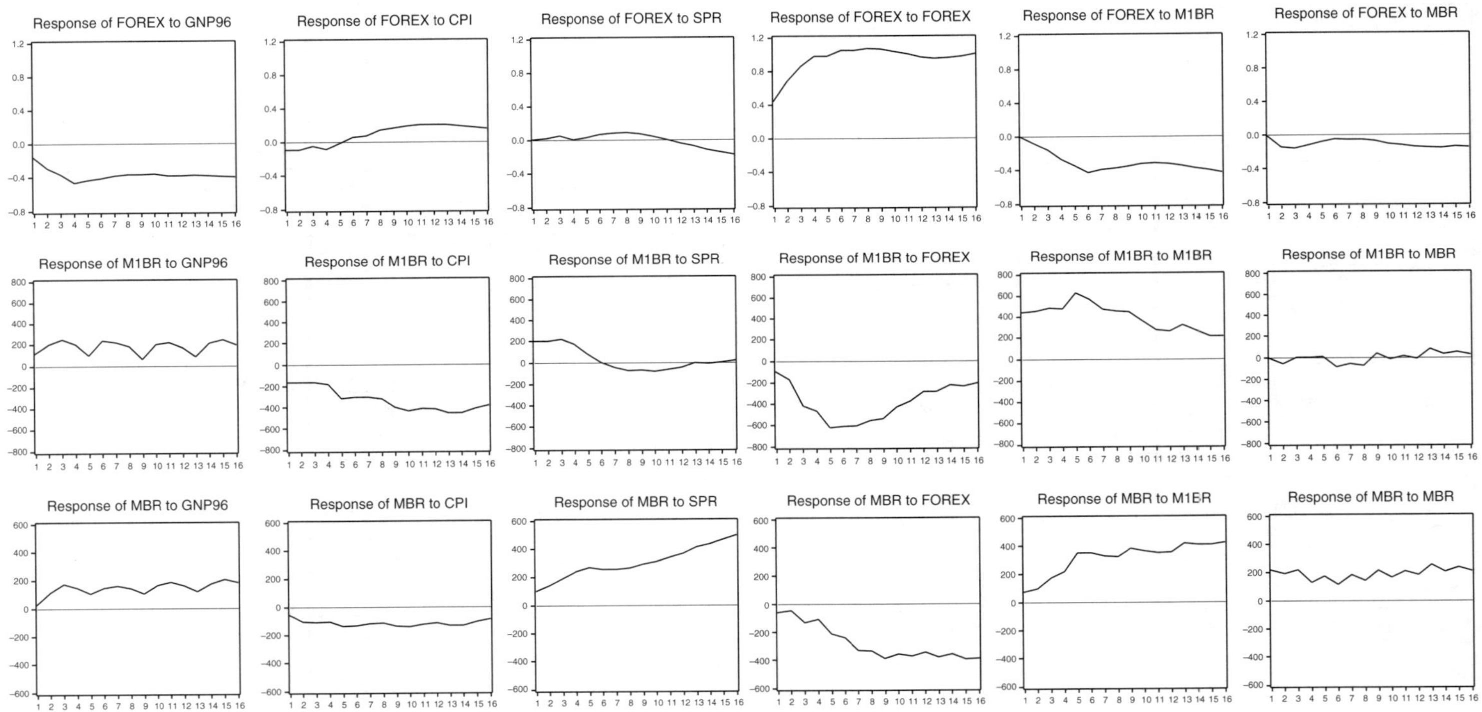

Figure 10.E2 M1B (2 cointegrating vectors).

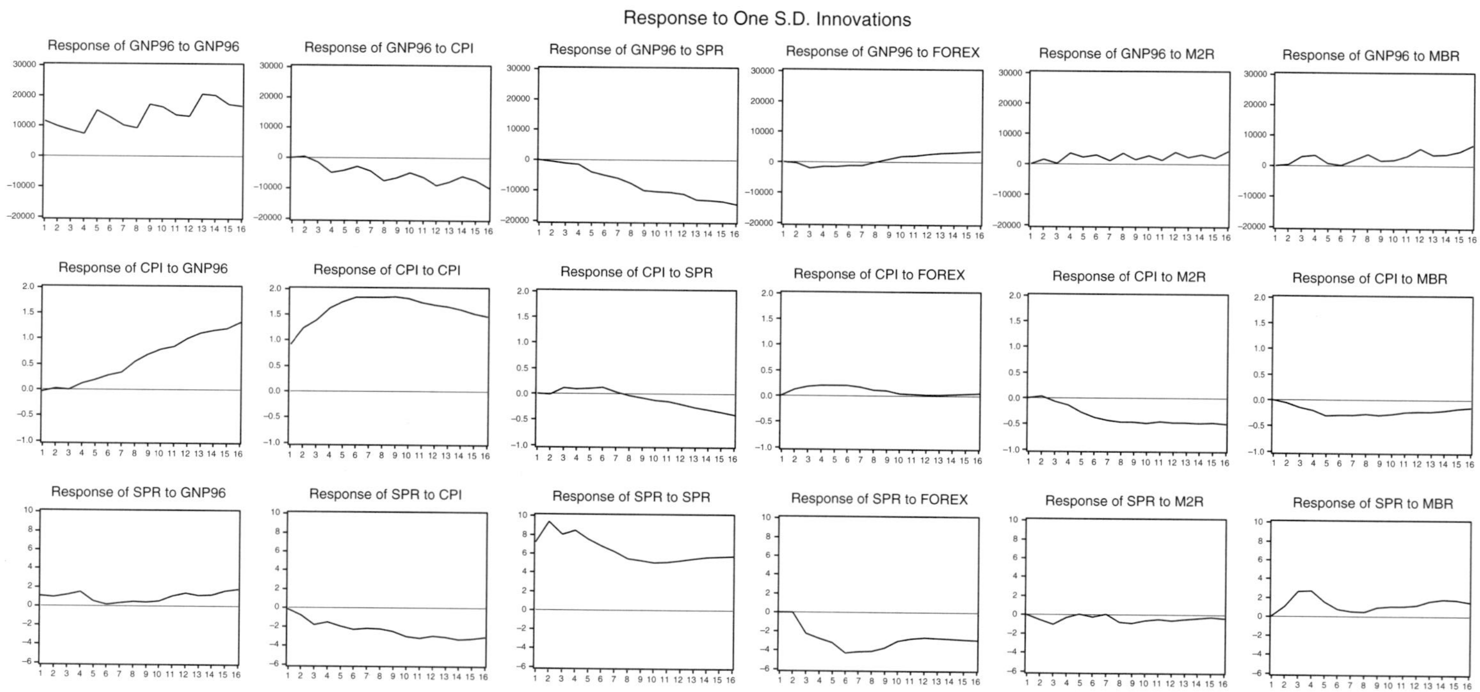
Response to One S.D. Innovations
Response of GNP96 to GNP96
Response of GNP96 to CPI
Response of GNP96 to SPR
Response of GNP96 to FOREX
Response of GNP96 to M2R
Response of GNP96 to MBR
Response of CPI to GNP96
Response of CPI to CPI
Response of CPI to SPR
Response of CPI to FOREX
Response of CPI to M2R
Response of CPI to MBR
Response of SPR to GNP96
Response of SPR to CPI
Response of SPR to SPR
Response of SPR to FOREX
Response of SPR to M2R
Response of SPR to MBR

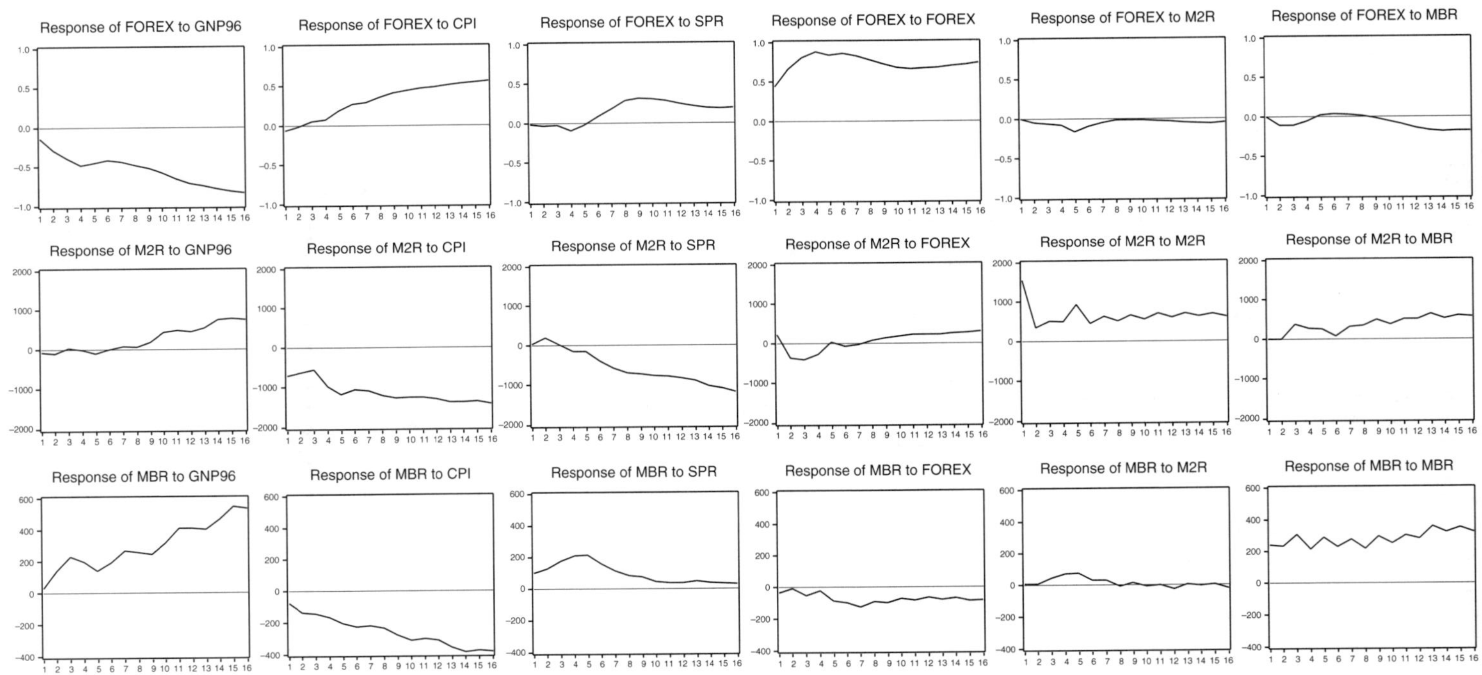

Figure 10.E3 M2 (3 cointegrating vectors).

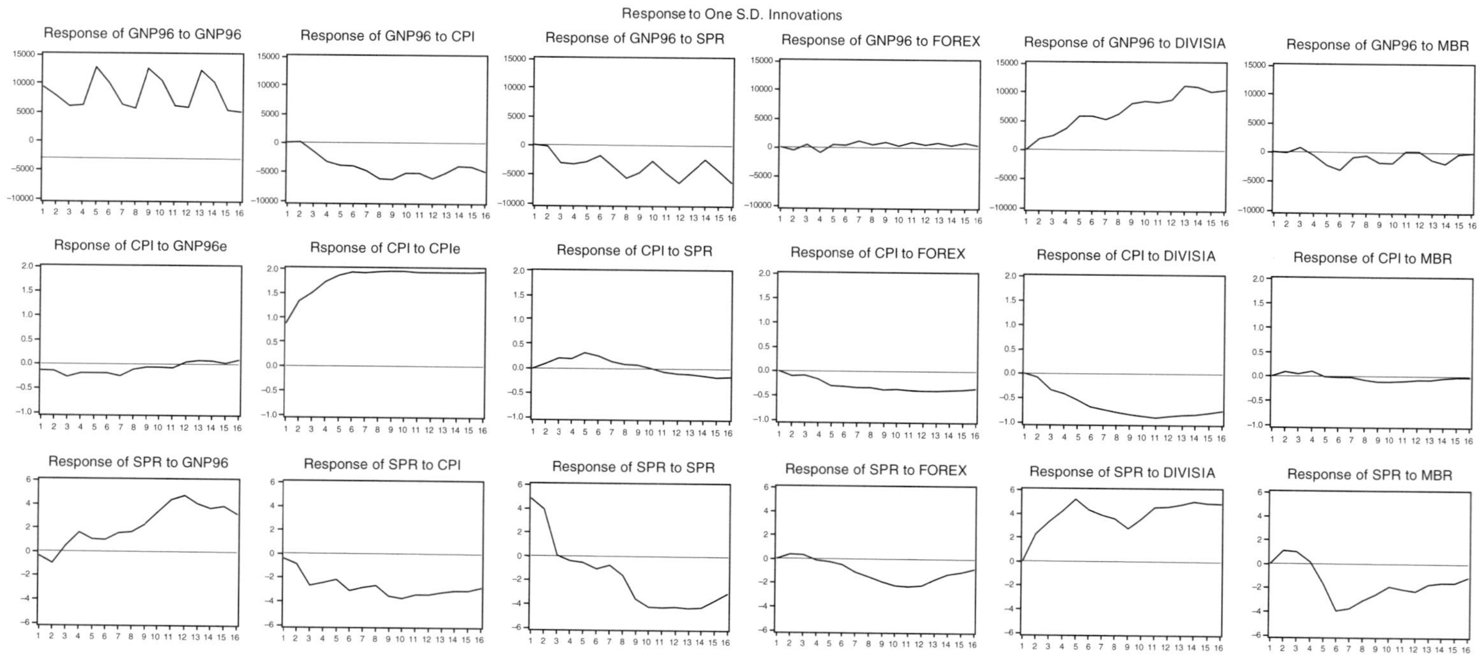
Response to One S.D. Innovations
Response of GNP96 to GNP96
Response of GNP96 to CPI
Response of GNP96 to SPR
Response of GNP96 to FOREX
Response of GNP96 to DIVISIA
Response of GNP96 to MBR
Rsponse of CPI to GNP96e
Rsponse of CPI to CPIe
Response of CPI to SPR
Response of CPI to FOREX
Response of CPI to DIVISIA
Response of CPI to MBR
Response of SPR to GNP96
Response of SPR to CPI
Response of SPR to SPR
Response of SPR to FOREX
Response of SPR to DIVISIA
Response of SPR to MBR

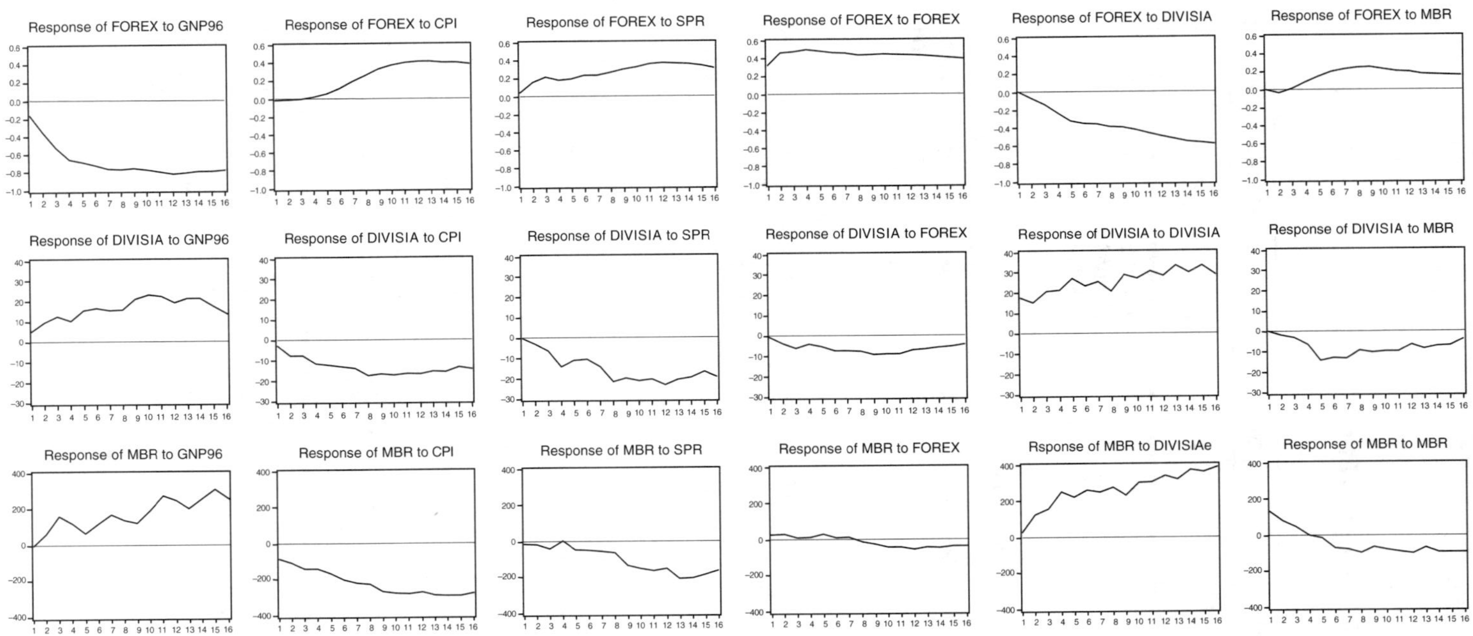

Figure 10.E4 Divisia (2 cointegrating vectors).

Appendix F

Variance decompositions for the VECs

Table 10.F1 M1A

Period	*S.E.*	*GNP96*	*CPI*	*SPR*	*FOREX*	*M1AR*	*MBR*
Variance decomposition of GNP96							
1	10943.29	100	0	0	0	0	0
4	17927.28	64.59878	10.37211	0.068572	8.886963	15.14193	0.931641
8	29558.81	49.13442	16.03458	1.357324	11.65992	20.01527	1.798477
12	38992.62	45.33226	17.82064	1.174628	10.25053	23.84319	1.578755
16	46788.43	42.20477	18.03817	1.145634	9.062409	27.42899	2.12003
Variance decomposition of CPI							
1	0.920412	0.309423	99.69058	0	0	0	0
4	2.690303	0.422199	95.70265	0.400177	1.236299	0.034728	2.203945
8	4.607671	0.641373	90.21838	2.908918	1.216942	0.097868	4.916517
12	6.143479	0.429891	82.19023	7.846809	0.770883	1.218186	7.544005
16	7.485483	0.301322	73.564	12.38256	0.567715	3.629285	9.555118
Variance decomposition of SPR							
1	6.531832	4.080639	0.424712	95.49465	0	0	0
4	12.94993	2.197182	11.59008	76.86305	0.835809	7.216614	1.297262
8	16.34376	2.014061	22.08572	50.64642	1.886252	18.76204	4.605509
12	20.3927	3.884311	23.9394	35.94245	5.097314	25.31489	5.821636
16	23.32242	4.873389	27.46144	28.61507	6.645695	26.49932	5.905087
Variance decomposition of FOREX							
1	0.452756	8.29165	1.224443	0.426727	90.05718	0	0
4	1.495191	10.47143	1.159639	3.883215	77.94022	5.926656	0.618832
8	2.734874	6.943516	3.992127	13.56012	54.99143	16.03222	4.480594
12	3.766903	7.545848	5.767514	13.46692	48.49215	20.82933	3.898237
16	4.640509	7.406596	7.17442	12.26492	45.76196	23.71305	3.679055
Variance decomposition of M1AR							
1	274.4914	7.088689	10.86145	24.11947	0.738324	57.19207	0
4	727.0753	8.991258	18.91612	8.886326	5.326656	57.48932	0.39032
8	1336.431	6.087299	19.75638	5.51215	7.459729	58.25636	2.928088
12	1877.263	6.416996	19.02342	5.636149	8.556568	57.26462	3.102248
16	2288.611	6.609077	19.66037	5.158805	9.032546	56.69462	2.844578
Variance decomposition of MBR							
1	265.2218	0.538492	9.972615	9.98198	1.101963	18.04329	60.36166
4	658.0943	9.490667	21.95735	11.37368	0.951074	30.96084	25.26639
8	1123.719	5.49471	25.3839	4.903912	3.529158	51.25682	9.431506
12	1668.54	5.26105	23.23295	2.618944	4.698392	59.59247	4.596194
16	2235.383	4.837582	22.02522	2.201808	5.547311	62.75184	2.636238

Ordering: GNP96 CPI SPR FOREX M1AR MBR.

Table 10.F2 M1B

Period	*S.E.*	*GNP96*	*CPI*	*SPR*	*FOREX*	*M1BR*	*MBR*
Variance decomposition of GNP96							
1	10954.03	100	0	0	0	0	0
4	19206.81	69.61868	7.531596	2.003089	8.816083	7.681651	4.348905
8	32260.94	61.07188	14.5669	2.479765	12.76768	4.898669	4.215106
12	43837.04	57.14992	16.51163	7.495913	8.658008	3.031286	7.153234
16	57939.3	51.11375	12.71288	18.56123	5.384489	2.133566	10.09409
Variance decomposition of CPI							
1	0.947972	0.505673	99.49433	0	0	0	0
4	2.860959	0.312495	98.33296	1.029083	0.077093	0.057135	0.191236
8	5.098489	0.131158	95.45125	3.529372	0.669446	0.028294	0.190478
12	6.955611	0.171993	92.1757	5.971111	1.452808	0.122482	0.105904
16	8.653845	0.288566	87.7909	9.182289	2.304314	0.31065	0.12328
Variance decomposition of SPR							
1	6.321444	8.669526	0.208934	91.12154	0	0	0
4	15.16979	8.065952	0.908064	80.14692	3.619955	3.507337	3.751771
8	20.95076	7.708241	0.906402	58.66518	14.8951	15.3095	2.51557
12	23.99927	7.757814	2.027453	50.20703	22.82812	15.19116	1.988427
16	25.36021	8.205108	4.195936	48.56222	22.4952	14.69893	1.842609
Variance decomposition of FOREX							
1	0.48233	10.37339	3.283141	0.030408	86.31306	0	0
4	1.736203	15.24524	0.807102	0.127193	78.64098	3.413664	1.765813
8	2.933722	12.83516	0.635369	0.29725	77.40891	8.052623	0.770692
12	3.730713	11.9129	1.442814	0.251496	77.49536	8.062249	0.835176
16	4.377467	11.77949	1.742274	0.531555	75.8847	8.992887	1.069096
Variance decomposition of M1BR							
1	534.4217	4.87754	9.544461	13.96707	2.893135	68.7178	0
4	1314.762	9.178884	6.727654	9.024999	24.88492	49.99163	0.191909
8	2207.684	6.276265	10.40529	3.485833	38.21032	41.20736	0.414933
12	2622.346	6.220355	17.46263	2.716337	37.15297	36.12516	0.322548
16	2874.553	6.986427	23.36118	2.266654	33.70398	33.27313	0.408629
Variance decomposition of MBR							
1	268.4066	0.956364	4.747794	13.73653	4.931514	8.039506	67.58829
4	712.9215	13.06912	7.461192	24.52011	7.052087	18.22647	29.67102
8	1343.45	8.086311	5.658784	22.02649	20.08549	30.38003	13.76288
12	1902.263	6.813888	4.702253	23.01995	24.84006	29.62276	11.0011
16	2469.495	5.998177	3.685414	27.27937	24.32641	28.7949	9.915734

Ordering: GNP96 CPI SPR FOREX M1BR MBR.

Table 10.F3 M2

Period	*S.E.*	*GNP96*	*CPI*	*SPR*	*FOREX*	*M2R*	*MBR*
Variance decomposition of GNP96							
1	10811.81	100	0	0	0	0	0
4	18630.84	75.28541	7.69631	0.966966	8.2648	4.347152	3.439364
8	28923.39	62.38242	16.73209	0.749332	11.14133	5.743513	3.251313
12	36601.17	57.34798	22.13213	1.114813	8.262146	6.271264	4.871669
16	44239.97	54.50407	22.87089	1.72656	7.072125	6.161417	7.664938
Variance decomposition of CPI							
1	0.909701	0.287271	99.71273	0	0	0	0
4	2.66362	0.105915	97.0225	0.483069	0.991722	0.379833	1.016958
8	4.638011	1.080647	92.39464	0.733703	0.53151	2.960248	2.299252
12	6.045833	3.671937	88.28969	0.954509	0.618942	4.021827	2.443097
16	7.100422	6.232995	84.12072	1.757086	1.037769	4.645394	2.206033
Variance decomposition of SPR							
1	7.155002	5.320932	0.004088	94.67498	0	0	0
4	16.432	7.655505	2.098854	80.4435	2.119576	0.588293	7.094275
8	20.36144	12.14978	4.744155	69.03804	6.843954	0.599767	6.624301
12	23.12945	18.06132	11.47693	55.28057	8.497757	0.971629	5.711793
16	26.32246	20.21746	19.43725	44.82559	9.574189	0.780004	5.165507
Variance decomposition of FOREX							
1	0.46442	12.97612	2.317597	0.005675	84.70061	0	0
4	1.599746	24.47251	0.443306	0.074611	73.35781	0.473028	1.178732
8	2.55719	24.85409	4.770584	3.161451	65.99252	0.727654	0.493705
12	3.340333	26.60533	10.52701	4.514638	57.51412	0.459213	0.379689
16	4.103992	27.47942	14.41768	3.072418	53.88154	0.433063	0.715883
Variance decomposition of M2R							
1	1705.343	0.064808	17.33376	0.000782	1.820615	80.78004	0
4	2414.115	0.31569	37.84263	1.690232	5.25332	50.73846	4.159669
8	3757.473	0.248883	51.54999	9.551921	2.282592	32.73873	3.627888
12	5029.504	0.848224	57.0908	11.98452	1.284995	24.65075	4.140712
16	6168.359	1.067085	60.07125	10.941	0.874923	21.70972	5.336025
Variance decomposition of MBR							
1	276.0665	1.265177	7.086523	14.35149	2.030172	0.102107	75.16453
4	742.6488	18.54138	12.71413	21.48948	1.439202	1.465251	44.35055
8	1157.547	18.97983	20.01435	18.11337	5.452532	1.246469	36.19344
12	1563.827	22.9484	25.40394	13.39373	5.670366	0.714937	31.86862
16	2057.905	24.63436	27.54637	12.89253	6.53837	0.421983	27.96639

Ordering: GNP96 CPI SPR FOREX M2R MBR.

Table 10.F4 Divisia

Period	*S.E.*	*GNP96*	*CPI*	*SPR*	*FOREX*	*DIVISIA*	*MBR*
Variance decomposition of GNP96							
1	9176.695	100	0	0	0	0	0
4	16696.98	78.53554	4.719096	7.340105	0.450607	8.57434	0.380314
8	30310.66	60.41284	11.66868	8.423917	0.35007	17.30033	1.844156
12	42146.19	50.34359	13.41158	9.72105	0.307689	24.8791	1.336997
16	52128.84	44.3437	11.91192	9.556718	0.266186	32.83185	1.089629
Variance decomposition of CPI							
1	0.878083	2.356806	97.64319	0	0	0	0
4	2.885924	1.724054	92.82961	1.158397	0.600696	3.454996	0.232247
8	5.053784	1.140568	87.26016	1.141766	1.8009	8.548518	0.108085
12	6.647679	0.702676	84.46737	0.708523	2.356122	11.60382	0.161489
16	7.89828	0.525457	83.75591	0.660642	2.579441	12.34536	0.133189
Variance decomposition of SPR							
1	4.86274	0.599387	0.982341	98.41827	0	0	0
4	9.702589	4.049241	15.31522	41.54999	0.244548	36.61532	2.225691
8	15.94361	4.27535	17.31639	17.16891	1.617674	42.57786	17.04382
12	23.02351	13.01895	17.70212	20.79644	4.375177	32.08103	12.02627
16	28.18058	15.63559	16.58656	21.39833	3.74144	33.42746	9.210615
Variance decomposition of FOREX							
1	0.362756	19.87581	0.142114	1.622631	78.35944	0	0
4	1.359658	46.50492	0.039802	5.416788	43.23761	4.33164	0.46924
8	2.422961	51.66486	1.96086	5.253156	28.05961	10.04546	3.016058
12	3.339287	49.6147	6.134712	6.880578	21.74196	12.33831	3.28974
16	4.095221	47.99858	7.819053	7.362151	18.46464	15.55135	2.804222
Variance decomposition of DIVISIA							
1	18.46263	6.855592	2.278636	0.033724	0.108115	90.72393	0
4	49.45058	15.69914	10.87585	10.38543	2.828417	57.81587	2.395301
8	91.29936	16.40474	13.20092	14.00873	3.278551	44.67668	8.430386
12	130.2665	18.85051	13.09419	17.45836	3.399565	41.02977	6.167607
16	157.9219	18.37082	12.45664	17.73286	2.829327	43.64895	4.961401
Variance decomposition of MBR							
1	162.3443	0.085479	28.06829	1.205651	2.711507	2.827389	65.10169
4	482.7104	17.7756	25.66243	1.149203	0.755793	43.61288	11.0441
8	866.1138	14.05052	30.70955	2.04653	0.393976	46.63748	6.161949
12	1309.736	16.76761	31.07242	6.402807	0.666955	40.69702	4.393194
16	1736.697	18.08209	28.80002	8.625917	0.643216	40.29779	3.550965

Ordering: GNP96 CPI SPR FOREX DIVISIA MBR.

Notes

1 Including the encouragement of foreign direct investment; and evaluation of the effect of the latter on the Taiwanese economy and vice-versa is given in Bende and Ford (1998).

2 The essential commitment of the Central Bank in Taiwan to the private sectors protects the economy as a whole from the possibility that the domestic industry fails to adapt itself to face the impact of a once-and-for-all appreciation of local currency.

3 Their definitions are: M1A, cash in circulation with the public, checking accounts, and passbook deposits; M1B, is M1A plus passbook-savings deposits; and, M2, is M1A plus time and savings deposits.

4 A summary of financial liberalisation can be found in Agung and Ford (1999) and in Ford (2000). See also, Jia-Dong Shea (1994) and Ya-Hwei Yang (1994).

5 An alternative approach to identifying the structural innovations is that of King *et al.* (1991), using a variant of that proposed by Blanchard and Quah (1989). This is based on the exploitation of the presence of cointegrating relationships within the vector, or sub-sets of the vector, of endogenous variables (but arrived at *outside* the system, in the sense that the cointegrating equations are not obtained by estimating the VAR itself as a system (as in the section 'Empirical results' below), by say the Johansen approach). The cointegrating vectors are used to identify the number of innovations to the variables that produce only transitory effects on the variables, whilst the remaining common stochastic trends exhibited by the vector of variables are used to quantify the permanent innovations in the system. The cointegrating equations are exploited to measure and incorporate the permanent innovations into the decomposition matrix used to generate the impulse-response functions arising from the permanent innovations. Those impulse responses are generated from the ECM form of the system with the error-correction terms from the cointegrating equations used as (exogenous) regressors. We have used this approach to examine the monetary versus banking channel views of the transmission mechanism for Japan; however, it is problematic, not least in its identification of the so-called permanent innovations (for example, productivity innovations,...), and it requires further extensive econometric work to develop our modelling along such lines.

6 In their work of the CBC's reaction function, Shen and Hakes (1995) find that the variables associated with the open economy, such as the exchange rate and the foreign assets, are insignificant statistically while the internal objectives of both inflation and output are significant to the responses of policy instruments.

7 There are numerous surveys now in available on the monetary policies and controls, as well as on general economic policy in Taiwan. However, perhaps we can make bold to note some of our own work, which we do since it embraces aspects of our current topic and offers some other econometric study of the Taiwanese economy. Thus, we note as examples, Ford (1997), Agung and Ford (1999) and Ford (2000).

8 The VAR system performs worse if the required ratio is selected as the policy instrument in response to the overall state of Taiwan economy, regardless of whether it is jointly included with other instruments such as the monetary base or the rediscount rate. Therefore, we exclude the required-ratio from our analysis in the ensuing discussion. In fact, we could find no evidence to persuade us that the Central Bank of China frequently sets the required-ratio in pursuit of our predetermined final goals. The disadvantage of using reserve requirements to control the money supply is that raising the requirements can cause immediate liquidity problems for banks with low excess reserves. Continually fluctuating required ratio would create more uncertainty for monetary institutions and make their liquidity management more difficult.

9 These tests are now so commonplace that we do not cite any references; and neither do we report here the detailed findings. They consume unnecessary space; but can be obtained from the authors upon request. We might perhaps add, however, that in the presence of possible structural changes, such as might have occurred with the 1985 (Plaza Accord) appreciation of the exchange rate, and the changes in the banking system and interest rates consequent upon deregulation, that the Zivot and Andrews (1992) test for unit roots be employed. However, that test is nested within the conventional tests, in that if they indicate unit roots (non-stationarity) there is no need to test further by using the variable trend function of Zivot and Andrews. If we do we obtain the outcome reported here.

10 We have done so on several occasions, and we make reference to one of those publications since provides the information on the construction of the Divisia index used in this paper. See, Agung and Ford (1999).

11 See the reference in note (10) for innovation and the Divisia for Taiwan; and also on innovation and the Divisia, see Ford, Peng and Mullineux (1992).

12 The procedure adopted was to test for no trend, linear trend and then quadratic trends in that order; so that we moved from the most-restrictive to the least-restrictive model in respect of the role accorded to time. In effect, adopting the Pantula principle as suggested by Johansen (1992) (see also Johansen (1995)). That role was evaluated with reference to the trace statistic, maximum eigenvalue test statistic and information criteria. Essentially, cointegration was present for the four systems (that is with the four different monetary aggregates) in the first system, the most restricted model. Again, as with the test statistics for unit roots, these are too extensive to be listed here and can be obtained from the authors on request.

13 Details of the diagnostic statistics (Jacque-Bera, LM, ARCH, information criteria,...) for the VARs in levels that were used in the following and for the tests for cointegration are also too extensive to include here. They can be obtained from the authors upon request.

14 The trace statistics are:

Cvectors	*M1AR*	*M1BR*	*M2R*	*Divisia*	*5% crit. val.*	*1% crit. val.*
None	132.91	130.43	144.22	132.00	82.49	90.45
At most 1	84.05	80.17	93.73	79.17	59.46	66.52
At most 2	40.97	38.37	51.60	36.16	39.89	45.58
At most 3	16.65	14.28	20.15	17.86	24.31	29.75
At most 4	6.02	7.11	6.15	8.23	12.53	16.31

15 Here we are treating the six innovations as permanent innovations: that is, they potentially have permanent effects on the system. If we adopt the methodology summarised in note 5, we could use the cointegrating vectors to partition the innovations to the system into permanent and transitory components.

16 The tests conducted were standard ones, being Wald tests. As Toda and Phillips (1994) point out the Wald test for causality should be conducted in the VEC and not in the VAR in levels (as they frequently are), since only in the presence of some cointegration between the variables will the Wald test be asymptotically χ^2.

17 In some of the equations in the VAR systems the discount rate is significantly different from zero when it is entered as a conditioning, that is, exogenous, variable. However, its presence does not alter the impulse-response functions and the variance decompositions significantly: the broad picture depicted here is retained.

18 This accords with the findings of Shen and Hakes (1995). Our next conclusion, though weaker than our first, differs slightly, therefore, from theirs.

References

Agung, J. and Ford, J. L. (1999) 'The money multiplier for broad money, Divisia money, and innovation (liberalisation) adjusted Divisia money: a cointegration and ECM study for Taiwan, 1969 to 1996', *Rivista Intenazionale di Scienze Economiche e Commerciali (RISEC)*, xlvi(4), 725–49.

Barnett, W. A. (1978) 'The user cost of money', *Economics Letters*, 6(2), 145–9.

Barnett, W. A. (1980) 'Economic monetary aggregates: an application of index number and economic aggregation theory', *Journal of Econometrics*, 14(3), 11–48.

Bende-Nabende, A. and Ford, J. L. (1998) 'FDI, policy adjustment and endogenous growth: multiplier effects from a small dynamic model for Taiwan, 1959–1995', *World Development*, 26(7), 1315–30.

Blanchard, O. J. and Quay, D. (1989) 'The dynamic effects of aggregate supply and demand fluctuations', *American Economic Review*, 79(4), 655–73.

Chinn, M. D. and Dooley, M. P. (1997) 'Monetary policy in Japan, Germany and the United States: does one size fit all?' *NBER Working Paper*, 6092.

Chiu, P. C. H. and Hou, T.-C. (1992) 'Prices, money and monetary policy implementation under financial liberalisation – the case of Taiwan', in H. Reisen and B. Fischer (eds), *Financial Opening: Policy Issues and Experiences in Developing Countries*, pp. 173–200 OECD.

Chiu, P. C. H. and Hou, T.-C. (1995) 'Prices, monetary indicators and monetary policy implementation: the case of Taiwan', *The Central Bank of China, Quarterly Review*, 17(2), 23–41.

Clarida, R. and Gertler, M. (1996) 'How the Bundesbank conducts monetary policy', *NBER Working Paper*, 5581.

Clarida, R., Gali, J. and Gertler, M. (1997) 'Monetary policy rules in practice: some international evidence', *Centre for Economic Policy Research (CEPR) Working Paper*, 1750.

Doan, T. (1992) *RATS Users's Manual*, Evanston, Illinois: Estima.

Ford, J. L., Peng, W. S. and Mullineux, A. W. (1992) 'Financial innovation and Divisia monetary aggregates', *Oxford Bulletin of Economics and Statistics*, 54(1), 97–112.

Ford, J. L. (1997) 'The targets and instruments of monetary control: long-run trade-offs, multiplier effects, and Central Bank preferences, Taiwan, 1995–1995', Department of Economics, University of Birmingham, Discussion Paper, 97-21.

Ford, J. L. (2000) 'Economic development, financial development and liberalisation: Taiwan, 1960–1995', in D. G. Dickinson, J. L. Ford, M. J. Fry, A. W. Mullineux and S. Sen (eds), *Finance, Governance and Economic Performance in Pacific and South East Asia*, pp. 26–62, Cheltenham, United Kingdom: Edward Elgar.

Friedman, M. (1988) 'Money and the stock market', *Journal of Political Economy*, 96, 221–45.

Granger, C. W. J. and Newbold, P. (1974) 'Spurious regressions in econometrics', *Journal of Econometrics*, 2, 111–20.

Hsu, C.-M. (1996) 'The Taiwanese monetary policy in a decade', in the conference in memory of Prof. Liang Kuo-Shu, the Economics Department of the National Taiwan University, August 17, 1996.

Hwung, F.-Y. (1996) 'The investigation on the effects of intermediate targets to monetary policy', National Cheng-Chih University, M.A. dissertation.

Johansen, S. (1992) 'Determination of cointegration rank in the presence of a linear trend', *Oxford Bulletin of Economics and Statistics*, 54, 383–97.

Johansen, S. (1995) *Cointegration*, Oxford: Oxford University Press.

King, R. G., Plosser, C. I. and Watson, M. W. (1991) 'Stochastic trends and fluctuations', *American Economic Review*, 81(4), 819–40.

Lin, T.-Y. (1996) 'The set-up of target zone of monetary aggregate for 1995 – the effects of structural factors on demand for M2', Department of Economics Research, The Central Bank of China.

Lin, T.-Y. and Lee, J.-C. (1989*a*) 'The relation between velocity of income and the stock market', The Central Bank of China, *Quarterly Review*, 11(4), 38–45.

McCallum, B. T. (1984) 'Monetarist rules in the light of recent experience', *American Economic Review Papers and Proceedings*, 74(2), 388–91.

McCallum, B. T. (1987) 'The case for rules in the conduct of monetary policy: a concrete example', *Weltwirtschaftliches Archiv*, 123, 415–29.

McCallum, B. T. (1988) 'Robustness properties of a rule for monetary policy', *Carnegie-Rochester Conference Series on Public Policy*, 29, 173–204.

McCallum, B. T. (1993*a*) 'Discretion versus policy rules in practice: two critical points, a comment', *Carnegie-Rochester Conference Series on Public Policy*, 39, 215–20.

McCallum, B. T. (1993*b*) 'Specification and analysis of a monetary policy rule for Japan', *Bank of Japan Monetary and Economic Studies*, 11(2), 1–45.

McCallum, B. T. (1994*a*) 'Specification of policy rules and performance measures in multicountry simulation studies', *Journal of International Money and Finance*, 13(3), 259–75.

McCallum, B. T. (1994*b*) 'Monetary policy without monetary aggregates', Federal Reserve Bank of St. Louis, *Review*, 76(2), 216–18.

Patrick, H. T. and Park, C. Y. (eds) (1994) *The Financial Development of Japan, Korea, and Taiwan*, Oxford: Oxford University Press.

Sellin, P. (1998) 'Asset prices and monetary policy in Sweden', *Bank for International Settlements, Conference Papers*, 5, 166–77.

Shea, J.-D. (1994) 'Taiwan: development and structural change of the financial system', in H. T. Patrick and Y. C. Park (eds), pp. 222–87.

Shen, C.-H. and Hakes, D. R. (1995) 'Monetary policy as a decision-making hierarchy: the case of Taiwan', *Journal of Macroeconomics*, 17(2), 357–68.

Shen, C.-H. and Wai, W.-C. (1993) 'Selection of the intermediate target in Taiwan: comparison between M1A, M1B, M1C and M2', The Bank of Taiwan, *Quarterly Review*, 44(1), 56–87.

Shih, Y. (1994) 'The estimation and test of the demand for M1A, M1B and M2; the set-up of target zone of monetary aggregate for 1995', Department of Economics Research, The Central Bank of China.

Sims, C. A. (1980) 'Macroeconomics and reality', *Econometrica*, 48(1), 1–48.

Sims, C. A. (1986) 'Are forecasting models usable for policy analysis?' Federal Reserve Bank of Minneapolis, *Quarterly Review* (Winter), 3–16.

Sims, C. A. (1992) 'Interpreting the macroeconomic time series facts, the effects of monetary policy', *European Economic Review*, 36, 975–1011.

Toda, H. Y. and Phillips, P. C. B. (1994) 'Vector autoregression and causality: a theoretical overview and simulation study', *Econometric Reviews*, 13, 259–85.

Wenninger, J. and Radecki, L. J. (1986) 'Financial transactions and the demand for M1', Federal Reserve Bank of New York, *Quarterly Review*, 11(2), 24–9.

Wu, C.-S. and Hwung, T.-H. (1990) 'The components of money stock and movements of price – a case study of Taiwan', in the Conference on Taiwan Financial and Price Issues, Department of Economics, *Academia Sinica*, June.

Yang, Y.-H. (1994) 'Taiwan: development and structural change of the banking system', in H. T. Patrick and Y. C. Park (eds), pp. 288–324.

Zivot, E. and Andrews, D. W. K. (1992) 'Further evidence on the Great Crash, the oil-price shock, and the unit-root hypotheis', *Journal of Business and Economics*, 10(3), 251–70.

11 New transmission mechanisms and instruments of monetary policy at near zero-interest rates

The case of Japan in the late 1990s*

Eric Girardin and Nicholas Horsewood

Introduction

Monetary policy in Asia was one of the central themes of Max Fry's work. He had first-hand knowledge and experience of many east and south-Asian countries. Concerned mainly with developing Asia, he dealt with monetary policy reaction functions (e.g. Fry, 1995), as well as the effects of monetary policy on output dynamics (e.g. Fry and Lilien, 1986). He stressed that greater monetary discipline in the Pacific Basin developing economies was a major factor behind their superior economic performance. We will here examine the effects of monetary policy by focusing on the case of Japan.

Since the mid-1990s, the Japanese economy has entered a new stage characterised by very low interest rates, with the lower bound of zero reached from early 1999 until August 2000. Since then the Bank of Japan has tried to lift interest rates back to positive territory, but retreated to its earlier stance in late March 2001. Given that the restart of positive Japanese economic growth is quite fragile and that deflation is still going on, such decisions raise heated controversy among both academics and policy makers (see Amirault and O'Reilly (2001) or Oda and Okina (2001) for a survey of the proposed policy options). The latter disagree on the likely effects of such rate-changes both on output and prices in the short as well as in the medium run. The main issue to be addressed is whether, with such near-zero (less than 1 per cent) interest rates, during the second half of the 1990s, the transmission mechanisms of monetary policy were any different from what they are under more 'normal' circumstances.

The unique experience of Japan in the late 1990s has justifiably raised the interest of many academics. Such contributions stress that if the interest rate is stuck close to zero, there is still a route for monetary-stabilisation policy operating through the monetary base and/or via the foreign-exchange market. Thus,

*The present version of the chapter benefited from comments by Michael Hutchison and participants at the Oxford 2001 meeting of the CEPR European Network on the Japanese Economy. We also thank Alistair Barr both for his comments and his providing data on all-industry output and the broad index of share prices. However we remain solely responsible for all remaining errors.

some argue that a rise in monetary base can stimulate real income even in periods with near-zero interest rates (Meltzer, 1998, 2000). Others (e.g. Bernanke, 2000; McCallum, 2000; Svensson, 2000; etc.) support the view that a depreciation in the yen, engineered by central bank intervention in the foreign-exchange market, can similarly reflate the economy. Considering the lack of success of Krugman (1998) style reflationary policies, based on a restart of inflation expectations, in convincing the board of the Bank of Japan (BOJ), the impact of alternative instruments of monetary policy is worth considering as a potential basis for an escape route for Japan.

The present chapter focuses exclusively on the effects of policy shocks, that is, temporary measures, and may thus seem ill-suited to assess the impact of supposedly 'permanent' measures. However, one should be cautious about dubbing as permanent monetary-policy measures which may be reversed in the near future. One example is the assertion in late March 2001 by the BOJ that it would keep its key interest rate at zero until CPI inflation started to be positive again. It is worth recalling that a year ago (13 April 2000) the BOJ similarly announced that it would pursue a zero interest rate policy until deflationary concerns disappeared (Oda and Okina, 2001, p. 328), and yet four months later it lifted interest rates back to positive territory.

Given the scant empirical evidence available, compared to the explosion of proposals and recent wave of theoretical modelling, there is a need to provide an empirical basis in order to assess three series of issues in the second half of the 1990s in Japan. Do interest rate changes have any impact on output and prices? Do changes in bank reserves have an impact even at near-zero interest rates? Can exchange-rate depreciation be the 'foolproof' (Svensson, 2000) way out of the liquidity trap?

The empirical study of the output and price effects of monetary policy using the workhorse in macroeconomic time series analysis, that is, VARs (vector autoregressive models), has been a very intensive area over the last decade (Favero, 2000; Sims *et al.*, 1990). Such work has usually put a lot of emphasis on the interest rate and money transmission channels. However, one may wonder, particularly in the case of Japan, whether some other transmission channels could not play a role. Among these, asset price and to a lesser extent credit channels are typical candidates.

We will argue that the study of the role played by asset prices should not be confined to the exchange rate. Indeed, given the prominent role played by share prices in the Japanese economy, through wealth effects on consumption, Tobin's *q* type effects on investment or possibly through the asset side of banks' balance sheets, we will consider to what extent share prices represent a key variable and whether supporting them can also play a role in stimulating output. The various ways in which such a support can be provided are currently a hotly-debated issue in Japan.

The present paper will consider these issues in the light of the approach advocated by Christiano *et al.* (1999), and will focus on the second half of the 1990s. We will briefly review the main transmission channels of monetary policy as isolated by theoretical work in this area. Then, we will present the results of our empirical work on the transmission channels of monetary policy shocks. Next, we will briefly review the argument in favour of an intervention-led yen depreciation as a way to reflate the Japanese economy and empirically assess its validity as well as the efficacy of an alternative policy of share price support. Finally we will offer some conclusions and will give some details on some recent proposals aiming at lifting share prices in Japan.

Monetary policy in Japan and its channels of transmission

Transmission channels of monetary policy

Existing theoretical work on the transmission of monetary-policy shocks to the real economy has emphasised three series of channels (Mishkin, 1996), the relevance of which has recently received renewed interest in Japan (Oda and Okina, 2001). In the first, or money transmission, channel, contractionary monetary policy leads to a rise in real interest rates, which itself triggers an increase in the cost of capital, leading to a fall in aggregate demand through lower investment spending by both consumers and firms (Taylor, 1995).

The second series of channels questions the almost exclusive focus of the money transmission channel on one asset price, the interest rate. Indeed, both the exchange rate and share prices can play a major role. In an open economy an asset-price channel operates through the exchange rate, which impacts directly on the consumer price index via changes in the domestic value of imports. To the extent that the exchange rate usually responds quickly to interest rate changes, this leads to a faster transmission of monetary policy to domestic inflation. Moreover, given sticky nominal wages and prices, real exchange rate effects lead to a substitution between domestic and foreign goods, and in turn to changes in domestic economic activity (Taylor, 1995).

Monetary policy can affect the whole spectrum of relative asset-prices and real wealth through share prices (Meltzer, 1995). A fall in money supply (associated with a rise in short-term interest rates), thus, leads agents to sell equities in order to obtain the cash balances that are now in short supply. The fall in share prices can dampen private spending through two channels, involving respectively Tobin's q-theory of investment and wealth effects. According to the former, the fall in stock prices leads to a lower market value of firms relative to the replacement cost of capital (the q-ratio) generating a fall in investment by firms. The latter channel implies that the fall in financial wealth of consumers associated with lower equity prices leads them to cut their consumption in line with the fall in their lifetime resources.

Portfolio-rebalancing effects play a major role in the transmission mechanisms of quantitative easing through short-term or long-term market operations. In both cases the central bank purchases government bonds with base money. The extent to which portfolio effects can play a role depends on the difference in the 'moneyness' between the assets bought and sold by the bank. Moneyness is defined as the marginal cost for a money holder, that is, the opportunity cost of holding each monetary asset. Short-term government bonds have the same moneyness as base money when interest rates are very close or equal to zero. As a result, no portfolio effect can operate through a money-market operation involving such assets because the latter are almost perfect substitutes with base money under such conditions (Meltzer, 1999; Oda and Okina, 2001). However, portfolio effects could still be present if the central bank decided to operate on the long-term government bond market.

The third series of channels involves credit markets where imperfect information is a major feature. The emphasis is then put either on the bank lending channel or on the balance-sheet channel (e.g. Bernanke and Gertler, 1995). A restrictive monetary policy shock can generate a fall in bank deposits which will lead banks to reduce their lending. As a result investment by firms, or consumers, will fall, resulting in a decline in output. Besides, the balance-sheet channel stresses both the fall in collateral as well as the rise in moral hazard associated with a fall in the net worth of firms. The impact of monetary policy may be substantially different depending on the degree of weakness of banks' balance sheets, or on the type of borrowers (e.g. small vs large firms, Kasyap and Stein, 1994).

Some of these different channels may very well coexist and complement each other, as exemplified by Kashyap and Stein (1994) in the case of the credit channel and the traditional money channel. Moreover, in the Japanese case, the asset-price channel may interact with the credit channel through changes in the value of shares held by banks.

Monetary policy and financial asset prices in Japan

The main series used in the empirical analysis are presented in Figure 11.1. Monthly data are employed to identify the salient features of the transmission mechanism in a very disturbed and unique period. Apart from the sharp upheavals[1] in the late 1980s and the early 1990s, the mid-1990s represent a major turning point in monetary policy and financial price movements in Japan (for an overview, see Cargill *et al.*, 2000). Indeed, the second half of the 1990s stands out as a period where deflationary forces were strongly at work (Bernanke, 2000). Except for part of 1997, CPI inflation was zero and headline deflation set in as of late 1999. This was accompanied by declining nominal asset values, like share prices from 1996 to late 1998, even though such a fall is less sharp with a broad share-price index than with the usual Nikkei or Topix indices. Initially, the yen depreciated, but it started appreciating in mid-1998.

Meanwhile the Bank of Japan cut its call money rate from over 200 basis points in early 1995 to half this level in the summer and again by half in the early autumn. The money-market interest rate levelled off for almost 3 years, hovering around 30 basis points, until, in the autumn 1998, it started falling to reach around 3 basis points in February 1990. Such a 'zero' interest rate policy (money-market rates between 3 and 4 basis points) was pursued until the Bank of Japan decided to lift its rate to 25 basis points in August 2000. Associated with this interest rate policy was a huge injection of reserves in the banking system by the BOJ (Figure 11.1).

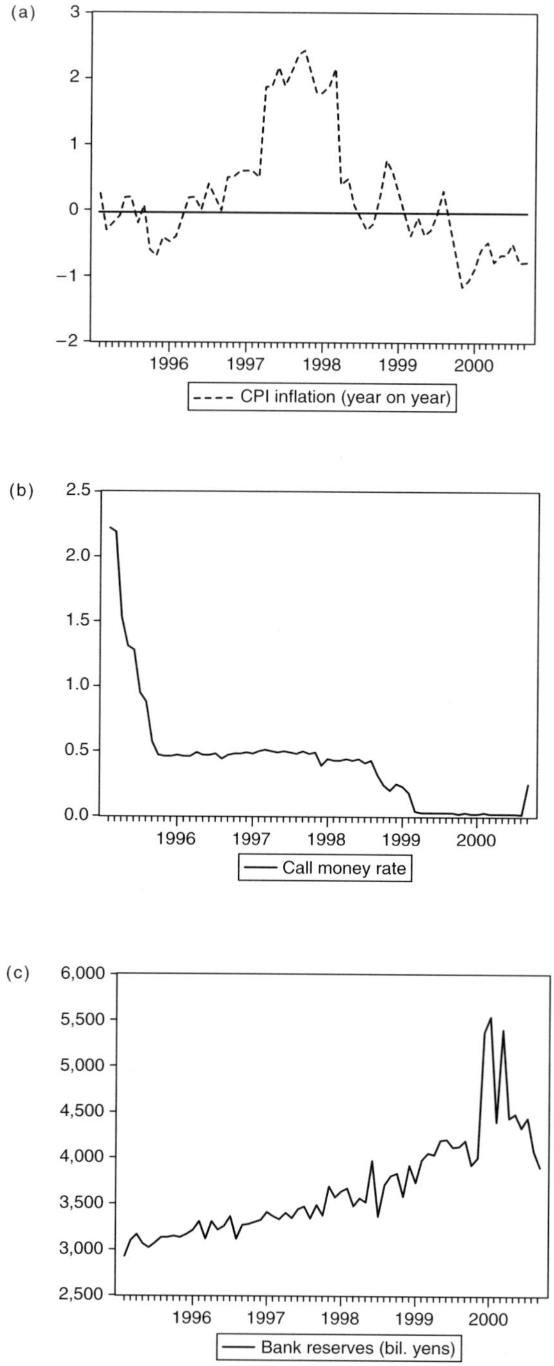

Figure 11.1 (a)–(f) The data.

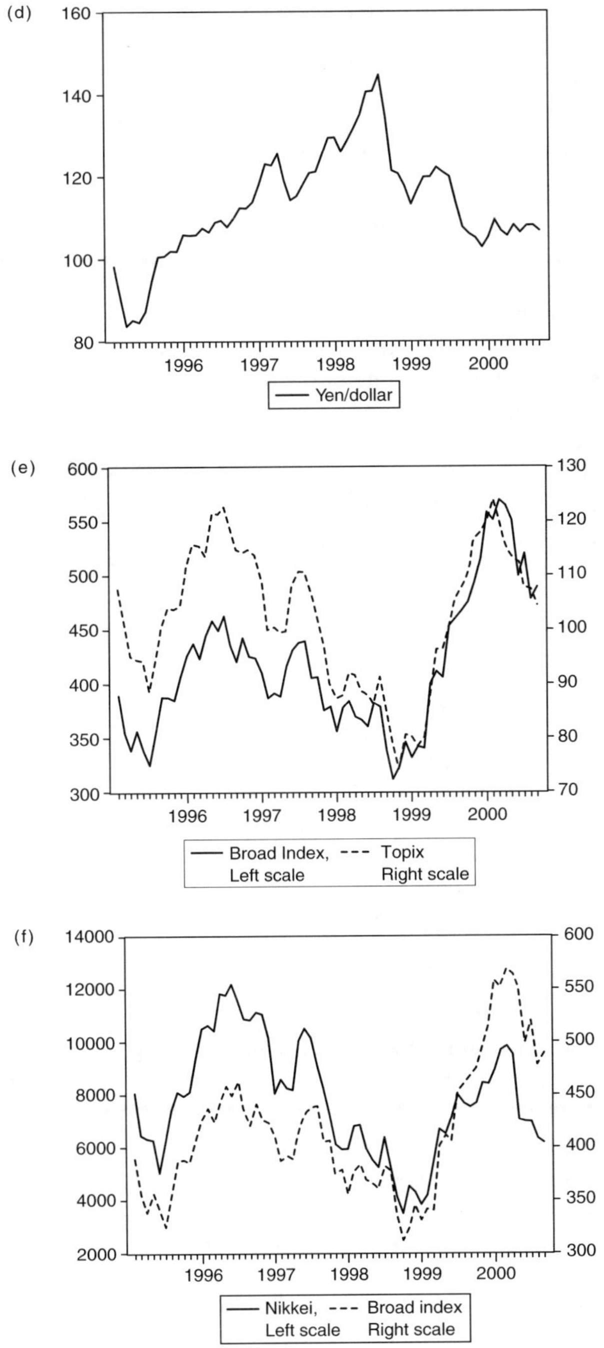

Figure 11.1 (Continued)

Evaluating the respective role of the different channels in the late 1990s

Methodological approach

We are concerned here with the unanticipated effect of monetary policy and rely on the identification of monetary policy shocks. Such a focus is synonymous with a concern with the unsystematic part of interest rate movements (for a concern with the systematic part, see McCallum, 1999; on the alternative approach implemented here, see Favero, 2000), defined as all variations in central bank policy that cannot be accounted for by a rule-based reaction to the state of the economy. Such a study of the effects of deviations from rules is a means to collect information on the response of macroeconomic variables to monetary impulses that are not expected by the market.

In the tradition of Sims *et al.* (1990), the specification of a VAR system considers variables in levels since we are only interested in studying the impact of shocks within impulse-response functions exercises (Christiano *et al.*, 1999). An alternative route would consist in focusing on target variables such as the output gap rather than the level of output, and inflation rather than the price level. However, both would raise problems. In the case of Japan, the output gap is a loosely-defined concept since there is much uncertainty on the level of potential output (Bayoumi, 2000). Similarly, focusing on the rate of inflation would not seem adequate when examining a period of price stability. Movements in the price level then seem to be the relevant variable of interest.

The structure in the VAR that we use ranks first non-policy variables such as the consumer price index and industrial output. Policy variables are ranked second since they are considered to be affected contemporaneously by non-policy variables, but the latter are affected by monetary policy shocks only with a one-period lag (Christiano *et al.*, 1999).

The monthly data that we use are extracted from the I.M.F. International Financial Statistics CD-Rom, except for commercial bank reserves with the BOJ and interest rates on loans which are extracted from the BOJ database. The estimations were carried out with E-Views, a software for which Max Fry was UK representative. Rather than industrial output (available in IFS), we used a broader measure of economic activity, that is, the all-industry output (compiled by the METI). The all-industry index takes a reading of activity in six tertiary industries (utilities, transport and telecommunications, wholesale and retail, finance and insurance, real estate and services), combined with activity in the construction, agricultural and fisheries industries, the public sector and industrial production. This index is considered a close approximation for Gross Domestic Product as measured by industrial and service sector output. Besides, given the unavailability of land prices on a monthly basis, we had to neglect such a variable in the empirical work. We included a dummy variable to partial out the impact on the Consumer Price Index of the April 1997 increase in the sales tax from 3 to 5 per cent.

When assessing the asset-price transmission mechanism, three share-price indices were considered: the Nikkei index, the Topix index and the Datastream broad-market index. The results appeared robust to the use of the share-price index and the analysis presented below employs the broad-market index, a capitalisation-weighted average of the 1200 shares on the first section of the Tokyo Stock exchange.

A substantive issue relates to the appropriate sample to be considered in the econometric study. It is often emphasised that VAR models of the monetary-transmission mechanism should be estimated within a single policy regime (Favero, 2000) because regime shifts require different parameterisations (see also Bagliano and Favero, 1998). When estimated over different policy regimes, VAR models of the monetary-transmission mechanism show evidence of structural instability. This is something that we certainly verified with prior tests in the case of Japan, which showed the presence of structural instability of such VARs in early 1990. It thus seemed that examining the transmission mechanisms of monetary policy in Japan over the 1980s and 1990s (as, for instance, in Morsink and Bayoumi, 2000) would not yield any meaningful result. However, even focusing on the 1990s does not seem adequate. Indeed in a standard stochastic model, Orphanides and Wieland (1998) show that, when inflation is lower than one per cent, non-linearities in the transmission process of monetary policy arise solely from the presence of the zero-bound on nominal interest rates. Indeed, these effects become increasingly important for determining the outcome of policy in circumstances with such low-inflation rates. In the light of these arguments, we decided to focus on the period of near-zero interest rate by using the sample period February 1995 through September 2000.

In line with most existing work in this area (Christiano *et al.*, 1999; and Favero, 2000 for a survey), we consider the effects of monetary policy shocks on both real economic activity and prices. Leaving out prices, as in Miyigawa and Morita (1998), particularly in the case of Japan, would miss the possible role of deflation induced by restrictive monetary policy as a transmission channel of policy. We start from a core VAR system with two lags, chosen on the basis of whitening the residuals and getting rid of non-normality and heteroscedasticity (for a similar choice, see Braun and Shioji, 2000).

The effectiveness of bank reserve expansion

The core VAR comprises (seasonally adjusted) all-industry production (LINDALLA), the consumer price index (LCPI), the call money rate (CALL), and commercial bank reserves (LRESBK) with the BOJ (adjusted for changes in reserve requirements), and broad money (LMQMCD) with all variables in logarithm except interest rates. This enables us to check whether the model matches the stylised facts on the effects of a contractionary policy shocks, as established by Christiano *et al.* (1999) using impulse response functions. They conclude that plausible models of the transmission mechanism of a monetary contraction should be consistent at least with the following evidence on price, output and interest rates: (a) the aggregate price level initially responds very little, (b) output initially falls, with a j-shaped response, with a zero long-run effect of the monetary impulse, and (c) interest rates initially rise. Figure 11.2 presents the results from a positive bank reserve shock. Over the 1995–2000 period, a shock on bank reserves of one standard deviation has no significant effect on the price level and on the interest rate and leads to an almost insignificant rise in all-industry output. The significance of the output effect would be

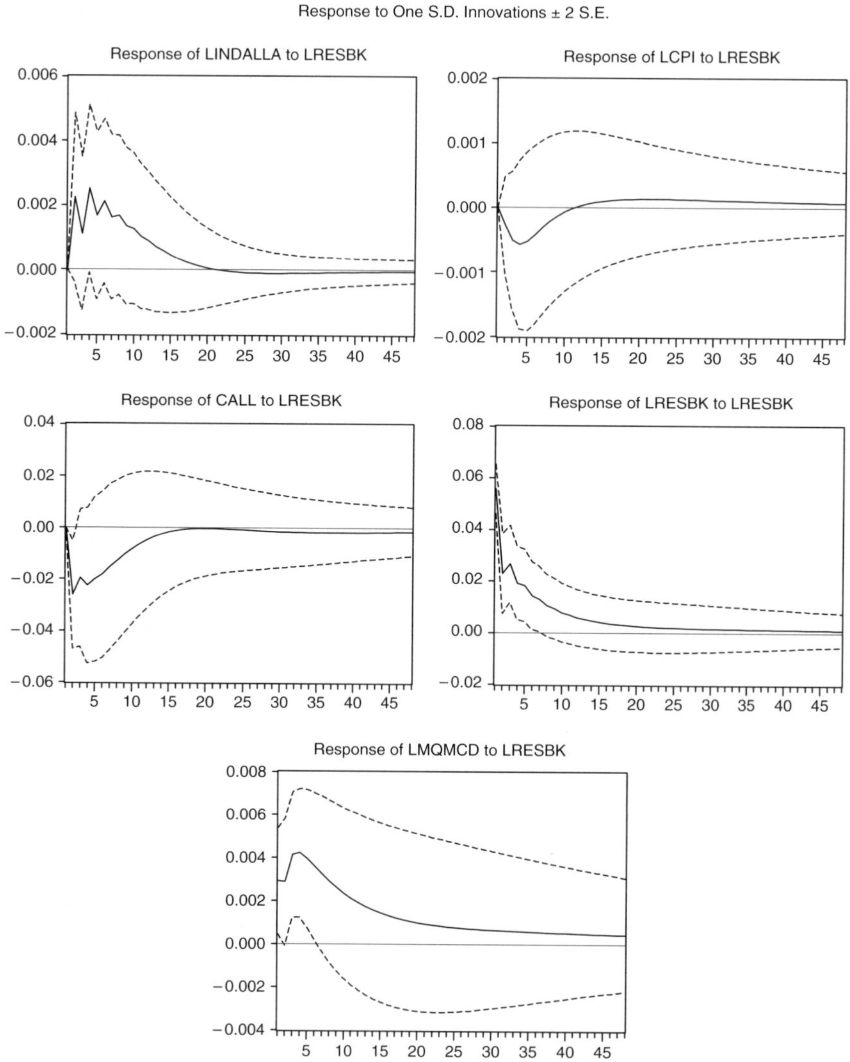

Figure 11.2 Impulse responses to a bank reserve shock with broad money.

a little surprising in the case of Japan in the second half of the 1990s since, as discussed in the previous section, at near-zero interest rates base-money and short-term bills should be perfect substitutes. Broad money, in its usual definition in Japan (M2 plus certificates of deposit) rises significantly over the first quarter after the bank reserve shock, although the magnitude of this effect is small. This vindicates the observation by Bernanke (2000) to the effect that, since 1995 in Japan a rise in base money does not lead to equivalent increases in broad money. We checked that the bank reserve shock has no (significant) effect on the government bond yield.

Some authors (e.g. Meltzer, 2000) argue that a large depreciation of the yen should result from the expansion in bank reserves. In order to assess this argument, we focus on the yen–dollar exchange rate since Japan's nominal effective exchange rate moves in close synchronisation with the former (Ramaswamy and Samei, 2000). The core model is extended by including the yen–dollar exchange rate and the share price to capture other transmission mechanisms. By contrast with Meltzer's view, the inclusion of the yen–dollar rate in our VAR system shows that the yen would seem to respond to the bank reserve shock with an appreciation (Figure 11.3), although such an effect is insignificant.

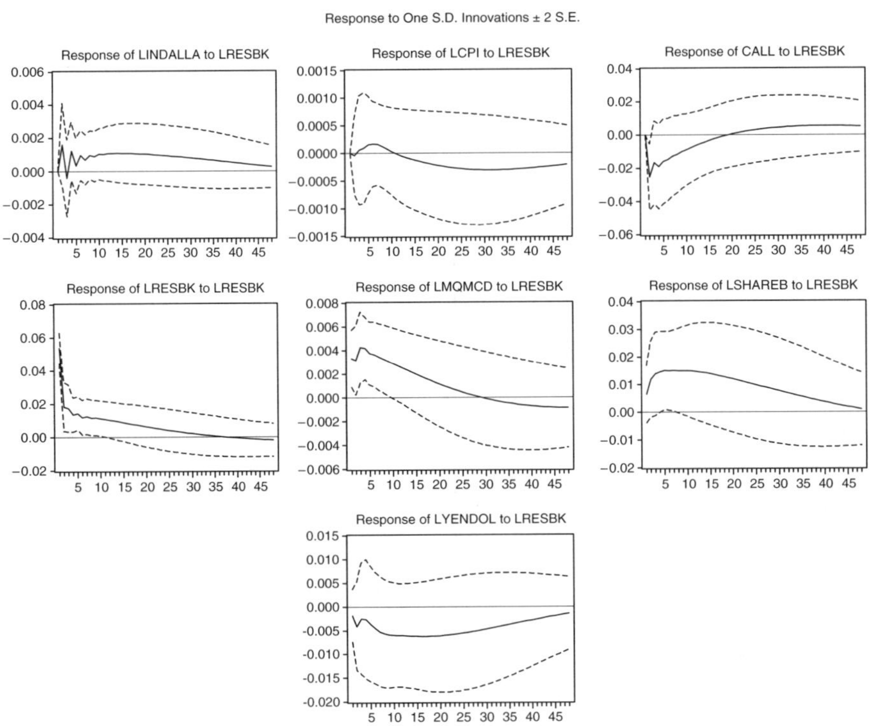

Figure 11.3 Impulse responses to a bank reserve shock with broad money, yen–dollar and share price.

It thus does not seem valid to assert in the case of Japan in the second half of the 1990s that: 'The exchange rate appears to be an important variable in the transmission of monetary changes' (Meltzer, 2000). By contrast, share prices are significantly and positively affected by a bank reserve shock, implying that the output effects of the reserve shock are longer-lived, but remain small (and insignificant).

The transmission mechanisms of interest rate shocks

The core model was altered to a four-variable VAR, with broad money excluded, to analyse the effects of a shock to the call money rate. The results are presented in Figure 11.4, and the response of consumer prices is seen to be insignificant. All-industry output falls in an increasing way over the first semester and gets back to its initial level after 2 years. An 8 basis-points rise in the call rate leads to at most a 0.1 per cent fall in all-industry output. In such a

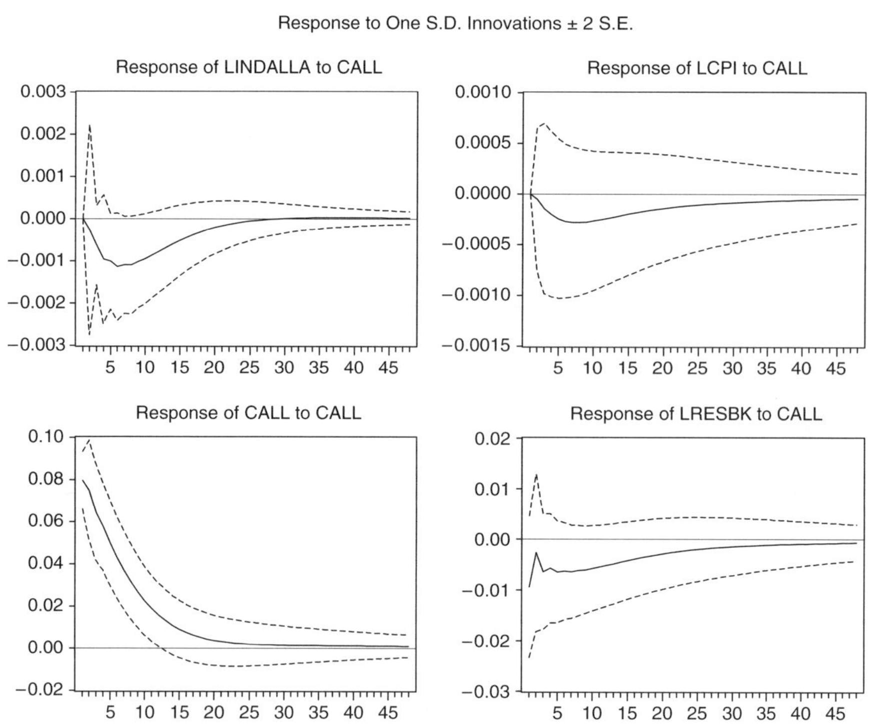

Figure 11.4 Impulse responses to an interest rate shock

simple system no output puzzle is apparent. Here, as well as in more complex systems, we experimented with the inclusion of a commodity price index (IMF series of export price of commodities) but there were no substantive changes in the transmission channel, so that we decided to drop such a variable in order to save on degrees of freedom. The traditional money channel, through bank reserves does not operate, since the impact of the shock in the call money rate on such reserves is insignificant.

We specified the interest rate channel by examining separately (results not reported) the impact of the interest shock on the bank spread as measured by the difference between the average interest rate on long-term loans and the call rate. The spread falls on impact and gets back to its initial level after a year. The presence of this channel magnifies the fall in output generated by the call-rate shock.

In order to examine the relevance of the various transmission channels highlighted in the previous section, we experimented by adding the extra variables to the VAR: bank credit to the private sector (lcredit), share prices (lsharex) the yen–dollar exchange rate (lyendol) and the government-bond yield (govy). The inclusion of bank credit did not make any difference to the effects of an interest-rate shock. Bank credit to the private sector, if at all, is affected (though non-significantly) in a positive way. Including bank credit as an exogenous variable (with two lags) did not change the results presented above, and so it was excluded from the VAR. We also examined the impact of interest-rate shocks on loans disaggregated between different type of banks (city, trust, or regional, taken from the BOJ database), but this proved insignificant.

When the government-bond yield was included in the VAR framework (see Figure 11.5 or Figure 11.6) it was not significantly affected by an interest-rate shock, except for the first two months after the shock and the impact was almost one for one. There is thus little evidence that the transmission mechanism of Japanese monetary policy at a time of near-zero interest rates would work essentially through the effects on the term structure of interest rates (for a contrary view, see Ueda, 2000).

Figure 11.5 presents results from a system comprising share prices, LSHAREB, (with the yen–dollar, lagged 1 and 2 months, exogenous). The latter fell sharply for 9 months after the interest rate shock and recovered over the subsequent 16 months (with a similar response by the Topix and Nikkei). Industrial output responds in a delayed way to the decline in share prices, and the maximum fall in output is larger than without the share-price channel in action.

The impact of the inclusion of the yen–dollar rate, among the endogenous variables (with share prices, lagged 1 and 2 months, exogenous), is given in Figure 11.6 and is very striking. The appreciation in the yen *vis à vis* the dollar following a positive interest-rate shock is in line with consensus effects of well-specified VAR systems emphasised by Christiano *et al.* (1999). However, such an

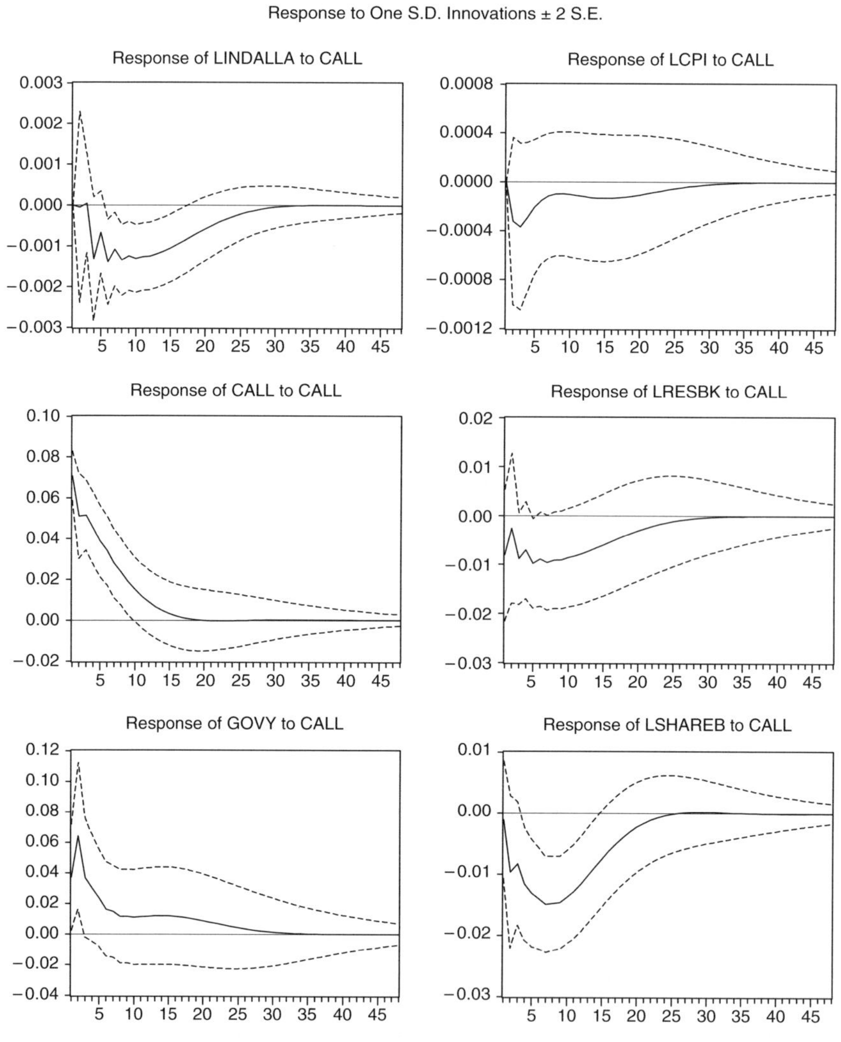

Figure 11.5 Impulse responses to an interest rate shock with government-bond yield and (broad) share prices.

exchange-rate effect is insignificant within the system and indicates the lack of role of this variable in the transmission mechanism. There is also insignificant evidence of imported deflation. The surprising result is that industrial output is now unaffected.

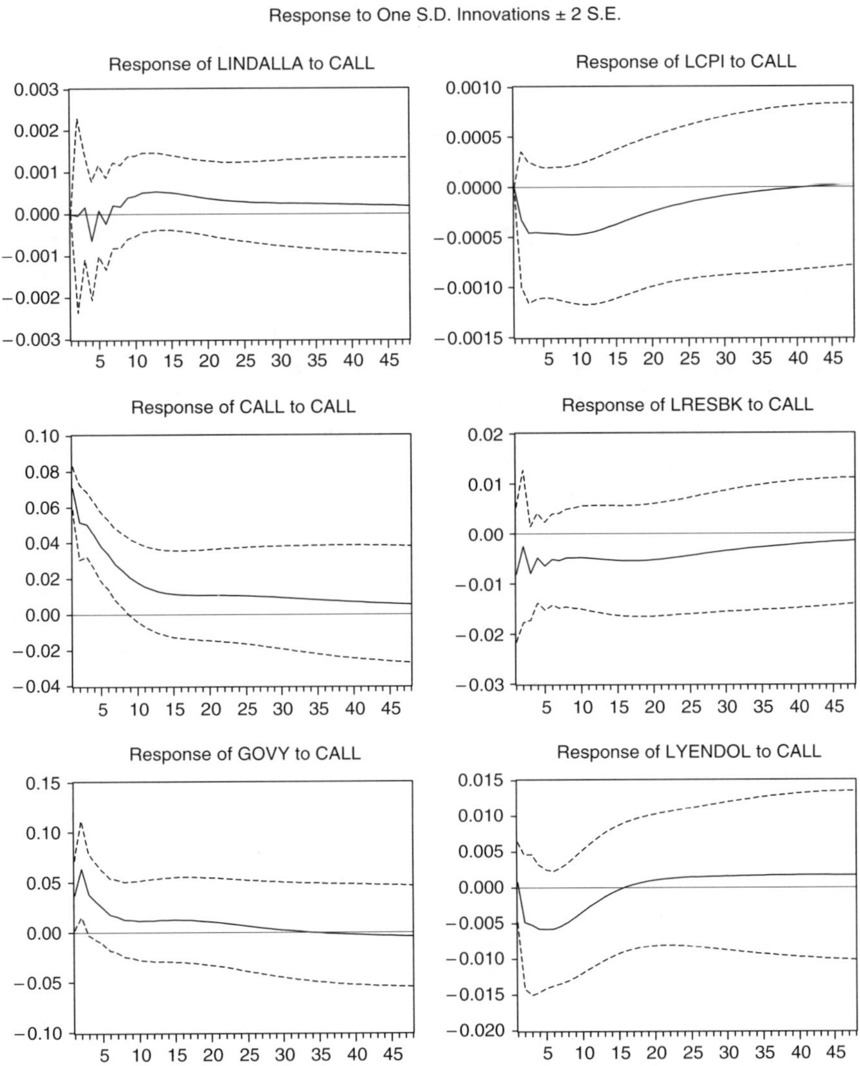

Figure 11.6 Impulse responses to an interest-rate shock with government-bond yield and yen–dollar.

Can asset-price changes be the new hidden weapon of Japanese monetary authorities?

Yen depreciation as an instrument of Japanese monetary policy

It was recently suggested that in a situation of zero interest-rate policy, the central bank could reflate the economy by pushing towards a depreciation of the yen via purchases of foreign exchange with high-powered money. According to its advocates, such 'a policy of aggressive foreign-exchange intervention to put downward pressure on the yen would by itself probably suffice to get the Japanese economy moving again' (Bernanke, 2000, p. 15).

The standard objection to this proposal is that since monetary policy would have been made ineffective by the liquidity trap, foreign-exchange market intervention by the Bank of Japan would be nothing other than sterilised intervention. There is a consensus view in the literature (see the survey by Girardin, 2000) to the effect that sterilised interventions are unable to influence the value of a currency (i.e. the level of the exchange rate), in a lasting and substantial way.[2] Available empirical evidence concludes that if intervention works, it only impacts on exchange-rate volatility. In the light of such evidence, it is likely that intervention aimed at changing the level of the yen-exchange rate may end up influencing only its volatility, which may increase the volatility of output and not its level.

Evidence on the efficacy of Japanese intervention is scant, given the past refusal of the Bank of Japan to publish its intervention data. However, a recent econometric study of the 1995–99 period uses information on the occurrence of foreign-exchange interventions in the yen–dollar market collected from the electronic archives of the financial press (Ramaswamy and Samiei, 2000). This study concludes that 'there may indeed be a role for foreign exchange interventions . . . given that interventions have succeeded on a number of occasions during 1995–99 in changing the path of the yen–dollar rate in the desired direction' . . . 'even though the interventions in the yen–dollar market were routinely sterilised'(op. cit. p. 78 and 59). One should stress that 'the typical intervention when successful has a relatively small, though persistent, impact on the yen–dollar' (ibid.).

For some reason, the justifications recently put forward for the efficacy of potential intervention by the Bank of Japan on the foreign-exchange market completely ignore the teachings of existing work on the subject. The ability of large-scale intervention to lead to a depreciation in the yen is defended by Bernanke (2000) as '*reductio ad absurdum*' argument. We should imagine that the BOJ prints domestic currency in order to buy foreign currency. A depreciation of the yen should result. Otherwise, the BOJ could be led to acquire infinite quantities of foreign assets, with the end result that foreigners would be left with yen holdings. Since this is impossible in equilibrium, it will not happen.

The argument presented by McCallum (2000) seems to be of a different nature, since it focuses on the systematic part of monetary policy, in the shape of a feedback rule with an exchange-rate instrument. However, it relies in a similar way on the portfolio-balance channel for the efficacy of intervention in the foreign-exchange market. Similarly, Svensson (2000) claims to offer a 'foolproof' way for Japan to escape from the liquidity trap and recession, a combination of a price-level target path with positive inflation and a yen devaluation with a temporary exchange-rate peg. In his view, such a package is more general than McCallum's suggestion since its efficacy would not depend on any portfolio-balance effects of foreign-exchange interventions (Svensson, 2000). However, even for Svensson, 'one can think of the temporary peg as supported by a threat of foreign exchange interventions of huge volumes, at which a portfolio-balance effect would realistically appear and depreciate the currency. This threat would exclude the possibility that the peg would fail'(op.cit. p.25). The latter assumes that the upper limit to how much domestic currency the central bank is willing to issue (anticipated by the market) is very large. 'It is realistic at such volumes of currency issue that domestic currency would no longer be a perfect substitute for foreign assets and some portfolio-balance effect would appear and depreciate the domestic currency' (ibid. p. 35).

Such proposals refer to (hopefully) lasting monetary-policy measures by the Bank of Japan, and thus involve permanent measures as opposed to the temporary monetary-policy shocks as considered in the present chapter. However, the methodology we use can still shed some light at least on the transmission mechanisms of the proposed measures.

Would a yen depreciation or a boost to share prices reflate the Japanese economy?

We can use our enlarged VAR system[3] to examine the macroeconomic response of the Japanese economy to a shock in the yen–dollar exchange rate with the results displayed in Figure 11.7. A shock to the yen–dollar, equivalent to a

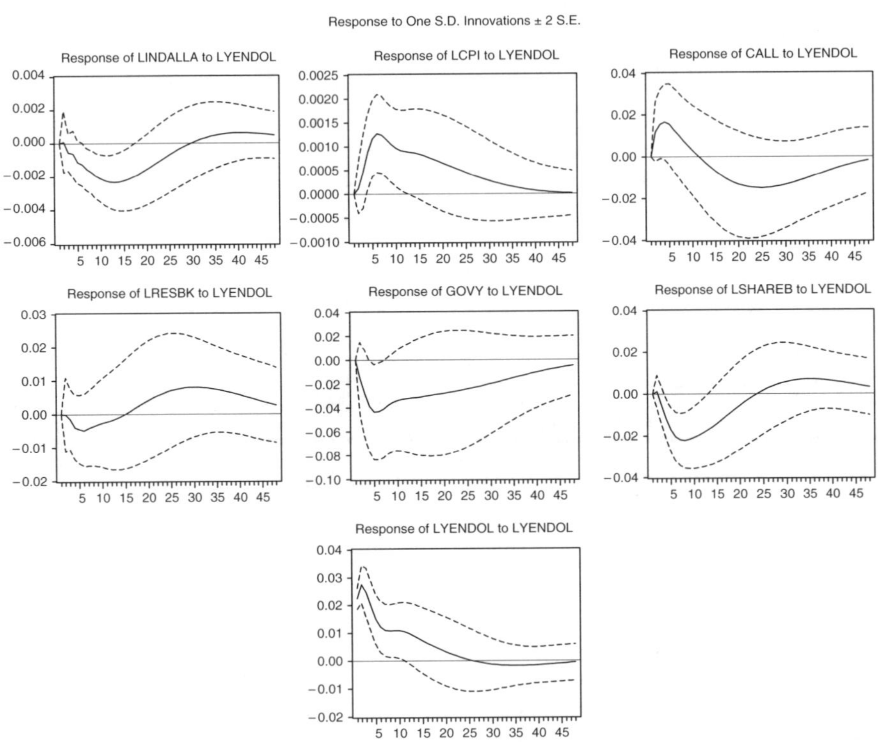

Figure 11.7 Impulse responses to a yen–dollar shock.

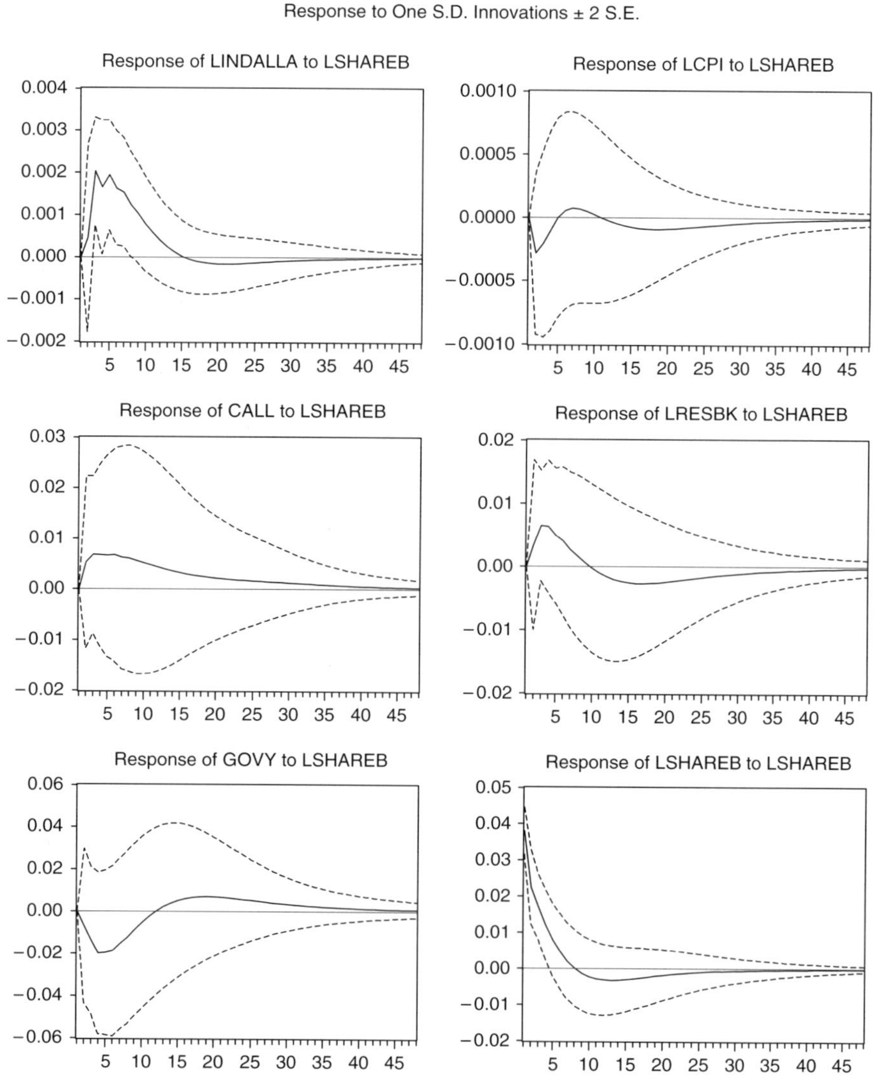

Figure 11.8 Impulse responses to a share price shock in the 1990s.

depreciation of the yen, generates in turn a rise and an insignificant fall in the call rate, a lasting, but insignificant, fall in the government-bond yield as well as a significant fall in share prices. It also leads to a fall in all-industry output, reaching its maximum after a year and a rise in the CPI. A 10 per cent depreciation in the yen leads to a 0.66 per cent fall in all-industry output and 0.3 per cent CPI inflation. The rise in the call rate responds to the initial rise in output and to the inflationary impact of the yen depreciation, as well as possibly to the yen depreciation itself. However, this response is not very significant, and we checked that the effects of the depreciation in the yen are hardly altered when the call rate enters exogenously. The negative effects of the yen depreciation on output are channelled on the one side via the deterioration of competitiveness induced by inflation and on the other by the fall in share prices. The latter may be explained by the exchange-rate loss made by non-residents holding shares quoted in Japan, which leads them to sell part of their portfolio, possibly in association with capital outflows.

The lesson from the study of the transmission of interest-rate shocks (discussed above) was that these lead to a fall in share prices, which depresses output. An extended VAR was estimated, with the yen–dollar exchange rate exogenous, to consider to what extent a positive shock in share prices would stimulate output. Figure 11.8 implies that a 10 per cent rise in share prices leads to a 0.5 per cent rise in all-industry output after a few months which dies out after a little more than a year. The response of all other variables is insignificant.

Given that the negative output effects of a yen depreciation work partly through a fall in share prices, and that a falling yen boosts the CPI, any policy aimed at depreciating the yen should be supplemented with a support of share prices, which has a positive effect on output.

The Japanese experience of interest-rate policy destabilising the stock market prior to 1990 and attempting to stabilise it thereafter, was severely criticised by some observers. Thus, Bernanke and Gertler (1999) find in their estimates of interest-rate reaction functions for Japan that stock prices in turn have a negative and a positive coefficient. However, the point we stress here is different since the stimulation of share prices we are concerned with is relevant at a time of near-zero interest rates and where a stock market bubble is long ago collapsed.

Conclusion

This chapter aimed at giving some empirical evidence on the nature of the transmission channel of monetary policy at a time of very low interest rates, as in Japan in the second half of the 1990s, as well as at providing some empirical basis in order to start assessing the transmission mechanisms through which alternative instruments of monetary policy may help reflating the economy.

The use of impulse-response functions in a VAR in levels enabled us to establish that the main channels of transmission of interest-rate shocks do not involve bank lending but mainly asset-prices, both via the share price and the exchange rate. Shocks on bank reserves have no significant effect on prices or exchange rates, and an almost insignificant impact on output which is not surprising at near-zero interest rates, where base money and short-term bills are perfect substitutes.

Our results lead us to recommend some caution in evaluating the often advocated 'quick fix' out of the liquidity trap in Japan, in the shape of an intervention-led depreciation in the yen. Existing literature implies that such intervention is unlikely to influence the level of the yen through portfolio-balance effects. We find that exchange-rate shocks would certainly help the country to get out of price deflation, but would, at best, have insignificant effects on output in part because of the negative impact on the stock-market price. By contrast, a positive shock on share prices would lead to a boost in output. This may lead to the tentative conclusion that to get a positive effect on both output and prices in Japan a yen depreciation should be supplemented with a support to share prices.

The possibility of reflating the economy through public share-price support seems to have been overlooked by most researchers (though not by all observers) in this area, even though it may be by far a better 'foolproof' way out of the liquidity trap than yen depreciation. The details of implementation can involve the purchase of sizeable amounts of shares by publicly-owned financial institutions. Something similar to the action of the Hong Kong government in its successful defence against speculative attacks would be conceivable. However, the Japanese public opinion may not be ready to accept such policies. Indeed, it seems that 'ideas initially floated by the politicians, such as using public funds to buy shares, were met with horror by investors and appear to have been dropped' (Rahman, 2001). Alternative schemes[4] have been floated by a coalition-government panel, among those we can mention the easing of restrictions on share buybacks by companies, developing stock-option schemes, encouraging companies to swap cross-held shares outside the market, and the accelerated introduction of US-type defined contribution plans. However, such schemes would be slow to make their effects felt. For share prices to go up quickly, expectations of future dividends should improve (for empirical evidence on the close link between expected future dividends and share prices in Japan, see Girardin, 2001).

Of course one should keep in mind (as stressed by Oda and Okina, 2001) that the desirability of policy actions should be assessed not only on the basis of their ability to stimulate output but also by taking into account their feasibility, their costs and associated risks, as well as the danger of a deflationary spiral developing if nothing is done.

Appendix A

The pattern of monetary policy and asset price shocks

The monetary policy shocks in the late nineties, in the shape of shocks to the money-market interest rate and bank reserves, associated with our enlarged VAR model for the second half of the nineties are displayed in Figure A11.1. In order to correct for the intrinsically noisy character of such residuals of the interest-rate equation in the VAR, we show on such a graph their 3-month centred moving average. We also display in Figure A11.2. the (broad) share-price shocks and yen–dollar shocks.

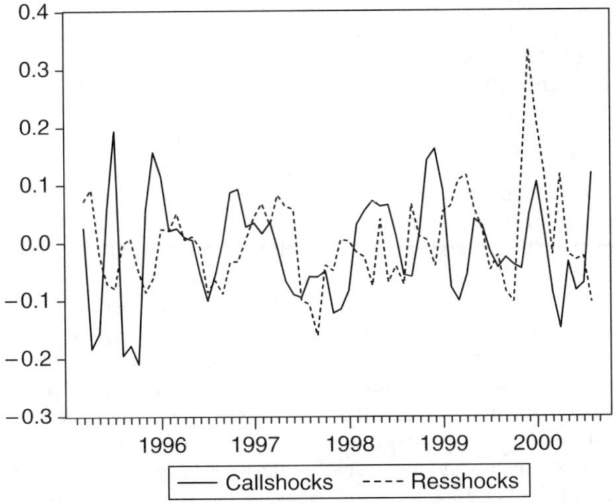

Figure 11.A1 Interest rate shocks and bank reserve shocks in the second half of the 1990s.

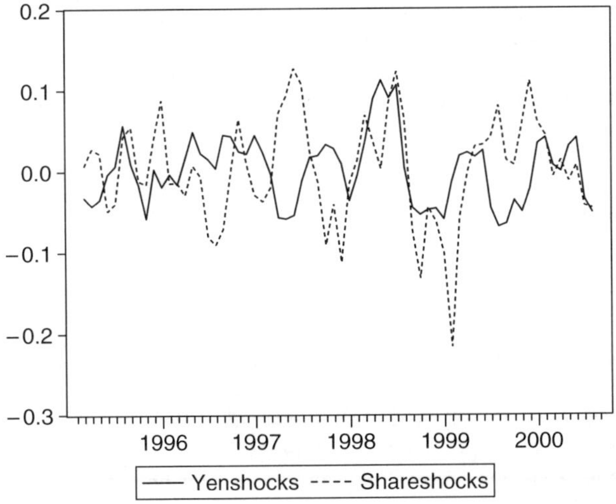

Figure 11.A2 Share price and yen–dollar shocks in the second half of the 1990s.

Notes

1 Until the early 1990s the BOJ was concerned that it might not be able to control an acceleration of bank lending without direct measures, leading it to officially abandon Window guidance only in July 1991 (Cargill, Hutchison and Ito, 1997). Besides, while the second half of the 1980s was characterised by the formation and expansion of a

financial bubble both in stock and land prices, the shift to restrictive monetary policy in 1989 led to a subsequent collapse of the bubble.

2 While there is currently a near-consensus on the negligible size of the effects associated with the portfolio channel, the 'signaling of future changes in monetary policy' channel is often considered as the only alternative channel through which central banks should rely in the hope of their intervention to have any effectiveness (Girardin, 2000). Recent theoretical work shows that a third channel should be considered more relevant. Such a channel is based on the release by the central bank through its interventions of information on its exchange-rate target. The two types of signalling channels generate conflicting predictions with respect to the effects of intervention on the level as well as the volatility of the exchange-rate, and on the profitability of interventions. Empirical work on daily data mostly validates the alternative signalling channel.

3 Using forecast error variance decomposition we found that during the second half of the 1990s, a third of output variance as well as of the variance of consumer prices is accounted for by exchange-rate movements after a year and a half (not reported). Movements in share prices and in government-bond yields account each for 7 per cent of output variance. Both the exchange rate and the government-bond yield account for a fifth of the variance of the call rate. The government-bond yield accounts for a quarter of the variance in share prices over short horizons, while over long horizons, the yen–dollar rate explains half of the variance in share prices. Japanese bank reserves are the dominant factor behind the forecast error variance of the yen–dollar. This may represent a channel through which monetary policy can affect the exchange rate in Japan.

During the January 1980–January 1991 period, the transmission channel of monetary policy seemed to involve in a dominant way the term-structure channel. Indeed the government-bond yield accounts for 40 per cent of output variance and a fifth of price variance after 4 years. The same is true for the money channel in the case of consumer prices, while the role of asset prices is more limited.

4 An action to boost the stock market would be very timely given that starting with fiscal year 2001 the Japanese Financial Services Agency will compel banks to mark to market their portfolio of shares. Given the current level of the Nikkei, banks will have to acknowledge capital losses on such portfolios and will be forced to sell assets or scale down loans. An action aiming at raising the stock-market price would thus enable the authorities to kill two birds with one stone.

References

Amirault, D. and O'Reilly, B. (2001) 'The zero bound on nominal interest rates: how important is it?' *Bank of Canada, Working paper*, 6 (April).

Bagliano, F. C. and Favero, C. A. (1998) 'Measuring monetary policy with VAR models: an evaluation,' *European Economic Review*, 42, 1069–112.

Bayoumi, T. (2000) 'Where are we going? The output gap and potential growth,' in T. Bayoumi and C. Collins (eds) *Post-Bubble Blues: How Japan Responded to Asset Price Collapse*. Washington DC: IMF.

Bernanke, B. S. (2000), 'Japanese monetary policy: a case of self-induced paralysis,' revised version of a paper presented at the AEA meeting (January).

Bernanke, B. S. and Gertler, M. (1995) 'Inside the black box: the credit channel of monetary policy transmission,' *Journal of Economic Perspectives*, 9(4), 27–48.

Bernanke, B. S. and Gertler, M. (1999) 'Monetary policy and asset price volatility,' Conference of the Federal Reserve System, Jackson Hole, Wyoming (August).

Braun, R. A. and Shioji, E. (2000) 'Monetary policy and the term structure of interest rates in Japan.' Japan Project Joint Meeting NBER-CEPR, Tokyo (September).

Cargill, T. F., Hutchison, M. M. and Ito, T. (1997) *The Political Economy of Japanese Monetary Policy*. Cambridge, MA: MIT Press.

Cargill, T. F., Hutchison, M. M. and Ito, T. (2000) *Financial Policy and Central Banking in Japan*. Cambridge, MA: MIT Press.

Christiano, L. J., Eichenbaum, M. and Evans, C. L. (1999) 'Monetary policy shocks: what have we learned and to what end?' in J. B. Taylor and M. Woodford (eds) *Handbook of Macroeconomics*.

Favero, C. (2000) *Applied Macroeconometrics*, Oxford, United Kingdom: Oxford University Press.

Fujiki, H., Okina, K. and Shiratsuka, S. (2001) 'Monetary policy under zero interest rates: viewpoints of central bank economists,' Bank of Japan, *Monetary and Economic Studies* (February), pp. 89–130.

Girardin, E. (2000) 'Conditions for the effectiveness of central bank intervention in the foreign exchange market: a survey,' Western Economic Association Annual Conference, Vancouver (July).

Girardin, E. (2001) 'Do traditional bubble tests forget about fundamentals? An application to the Japanese stock market in the eighties and nineties,' *Working Paper*, Université de la Méditerranée (March).

Kasyap, A. K. and Stein J. C. (1994) 'Monetary policy and bank lending,' in N. G. Mankiw (ed.) *Monetary Policy*, pp. 221–62. The University of Chicago Press.

Krugman, P. (1998) 'It's baaack: Japan's slump and the return of the liquidity trap,' *Brookings papers on Economic Activity*, 2, 137–87.

McCallum, B. T. (1999) 'Analysis of the monetary transmission mechanism: methodological issues,' *NBER Working Paper*, 7395 (October).

McCallum, B. T. (2000) 'Theoretical analysis regarding a zero lower bound on nominal interest rates,' *NBER Working Paper*, 7677 (April).

Meltzer, A. H. (1995) 'Monetary, credit and (other) transmission processes: a monetarist perspective,' *Journal of Economic Perspectives*, 9(4), 49–72.

Meltzer, A. H. (1998) 'The transmission process,' proceedings of a conference on the Monetary transmission process: recent developments and lessons for Europe, Bundesbank, MacMillan (Forthcoming).

Meltzer, A. H. (2000) 'Monetary transmission at low inflation: some clues from Japan in the 1990s,' Bank of Japan, Institute for Monetary and Economic Studies, Discussion paper, E25.

Mishkin, F. S. (1996) 'The channels of monetary transmission: lessons for monetary policy,' *NBER Working Paper*, 5464 (February).

Miyagawa, S. and Morita, Y. (1998) 'The transmission mechanism of monetary policy.' Working paper, Faculty of Economics, Kyoto Gakuen university (Summer).

Morsink, J. and Bayoumi, T. (2000) 'Monetary policy transmission in Japan.' in T. Bayoumiu and C. Collins (eds) *Post-Bubble Blues: How Japan Responded to Asset Price Collapse*, Chapter 7. Washington DC: IMF.

Oda, N. and Okina, K. (2001) 'Further monetary easing policies under the non-negativity constraints of nominal interest rates: summary of the discussion based on Japan's experience.' Bank of Japan, *Monetary and Economic Studies* (Special Edition). (February), pp. 323–69.

Orphanides, A. and Wieland, V. (1998) 'Price stability and monetary policy effectiveness when nominal interest rates are bounded at zero.' *Working paper*, Federal Reserve Board.

Rahman, B. (2001) 'Japan moves to end "horror show",' *Financial Times*, 12 February.

Ramaswamy, R. and Samiei, H. (2000) 'The yen–dollar rate: have interventions mattered?' *IMF Working Paper* (June), Washington DC.

Sims, C., Stock, J. and Watson, M. (1990) 'Inference in linear time series models with some unit roots,' *Econometrica*, 58, 113–44.

Svensson, L. E. O. (2000) 'The zero bound in an open economy : a foolproof way of escaping from a liquidity trap,' *NBER Working Paper*, 7957 (October).

Taylor, J. B. (1995) 'The monetary transmission mechanism: an empirical framework,' *Journal of Economic Perspectives*, 9(4), 11–26.

Ueda, K. (2000) 'The transmission mechanism of monetary policy near zero interest rates: the Japanese experience 1998–2000.' Speech given to the Japan Project Joint Meeting NBER-CEPR, Tokyo (September).

12 Real exchange rates and capital flows

Chang Shu

The real exchange rate is one of the most important macroeconomic variables, and has been at the centre of policy discussions in both developed and developing economies. It is important for policy-conduct purposes to evaluate the 'appropriateness' of the real exchange rate and understand the causes of deviation of the real exchange rate from its long equilibrium. This chapter follows the strand of literature on the equilibrium real exchange rate to model empirically both the short-run and long-run dynamics of the real exchange rate for groups of developing countries. Special attention is given to the impact of capital flows on real exchange rates. The phenomenal growth of capital flows to less developed countries has been one of the most far-reaching developments in the world economy in the past two decades. While capital flows can bring to those countries much-needed resources and embedded technological transfer and managerial know-how, they frequently pose difficulties to the recipient country's macroeconomic management. Real appreciation is a major difficulty that capital flows cause (see Calvo *et al.*, 1993; Edwards, 1998). However, no study has used disaggregated capital-flow data to investigate the effects of different types of capital flows on the real exchange rate in different countries.

In this chapter, I intend to address the following two questions within an equilibrium real exchange-rate framework:

1 Do different types of capital flows have different effects on real exchange rates? Five measures of capital flows will be used in gauging the impact of capital flows on the real exchange rate – FDI, portfolio investment and bank loans and two aggregate measures of capital flows.
2 Do different types of capital flows into different countries groups/regions, for example, Africa, Asia and Latin America, have different effects on real exchange rates?

This chapter will be organised as follows. The first section will briefly review the different approaches to modelling the equilibrium real exchange rate. The second section presents the empirical model, and describes the panel unit root and cointegration methodology which is employed in the empirical work. The third section presents the empirical results while the fourth section describes the policy implications.

Approaches to the equilibrium real exchange rate

Purchasing power parity (PPP) is one of the oldest exchange-rate determination theories. There is a voluminous and ever-growing literature on testing the PPP theory (see Rogoff (1996) for a survey). It is generally recognised that although the real exchange rate does seem to tend toward PPP in the very long run, PPP is unable to account for short-run fluctuations in exchange rates, and deviations from PPP are frequently large and volatile.

The more recent methods of modelling the equilibrium real exchange rate include Williamson's 'fundamental real exchange rate' (1994) and Bayoumi *et al.*'s 'desired real exchange rate' (1994), Stein's (1994, 1995) 'natural real exchange rate' and Edwards' (1989, 1994) and Elbadawi's (1994) 'equilibrium real exchange rate'. These studies all define the equilibrium real exchange rate as the rate that attains the internal and external equilibria of an economy. One common feature is that these studies tend to use a small set of economic variables to explain the evolution of the real exchange rate. Where they differ is the operational definitions of internal and external equilibria in their modelling, and the set of economic fundamentals they use to explain the equilibrium real exchange rate.

Edwards' ERER approach

Edwards' 'equilibrium real exchange rate' approach has been mentioned in the context of comparing different methods of assessing the appropriate level of the real exchange rate. Similar to other approaches to the equilibrium real exchange rate, this approach relates the real exchange rate to a small number of economic fundamentals. Its characteristic is that it distinguishes the long-run equilibrium and short-run dynamics of the real exchange rate. As this paper will apply this framework, this section will discuss Edwards' equilibrium real exchange rate approach in a little more detail.

The 'equilibrium real exchange rate' approach postulates that in the long run, the real exchange rate is only affected by economic fundamentals and evolves as the economic fundamentals change. In a reduced form it is:

$$\text{RER}^* = f(\text{Fundamental}). \tag{1}$$

The economic fundamentals can include openness in trade regimes, terms of trade, fiscal policy, technological progress, and capital flows.

The short-run dynamics of the real exchange rate can be given as:

$$\Delta\text{RER} = f((\text{RER} * -\text{RER}),\ \Delta \text{ Fundamentals},\ Z_t,\ \text{nominal depreciation}). \tag{2}$$

In the short run, the actual real exchange rate has the tendency to return to its long-run equilibrium level. Moreover, it also responds to the changes in economic fundamentals, macroeconomic policy, Z_t, and changes in the nominal exchange rate.

Edward's approach has been widely applied in the empirical literature to assess the equilibrium real exchange rate, misalignment and policy action of an individual country. Most empirical studies employ an error-correction modelling-technique (see Elbadawi, 1994; Feyzioglu, 1997; Mongardini, 1998; Nyoni, 1998; Sorsa, 1999). Although not common, this approach has also been tested using panel data. Edwards' original empirical work (1989, 1994) is carried out on a group of twelve developing countries in 1962–84. However, Edwards' studies do not use the cointegration approach, and are unable to distinguish the short-run and long-run effects of the determinants of the real exchange rate.

Recent developments in panel unit roots and cointegration tests studies have enabled application of an error-correction modelling procedure in a panel setting. Chinn and Johnston (1996) apply this procedure to studying effects of productivity and demand shocks on the real exchange rate. Chinn (1997) shows that it is difficult to find a cointegrating relationship between the real exchange rate and sectoral productivity levels when analysis is carried out on a single-country basis. However panel cointegration tests seem to provide more evidence of a long-run relationship between the equilibrium real exchange rate and its fundamentals.

The empirical model of ERER and modelling procedure

Engle and Granger (1987) suggest a two-step approach to modelling cointegration processes, which can link the long-run equilibrium with short-run dynamics. Until recently, this empirical modelling procedure could only be applied on time-series. Levin and Lin (1992) compile the critical value for the equivalent of ADF statistics in a panel for different lengths of time-periods and different numbers of cross-section units. As the single-series ADF test is widely acknowledged to have low power in rejecting a false null, using a panel approach has the advantage of exploring the cross-section variations to increase the power of unit root tests. This paper follows Chinn and Johnston (1996) and Chinn (1997) who extend the Engle–Granger two-step modelling into a panel setting. It allows specification of both long-run relationships and short-run dynamics, while at the same time, it takes into account heterogeneity in a panel. This two-step empirical modelling procedure is suitable for testing the Edwards' model which makes a distinction between determination of the long-run equilibrium real exchange rate and short-run dynamics of the real exchange rate.

In applying Edwards' equilibrium real exchange rate framework, this paper focuses on the real exchange rate determination in developing countries. It covers thirty developing countries and employs annual data between 1970–96. More interestingly, the real exchange rate determination is studied for three geographic regions that make up the whole sample – Africa, Asia and Latin

America. The countries in the sample can be found in Tables 12.A1–3. Particular interests are paid to the impact of different types of capital flows on the real exchange rate.

The data used for this study include the real exchange rate, variables representing the economic fundamentals, monetary and fiscal policy, the nominal exchange rate and exchange rate regimes. The real exchange rates are trade-weighted multilateral rates calculated based on the *IFS* data. An increase in the real exchange rate is a depreciation. The precise definitions of the explanatory variables will be given shortly in conjunction with explanations of the long-run and short-run specifications, and Appendix B provides detailed information on the data sources.

The modelling procedure of the paper is as follows:

Step 1: Investigate the time-series properties of the real exchange rate and the explanatory variables using Levin and Lin's panel ADF test.
Step 2: Explore long-run relationships between the real exchange rate and its fundamentals, and test the existence of cointegration among the variables.
Step 3: If long-run relationships exist, employ an error-correction model to explore the short-run dynamics of the real exchange rate.
Step 4: Some specification tests.

The four steps of the modelling procedure will be discussed in greater detail in turn.

Step 1: Panel unit root tests[1]

Panel unit root tests are first conducted on the real exchange rate and its explanatory variables both in their levels and first differences. Following the approach by Levin and Lin (1992), and a panel ADF test regression is run as follows:

$$\Delta y_{i,t} = \beta y_{i,t-1} + \text{currency dummies} + \sum_{i=1}^{p} \phi_i \Delta y_{t-i} + \epsilon_{i,t}. \tag{3}$$

Equation (3) is the panel data equivalent of a single-series ADF test. In (3) y_t is the variable of interest either in its level or differences. The model is estimated by the fixed-effects model, and has different constants for different countries. These different constants are referred to as currency dummies in this context of modelling the real exchange rate. By using a fixed-effects model, heterogeneity within a panel is accounted for by the different constants for individual countries, while keeping the model tractable.

The null hypothesis and alternative hypothesis are given by:

H_0: $\beta = 0$, H_1: $\beta < 0$.

That is, the null hypothesis that each series in the panel contains a unit root is tested against the alternative that all individual series in the panel are stationary. The panel ADF statistics are then compared to critical values compiled by Levin and Lin.

However, it should be noted that the results of panel unit root tests need to be treated with caution. Karlsson and Löthgren (2000) evaluate the power of different panel unit root tests and warn against imposing stationary and non-stationary homogeneity based solely on panel unit root tests.

Step 2: The long-run relationship

After the stationarity properties of variables are determined, the next step is to explore the long-run relation between the real exchange rate and its fundamentals. Based on the models presented in the previous section, the empirical model of the long-run equilibrium real exchange rate determination can be given as:

$$\begin{aligned} \text{RER} = \alpha_0 + \alpha_1 \cdot (\text{capital flows}) + \alpha_2 \cdot (\text{technological progress}) \\ + \alpha_3 \cdot \text{tt} + \alpha_4 \cdot \text{opy} + \alpha_5 \cdot (\text{trade barriers}) + \alpha_6 \cdot (\text{fiscal policy}). \end{aligned} \tag{4}$$

The fundamentals considered include capital flows, technological progress, terms of trade (tt), openness (opy), trade barriers and fiscal policy.

Capital flows

This paper tests the effects of total capital flows as well as different types of capital flows on the real exchange rate. Five measures of capital flows are tested: FDI (fdy), portfolio investment (pfy), bank loans (oky), capital flows other than FDI (poy = pfy + oky) and total capital flows (tpky = fdy + pfy + oky). The measures of capital flows are scaled by GDP. As capital flows often lead to real appreciation, α_1 is expected to carry a negative sign.

Capital flows into less-developed countries are desirable as they can increase investment and capital formation, and facilitate productivity growth. However, they are not an unmixed blessing as they often pose difficulties in macroeconomic management. One issue of concern is that they might lead to real appreciation. Capital flows into a country in response to a host of factors. If they are a response to increases in domestic consumption due to changes such as a reduction in capital controls and the consequent lowering of domestic-interest rate, an inflow of capital and real appreciation will be observed simultaneously. If capital flows are exogenous and the income elasticity of demand for nontradables is not zero, capital inflows will directly lead to increases in absorption and real appreciation. Real appreciation causes a loss of external competitiveness, and consequently a decline in exports and manufacturing production. This is known as the Dutch disease (Edwards and van Wijnbergen, 1989).

However among different types of capital flows, foreign direct investment may merit special analysis. Like any other type of capital flow, it can lead to increases in aggregate demand, and thus, real appreciation. But what differentiates it from others is that foreign direct investment is one type of capital flow that is most likely to lead to capital formation in the host country. In this case, its effects on the equilibrium real exchange rate can be more complex than other types of capital flows. It might facilitate productivity improvement due to increased capital formation as well as the embedded technological transfer and managerial know-how. Whether technological progress leads to appreciation or depreciation depends on the relative strength of its demand and supply side effects. In addition, foreign direct investment often requires imports of capital equipment in the short and medium run. The increase in demand for imports can contribute to a depreciation.

Other economic fundamentals

Technological progress is included in the long-run relationship between the real exchange rate and its fundamentals to test the Balassa–Samuelson hypothesis. According to this hypothesis, due to different rates of productivity growth in different sectors, countries experiencing a faster rate of technological progress will experience an equilibrium real exchange-rate appreciation. Following studies such as Edwards (1994) and Nyoni (1998), technological progress is alternatively proxied by a time-trend (trend) or real GDP growth (gdg). If α_2 is negative, it gives support to the Balassa–Samuelson hypothesis.

The impact of changes in terms of trade (tt) on the real exchange rate depends on the relative magnitude of the income and substitution effects. In the event, that the income effect of terms of trade improvement dominates the substitution effect, the improvement will lead to real appreciation, that is, $\alpha_3 < 0$.

Openness (opy) is defined as the sum of imports and exports over GDP. Two tax measures are used. One is taxes on international trade (ty), and the other is import tariffs (imty). They are scaled by GDP, and used as alternatives in the regressions. The measures of taxes on trade explicitly measure quantitative distortions in a trade regime, while openness accounts for implicit factors such as quotas and exchange controls (Elbadawi, 1994). Tariffs are a major source of revenue in developing countries. The effect of a rise in tariffs on the equilibrium real exchange rate depends on the degree of substitutability between different goods within the consumption bundle, and the income effect. The sign on a tax measure is ambiguous due to the forces of income and substitution effects a tax change can bring. However, more open regimes are often found to be associated with more depreciated currency, and lowering trade barriers leads to real depreciation, that is, $\alpha_4 > 0$, $\alpha_5 < 0$.

The long-run relationship also includes a variable to assess the impact of fiscal policy on the equilibrium real exchange rate. The level, composition and financing of government expenditure can have an impact on the equilibrium real exchange rate. Increases in government expenditure lead to rises in aggregate demand, and thereby, increases in prices. If the government has a higher propensity to spend on nontraded goods than the private sector does, the rise in the nontradable price will be sharper, resulting in real appreciation. However, if an increase in the taxes is expected in later periods to repay the government debt to the foreign sector, disposable income is reduced over all horizons, reducing demand in all periods. This fall in demand may lead to a price fall and real depreciation. Two measures are used to test the effect of fiscal policy on the real exchange rate, and employed as alternatives in estimation. One is the government expenditure to GDP ratio (gexy), and the other is the government consumption to GDP ratio (gcy). In the case of government expenditure bias towards non-tradables, α_6 will carry a negative sign.

To explore this long-run relationship, regressions will be estimated in levels using the fixed-effects model. The general-to-specific approach is used to select the suitable model. When a long-run relationship is established, a residual-based panel ADF test will be used to find out whether a long-run relationship exists between the real exchange rate and its fundamentals. To determine whether the variables are cointegrated in a panel, the residuals are extracted from the long-run regression, and an equivalent of the ADF is run for the panel:

$$\Delta \mathrm{ECM}_{i,t} = \beta \, \mathrm{ECM}_{i,t-1} + \text{currency dummies} + \sum_{i=1}^{p} \phi_i \Delta \mathrm{ECM}_{t-i} + \epsilon_{i,t}. \qquad (5)$$

If the null hypothesis of no cointegration is rejected, a long-run relationship exists between the real exchange rate and the fundamentals that appear in the regression. One characteristic of cointegration is that the relationship found between the variables will hold in the long run. It is, therefore, appropriate to investigate the link between the real exchange rate and its fundamentals.

Step 3: Short-run determination of real exchange-rate movement

If a long-run relationship does exist between the real exchange rate and its fundamentals, the short-run dynamics of the real exchange-rate movement can then be captured by:

$$\begin{aligned} \Delta \mathrm{RER} = & \beta_0 + \beta_1 \cdot \mathrm{ECM}_{t-1} + \beta_2 \cdot \Delta \mathrm{Fundamental}_t \\ & + \beta_3 \cdot Z_t + \beta_4 \cdot \mathrm{d(exa)}_t. \end{aligned} \qquad (6)$$

Following the Engle–Granger two-step modelling procedure, the short-run dynamics is given as a regression of changes in the real exchange rate on the lagged error correction term (ECM_{t-1}), changes in the fundamentals ($\Delta\mathrm{Fundamental}_t$) plus other macroeconomic measures, Z_t, and nominal depreciation ($\mathrm{d(exa)}_t$). Again the fixed effects model are applied for estimation, and the general-to-specific approach is used for model selection.

The ECM term is the deviation of the real exchange rate from its long-run equilibrium level. When a long-run relationship exists between the real exchange rate and the fundamentals, there is a tendency for the real exchange rate to return to its long-run equilibrium level. This is consistent with the cointegration concept in econometrics. If the real exchange rate always tends to its long-run value, β_1 should be negative. The speed at which the real exchange rate returns to the equilibrium value is reflected by the magnitude of β_1. The model also tests whether fundamentals have any short-run effects on real exchange rate movement by including changes of the fundamentals in the short-run dynamics.

Z_t stands for a set of macroeconomic policy. Excessively expansionary policy is likely to increase demand for both tradables and nontradables. If there is a bias towards domestic consumption, the price of nontradables will increase faster than tradables, leading to real appreciation. The variables used as proxies of macroeconomic policy include excess credit supply (excr), the ratio of deficits to reserve money (ddh) and changes in debt (tdg) and changes in debt-service (tdsg). Excess credit supply is measured as the rate of domestic credit over the lagged rate of growth of real GDP. The coefficients on these variables are expected to be negative.

Nominal devaluation (d(exa)) may lead to real depreciation, and thus β_4 will be positive. There are three channels through which nominal devaluation affects an economy. The first is the wealth effect. The second channel is the substitution effect which induces more spending on the domestic nontradable goods. This increases demand for nontradables while the wealth effect is to reduce it. Finally, nominal devaluation increases the cost of imported intermediate inputs. The exchange rate passthrough effect gives rise to conflicting forces in real exchange rate adjustment. On the one hand, nominal devaluation points to a lower real exchange rate, but on the other hand, higher-price levels, resulting from the exchange rate passthrough, will partially offset the fall in the real exchange rate value. Therefore, the speed and degree of exchange-rate passthrough will be an important determinant of the real exchange-rate adjustment process. As exchange-rate regimes might have impact on the adjustment process of the real exchange rate as they may lead to different adjustment speeds of the nominal exchange rate and prices. Tables 12.A1–3 trace the changes in the exchange-rate regimes in the selected economies from 1982 to 1996. The information is taken from various issues of the *Annual Report on Exchange Arrangements and Exchange Restrictions* published by the International Monetary Fund. The first row for each country classifies the exchange rate regime. F1 refers to an exchange-rate regime that is pegged to a currency or a composite of currencies. The exchange-rate regimes that are classified as 'flexibility limited' and 'managed floating' are referred to as F2. F3 is the independent floating regime. The second row classifies the exchange-rate structure. If there is one exchange rate for all transactions and all economic entities, the system is referred to as unitary; if there are more than one exchange rate, the system is referred to as multiple.

Step 4: Checks on specifications

The fixed-effects model is chosen for estimation in this paper. An F test can be applied to examine whether there are significant differences between the individual countries within a group and whether the application of the fixed-effects model is justified. The unrestricted regression is the fixed-effects model while the restricted model is the pooled regression.

Empirical results

Real exchange rate movement, capital flows and economic fundamentals

The real exchange rate (RER) movements of the selected countries in Africa, Asia and Latin America are summarised in Table 12.1. Over the whole sample period of 1970–96 currencies in Africa, Asia and Latin America experienced real depreciation. The Asian currencies depreciated by around 3 per cent in 1970–80 and 1981–90. In the first half of 1990s, they had a mild appreciation. Both African and Latin American countries had substantial real depreciation in the 1980s. Latin American currencies then experienced the biggest real appreciation in the 1990s. Volatility of the currencies has decreased in the early part of the 1990s in all the three regions. Real exchange rate volatility is the highest in Latin America throughout the whole period. Overall, the Asian currencies are the most stable, particularly in the 1980s and 1990s prior to the currency crisis in 1997.

Capital flows

Table 12.2 summarises capital movement to Africa, Asia and Latin America during 1970–96. The past two decades have witnessed a surge in international investment in less developed countries. However, capital flows to developing countries have been extremely erratic and highly unevenly spread. A further prominent feature in recent capital movement to developing countries is the steady growth of foreign direct investment. An average African country

Table 12.1 Real exchange rates

	1970–96	*1970–80*	*1981–90*	*1991–96*
Africa				
Average real devaluation	1.4	−0.5	4.4	−0.4
Real exchange rates volatility	22.9	16.1	26.6	12.6
Asia				
Average real devaluation	2.0	3.0	3.0	−1.2
Real exchange rates volatility	20.1	20.7	17.7	6.9
Latin America				
Average real devaluation	1.3	0.9	4.1	−2.7
Real exchange rates volatility	37.4	40.3	41.5	9.0

Table 12.2 Averages of different types of capital flows by country groups ($millions)

	1971–96	*1970–80*	*1981–90*	*1991–96*
Africa				
FDI (fd)	55.8	35.6	44.1	106
Portfolio Investment (pf)	4.6	0.2	4.0	11.2
Bank loans (oky)	218	322	170	182
Asia				
FDI (fd)	672	200	567	1400
Portfolio Investment (pf)	306	34.1	126	985
Bank loans (oky)	1240	864	798	2580
Latin America				
FDI (fd)	588	208	436	1370
Portfolio Investment (pf)	711	39.4	26.3	3000
Bank loans (oky)	−292	1000	−821	−838

received nearly three times as much FDI per annum in the 1990s as in the 1970s. The increase in the FDI was even more dramatic in Asia and Latin America. On an average, an Asian or Latin American country received $1.4 billion each year in the 1990s, seven times the level in the 1970s. Asia received the highest level of FDI per country, with Latin America closely behind. An average African country only received 7.5 per cent of the amount of FDI that goes to an average Asian country. Unlike the trend growth in FDI, the movement in portfolio and other types of capital flows was less predictable. Portfolio investment grew steadily in Asia, increasing nearly threefold in the 1980s and then almost sevenfold in the 1990s. Other types of capital flows to Asia decreased in the 1980s compared to the 1970s level, but soared in the 1990s. Portfolio investment in Latin America decreased in the 1980s, and yet reached a record high in the 1990s. Latin America saw an outflow of other types of capital flows, which mainly consisted of bank loans in the last two decades. This probably reflects the extent of capital flight in these countries. Like FDI, portfolio investment and other types of capital flows to Africa were much less than to Asia and Latin America.

The panel unit root tests

The panel unit root test results are presented in Table 12.3. Panel A reports the test statistics for the variables that will enter the long-run equations, while Panel B are for variables that will enter the short-run equations. As the long-run relationships include the real exchange rate and economic fundamentals in their levels while short-run equations include these variables in their first differences

Table 12.3 Panel unit root tests

	World	*Africa*	*Asia*	*Latin America*
Variables in the long-run equations				
RER	−6.75	−5.26[a]	−4.94	−5.29
fdy	−13.70[c]	−8.02[c]	−5.34[a]	−3.22
pfy	−10.48[c]	−5.28[a]	−2.99	−4.77
oky	−12.83[c]	−6.08[c]	−6.70[c]	−9.55[c]
poy	−10.69[c]	−5.06	−3.77	−8.70[c]
tpky	−12.68[c]	−7.60[c]	−5.61[b]	−7.17[c]
gdg	−21.83[c]	−9.51[c]	−9.45[c]	−13.28[c]
tt	−5.84	−4.32	−2.05	−7.25[c]
opy	−6.77	−5.27[a]	−3.01	−4.38
ty	−2.34	5.27	−3.96	−2.69
imty	−8.51[b]	−5.44[a]	−4.78	−4.10
gexy	−8.30[b]	−5.06	−5.93[c]	−5.15
gcy	−6.76	−5.00	−4.16	−2.89
Variables in the short-run equations				
d(real exchange rate)	−9.46[c]	−12.91[c]	−6.98[c]	−5.61
d(fdy)	−17.99[c]	−9.99[c]	−10.88[c]	−8.51[c]
d(pfy)	−12.66[c]	−8.75[c]	−4.81	−11.43[c]
d(oky)	−14.51[c]	−13.83[c]	−9.39[c]	−8.60[c]
d(poy)	−13.48[c]	−11.96[c]	−7.92[c]	−8.39[c]
d(tpky)	−12.79[c]	−9.11[c]	−7.79[c]	−8.99[c]
d(tt)	−14.93[c]	−14.20[c]	−8.03[c]	−16.74[c]
d(opy)	−13.99[c]	−10.00[c]	−8.59[c]	−7.37[c]
d(ty)	−9.51[c]	−9.85[c]	−11.33[c]	−5.59
d(imty)	−8.61[b]	−6.17[c]	−8.78[c]	−4.27
d(gexy)	−7.12	−5.33[a]	−9.17[c]	−4.22
d(gcy)	−10.44[c]	−7.73[c]	−11.95[c]	−6.91[c]
excr	−11.1[c]	−6.50[c]	−6.20[c]	−7.74[c]
tdy	−6.75	−3.60	−3.64	−5.19
d(tdy)	−7.52[a]	−3.65	−6.46[c]	−7.80[c]
tdsy	−7.74[a]	−5.40[b]	−4.08	−5.55
d(tdsy)	−7.91[a]	−2.03	−6.18[c]	−10.40[c]
ddh	−8.49[b]	−3.45	−7.04[c]	−11.20[c]
d(exa)	−13.77[c]	−8.79[c]	−11.65[c]	−8.18[c]

Note: a, b, and c indicate that the null hypothesis is rejected at the 10%, 5% and 1% levels respectively.

along with other variables, analysis combining the results from Panels A and B can reveal the time-series properties of the real exchange rate and economic fundamentals.

Table 12.3 shows that for the whole sample, the African and Asian groups, the levels of the real exchange rate are nonstationary while its first differences are. This suggests that the real exchange rate exchange rate is an I(1) process, and thus, the PPP is refuted. This corroborates with Chinn (1999) that the multilateral real exchange rate is never found to be stationary. PPP does not hold for the Latin American group either, as its real exchange rate does not appear to be stationary even in the first differences.

There are some indications that some types of capital flows may be I(0) processes. When the overall sample is considered, the five types of capital flows series are all stationary in their levels. However, when individual country groups are considered, only two types of capital flows are stationary in their levels for all individual groups. They are bank loans (oky) and total private capital flows (tpky). For the other three types of capital flows, there are some cases where they may be I(0) for some country groups, for example, FDI in the case of the African group.

Among the economic fundamentals, real GDP growth (gdg) is I(0). Other economic fundamentals such as openness (opy), import tariffs (imty), taxes on international trade (ty), government consumption (gcy) and terms of trade (tt) are I(1) in nearly all cases as they are nonstationary in levels, but stationary in first differences. There are a number of exceptions. For the Latin American group, ty and imty may not be stationary even in their first differences. The time-series properties of government expenditure (gexy) is more problematic. It may be stationary in its levels in the case of the overall sample and the Asian group, but nonstationary even in its first differences for Africa and Latin America.

Among other variables that enter the short-run equations, excess credit supply (excr), the ratio of deficits to high-powered money (ddh), changes in debt (d(tdy)), changes in debt services (d(tdsy)) and nominal devaluation (d(exa)) are mostly stationary. However, ddh and d(tdsy) may not be stationary for the African country group.

The panel unit root tests seem to indicate that some of the fundamentals that are suggested by the theories, and thus, used for long-run relationships may be stationary in their levels. If this is indeed the case, they can only have transitory effects on the real exchange rate and cannot enter the long-run relationships. Since the real exchange rate is nonstationary, any stationary variable cannot be a fundamental. However, as pointed out by Karlson and Löthgren (2000), one cannot solely rely on panel unit root test results to make judgement on the stationarity property of variables. It is also widely known that within finite samples I(0) and I(1) processes are difficult to distinguish, and in fact, may be good approximates for each other for short sample-periods. Therefore I first carry out an analysis that is based on the estimation that closely follow the theoretical motivation and empirical studies in this area and treat these variables as I(1). Thus the variables such as capital flows enter the long-run relationships in levels, and appear as differences in the ECM of short-run dynamics, as in, for example, Elbadawi(1994), Nyoni (1998) and Feyzioglu (1997).

However, to check the robustness of the analysis, I have also carried out alternative estimations in which the fundamentals indicated as I(0) by the panel unit root tests will be treated as such. In that event, they will not be included as long-run relationships, but appear in levels in the ECM specification of the short-run real exchange rate. As it turns out, the main conclusion of the empirical analysis is highly robust no matter which modelling procedure is followed.

The long-run relationships

After the time-series properties of the variables are determined, the long-run relationships between are the real exchange rate and its fundamentals are estimated for the overall sample, and the three individual groups – the African, Asian and Latin American groups. After the best specifications for the long-run relationships are chosen, the panel cointegration tests described in the section on 'The empirical model of ERER' are performed on the residuals from these equations for individual groups. The test statistics are reported in Table 12.4 in the second row from the bottom of the table. They reveal that in all cases, some long-run relationships have been found between the real exchange rate and its fundamentals for the groups, as the test statistics clearly reject the null hypothesis of no cointegration. The estimates for the long-run relationships for the groups are also reported in Table 12.4 where each column is an established long-run equation.

Capital flows and the equilibrium real exchange rate

In the long-run relationship between the real exchange rate and the economic fundamentals for the whole sample which includes the countries in Africa, Asia and Latin America, capital flows do not feature at all in the relationship. This might be explained by the fact that the recent surge of capital inflows tends to concentrate in a small number of countries, rather than spread evenly across the whole developing world. The long-run relationship for the countries in Africa shows that capital flows are not a significant determinant in the equilibrium real exchange rate of this group. In contrast to the case of Africa, capital flows played a significant role in determining the equilibrium real exchange rate in Asia and Latin America. As examined in the earlier section, Asia and Latin America have received huge capital flows in the past two decades, although the spread of capital flows within these continents were not even either. These findings seem to suggest that for countries which have not benefited from the increasing globalisation of capital markets and investment from foreign countries, capital flows have not yet become a force in moving the equilibrium real exchange rate, while in countries which have received substantial capital flows, capital flows are of importance in affecting the equilibrium real exchange rate.

Corroborating findings from the existing literature, the coefficients of all different types of capital flows are all found to be negative. This has confirmed the emerging consensus that capital flows tend to appreciate currency, (see Calvo *et al.*, 1993 and Edwards, 1998). However some very interesting observations can be made from the estimated long-run relationships.

Foreign direct investment on its own never enters any of the long run relationships, even for the Asian and Latin American groups where capital flows are an important factor in determining the equilibrium real exchange rate. The two aggregates, capital flows other than FDI (po = pf + ok) and total private capital flows (tpk = fd + pf + ok) are found to lead to real appreciation of the

Table 12.4 Long-run determination of the equilibrium real exchange rate

	Africa	*Asia*			*Latin America*			*Whole*
Capital flows								
Portfolio investment (pf)					-4.63^{c}			
Bank loans (oky)		-0.97^{c}						
Capital flows other than FDI (po)			-0.56^{b}			-5.03^{c}		
Total capital flows (tpky)				-0.53^{b}			-4.82^{c}	
Technological progress								
Trend	0.02^{c}				0.02^{c}			0.01^{c}
Real GDP growth		0.99^{c}	0.94^{c}	1.00^{c}				
Openness and trade regimes								
Openness	0.83^{c}	0.23^{c}	0.24^{c}	0.27^{c}	1.01^{c}	1.88^{c}	2.00^{c}	0.49^{c}
Import tariffs						5.74^{c}	6.86^{c}	
Taxes on international trade	0.01^{c}	0.01^{c}	0.03^{c}	0.01^{c}	0.01^{a}			0.02^{c}
Fiscal policy								
Government expenditure	0.57^{b}							
Government consumption					-2.72^{c}			
Terms of trade	-0.001^{a}	-0.002^{c}	-0.002^{c}	-0.002^{c}	-0.001^{b}			-0.001^{b}
R-bar squared	0.66	0.66	0.64	0.64	0.85	0.71	0.71	0.63
Panel ADF test	-6.53^{c}	-7.25^{c}	-7.14^{c}	-7.20^{c}	-6.81^{c}	-5.45^{b}	-6.14^{c}	-8.59^{b}
Fixed effects	5.77^{c}	9.88^{c}	9.90^{c}	9.53^{c}	76.26^{c}	49.21^{c}	50.32^{c}	10.20^{c}

Note: a, b and c indicate that the coefficient is significant, or the null hypothesis is rejected in the case of the test of fixed effects, at 10%, 5% and 1% levels respectively.

equilibrium real exchange rate in Asia. However, it is likely that their appreciation effect is driven by the category of bank loans amongst the different types of capital flows. For Latin America, the two aggregates of capital flows (po and tpk) are also important in the determination of the long run equilibrium real exchange rate. However, among the three categories of capital flows, only portfolio investment enters significantly on its own in the long-run relationship. This probably suggests that the major type of capital flows in driving appreciation in Latin America was portfolio investment.

Noticeably, in none of the cases is foreign direct investment found to be the type of capital flow that drives real appreciation of the equilibrium real exchange rate. This may be explained by the possibly conflicting effects of foreign direct investment on the equilibrium real exchange rate suggested in the section on 'The empirical model of ERER'. It could be because foreign direct investment has brought about technological progress, whose demand and supply-side effects have offset each other. As will be studied further later in the section, technological progress seems to have strong supply-side effects. Considering that real appreciation tends to lead to the loss of competitiveness of a country's product in the world market, this finding lends further support to the belief that foreign direct investment is more beneficial to a country's economic growth performance than other types of capital flows.

Another important observation is that capital flows to Latin America led to much sharper appreciation than in Asia. For example, for the two aggregate measures of capital flows, a 1 per cent increase in the capital flow to GDP ratio, would lead to five units of appreciation in terms of the real exchange rate index in Latin America. This is around ten times the magnitude of appreciation that will take place in Asia for a capital flow shock of the same magnitude. This again highlights the volatile nature of real exchange-rate movement and capital markets as well as unstable macroeconomic environment in general in Latin America.

Other fundamentals

In all the specifications for all the country groups as well as the whole sample, technological movement proxied by a trend (trend) or real GDP growth (gdg) is found to be an important determinant for the equilibrium real exchange rate. No matter which proxy is used, the estimated coefficients are positive, implying that faster technological improvement actually leads to real depreciation of the equilibrium real exchange rate. This does not support the Balassa–Samuelson hypothesis, and is at odds with Feyzioglu (1997) who finds that productivity improvement leads to real appreciation of the equilibrium real exchange rate in Finland. However, the same contradiction with the Balassa–Samuelson effect is found in Edwards (1989, 1994) in studying a panel of twelve developing countries.

The estimates for the terms of trade (tt) are fairly consistent across different groups and for different specifications. It tends to carry a significant negative sign, although its impact is fairly small. This finding is consistent with most studies in the existing literature, for example, Elbadawi (1994); Edwards (1989, 1994); Feyzioglu (1997); and implies that an improvement in the terms of trade tended to appreciate currencies. As the theoretical sign of the terms of trade on the equilibrium real exchange rate is ambiguous, this estimated sign of terms of trade (tt) suggests that the income effect might dominate the substitution effect.

Openness (opy) is another important fundamental. The result is similar to Elbadawi (1994) and reveals that a more open regime required a more depreciated currency in Asia and Latin American as well as for the whole group. An increase in openness in Latin America led to bigger real depreciation. Latin America was the least open among the three groups. The estimates of coefficients on openness may suggest that for less open economies, an improvement in openness might lead to larger depreciation than in a more open economy.

The effect of trade controls on the equilibrium real exchange rate is a little surprising. Both proxies, namely taxes on international trade(ty) and import tariffs (imty), are found to have a positive sign in specifications where they are significant. This implies that raising barriers on trade actually led to real appreciation in Asia and Latin America. The finding contradicts the results from Edwards' (1989, 1994). It may be the case that trade liberalisation in an environment of prevalent distortions may have highly conflicting effects, and not lead to the desired depreciation.

With regard to the effect of fiscal policy on the equilibrium real exchange rate, the result is similar to that of Chinn (1997) in this respect. The two proxies for fiscal policy, total government expenditure and government consumption, are not always significant for different groups or in different specifications. Government expenditure is significant in the long-run relationship for the African country group. It carries an unexpected positive sign, suggesting that a rise in the level of total government expenditure would lead to depreciation. Government consumption in Latin America led to substantial real appreciation, which implies a significant domestic bias in government consumption in these countries. As Latin America's level of government consumption is the highest among the groups, this might have contributed to real appreciation, leading to difficulties in macroeconomic management.

Short-run dynamics

In testing the short-run dynamics for the different regions, the lagged residuals from the cointegration relationship are used as error-correction terms. In addition, changes in the fundamentals, measures of macroeconomic policy and nominal devaluation are included to explain short-run real exchange-rate movement. The short-run dynamics are reported in Tables 12.5a–c.

In the tables, different ECM terms refer to the long-run cointegration vectors with different types of capital flows. ECM1, ECM2, ECM3 and ECM4

Table 12.5a Short-run dynamics of the real exchange rate: groups in which capital flows do not feature

	Africa	*Whole*
ECM(−1)	−0.38[c]	−0.18[c]
Technological progress		
Trend	−0.003[c]	
Real GDP growth		0.18[c]
Openness and trade regimes		
Changes in openness	0.26[c]	0.26[c]
Changes in import tariffs	−0.04[a]	
Changes in taxes on trade		0.05[c]
Fiscal and other macroeconomic policy		
Changes in government consumption	−0.07[a]	−0.22[c]
Excess credit supply	−0.05[c]	
Changes in debt	0.46[c]	0.37[c]
Changes in debt service	0.39[c]	0.48[c]
Changes in terms of trade		−0.0004[a]
Nominal devaluation	−0.31	
R-bar squared	0.82	0.60
Test of fixed effects	13.625[c]	3.07[c]

Note: a, b and c indicate that the coefficient is significant, or the null hypothesis is rejected in the case of the test of fixed effects, at 10%, 5% and 1% levels respectively.

refer to the cointegration vectors that contain portfolio investment (pfy), bank loans (oky), capital flows other than foreign direct investment (poy = pfy + oky) and total private capital flows (tpky = fdy + pfy + oky) respectively. For Asia and Latin America, with each long-run cointegration vector, different types of capital flows enter into the short-run specification one at a time. This gives rise to several possible short-run specifications for the two groups. The estimates of the different specifications are fairly consistent for both Asia and Latin America.

For all the three regions of Africa, Asia and Latin America as well as for the whole sample, the error-correction terms have been found to be highly significant and carry the expected negative sign. This means real exchange rates did tend to adjust to their long-run values. The speed of adjustment was highest in Africa, and lower for Asia and Latin America. In Africa, the deviation of the actual real exchange rate from the equilibrium real exchange rate determined by the fundamentals could be corrected by 40 per cent in a year. In Asia and Latin America, misalignment would be reduced by about 20 per cent per annum, as indicated by all specifications but one. This rate of mean reversion is close to those found by Frankel and Rose (1995), which is −0.15, and by Chinn (1997) and Johnston and Chinn (1996), which is −0.17.

Consistent with long-run findings, changes in capital flows did not affect the short-run real exchange-rate movement in Africa either. This seems to confirm

Table 12.5b Short-run dynamics of the real exchange rate: Asia

	ECM2		*ECM3*		*ECM4*	
ECM(−1)	−0.23[c]	−0.23[c]	−0.21[c]	−0.20[c]	−0.21[c]	−0.20[c]
Capital flows						
Changes in capital flows other than FDI (po)	−0.42[c]		−0.33[b]		−0.31[b]	
Changes total capital flows (tpky)		−0.39[c]		−0.33[c]		−0.32[b]
Technological progress						
Trend	0.002[c]	0.002[c]	0.002[c]	0.002[a]	0.002[b]	0.002[b]
Openness and trade regimes						
Changes in openness	0.27[c]	0.28[c]	0.27[c]	0.28[c]	0.27[c]	0.28[b]
Changes in taxes on trade			0.04[a]	0.04[a]	0.04[a]	0.04[a]
Changes in import tariffs	0.05[a]	0.05[a]				
Fiscal and macroeconomic policy						
Changes in government consumption	−0.20[c]	−0.20[c]	−0.20[c]	−0.20[c]	−0.20[c]	−0.20[b]
Deficit to high powered money	−0.05[b]	−0.04[b]	−0.05[b]	−0.05[b]	−0.05[b]	−0.05[b]
Nominal devaluation	0.33[c]	0.32[c]	0.27[c]	0.27[c]	0.27[c]	0.27[c]
R-bar squared	0.51	0.51	0.50	0.49	0.49	0.49
Test of fixed effects	1.01	1.28	0.63	0.63	0.63	0.63

Note: a, b and c indicate that the coefficient is significant, or the null hypothesis is rejected in the case of the test of fixed effects, at 10%, 5% and 1% levels respectively. In the table, ECM2, ECM3, ECM4 refer to cointegration vectors that contain bank loans (oky), capital flows other than FDI (poy = pfy + oky) and total capital flows (tpky = fd + pf + oky) respectively.

Table 12.5c Short-run dynamics of the real exchange rate: Latin America

	ECM1	*ECM3*		*ECM4*		
ECM(−1)	−0.29[c]	−0.16[c]	−0.17[c]	−0.17[c]	−0.17[c]	−0.17[c]
Capital flows						
Changes in bank loans (oky)		−1.23[c]		−1.25[b]		
Changes in capital flows other than FDI (po)			−1.06[b]		−1.05[b]	
Changes in total capital flows (tpky)						−1.01[b]
Technological progress						
Trend	−0.002[b]					
Openness and trade regimes						
Changes in openness	0.41[c]	0.41[c]	0.41[c]	0.42[c]	0.41[c]	0.42[c]
Changes in taxes on trade	0.05[c]	0.05[b]	0.05[b]	0.05[b]	0.05[b]	0.05[c]
Fiscal and macroeconomic policy						
Changes in government consumption	−0.23[c]	−0.23[c]	−0.23[c]	−0.23[c]	−0.23[c]	−0.24[c]
Deficit to high powered money	−0.05[c]					
Changes in debt		0.55[c]	0.54[c]	0.55[c]	0.54[c]	0.54[c]
Nominal devaluation	0.33					
R-bar squared	0.69	0.64	0.63	0.64	0.64	0.64
Test of fixed effects	1.01	3.30[c]	3.30[c]	3.32[c]	3.32[c]	3.35[c]

Note: a, b and c indicate that the coefficient is significant, or the null hypothesis is rejected in the case of the test of fixed effects, at 10%, 5% and 1% levels respectively. In the table, ECM1, ECM3, ECM4 refer to cointegration vectors that contain portfolio flows (pf), capital flows other than FDI (po = pf + okay) and total capital flows (tpky = fd + pf + okay) respectively.

the earlier message that for countries which were not exposed to large capital movement, capital flows were not important in affecting the real exchange rate, not even in the short run.

In addition to their long-run effects, changes in capital flows also led to a short-run real appreciation of the real exchange rate of Asia and Latin America in the short-run. Changes in the two aggregate measures of capital flows, that is, capital flows other than foreign direct investment (po), and total private capital flows (tpky), are highly significant with any cointegration vector in Asia. When the long-run vector contains portfolio investment (pf), no capital flows measure features in the short-run determination of the real exchange rate for Latin America. However, when the other established cointegration vectors are used, changes in bank loans (oky), and the two capital flow aggregates become significant, implying that increases in these categories of capital flows would lead to short-run overvaluation of the real exchange rate. As in the long-run findings, under no specifications is foreign direct investment (fd) found to be the cause of overvaluation. The coefficients also show that a shock in capital flows of the same magnitude would result in greater real overvaluation in Latin America than in Asia.

Openness features prominently in all short-run relations. The variable carries the same sign as in the long-run relationship. This confirms that more openness tended to lead to a more depreciated currency. For the Asian and Latin American countries, the coefficients on changes in trade barriers carry the same sign as the long run. However, in Africa, the coefficient on import tariffs in the short-run specification carry a different sign from the long-run one.

Technological progress is one significant contributor to short-run real exchange-rate movement in Asia. The estimated coefficient carries a positive sign, which indicates that the Balassa–Samuelson effect was not supported in the short run either in this group of countries. However, in one short-run specification for the real exchange rate for Latin America, as well as in the specification for Africa, the estimates show that fast technological progress could lead to appreciation, and thus, give some support to the Balassa–Samuelson hypothesis.

Growth in government consumption led to real appreciation in all the country groups, supporting the hypothesis that government consumption has a bias towards domestic production. The estimated coefficient is around -0.2 for both Asia and Latin America for all specifications, but smaller for Africa.

In general, the findings for the short-run movement determination seem to be consistent with those for the equilibrium real exchange rate determination. Changes in the fundamentals tended to have a similar impact on both the long-run equilibrium real exchange rate and the short-run real exchange-rate movement.

In Asia, nominal devaluation was always translated into real depreciation. This suggests that nominal devaluation may be a useful tool in assisting quick adjustment towards the long-run equilibrium real exchange rate should a misalignment exist. For Latin America the effect of nominal devaluation is not robust, and only significant in one specification. In the African country group, nominal devaluation actually resulted in real appreciation. Therefore, for the latter two country groups, the authorities need to be cautious in using nominal devaluation as a tool of adjustment.

The estimates also show that reckless macroeconomic policy led to currency appreciation. Excess credit supply leads to real appreciation in Africa, and high levels of deficits result in overvaluation in Asia and Latin America. However, it is found that increases in debt and/or debt service burden have led to depreciation in Africa and Latin America. This differs from studies such as Lim (2000) which find that higher foreign debt led to real appreciation. One possible explanation for this finding is that increases in debt burden may weaken investors' confidence in the economy, and lead them to doubt the sustainability of the external position of the country.

Tests of fixed effects

The second row from the bottom in Table 12.4 reports the tests of fixed effects for the long-run specifications while the bottom rows in Tables 12.5a–c report those for the short-run specifications of the real exchange rate. In all the long-run specifications, the null hypothesis of a common constant is rejected, and the choice of the fixed effects model is supported. Most of the short-run specifications give strong support to the choice of the fixed effects model over the pooled regressions. The test statistics are significant, and reject the hypothesis of an identical constant in the whole group and the African group. For the Latin American group, there is only one case among the six different specifications where a common constant is accepted. The detection of fixed effects justifies the use of the fixed effects model to carry out the estimation. However, for the Asian group the common constant is accepted for all the short-run specifications. This seems to suggest that countries within this group are fairly homogenous. Under these circumstances, the efficient estimator for the Asian group is the pooled regression. Therefore, the real exchange rate determination equations are re-estimated for the Asian group using the fixed effects for the long-run relationship and the pooled regression estimator for the ECM of short-run dynamics. The estimates are very close to those of the fixed-effects models.

Experiments have also been carried out to see whether different exchange-rate regimes and structures have any effects on real exchange-rate dynamics utilising the information provided in Tables 12.A1–3. However, the dummy variables for the exchange regime and exchange structure are insignificant in most specifications. My interpretation is that, rather than indicating that the degree of flexibility in exchange-rate regimes or the exchange-rate structure does not matter, this result reflects the difficulty in describing the wide ranging exchange-rate practices in countries. Between the most rigid system of currency board arrangement and independent floating, there is a whole spectrum of exchange-rate regimes with varying degrees of flexibility including pegged but adjustable, crawling peg and managed floating. In a pegged, but adjustable exchange-rate regime, the degree of fixity depends on the width of the bands with which exchange rates are normally allowed to fluctuate, on the determination with which the limits of these bands are defended and on the frequency and magnitude of changes in the central parities. A tight crawling at a low speed with infrequent adjustment is more fixed than adjustable peg with weakly-defended wide bands and frequent changes in central parities. If the domestic currency is tightly linked to a currency or a basket of currencies, a managed-floating may function like a rigid peg with narrow bands. Even in independently floating regimes, exchange rates are hardly allowed to fluctuate unfettered in practice, (Eichengreen *et al.*, 1998). The IMF's simple classification is not able to capture the degree of flexibility of an exchange rate regime.

Concluding remarks

This paper has studied real exchange-rate determination using panel data for Africa, Asia and Latin America. Working within the Edwards' framework of equilibrium real exchange-rate determination, the relationship between capital flows and real exchange rate is particularly addressed. For this purpose, the Engle–Granger two-step modelling procedure is applied on the panel data in the empirical work. There have emerged some interesting results that are fairly robust to different estimation procedures.

Long-run relationships are found between real exchange rates and their fundamentals for all the three regions of Africa, Asia and Latin America. Interestingly, for countries which have not received substantial capital flows such as those in Africa, capital movement is not a significant determinant of the long-run equilibrium real exchange rate. In contrast, capital flows are important in affecting the value of the long-run equilibrium real exchange rate as well as the short-run dynamics of the real exchange rate. Corroborating earlier studies such as Calvo *et al.* (1993) and Edwards (1998), most types of capital flows are found to lead to real appreciation in Asia and Latin America which have seen surges in capital flows in the past two decades. However, the approach of using disaggregated capital flows proves fruitful in establishing that, among different types of capital flows, foreign direct investment is unlikely to be the force driving real appreciation.

Some other important factors in explaining real exchange-rate movements include openness, technological progress, restrictions on trade, government consumption/expenditure, excess credit supply, government deficits.

The major findings with regard to the effects of capital flows on the real exchange rate reinforce the lesson from earlier studies that capital flows are indeed mixed blessings. On the one hand, they bring to developing countries much-needed resources as well as technological transfer and managerial knowhow. But on the other hand, they are known to be highly volatile and often pose difficulties to macroeconomic management. Real appreciation is one of the major difficulties that capital flows cause. As a result, some countries are

Appendix A

Table 12.A1 Changes in the exchange regime and structure in the selected African economies

	1982	*1983*	*1984*	*1985*	*1986*	*1987*	*1988*	*1989*	*1990*	*1991*	*1992*	*1993*	*1994*	*1995*	*1996*
Botswana	F1	--->													
	U	--->													M
Ghana	F2	--->		F1	F3	--->									
	M	--->												U	--->
Kenya	F1	--->										F3	--->		
	M	--->													U
Mauritius	F1	--->						F2	--->		F1	--->	F2	--->	F3
	U	--->													
Morocco	F2	--->								F1	--->				
	U	--->			M	--->									
Sierra Leone	F2	F1	--->		F3	F1	--->		F3	--->					
	U	--->													
Swaziland	F1	--->													
	U	--->													
Tunisia	F1	--->			F2	--->									
	U	--->													
Zambia	F1	--->		F3	--->	F1	--->		F2	--->		F3	--->		
	M	--->		U	M	U	--->				M	--->			U

Note: The first row for each country traces the changes in the country's exchange rate regime. F1, F2 and F3 refer a fixed exchange rate regime, exchange rate regimes with some flexibility and an independent floating exchange rate regime, respectively. The second row shows the development of the exchange rate structure. U indicates that the country has one exchange rate in the system while M indicates that it has more than one exchange rate for different transactions.

Table 12.A2 Exchange rate regime and structure in the selected Latin American economies

	1982	*1983*	*1984*	*1985*	*1986*	*1987*	*1988*	*1989*	*1990*	*1991*	*1992*	*1993*	*1994*	*1995*	*1996*
Argentina	F2	--->						F3	--->	F1	--->				
	M	--->													
Brazil	F2					F1	F2		F3				F2		
	M	--->													
Chile	F2	--->													
	M	--->													
Colombia	F2	--->													
	M	--->													U
Costa Rica	F2	--->									F3	--->			F2
	M	--->								U	--->				
Dominican Rep.	F1	--->		F3	--->		F2	F1	--->	F3	--->		F3	--->	
	M	--->									U	--->			M
Ecuador	F1	F2	--->				F1	--->		F2	--->				
	M	--->													
Guatemala	F1	--->						F3	--->						
	U	--->	M	--->									U	--->	
Honduras	F1	--->							F2	--->	F3	--->	F2	--->	
	U	--->		M	--->							U	--->		M
Mexico	F2	--->											F3	--->	
	M	--->								U	--->				
Paraguay	F1	--->						F3	--->						
	M	--->						U	--->						
Peru	F2	--->		F1	--->				F3	--->					
	M	--->								U	--->				
Venezuela	F1	--->						F3	--->			F2	F1	--->	F2
	M	--->								U	--->				

Table 12.A3 Exchange rate regime and structure in the selected Asian economies

	Exchange rate regimes	*Unitary or multiple exchange rates*
Indonesia	Some flexibility	Unitary
Korea	Some flexibility	Unitary
Malaysia	Fixed (1982–91) Some flexibility (1991–96)	Unitary
Pakistan	Some flexibility	Unitary
Philippines	Some flexibility (1982–83) Floating (1984–96)	Unitary
Singapore	Fixed (1982–86) Some flexibility (1987–96)	Unitary
Sri Lanka	Some flexibility	Unitary
Thailand	Some flexibility (1982–84) Fixed (1985–96)	Unitary

reluctant to open up to capital flows. However, the findings of this paper suggest that different types of capital flows should not be treated equally in the policy-making process. FDI has long been known to be a desirable type of capital flows. It is more likely to lead to capital formation, and less likely to be speculative in nature. This paper has provided another argument in favour of FDI. In addition to other benefits it provides, FDI does not appear to lead to undesirable real appreciation. Therefore, governments should actively encourage FDI.

Appendix B

Data sources

The variables used as fundamentals are:

- Real exchange rates: calculated from the *IFS*;
- Terms of trade: from *IFS, World Tables* CD-ROM and various issues *of UN Statistical Yearbook*;
- Capital flow: net FDI, portfolio investment and other types of capital flows from the *IFS* and the *World Table*;
- Openness: defined as the ratio of (imports + exports) to GDP; data are extracted from the *IFS*;
- Technological progress: proxied by a time trend or real GDP growth;
- Restrictions on trade: two measures are used; one is import duties and the other taxes on international trade; both series are from *World Table* CD-ROM;
- Government consumption and government expenditure: from the *IFS and World Table* CD-ROM;
- Nominal and real GDP: from the *IFS* and *World Tables*.

In addition, the following variables are used in the short run relationships:

- Excess credit supply: defined as growth of domestic credit in excess of the previous year's GDP growth; domestic credit and GDP data are from the *IFS* and *World Tables* CD-ROM;
- Deficits/high powered money: this is a measure of fiscal stance; data are from the *IFS* and *World Tables* CD-ROM;
- Total debt: mostly from the *World Tables*; for Korea and Singapore data on total debt are not readily available; accumulation of balance of payments definition of current account is used as a proxy of total debt.
- Debt service ratio: from the *World Tables* CD-ROM.

Notes

1 Levin and Lin (1992) test employed in this paper is among the first generation of panel unit root tests, and has been widely employed in applied work. There are a number of unit root tests being proposed more recently such as Breuer *et al.* (2000); Im *et al.* (1997); Maddala and Wu's (1997); Sarno and Taylor (1998) and Taylor and Sarno (1998). Some of them allow for greater heterogeneity, while others take into account cross unit correlations. See Breuer *et al.* (2000) for an evaluation of different panel unit root tests. In addition, Pedroni (1995, 1999) propose a series of panel cointegration tests that can be applied to bivariate and multivariate regressions.

2 See, for example, Fry (1993) for using accumulating balance of payments definition of current account as a proxy for total debt.

References

Balassa, B. (1964) 'The purchasing power parity doctrine: a reappraisal', *Journal of Political Economy*, 72(6), 244–67.

Bayoumi, T., Clark, P., Symansky, S. and Taylor, M. (1994) 'The robustness of equilibrium exchange rate calculations to alternative assumptions and methodologies', in J. Williamson (ed.), *Estimating Equilibrium Exchange Rates*, pp. 19–59. Washington DC: Institute for International Economics.

Breuer, J. B., McNown, R. and Wallace, M. (2000) 'The quest for purchasing power parity with a series-specific test using panel data', Universtiy of South Carolina, mimeo.

Calvo, G. A., Leiderman, L. and Reinhart, C. M. (1993) 'Capital inflows and real exchange rate appreciation in Latin America', *IMF Staff Papers*, 40(1), 108–51.

Chinn, M. D. (1997) 'Sectoral productivity, government spending and real exchange rates: empirical evidence for OECD countries', *NBER Working Paper*, 6017, April.

Chinn, M. D. (1999) 'Measuring misalignment: purchasing power parity and East Asian currencies in the 1990s', *IMF Working Paper*, WP/99/120, September.

Chinn, M. and Johnston, L. (1996) 'Real exchange rate levels, productivity and demand shocks: evidence from a panel of 14 countries', *NBER Working Paper*, 5709, August.

Edwards, S. (1989) *Real Exchange Rates, Devaluation, And Adjustment: Exchange Rate Policy in Developing Countries*, Cambridge, MA: MIT Press.

Edwards, S. (1994) 'Real and monetary determinants of real exchange rate behaviour: theory and evidence from developing countries', in J. Williamson (ed.), *Estimating Equilibrium Exchange Rates*, pp. 61–91. Washington DC: Institute of International Economics.

Edwards, S. (1998) 'Capital flows, real exchange rates, and capital controls: some Latin American experiences', *NBER Working Paper*, 6800, November.

Edwards, S. and van Wijnbergen, S. (1989) 'Disequilibririum and structural adjustment', in H. Chennery and T. N. Srinivasan (eds), *Handbook of Development Economics*, Amsterdam: North-Holland.

Eichengreen, B., Masson, P., Bredenkamp, H., Johnston, B., Hamann, J., Jadresic, E. and Ötker, I. (1998) 'Exit strategies: policy options for countries seeking greater exchange rate flexibility', *IMF Occasional Paper*, 168.

Elbadawi, I. A. (1994) 'Estimating long-run equilibrium real exchange rates', in J. Williamson (ed.), *Estimating Equilibrium Exchange Rates*, pp. 93–131. Washington DC: Institute for International Economics.

Engle, R. and Granger, C. (1987) 'Co-integration and error correction: representation, estimation and testing', *Econometrica*, 55(2), 251–76, March.

Feyzioglu, T. (1997) 'Estimating the equilibrium real exchange rate: an application to Finland', *IMF Working Paper*, WP/97/109.

Frankel, J. A. and Rose, A. K. (1995) 'A panel project on purchasing power parity: mean reversion within and between countries', *NBER Working Paper*, 5006.

Fry, M. J. (1993) 'Foreign debt accumulation: financial and fiscal effects and monetary policy reactions in developing countries', *Journal of International Money and Finance*, 12(4), 347–67.

Im, K. S., Persaram, M. H. and Shin, Y. (1997) 'Testing for unit roots in heterogenous panels, University of Cambridge, Department of Economics, mimeo.

International Monetary Fund. *International Financial Statistics CD-ROM*.

Karlsson, S. and Löthgren, M. (2000) 'On the power and interpretation of panel unit root tests', *Economics Letters*, 66(3), 249–55.

Levin, A. and Lin, C.-F. (1992) 'Unit root tests in panel data: asymptotic and finite-sample properties', University of California at San Diego, Department of Economics, Discussion Paper, 92-23, May.

Lim, G.-C. (2000) 'Misalignment and managed exchange rates: an application to the Thai Baht', *IMF Working Paper*, WP/00/63, March.

Maddala, G. S. and Wu, S. (1997) 'A comparative study of unit root tests with panel data and a new simple test', Ohio State University, mimeo.

Mongardini, J. (1998) 'Estimating Egypt's equilibrium real exchange rates', *IMF Working Paper*, WP/98/5, January.

Nyoni, T. S. (1998) 'Foreign aid and economic performance in Tanzania', *World Development*, 27(7), 1235–40.

Pedroni, P. (1995) 'Panel cointegration: asymptotic and finite sample properties of pooled time series tests with an application to the PPP hypothesis', Indiana University Department of Economics, Discussion Paper, 95-013.

Pedroni, P. (1999) 'Critical values for cointegration tests in heterogeneous panels with multiple regressors', *Oxford Bulletin of Economics and Statistics*, 61, 653–70.

Rogoff, K. (1996) 'The purchasing power parity puzzle', *Journal of Economic Literature*, 34(2), 647–68, June.

Samuelson, P. A. (1964) 'Theoretical notes on trade problems', *Review of Economic Statistics*, 46(2), 145–54.

Sarno, L. and Taylor, M. (1998) 'Real exchange rates under the recent float: unequivocal evidence of mean reversion', *Economics Letters*, 60(2), 131–7, August.

Sorsa, P. (1999) Algeria – the real exchange, export diversification, and trade protection, *IMF Working Paper*, WP/99/49, April.

Stein, J. L. (1994) 'The natural real exchange rate of the US dollar and determinants of capital flows', in J. Williamson (ed.), *Estimating Equilibrium Exchange Rates*, pp. 133–75. Washington DC: Institute for International Economics.

Stein, J. L. and Allen, P. R. (1995) *Fundamental Determinants of Exchange Rates*, Oxford: Clarendon Press.

Taylor, M. and Sarno, L. (1998) 'The behaviour of real exchange rates during the post Bretton Woods period', *Journal of International Economics*, 46(2), 281–312, December.

Williamson, J. (1994) 'Estimates of FEERs' in J. Williamson (ed.) *Estimating Equilibrium Exchange Rates*, pp. 177–243. Washington DC: Institute of International Economics.

World Bank. *World Economic Indicators CD-ROM*.

13 Foreign investment and macroeconomic uncertainty

An empirical analysis of recent experience from the European Union

David G. Dickinson

Introduction

This paper looks at issues relating to the performance of foreign direct investment (FDI)) into four European Union (EU) countries from 1980 to 1998. Its purpose is to explore the impact of uncertainty on the investment that has been made. Some of the countries chosen (Spain and Portugal) have experienced more stable macroeconomic regimes as a result of becoming members of the European Union (EU), as well as later in the period of European Monetary Union while others (Netherlands and Italy) have experienced the benefits of EU membership over much longer periods of time.

An objective of the analysis is to consider what the implications of EU membership are for the countries of Central and East Europe (CEE) which are currently in the process of preparing themselves for accession to the EU. Since inflows of capital are likely to be an important component of the benefits which will be achieved, analysis of the experience of countries which 15 or 20 years ago were in a similar position to a number of CEE countries should therefore provide some insights into what the future holds for these aspiring members.

The paper is divided into three further sections. In the next we consider the likely influences on foreign investment. In the third section we report the empirical results and the fourth section provides a summary of our analysis and draws the implications for the potential new EU members from CEE.

The influences on FDI

Numerous studies of FDI provide testimony to the importance attached both by policy-makers and economists to this flow as a source of increasing domestic economic growth (for analysis of the relationship between FDI and economic growth see Borensztein *et al.*, 1998). There have been studies of both developed and developing economies. They have tackled the issue across a wide range of viewpoints, from the perspective of the motives and strategy of the multinational enterprise (e.g. Dunning, 1993), through to the implications of the standard neoclassical-growth model (Zebregs, 1998). The interlinking between trade and

FDI has provided a further perspective and has led to a branch which emphasises economic-geography aspects behind the decision to build plants overseas (see Krugman, 1991; Markusen, 1995). This literature highlights that there are external economies associated with the geographical concentration of production (so-called agglomeration economies[1]). However, it must be recognised also that observed capital flows can be a reflection of economic conditions in the originating countries rather than in the host country.[2]

Taking an eclectic view leads one to conclude that FDI is likely to be influenced by both the characteristics of the domestic economy (e.g. its infrastructure, the average level of skill of its workforce and special abilities it has, the level of capital currently, the political stance towards inward investment, the fiscal incentives offered and the size of the market available for domestically-based production[3]) as well as the objectives and constraints under which the investors, often multinational enterprises, operate (e.g. the economies of scale which can be exploited, the transport costs incurred in engaging in trade, the gains from internalisation of costs in a world with imperfect markets, and there may also be momentum effects where large investments create persistent effects through improvements in profit expectations).

Certainly, the theory which argues that FDI is all about the transfer of abundant capital from rich countries with high real-wages to poor countries with low real-wages is found to be inadequate in the face of the actual capital flows which are seen to take place (much of it between countries of similar income and the concentration of capital flows to a small number of countries).[4]

The particular focus of this paper is to consider the impact of uncertainty (of the macroeconomic variety) on the flows of FDI. The importance of uncertainty for a forward-looking decision such as investment seems undeniable.[5] However establishing this in a formal empirical study has proved somewhat elusive although recent work has been somewhat more helpful. One of the problems is that, from a theoretical perspective, uncertainty does not have a clearly-signed effect (see Nickell, 1978). The more recent work on irreversible investment has provided stronger theoretical foundation for a negative impact of uncertainty on investment, although consideration of partial reversibility and expandability makes this a more tentative conclusion (see Abel *et al.*, 1996; Carruth *et al.*, 2000; Pindyck and Dixit, 1994 for more extensive discussion). Pennings and Sleuwaegen (2000) have analysed the decision of a multinational utilising the real-option approach developed by Pindyck and Dixit. Using this approach leads them to conclude that the timing of foreign direct investment (and hence, in the aggregate, the total amount that is undertaken) will be dependent on uncertainty about future profits as well as the other institutional/competitiveness features found in the OLI (ownership/location/internalisation) model (such as tax advantages, cost differentials, labour market flexibility and so on).

We may also note that exchange-rate uncertainty has appeared in a number of studies as an influence on investment. Darby *et al.* (1998) have examined the impact of exchange rate uncertainty on total investment from both a theoretical and empirical perspective. They develop a model which demonstrates that exchange-rate uncertainty can have both positive and negative effects on investment. They then test this model for a number of OECD countries. They find that uncertainty is a significant determinant of investment with a negative sign. Aizenman (1992) has also investigated the influence of exchange-rate volatility on foreign direct investment. In particular, he is interested in the effect of exchange-rate *regime* on the decision to invest. He argues that the source of shocks is important since the ability of the economy to absorb these shocks is a function of the exchange-rate regime. He shows that a fixed exchange-rate regime is better at absorbing both monetary and productivity shocks, and hence, will encourage more foreign direct investment if these are the main disturbances affecting the economy.[6]

We wish to investigate exactly what sort of uncertainty is found to influence the amount of foreign direct investment undertaken. Our approach is empirical; we wish to find the specification which provides a statistically appropriate representation of the data and which encompasses the considerations which have been argued to be important theoretically. In this regard, there are a number of aspects which we shall wish to capture:

(a) Foreign direct investment is made mainly by multinational companies in pursuit of long-run profitable opportunities;
(b) Foreign direct investment has been increasing during the last twenty years as a result of economic globalisation and may be driven by the factors identified in the economic-geography literature;
(c) Foreign direct investment has been concentrated in a relatively small number of countries and does not appear to rely exclusively upon low wages or, more generally, costs of production and may be more dependent on the size of the market available to domestically-based producers;
(d) FDI is lumpy in nature and any empirical specification must control for this aspect in order to successfully identify the determining variables. In addition, there may be momentum effects where large investments by one firm encourage others to enter the market;
(e) The impact of uncertainty could influence both the short run (by affecting the value of the option to invest, and hence, changing the timing of investment), as well as the long run (countries with more uncertain economic conditions are less attractive as destinations for foreign investors).

This last point seems to suggest that we will wish to model both the short and long-run specifications. The long run will be dependent upon among other things, relative costs of production, the potential for external economies of scale, the size of the market for domestic producers and uncertainty about the benefits of producing in the particular economy. The short run will reflect adjustment to this long-run equilibrium taking into account the impact of uncertainty on the timing of investment as well as the dynamics of the investment process which will reflect the costs of making lumpy investment as well as the possibility of momentum effects where large-scale investment by one company encourages others to follow.

We shall adopt a parsimonious approach to our empirical specification. We have highlighted that domestic economic conditions can be important determinants of FDI. Two particular variables are competitiveness and overall size of the domestic market. We might expect that, since we are looking exclusively at EU economies, the size of the market is not going to be a determining factor (FDI into any of our countries has the EU market available). Whilst individual countries can offer inducements to encourage FDI, they are, to some extent, hampered by EU regulations. Hence, we do not consider this to be an important variable explaining the different performance of the selected EU economies. A key factor is the overall profitability of investment which depends on productivity. We would normally regard this as diminishing as the capital stock (production) grows. However, agglomeration economies suggest that there may be increasing returns to investment. Therefore, the relationship between scale and FDI may be influenced by opposing forces. Our basic specification (using error-correction methodology) can then be written as follows:

$$\mathrm{FDI} = \mathrm{F}(\text{scale variable, competitiveness, uncertainty variables})$$

$$\Delta\mathrm{FDI} = \mathrm{f}(\Delta\text{scale variables}, \Delta\text{competitiveness, uncertainty variables}, \mathrm{ECM}(-1))$$

where

$$\mathrm{ECM}(-1) = \mathrm{FDI}(-1) - \mathrm{F}(\text{scale variable}(-1), \text{competitiveness}(-1), \text{uncertainty variables}(-1))$$

is the equation modelling the error-correction specification. We now turn to reporting the results of this empirical investigation.

Empirical analysis

In considering our analysis of foreign direct investment we examine each country individually. This is because we recognise that many factors which are country-specific are not directly modelled and hence an attempt to construct a multi-country approach is likely to founder. However, we wish to retain a narrow focus to our analysis and so we keep explanatory variables to as small a number as possible. We use the specification suggested at the end of the last section and measure a country's competitiveness using the effective exchange-rate basis calculated on a unit labour cost basis, as well as incorporating independent effects of inflation (domestic) and (nominal) exchange-rate changes. To measure scale, we use industrial production (on the grounds that much FDI is in the manufacturing sector). For the uncertainty variables, we construct measures using GARCH procedures (although some experimentation suggested that the exact procedure used may not make much difference) on a number of variables (effective exchange rate, inflation, nominal exchange rate, money supply (M1), interest rates (real and nominal)). The chosen specification is the one which we find represents the data in a parsimonious way. Our data is taken from the IMF International Financial Statistics, where we use the same variable across each country in order to ensure comparability. The data is quarterly from 1980Q1 to 1998Q4. Our testing procedure consists of preliminary analysis of the data, followed by construction of our uncertainty variables, and then, the estimation of our equation to explain foreign direct investment.

In order to get a handle on whether our approach to the problem is likely to be successful, we present below some statistics for two periods 1980–89 and 1990–99. (Note that we use the following notation: ES, Spain; IT, Italy; NL, Holland; PT, Portugal; IP, industrial production; INF, inflation; EFFER, real effective exchange rate on a unit labour cost basis.)

	ESFDI	*ITFDI*	*NLFDI*	*PTFDI*
FDI for the period 1980–89 ($US)				
Mean	858.5385	480.8462	727.5641	113.5128
Std. Dev.	632.8716	714.8816	743.7040	129.8406
FDI for the period 1990–99 ($US)				
Mean	2446.550	939.2250	3967.125	416.3750
Std. Dev.	937.7009	678.6463	3804.869	289.4659

Hence, we can see that Spain had a large increase in FDI over the two periods in levels, and proportionately, as did the Netherlands, while Portugal saw a large proportionate increase although from a low base. Italy saw a doubling of FDI, but in the context of the other countries, this was quite modest. We can now look at the behaviour of key variables likely to explain these flows:

Spanish macroeconomic data

	1980–89			*1990–99*		
	ESIP	*ESINF*	*ESEFFER*	*ESIP*	*ESINF*	*ESEFFER*
Mean	85.2	9.36	95.8	100.3	4.86	107.8
Std. Dev.	5.98	3.45	6.87	8.05	1.40	6.62

Italian macroeconomic data

	1980–89			*1990–99*		
	ITIP	*ITINF*	*ITEFFER*	*ITIP*	*ITINF*	*ITEFFER*
Mean	82.7	10.03	129.8	97.4	4.12	122.9
Std. Dev.	5.55	5.10	4.38	5.31	1.72	14.99

Dutch macroeconomic data

	1980–89			*1990–99*		
	NLIP	*NLINF*	*NLEFFER*	*NLIP*	*NLINF*	*NLEFFER*
Mean	81.0	2.34	106.0	99.6	2.45	97.4
Std. Dev.	4.5	2.4	6.7	6.34	0.54	4.14

Portuguese macroeconomic data

	1980–89			*1990–99*		
	PTIP	*PTINF*	*PTEFFER*	*PTIP*	*PTINF*	*PTEFFER*
Mean	102.5	17.9	107.3	124.4	5.99	121.0
Std. Dev.	9.65	7.51	5.33	7.05	3.89	10.41

The data reported above demonstrates that there was increasing economic stability from the former to the latter period as measured by the rate of inflation as well as in terms of its variability. However, there is no evidence of increasing exchange rate stability (note that we use the real effective exchange rate index) and also overall stability of industrial production (again an index) shows no marked decline. For both Portugal and Spain, we observe real exchange-rate appreciation while for the Netherlands and Italy, there is a real depreciation. Overall, given the different experience of the four countries chosen it seems that a multi-country study will provide us with some insight into the process of FDI, at least at the aggregate level.

Before reporting the results of this procedure, we shall outline how we have determined our uncertainty variables. For each of the variables (inflation, effective exchange rate, industrial production, and so on), differenced if necessary to ensure stationary, we run a simple model with a constant, a time-trend and one lagged-value of the endogenous variable including a GARCH(1,1) specification for the conditional variance of the residuals. The uncertainty variable is then the series generated by the GARCH specification.

We now turn to our empirical results. Consider first the case of Spain. We shall present the results in detail to illustrate our approach. For other countries we have adopted a similar empirical strategy. We start with unit root tests (allowing for two lags for the Augmented Dickey–Fuller (ADF) test and three lags for Phillips–Perron (PP) test; other lag-lengths gave similar results). Note that VAR attached to the variable refers to the variance calculated from the GARCH model.[7]

Given the results in Table 13.1 then we can see that we should estimate the short run using an error-correction model. A parsimonious model is as follows (*t*-statistics are shown in brackets under the appropriate

Table 13.1 Unit root tests for Spanish variables

	Level		*First difference*		*Second difference*	
Variable	*ADF*	*PP*	*ADF*	*PP*	*ADF*	*PP*
FDI	−1.39	−2.29	−6.99[a]	−17.30[a]	−37.63[a]	−11.61[a]
INF	−1.58	−1.34	−3.50[b]	−8.63[a]	−4.92[a]	−17.10[a]
EFFER	−1.70	−1.48	−3.86[a]	−6.05[a]	−6.74[a]	−14.65[a]
IP	−0.39	−0.10	−2.97[b]	−4.55[a]	−4.53[a]	−12.58[a]
INFVAR	−0.88	−1.07	−5.04[a]	−10.25[a]	−8.14[a]	−23.5[a]
IPVAR	−4.41[a]	−8.46[a]	−7.29[a]	−18.51[a]	–	–
EFFERVAR	−4.09[a]	−7.45[a]	−6.32[a]	−16.10	–	–

Note: a and b indicate rejection of unit root at 1% and 5% levels respectively.

coefficient):

$$\begin{aligned} \text{ESDFDI} = &- \underset{(-3.75)}{51387} - \underset{(-3.18)}{0.40}{}^{*}\text{ESDFDI}(-1) - \underset{(-3.50)}{146.5}{}^{*}\text{ESIPVAR} \\ &- \underset{(-2.03)}{120.9}{}^{*}\text{ESIPVAR}(-1) - \underset{(-4.43)}{0.622}{}^{*}\text{ESFDI}(-1) \\ &+ \underset{(3.52)}{41.97}{}^{*}\text{ESEFFER}(-1) + \underset{(3.66)}{1046}{}^{*}\text{ESIP}(-1) \\ &- \underset{(-3.56)}{5.60}{}^{*}\text{ESIPSQ}(-1) + \underset{(12.28)}{1812.94}{}^{*}\text{DUM90Q4} \\ &- \underset{(-11.79)}{1493}{}^{*}\text{DUM94Q3} - \underset{(-5.20)}{1338}{}^{*}\text{DUM91Q2} + \underset{(8.93)}{980.8}{}^{*}\text{DUM94Q2} \end{aligned}$$

R-bar squared 0.734
Standard error of regression 362.2

Specification Tests[8] (the probability of the test statistic is shown where the null hypothesis is that the test holds)

Test for normality = 0.32
Test for no serial correlation = 0.99
Test for no ARCH effects = 0.14
Test for no heteroscedasticity = 0.12

Note that it was necessary to correct for abnormal flows in particular quarters by adding dummy variables (i.e. DUM904 means a dummy variable with zeros everywhere except the fourth quarter of 1990). D associated with a variable means the first difference. The specification of the equation is satisfactory although the tests for ARCH and heteroscedasticity are not overwhelming. The result suggests a relatively moderate speed of adjustment to the long-run equilibrium, while the overall volatility of the economy (as represented by IPVAR) generates a negative effect in the short run. The effect of the overall level of economic activity (as represented by IP) is non-linear and shows that as IP increases the marginal effects of growth decreases and, for the latter part of the period, is negative. As industrial production grows, there is increasing profitability (perhaps due to externalities, and hence, an improved environment for additional investment; but eventually, it seems that profitability declines as economic activity increases. The positive effect of the real exchange rate can be explained by reference to confidence effects that is, an increase in the real exchange rate raises expectations of economic stability and improved corporate performance.

Italy

Italy is included in our study since it has been a long-time member of the EU and has experienced strong economic growth as a result, but has been relatively unstable from a macroeconomic perspective. However, empirically it is a different case since the unit root tests for FDI indicate that stationarity holds. Therefore, we can estimate the equation in levels. After checking for unit roots in the exogenous variables our final specification is as follows:[9]

$$\begin{aligned} \text{ITFDI} = & \underset{(9.15)}{2115} - \underset{(-3.69)}{0.239^{*}\text{ITFDI}(-1)} - \underset{(-3.26)}{37.2^{*}\text{ITDEFER}} \\ & - \underset{(-7.02)}{8754^{*}\text{ITINFVAR}} - \underset{(-2.91)}{248.2^{*}\text{ITDIPVAR}(-1)} \\ & - \underset{(-8.55)}{1745^{*}\text{LOW}} + \underset{(8.72)}{1531^{*}\text{HIGH}} \end{aligned}$$

R-bar squared 0.82
Standard error of regression 319.5

Specification tests (see discussion above for details).

Test for normality	= 0.28
Test for no serial correlation	= 0.35
Test for no ARCH effects	= 0.70
Test for no heteroscedasticity	= 0.30

As with the case of Spain, we have had to control for abnormal FDI in particular quarters by using dummy variables. In this case we have defined two dummy variables HIGH and LOW where abnormal positive and negative values of FDI were observed.[10] The results of the estimation for Italy demonstrate similar results to the case of Spain. There are negative effects of uncertainty, in this case not only from industrial production (as a measure of overall economic activity) but also from inflation. We find that changes in the effective exchange rate have effects on FDI with the opposite sign to that of Spain consistent with the idea that a rise in competitiveness increases the attractiveness of the country for foreign investment.

Netherlands

The Netherlands is useful as a comparator to the experiences of the other countries in the study. It is a long-term member of the EU, has always been open to foreign investment and has experienced significant levels through the whole of the data period. Furthermore, it has had much more stable macroeconomic conditions. When we run the unit root tests we find the following results (Table 13.2).

Table 13.2 Unit root tests for Dutch variables

	Level		*First difference*		*Second difference*	
Variable	*ADF*	*PP*	*ADF*	*PP*	*ADF*	*PP*
FDI	−1.34	−3.85[b]	−8.99[a]	−19.37[a]	−12.76[a]	−34.41[a]
INF	−5.32[a]	−2.54	−3.68[a]	−6.91[a]	−5.32[a]	−15.19[a]
EFFER	−2.19	−2.29	−4.49[a]	−8.62[a]	−7.62[a]	−21.25[a]
IP	0.37	0.37	−6.72[a]	−13.04[a]	−11.87[a]	−31.11[a]
INFVAR	−2.41	−2.41	−5.68[a]	−11.25[a]	−9.24[a]	−29.07[a]
IPVAR	−2.03	−2.36	−5.37[a]	−10.14[a]	−9.07[a]	−22.67[a]
EFFERVAR	−3.85[a]	−3.72[a]	−5.96[a]	−9.74[a]	–	–

Note: a and b indicate rejection of unit root at 1% and 5% levels respectively.

Although the test for FDI in levels is not conclusive, we use the ADF test to indicate that FDI is an I(1) variable since the PP test does not have reliable small sample properties. The error-correction model is:

$$\begin{aligned} \text{NLDFDI} = &- \underset{(-2.08)}{0.156}{}^{*}\text{NLDFDI}(-1) + \underset{(3.49)}{0.145}{}^{*}\text{NLDFDI}(-4) \\ &- \underset{(-4.65)}{0.581}{}^{*}\text{NLFDI}(-1) - \underset{(-3.70)}{27.56}{}^{*}\text{NLEFFER}(-1) \\ &+ \underset{(4.02)}{41.44}{}^{*}\text{NLIP}(-1) + \underset{(11.50)}{2641}{}^{*}\text{HIGH} - \underset{(-4.82)}{1835}{}^{*}\text{LOW} \end{aligned}$$

R-bar squared 0.87
Standard error of regression 611.2

Specification Tests (see discussion above for details)

Test for normality = 0.90
Test for no serial correlation = 0.78
Test for no ARCH effects = 0.72
Test for no heteroscedasticity = 0.32

As before, we have used dummy variables to control for abnormal flows of FDI in particular quarters.[11] First, for the error-correction component, we may note that IP has a linear relationship to FDI. Hence, as the economy (measured by IP) grows, FDI flows will grow proportionately. In addition, the real exchange rate has a negative influence on FDI (competitiveness issue). Second, we find that the speed of adjustment to the deviation from the long-run equilibrium is relatively fast and also that lagged-changes in industrial production have a negative influence on FDI. An explanation for this result is that a decline (increase) in economic activity in the period 3–6 months ago generates expectations of less (more) promising economic conditions in the future, and hence, a deteriorating investment environment. Finally, we may note that uncertainty variables do not have any significant effect.

Portugal

We now turn to the results for Portugal. The unit root test on relevant variables are reported as follows (Table 13.3).

Table 13.3 Unit root tests for Portuguese variables

	Level		*First difference*		*Second difference*	
Variable	*ADF*	*PP*	*ADF*	*PP*	*ADF*	*PP*
FDI	−1.53	−4.99[a]	−8.84[a]	−17.70[a]	−10.81[a]	−27.89[a]
INF	−1.68	−1.03	−3.77[a]	−6.04[a]	−4.46[a]	−13.54[a]
EFFER	−0.30	−0.79	−5.31[a]	−8.87[a]	−9.86[a]	−17.41[a]
IP	−0.30	−0.42	−7.45[a]	−16.30[a]	−13.17[a]	−37.28[a]
INFVAR	−2.03	−2.69	−4.04[a]	−9.32[a]	−7.07[a]	−21.45
EFFERVAR	−5.10[a]	−3.77[a]	−3.81[a]	−7.95[a]	–	–
IPVAR	−3.06[b]	−4.15[a]	−8.94[a]	−10.70[a]	–	–

Note: a and b indicate rejection of unit root at 1% and 5% levels respectively.

Although the PP test suggests that FDI is stationary, the ADF cannot reject a unit root and we follow this result and estimate an error-correction model. Our parsimonious specification is given by:

$$
\begin{aligned}
\text{PTDFDI} = {} & \underset{(4.66)}{5408} - \underset{(-9.90)}{0.417}{}^{*}\text{PTDFDI}(-1) - \underset{(-5.77)}{0.187}{}^{*}\text{PTDFDI}(-2) \\
& - \underset{(-2.15)}{37.57}{}^{*}\text{PTDINFDVAR} - \underset{(-5.49)}{0.312}{}^{*}\text{PTFDI}(-1) \\
& - \underset{(-4.72)}{100.1}{}^{*}\text{PTIP}(-1) + \underset{(4.91)}{0.489}{}^{*}\text{PTIPSQ}(-1) \\
& - \underset{(-2.72)}{2.65}{}^{*}\text{PTEFFER}(-1) - \underset{(-30.5)}{713.9}{}^{*}\text{LOW} + \underset{(17.6)}{216.2}{}^{*}\text{HIGH}
\end{aligned}
$$

R-bar squared 0.96
Standard error of regression 47.63

Specification Tests (see discussion above for details)

Test for normality = 0.90
Test for no serial correlation = 0.19
Test for no ARCH effects = 0.35
Test for no heteroscedasticity = 0.42

As previously, we have used dummy variables to deal with unusual FDI flows in specific quarters.[12] The short-run model indicates a fairly low speed of adjustment to the long-run equilibrium. As for Spain, the relationship between economic activity and FDI is non-linear. However, in the case of Portugal we find increases in economic activity (IP) have a negative influence on FDI initially but, as we move through the time-period and IP increases, this becomes positive and increases in size (this could be explained by the effects of an externality). Hence, Portugal does not seem to have suffered from the same situation as Spain, where economic growth has had an increasingly negative impact on FDI over the time-period. The real exchange rate has a negative effect on FDI (competitiveness arguments), once again different from the Spanish case. In the short run, changes in inflation uncertainty have the expected negative effect.

Summary

We now consider the general conclusions we can draw from the analysis of the four countries reported above. The first point we can note is that the experience of the different countries does not point towards a unified story of macroeconomic effects on the level of FDI. However, we will argue that there are some general messages that come from our analysis, particularly with regard to the effects of macroeconomic instability.

Firstly, the effects of the scale variable (IP) are non-linear in what we might call the emerging economies of the EU in the time-period considered (Spain and Portugal). However this non-linearity is of a different type in the two cases. For Portugal we find that there is a positive marginal effect. One explanation for this is the impact of positive externalities on the profitability of investment. In contrast, the results for Spain indicate a negative marginal effect of increases in scale, which is consistent with diminishing returns of production.[13]

Second, we find that the real exchange rate has a generally negative effect highlighting the importance of maintaining competitiveness if a country wishes to benefit from inward investment. However, Spain provides evidence that there is also a confidence effect which may operate. As the real exchange rate appreciates, this can improve expectations about future economic stability, and hence, encourage more capital inflows.

Third, we find that uncertainty is also important and has the expected negative impact on investment. Which variables are important varies across countries.

In the case of Spain, we find that the estimated volatility of industrial production is important while for Italy, we find effects of both industrial production and inflation variability. For Portugal, then, inflation seems to be the key uncertainty variable. Importantly, for Holland, we find that uncertainty variables do not play an important role, suggesting that the impact of volatility only becomes significant when it is at a certain level.

Conclusions

This paper has considered a simple specification to analyse the relationship between FDI and variables which represent key influences on the profitability of investment and variables which represent uncertainty about that profitability. It has maintained a number of hypotheses about FDI flows: that there are momentum effects or investment is lumpy, implying that lagged-FDI flows will be important explanatory variables, that competitiveness as measured by the effective exchange-rate index (in unit labour cost terms) is important and will be signed positively (i.e. a depreciation will be good for FDI), that economic growth may play a role through capacity constraints or through positive externalities, and that uncertainty is also an important determinant. The model has been empirically estimated for a number of EU coutries which have been chosen to represent different types of economic experience over the last twenty years. Our results support the contention that investment is lumpy, (we find lagged-investment flows exert negative influences on current investment), that competitiveness is important (although real exchange-rate appreciation may also signal increasing economic stability, and hence, encourage FDI), that emerging economies experience non-linear effects of economic growth, but that once they are mature and stable, the relationship becomes linear, and that uncertainty about inflation and economic growth have negative effects on FDI, which is consistent with the view that multinational firms are most concerned about overall economic stability. However, once economies are relatively stable the effects of uncertainty disappear.

What then are the lessons from this analysis for other countries (in Central and Eastern Europe)? Increased FDI flows are obviously of concern to them and they would wish to exploit the benefits of EU membership to maximise their impact. There seem to be two clear messages from the empirical analysis we have conducted. First, they should ensure that competitiveness is maintained once EU membership has been achieved. The dynamics of capital flows and economic growth are likely to put pressure on wages and prices, and hence, diminish the positive gains from the FDI in the first place. Second, they should be aware that exchange rate stability, of itself, does not seem to be the secret to receiving significant FDI flows. It is the attainment of a stable macroeconomy with low and predictable inflation rates and stable economic-growth rates, which is important. Hence, the attainment of a stable economic environment is of particular importance if membership of the EU is going to bring the desired large-scale capital inflows.

This raises an issue about future membership of EMU. Whilst EU membership can contribute positively to the achievement of economic stability, the decision to join EMU can also be seen as an accelerated way of achieving stability. At the same time, though, our results suggest that membership of the Euro (and the resulting intra-EU exchange-rate stability will not, of itself, encourage FDI. Indeed it can be argued that, until economic convergence has been achieved, it can be positively de-stabilising as the economy adapts to the constraints of the new exchange-rate regime. Furthermore, the path of the real exchange rate will also be important if it implies an increasingly uncompetitive domestic economy.

Beyond this, we may also note the asymmetric impacts of economic growth. For our two emerging economies, Spain and Portugal, we find evidence of negative effects of economic growth for Spain, suggesting reduced profitability of investment, while in the case of Portugal, it seems that the reverse effect operates, a potential sign of the increasing returns to scale reflecting positive externalities. Although this differential impact deserves further investigation, of equal interest is the case of the Netherlands which indicates that constant return to scale appear to operate for a mature and stable economy. Hence, whilst the short-run effects of increasing economic growth associated with EU membership may have positive or negative effects on FDI, it certainly seems plausible that the non-linearity will disappear over time.

Overall, the aspiring EU candidates from Central and Eastern Europe can expect FDI to increase as a result of EU membership. The transition to stable economies with low inflation rates will encourage this process of capital inflows and hasten economic growth. However, as growth continues, we may find feedback effects to FDI which may well be positive initially, but can turn negative as the per capita income increases. However, in the long run these non-linearities will disappear.

Notes

1 The use of these ideas to explain FDI has been discussed in Barrel and Pain (1999*a*), where they identify significant spill-over effects which increase the importance of FDI to domestic economic policy-makers.

2 For example, Kim (2000) has argued that explaining capital flows to developing countries requires paying attention to world interest rates and the economic prospects of the industrialised countries. In a similar vein, Barrell and Pain (1999*b*), have shown how Japanese monetary policy has had a significant influence on Japanese FDI around the world during the 1980s.

3 Barrell and Pain (1999*b*), discuss how trade restrictions have had a significant effect on Japanese FDI.

4 Note, however, that studies typically have found that relative unit labour costs are an important determinant of FDI flows (see Barrell and Pain, 1999*a,b*; Hatzius, 2000 as very recent examples).

5 We mean here both fixed investment as well as foreign direct investment and will refer to work mainly on the relationship between the former and uncertainty.

6 A recent paper on a related topic, Gourinchas (1999), has considered how foreign exchange rate volatility has affected job allocation across sectors, using micro-level

data, and finds that it has, indeed, had important effects. These impacts will, of course, be magnified if there is a long-run influence on foreign direct investment.

7 Note that we report results only for variables which are found to be significant in the estimated equation. Hence we do not observe any significant effects of uncertainty of money supply, nominal exchange rate or interest rates. This is a general result for all the countries examined.

8 The normality test is the Jacque–Bera test; the serial correlation test is the Breusch–Godfrey LM test (the statistic reported is for four lags); the test for ARCH is also the LM test where the result for four lags is shown; the heterscedasticity test is the White test, ignoring cross-terms.

9 Note that, as before we use a D to indicate first difference of the variable. We have had to use the first difference in some cases as a result of finding a unit root in levels.

10 The following quarters were HIGH: 88Q3, 88Q4, 90Q4, 95Q4 while for LOW: 86Q3, 86Q4, 89Q3.

11 In this case the dummy HIGH corresponds to: 89Q4, 90Q4, 93Q4, 95Q1, 95Q4, 96Q2 and for LOW we have: 91Q1, 93Q2, 94Q2, 95Q2, 97Q3.

12 For the LOW dummy we have: 92Q3, 95Q2, 96Q4 while the HIGH dummy corresponds to periods: 88Q4, 89Q4, 92Q2, 93Q3, 94Q4, 95Q3, 96Q3, 96Q4.

13 Since we are dealing with flows of FDI over a relatively short period of time we are looking at new, rather than replacement, investment so we do not find the stock of capital to be an important determinant of FDI flows.

References

Abel, A. B., Dixit, A. K., Eberley, J. C. and Pindyck, R. S. (1996) 'Options, the value of capital and investment', *Quarterly Journal of Economics*, 111, 753–77.

Aizenman, J. (1992) 'Exchange rate flexibility, volatility and domestic and foreign direct investment', *IMF Staff Papers*, 39, 890–922.

Barrell, R. and Pain, N. (1999) 'Domestic institutions, agglomerations and foreign direct investment in Europe', *European Economic Review*, 43, 925–34.

Barrell, R. and Pain, N. (1999) 'Trade restraints and Japanese direct investment flows', *European Economic Review*, 43, 29–45.

Borensztein, E., De Gregorio, J. and Lee, J. W. (1998) 'How does foreign direct investment affect growth?' *Journal of International Economics*, 45, 115–35.

Carruth, A., Dickerson, A. and Henley, A. (2000) 'What do we know about investment under uncertainty?' *Journal of Economic Surveys*, 14, 119–54.

Darby, J., Hughes Hallett, A., Ireland, J. and Piscitelli, L. (1998) 'The impact of exchange rate uncertainty on the level of investment', *CEPR Discussion Paper* 1896, CEPR, London.

Dixit, A. and Pindyck, R. (1994) *Investment under Uncertainty*, Princeton, N.J.: Princeton University Press.

Dunning, J. H. (1993) *Multinational Enterprises and the Global Economy*, New York: Addison Wesley.

Gourinchas, P.-O. (1999) 'Exchange rates do matter: French job re-allocation and exchange rate turbulence, 1984–92', *European Economic Review*, 43, 1279–1316.

Hatzius, J. (2000) 'Foreign direct investment and factor demand elasticities', *European Economic Review*, 44, 117–43.

Kim, Y. (2000) 'Causes of capital flows in developing countries', *Journal of International Money and Finance*, 19, 235–53.

Krugman, P. (1991) *Geography and Trade*, Cambridge, MA: MIT Press.

Markusen, J. R. (1995) 'The boundaries of multinational enterprises and the theory of international trade', *Journal of Economic Perspectives*, 9, 169–89.

Nickel, S. (1978) *Uncertainty and Investment*, Cambridge: Cambridge University Press.

Pennings, E. and Sleuwaegen, L. (2000) 'The choice of timing of foreign market entry under uncertainty,' *CEPR Discussion Paper*, 2470, London: CEPR.

Zebregs, H. (1998) 'Can the neoclassical model explain the distribution of FDI across developing countries?' *IMF Working Paper*, WP/98/139. Washington DC: International Monetary Fund.

Index